This book is sponsored by the Modern Chinese History Project of the Far Eastern and Russian Institute, whose members have taken an active interest in the work of the author.

FAR EASTERN AND RUSSIAN INSTITUTE
PUBLICATIONS ON ASIA

Number 18

The Land Revolution in China, 1930-1934

A STUDY OF DOCUMENTS

By

TSO-LIANG HSIAO

UNIVERSITY OF WASHINGTON PRESS

Seattle and London

Major parts of the translation of "Decisions Concerning
Some Problems Arising from the Agrarian Struggle" (Document 101, pages 257-82) are adapted from the English
version of the revised text of this document appearing
in the supplement to *People's China*, II, No. 8 (October
6, 1950), 5-14.

First printing 1969

The English translation of the
Preamble and Articles 1-7 of the Land Law of the
Chinese Soviet Republic (Document 34, pages 186–89) is adapted
from Conrad Brandt, Benjamin Schwartz, and John K. Fairbank,
A Documentary History of Chinese Communism (Cambridge, Mass.:
Harvard University Press, 1952), pp. 224–26.

Library of Congress Catalog Card Number 69-14205

Preface

This volume is the end result of a long process of work which was started at Taipei, Taiwan, in August, 1957, and completed at Seattle, Washington, in June, 1967. The task was at times suspended by the intervention of other aspects of my research, but this proved to be extremely helpful rather than harmful to my work. As the first draft of the manuscript of this volume was completed in the spring of 1958, it was found that many basic issues of the land revolution could not be seen in proper perspective until the wider subject of intraparty power struggle had been examined. Work on the latter subject was accordingly undertaken with the result that a volume entitled *Power Relations within the Chinese Communist Movement, 1930–1934: A Study of Documents* was published by the University of Washington Press in 1961.

As soon as I finished the volume on power relations, I resumed my work on land revolution. Over a hundred documents were examined and annotated. Because of their nature, some of them are also listed in my previous volume on power relations and are reproduced, in the original Chinese, in *Power Relations within the Chinese Communist Movement, 1930–1934: Vol. II, The Chinese Documents,* published by the University of Washington Press in 1967.

I visited Japan in 1963 and came to the United States in 1964. During these trips I gathered about a dozen new documents for this volume. Accordingly, the one hundred and seventeen documents annotated in this work and the two land laws included in the Appendix are all the primary sources of the Chinese land revolution of that I have been able to find for inclusion in this book.

Altogether twenty-six documents have been translated into English for this study. Two of them are placed in the Appendix since they were enacted prior to the period under study. In order not to subtract from their value, all the translations are given in full text. For the benefit of the reader, the longer paragraphs of the Chinese documents have been broken up into shorter ones in translation.

As this volume is in a sense a follow-up to my previous publications on power relations, what is said in the preface to the first volume of those publications is in large measure applicable here. Practically all those whose assistance I gratefully acknowledged in that book also aided me in the same manner in the preparation of this volume. The Asia Foundation granted me generous funds for a period of five years, and the Far Eastern and Russian Institute of the University of Washington, which was the sponsor of my research project, also gave me a grant in the last year of my work in Taiwan. In actual research Professors Chieh-ming Chu, Tse-cheng Hsiao, and Abraham E. Wu helped a good deal. Professor Chu, in particular, did the major part of the preliminary digging and checked most of my work. Dr. Wang Shih-chieh and the late Dr. Hu Shih read parts of the manuscript.

Professor Durham S. F. Chen, my former English teacher, deserves the major credit for the translations. Messrs. Chieh-ming Chu and James C. H. Shen gave me valuable assistance in some translations. A number of documents were translated by myself.

My debts of gratitude are due to Professors George E. Taylor, Kung-chuan Hsiao, and Hellmut Wilhelm for furthering the publication of this study. Miss Gladys Greenwood and Mrs. Margery Lang edited my manuscript for publication. When I put the finishing touches to the manuscript for publication in 1967, I was taking my time out of a research project under the joint sponsorship of the Far Eastern and Russian Institute of the University of Washington and the Institute for Sino-Soviet Studies of the George Washington University.

Microfilm copies of all the Chinese documents annotated in this work are on file in the Far Eastern and Russian Institute of the University of Washington. The items labeled SSC (standing for the Shih Sou collection of the late President Ch'en Ch'eng) are available on microfilm in the Hoover Institution at Stanford University. The documents labeled BIC are in the Bureau of Investigation collection on Taiwan.

Needless to say, I alone am responsible for the annotations and translations of the documents in this volume.

Seattle, Washington   TSO-LIANG HSIAO
June 28, 1967

Contents

The Land Revolution in China, 1930-1934

A STUDY OF DOCUMENTS

I

Li Li-san's Land Policy

SECTION 1. PROVISIONAL LAND LAW

DOCUMENT 1
*Translation on pages 127-30**

PROVISIONAL LAND LAW (土地暫行法 *T'u-ti chan-hsing fa*), adopted by the National Conference of Delegates from the Soviet Areas, May, 1930; printed in *The Red Flag*, No. 107 (June 4, 1930), pp. 2–3, on file in the Hoover Library, Stanford University; reproduced in: *A Collection of Red Bandit Documents*, I, 11–17, 008.2129/4070/V.1, SSC; *A Collection of Red Bandit Reactionary Documents*, III, 918–21, 008.2129/4077/V.3, SSC; Hsiao Tso-liang, *Power Relations within the Chinese Communist Movement, 1930–1934: Vol. II, The Chinese Documents;* approximately 1,400 words.

Land revolution was the main content of the Chinese Communist movement in the period between 1930 and 1934. To a large extent, it reflected intraparty power relations and Moscow's impact on them.

This land law was adopted by the National Conference of Delegates from the Soviet Areas held under the sponsorship of Li Li-san at Shanghai toward the end of May, 1930. It was called provisional because it was to operate until the establishment of the central Soviet government that Li Li-san had in mind as a part of his grand design known as the Li-san line.

The Li-san line was an event of international importance. It was in disagreement with Comintern policy in China.

On October 26, 1929, the Comintern issued a directive to the Chinese Communist Party, saying that China was entering upon the initial stage of a new revolutionary wave and that the strike and demonstration in the city and guerrilla warfare in the countryside should be strengthened

* Parenthetical and footnote references to documents in translation included in this volume are in **boldface type.**

and expanded.[1] This statement did not call for armed insurrection in the city nor military occupation of it. On the contrary, it warned against a repetition of the *putschist* mistakes made in 1927. Obviously, the new revolutionary wave in its initial stage as set forth in this statement was not the same thing as the high tide of the new revolutionary wave prescribed in the Comintern directive of February 25, 1928,[2] which called for armed insurrection in a future situation that, in the eyes of Moscow, was simply not present in China in 1930.

Despite the Comintern directive of October 26, 1929, Li Li-san on June 11, 1930, sponsored a Politburo resolution entitled "The New Revolutionary High Tide and Preliminary Success in One or More Provinces."[3] This resolution was the one document that presented what is commonly known as the Li-san line. In this document, Li Li-san announced the arrival of the new revolutionary high tide,[4] considering conditions ripe for a revolution throughout the country. Acting on his order, the Red Army captured Changsha on July 28 as the first step on the way to Wuhan for the purpose of a nationwide sweep. The Red Army was driven from Changsha after a week, and its second attack on the city in September also failed. Whether his military adventures succeeded or failed, Li Li-san evidently went beyond the scope of the Comintern directive of October 26, 1929.

On July 23, 1930, five days before the Communist capture of Changsha, the Comintern issued another directive to the Chinese Communist Party (Doc. 7). An examination of the complete texts of this Comintern directive and the Li Li-san-sponsored Politburo resolution of June 11 shows that these two statements represent two disparate approaches to the Chinese revolution. On one hand, the Comintern directive declared that the Chinese revolution had a weakness in the initial stage in that it was impossible to occupy the industrial centers at the outset. On the other, the CCP Politburo resolution maintained that once a gigantic struggle of workers was started in key cities, it would

[1] Letter from the Executive Committee of the Communist International to the Central Committee of the Chinese Communist Party, October 26, 1929, reprinted in *Red Documents*, pp. 334–45.

[2] "Comintern Resolution on the Chinese Problem," February 25, 1928, sec. 5, in *Red Documents*, pp. 289–96.

[3] Reproduced in Hsiao Tso-liang, *Power Relations within the Chinese Communist Movement, 1930–1934: Vol. II, The Chinese Documents* (hereafter cited as *Power Relations*, II).

[4] Richard Thornton distinguishes *High tide (kao ch'ao)* from *wave (lang ch'ao)* in "The Comintern and the Chinese Communists: 1928–1931," pp. 217, 232–33, nn. 65, 66.

inevitably lead to a revolutionary sweep all over the country.

Behind these opposing strategies of revolution lay different estimations of the Chinese situation. In its directive of February 25, 1928, the Comintern characterized the Chinese revolution as one of uneven development between the city and the countryside, that is, the peasant movement was outdistancing the labor movement. On the basis of this diagnosis of the Chinese scene, the Comintern directive of July 23, 1930, declared that only the peasant struggle in a few southern provinces could hope to succeed at this time and that the Red Army should be organized and strengthened to occupy one or more industrial and/or administrative centers in the future. In contrast, Li Li-san's Politburo resolution held that people had perceived only the superficial unevenness of the revolutionary development between the city and the countryside, and that they had overlooked the unusual acuteness of the struggle of the workers. If a gigantic struggle of the workers broke out in an industrial or political center, the resolution asserts, a direct revolutionary situation in the country would immediately follow.[5]

Of course, the Li-san line was not confined to immediate urban insurrection. It also deviated from Moscow's policy in China in the sphere of land revolution, as can be seen from the provisional land law under review. This law had the following characteristics, which were among the targets of attack during the liquidation of the Li-san line by Moscow. (Citations are from the original text in *Red Flag*, June 4, 1930.)

1. Prohibition of the purchase, sale, lease, or mortgage of land (art. IV);
2. Creation of collective farms (art. V, expl. nn. 10, 15);
3. Collaboration with the rich peasantry (art. I, expl. n. 2);
4. Denial of land allotments to Red Army men and hired farm hands (art. V, expl. nn. 14, 15).

A little more than seven weeks after the adoption of this land law, the Comintern in its directive of July 23, 1930, to the CCP declared:

> In the field of economic policies in the Soviet areas, the Party must avoid premature measures. It must not take measures which would simply serve to alienate the mass of peasants from our guidance. It may grant freedom in commerce. For the moment, it must not prohibit the purchase and sale of land. Nor must it enforce the concentration of supplies. Nor must it restrict commerce or regulate prices in the [Soviet]

[5] Cf. Hsiao Tso-liang, *Power Relations within the Chinese Communist Movement, 1930–1934: A Study of Documents*, pp. 25–26 (hereafter cited as *Power Relations*, I).

areas. Of course, it will have to make an exception of special cases (salt, coal, and kerosene) which stem from the wishes of the local people to meet military requirements or combat speculation and sabotage.[6]

As I commented on page 21 of *Power Relations within the Chinese Communist Movement, 1930–1934*, Vol. I, this Comintern directive ushered in a stream of Comintern and CCP denunciations of this land law. To the long list of Comintern and CCP statements given there we must add three more documents: (*1*) the statement of Pavel Mif,[7] (*2*) "The Land Problem and the Anti-Rich Peasant Tactics" (Doc. 25), and (*3*) "Resolution on the Land Problem" (Doc. 32).

Less than two months after the Comintern directive of July 23, 1930, had been issued, CCP officials met to prepare blueprints for the central Soviet government which had been contemplated by the Li Li-san leadership since May. Technically, the preparatory work was undertaken by a body known as the Central Preparatory Commission for the National Soviet Congress.[8] In the meeting of the Central Preparatory Commission, the present land law was revised at the suggestion of the representatives of the CCP Central Committee. The revisions were:

1. The words concerning the prohibition of the purchase, sale, or mortgage of land, as provided in article IV, were deleted.

2. The provisions of collective farms, as contained in article V, explanatory notes 10 and 15, were removed.

3. The criteria of land redistribution as listed in article V, explanatory note 9, were no longer specified. Instead, it was stipulated that the plots of the rich peasants, such as their proposition that farm implements should be used as a criterion for land redistribution, were to be smashed.

4. Red Army men, who under article V, explanatory note 14, had to wait for land allotments until the formation of a central Soviet government, were now given land.

Thus, it has become apparent that practically all the characteristics of the present land law which constituted a part of the Li-san line and were at variance with the July 23, 1930, Comintern directive, were removed by the Central Preparatory Commission. Interestingly, the Central Preparatory Commission declared that the revisions made were

[6] Document 7, "Resolution on the Chinese Problem," July, 1930, chap. ii, sec. 8, in *Red Documents*, p. 350.

[7] Mif, *Heroic China: Fifteen Years of the Communist Party of China;* Chinese version entitled *Ying-yung fen-tou ti shih-wu nien* (1936), pp. 92–93, 100.

[8] *Power Relations*, I, 39–40.

only "slight amendments, but no changes in basic principles at all."[9]

Accordingly, this land law with its Li-sanist traits was in force for only a little more than three months. As was seen in the Fu-t'ien incident,[10] it clashed with Mao's agrarian ideas in July, 1930, in Kiangsi, where Mao had been the controlling figure. Its influence came to a stop after a brief, prosperous hour in Oyuwan also.[11] It is therefore doubtful just how far this land law had been put into practice.

In the sphere of ideology, however, the revisions of this land law made by the Central Preparatory Commission marked the beginning of a series of CCP statements denouncing this law as a part of the Li-san line. The denunciations continued until August, 1931.

In Moscow, official attacks on this land law were made until July, 1931, and Pavel Mif's accusations appeared even as late as 1936. Under grilling by Kremlin officials during the Moscow trial in December, 1930, Li Li-san made abject confessions about this law. As the Comintern directive received on November 16 that year (Doc. 8) was the ideological background of the Moscow trial, it may be useful to give its passage bearing on this land law:

> Apart from these weaknesses in the Soviet movement, there were some premature, erroneous attempts at, say, creating collective farms and state farms, practicing planned economy, establishing monopolies, and regulating economic life where no military necessity warranted. The provisional land law adopted by the First Conference of Soviet Areas is basically wrong in its proposed solutions to many problems. It says that only the land taken from the landlord is subject to equal redistribution— that is wrong. It says that large farms should not be divided but should be converted into Soviet state farms—that is wrong. It says that the land assigned to hired farm hands should now be combined into collective farms—that is wrong. It says that Red Army men cannot be assigned land until the formation of Soviet regimes throughout the country— that is wrong, absolutely wrong.[12]

During the Moscow trial, specific points in this land law were singled out for attack, and Li Li-san pleaded guilty of having formulated them. The main charges made by Moscow may be summed up as follows:

[9] See the "Report on the Plenum of the Central Preparatory Commission for the National Soviet Congress," printed in the appendixes to *The Chinese Soviets*, Vol. I (compiled and printed by the Central Preparatory Commission for the National Soviet Congress, November 7, 1930, n.p.); cf. *Power Relations*, I, 48.

[10] *Power Relations*, I, 21, 99, 101, 106–7, 110, 111.

[11] Document 39, *How to Redistribute Land*, sec. I, art. 3; secs. II, III, in *A Collection of Red Bandit Documents*, I, 38–56.

[12] *Red Documents*, p. 368.

1. *The ban on the purchase, sale, lease, or mortgage of land.*

Moscow denounced Li Li-san's ban on the purchase, sale, lease, or mortgage of land as premature.[13]

2. *The formation of collective and state farms.*

This land law provides for collective farms in article V, explanatory notes 10 and 15. It is stated in explanatory note 10 that large-scale farms may not be divided into small pieces, but should be organized into collective farms, producers' cooperatives, and so on, in order to prevent the lessening of productive power. Explanatory note 15 states that the hired farm hands who enjoy special protection under labor law need not be allotted land, but that should they be allotted land, they must pool it to form collective farms. Evidently no all-out collectivization was intended under this land law.

It seems superfluous to point out that what Moscow denounced was not merely collective farms but state or Soviet farms as well.[14] The collective enterprises as enforced in Russia were of these two basic types; but their prohibition in China was predicated on the assumption that it was premature and that such steps would alienate the masses. Article V, explanatory notes 10 and 15, provides for the collective farm *per se*, while what is laid down in article VI is the state or Soviet farm. Of course, the provisions of article V, explanatory note 10, do not preclude the possibility of organizing state or Soviet farms under that article.

3. *Denial of land to Red Army men and hired farm hands.*

Article V, explanatory note 14, denies land allotments to Red Army men who have not received land before. Hired farm hands may not be allotted land under article V, explanatory note 15, on the ground that they are rural workers enjoying special protection under labor law. Denial of land allotments to these two categories of men drew severe criticisms from Comintern officials such as Kuchumov, Safarov, and Comrade P'i during the Moscow trial. According to Kuchumov, for example, the Chinese Red Army men and hired farm hands were denied land because it was feared that workers might become petty

[13] See Document 7; Document 35; "Report of the Comintern Eastern Department on the Errors of the Chinese Party Third Plenum and of Comrade Li Li-san," Moscow, December, 1930; Chinese version as appendix to "The Discussion of the Li-san Line by the Presidium of the ECCI," printed in *Bolshevik* (Shanghai), IV, No. 3 (May 10, 1931), 66–75; reprinted in *Power Relations*, II.

[14] See Document 8; Document 35; Document 36; "Report of the Comintern Eastern Department on the Errors of the Chinese Party Third Plenum and of Comrade Li Li-san," December, 1930.

bourgeoisie and Red Army men might no longer be willing to fight if they were all given land. Comrade P'i complained that these were just the kinds of men with whom the Communists should ally themselves, and yet they were denied land allotments.[15]

4. *Collaboration with the rich peasantry.*

Li Li-san's approach to the rich-peasant problem was attacked violently during the Moscow trial. To understand this matter clearly, it is necessary to realize just how his land law was more lenient to the rich peasantry than were the land laws sponsored by the Chu-Mao group in 1930 and by the Russian Returned Students on the occasion of the proclamation of the Chinese Soviet Republic in 1931. For convenience in discussion, this question may be viewed from two different angles: the *confiscation* and the *redistribution* of the property of a rich peasant.

Confiscation is decreed in this law for only that part of the land of a rich peasant which he rents out (art. I, expl. n. 2). By contrast, the land laws sponsored by the Chu-Mao group (**Doc. 9,** arts. 1, 11) and by the Russian Returned Students (**Doc. 34,** art. 3) deprive a rich peasant of all his land. Moreover, Li Li-san's law provides confiscation of the farm implements and houses of the reactionary rich peasants only (art. V, expl. n. 12), while Chu-Mao's land law deprives the rich peasants of all their houses as well as forests and ponds (art. 1), and the law of the Russian Returned Student leadership removes the surplus houses, farm implements, livestock, grain-husking water mills, oil-pressing mills, and so on, of all rich peasants (art. 8).

In the field of redistribution, the land law of the Chu-Mao group is vague with respect to the rich peasant. It provides only that a rich peasant, like a landlord, shall not be allowed to conceal land nor keep fertile land for himself (**Doc. 9,** art. 10). Another document which we attribute to the Chu-Mao group (see **Doc. 12,** sec. V, art. 15) provides that the rich peasant shall be allotted land in the same way as the middle peasant and the poor peasant, and that he shall neither be allowed to keep fertile land for himself, nor be given poor land purposely. In this connection, the land law of the Russian Returned Student leadership stipulates that a rich peasant may be allotted poor land if he cultivates it with his own labor (**Doc. 34,** art. 3).

In contrast, Li Li-san's land law contains no specific provision on redistribution for a rich peasant—perhaps because the question of re-

---

[15] See "The Discussion of the Li-san Line by the Presidium of the ECCI," *Bolshevik* (Shanghai), IV, No. 3 (May 10, 1931), 14, 31, 58.

distribution for a rich peasant would probably not arise so long as he was deprived of only that part of his land which he rented out. To all intents and purposes, as the Oyuwan Soviet charged, this would be in the interests of a rich peasant, since he would understandably keep fertile land for himself and rent out relatively poor land.[16]

Against this background, Li Li-san in the Moscow trial confessed:

> With regard to the agrarian problem, I made another mistake, that is, a mistake in the question of the rich peasantry. That was a mistake on the part of all the central leadership. At that time the central leadership took the position that collaboration with the rich peasantry should be achieved in the Chinese revolution. . . . The residue of the [influence] of this mistake regarding the rich-peasant problem is still reflected in the provisional land law adopted by the National Conference of Delegates from the Soviet Areas.[17]

Madyar, one of the interrogators in the Moscow trial, was of the opinion that Li Li-san's mistake in collaborating with the rich peasantry flowed from an erroneous statement emanating from the CCP Sixth National Congress of 1928, and that Li Li-san developed a pro-rich-peasant theory on the basis of that erroneous statement despite Moscow's warning.[18]

What was, then, that erroneous statement of the Sixth National Congress and what was Moscow's warning?

It will be recalled that the CCP Sixth National Congress of 1928 adopted several resolutions touching upon the question of the rich peasantry. The political resolution of that congress provides that it is wrong to step up the struggle against the rich peasant intentionally, but this does not mean that the struggle against the rich peasant as a semi-landlord should be abandoned.[19] Again, the resolution on the land problem adopted by that congress sets itself against the rich peasant, not because he is a rich peasant as such but because he has a part of his land for rent and therefore acquires the character of a semilandlord.[20] In addition, the resolution on the peasant problem adopted by the congress stipulates that it is necessary to neutralize or even absorb the rich peasant in the fight against the reactionary forces.[21]

[16] Document 39, *How to Redistribute Land*, sec. I, art. 3, secs. II, III, in *A Collection of Red Bandit Documents*, I, 38–56.

[17] "The Discussion of the Li-san Line by the Presidium of the ECCI," p. 8.

[18] *Ibid.*, p. 25.

[19] *Red Documents*, pp. 165–66.

[20] *Ibid.*, p. 206.

[21] *Ibid.*, p. 225.

All the foregoing points in the resolutions of the CCP Sixth National Congress were cited and criticized by the Comintern directive to the CCP dated June 7, 1929 (Doc. 26). That directive charged also that pro-rich-peasant tactics were even embodied in resolutions and papers of the CCP Central Committee. For instance, it was pointed out that the Central Committee had declared in a letter to Mao Tse-tung:

> In general tactics—in [our] stand against the landlords, it is necessary to cooperate with the rich peasantry. It is wrong to step up the struggle against the rich peasantry intentionally. . . .[22]

Thus, Li Li-san was right when he confessed in the Moscow trial that a pro-rich-peasant policy was not followed by him alone, but by the entire party leadership in China. It seems clear that he treated a rich peasant like a semilandlord as prescribed in the Sixth National Congress resolution on the peasant problem when he saw to it that a rich peasant was not deprived of all his land but only that part of his land that was rented out.

It must be remembered that when the CCP Sixth National Congress was held at Moscow in July, 1928, Stalin had not begun to liquidate the kulaks. The Russian peasants were still enjoying a measure of free economic life in the NEP stage. In May, 1928, Stalin declared that the "expropriation of the kulaks would be folly."[23] It was under such circumstances that the resolutions of the CCP Sixth National Congress were drafted.

In the summer of 1929, however, Stalin made a complete change in his policy toward the peasantry. The kulaks now must be destroyed. To that end, he ordered party workers to "liquidate the kulaks as a class."[24] In keeping with this policy switch in the Soviet Union, the Comintern issued its directive of June 7, 1929 (Doc. 26) to the Chinese Communist Party, urging an unprecedented campaign against the rich peasants in China, singling out documents of the CCP Sixth National Congress and of the CCP leadership for attack. Somehow or other, Li Li-san failed to follow this Comintern reorientation in China.

DOCUMENT 2

PROVISIONAL LAND LAW (土地暫行法 *T'u-ti chan-hsing fa*), adopted by the National Conference of Delegates from the Soviet Areas, May, 1930,

[22] *Ibid.*, pp. 326–27.
[23] Donald W. Treadgold, *Twentieth-Century Russia*, p. 268.
[24] *Ibid.*

and revised by the Central Preparatory Commission for the National Soviet Congress in September, 1930; printed in *The Chinese Soviets*, I, 10–12, 052.2/804, BIC; reprinted in Hsiao Tso-liang, *Power Relations within the Chinese Communist Movement, 1930-1934: Vol. II, The Chinese Documents;* approximately 1,400 words.

This is the text of the provisional land law as revised by the Central Preparatory Commission for the National Soviet Congress in September, 1930. As described in the preceding entry, all the traits of Li Li-sanism in the original text were removed. In addition, some slight changes in the wording of a few articles were also made.

Incidentally, it is interesting to note that the word *Li Li-sanism* appears more than once in the Comintern directive of July, 1931 (Doc. 36),[25] while the word *Maoism,* which is the subject of debate among some contemporary Western observers, has not been used in Comintern sources, nor in Chinese Communist documentations.[26]

SECTION 2. INFLUENCE OF LI LI-SANISM
DOCUMENT 3
LAND LAW OF THE SOUTHWEST KIANGSI SOVIET GOVERNMENT (贛西南蘇維埃政府土地法 *Kan-hsi-nan su-wei-ai cheng-fu t'u-ti fa*), reprinted by the North Route Office of the Southwest Kiangsi Soviet Government, May 26, 1930; mimeographed; 554.282/730, BIC; approximately 2,200 words.

As its title indicates, this land law was enacted by the Southwest Kiangsi Soviet Government, which was controlled by the group that unleashed the Fu-t'ien incident against Mao in December, 1930. That incident brought into the open a clash of land policies between Mao and the rebels, during which the Mao faction censured the rebels for promoting the interests of the rich peasantry.[27] That there were grounds for the censure is confirmed in the present document.

Superficially, this law appears very much like a reproduction of

[25] *Red Documents,* p. 391.

[26] For a debate on "Maoism," see Karl A. Wittfogel's article, "The Legend of 'Maoism,'" *China Quarterly,* Nos. 1, 2, 1960, and Benjamin Schwartz's reply, *China Quarterly,* No. 2, 1960; Conrad Brandt, Benjamin Schwartz, and John K. Fairbank, *A Documentary History of Chinese Communism,* p. 79; Karl Wittfogel, "A Short History of Chinese Communism," an unpublished manuscript on file in the Far Eastern and Russian Institute, University of Washington, chap. v; Boyd R. Compton, *Mao's China: Party Reform Documents, 1942–44,* pp. xxxix ff.; A. Doak Barnett, *Communist China and Asia,* pp. 69–70; John King Fairbank, *The United States and China,* pp. 232–33, 240–41, 304.

[27] *Power Relations,* I, 99, 101, 106–7, 109, 110, 111.

Document 9, the land law of the Chu-Mao group. The language and the arrangement of the articles of the two documents are virtually the same.

However, the differences of the two documents, though slight in terms of the number of the Chinese characters involved, are significant in the local context of the time. First and foremost, the term *rich peasant*, provided here and there in the land law of the Chu-Mao group, is removed altogether from the present document (arts. 1, 10, 11, 20, 24, 29). Unlike the land law of the Chu-Mao group, this document provides that labor power may be adopted as an alternative criterion to the number of persons in land redistribution under special circumstances (art. 9). According to the Mao group, this would operate in the interests of the rich peasants, who had superior labor power by virtue of their greater capital and better farming implements.[28] For the same reason, this document adopts only the principle of draw-on-the-plentiful-to-make-up-for-the-scarce, but not the principle of draw-on-the-fat-to-make-up-for-the-lean (art. 10).

Mao recorded that the rich peasants at Jui-chin and Yü-tu in southern Kiangsi cited article 14 of this land law to protect the interests of the original cultivators of land.

Article 14 reads:

> If land redistribution following an uprising takes place at a time when the peasants have already sown seeds [in the fields], the products of the current year shall be harvested by the peasants who have originally cultivated [the land], and others shall not be allowed to cut and gather them.

Those rich peasants were quoted as saying that whoever violated this land law was counterrevolutionary. To counter the rich peasants, the South Kiangsi Revolutionary Committee issued a proclamation which made known an eight-point land program put forward by Ch'en Yi, foreign minister of the present Chinese Communist regime, at the South Route Enlarged Conference on July 15, 1930. This land program included items like immediate land redistribution, draw-on-the-plentiful-to-make-up-for-the-scarce, draw-on-the-fat-to-make-up-for-the-lean, unconditional redistribution of houses, forests, ponds, and so on.[29]

The interests of the petty bourgeoisie are also safeguarded in the present document (arts. 21, 25). This confirms the charge brought by

[28] *Ibid.*, p. 106.
[29] Mao Tse-tung, *Investigations of the Rural Districts*, pp. 76–77.

the Mao group against the Fu-t'ien rebels that the party and political leadership in southwest Kiangsi was dominated by petty bourgeois intellectuals.[30]

Article 2 of this law provides that if an owner-peasant has more land than he needs for his own use, the excess portion of his land must be confiscated and redistributed. Though the term *owner-peasant* is used instead of *rich peasant,* this article sounds very much like Li Li-san's policy under which a rich peasant was deprived of that part of his land which he rented out. No wonder that Mao told Edgar Snow in 1936 that the incident at Fu-t'ien was essentially a conflict with Li Li-sanism.[31]

DOCUMENT 4

REGULATIONS GOVERNING THE LAND AND BUSINESS TAXES (土地商業稅則 *T'u-ti shang-yeh shui-tse*), a proclamation of the Hunan Provincial Soviet Government, 1930; reproduced in *A Collection of Red Bandit Secret Documents,* Vol. V, leaves 33–35, 008.2129/4074, SSC; mimeographed; approximately 1,100 words.

This proclamation announces the scales of the land and business taxes under the Hunan Provincial Soviet Government in 1930. The land tax was from 2 to 25 per cent of the rice harvested, or from 2 to more than $2\frac{1}{2}$ times as high as that provided in Mao's land law.

The proclamation was issued under the name of Li Li-san as chairman of the Standing Committee of the Hunan Provincial Soviet Government with P'eng Teh-huai and others as members. This leads one to wonder whether Li Li-san was in Hunan himself in the course of the Communist attacks on Changsha in July and September, 1930.[32]

DOCUMENT 5

THE LAND PROBLEM (土地問題 *T'u-ti wen-t'i*), a resolution adopted by the Presidium of the Action Committee, November 18, 1930, Chi-an, Kiangsi; reproduced in *A Collection of Red Bandit Secret Documents,* Vol. V, leaves 11–17; 008.2129/4074, SSC; mimeographed; approximately 4,000 words.

This document is a strange combination of conflicting land policies of the different cliques of the CCP at the time. On the one hand, it includes traits of Li Li-san's land policy, such as collective farms and

[30] *Power Relations,* I, 109.
[31] Edgar Snow, *Red Star over China,* p. 182.
[32] See *Power Relations,* I, 14–38; **Document 1.**

the prohibition of the purchase, sale, or lease of land. On the other, it incorporates some of Mao's ideas, such as redistribution according to the number of persons rather than labor power, and the twin principles of draw-on-the-plentiful-to-make-up-for-the-scarce and draw-on-the-fat-to-make-up-for-the-lean.

As this is a resolution adopted by a local party unit on the basis of a letter from a representative of a higher level party organization, it can scarcely be regarded as an authoritative statement. It seems to reflect the ideological confusion among the rank and file Communists during the transition period marked by the decline of the Li Li-san leadership.

DOCUMENT 6

SIGNIFICANCE OF THE COLLECTING OF THE AGRICULTURAL PROGRESSIVE TAX IN WAN-TSAI COUNTY (萬載縣蘇府徵收農業累進稅之意義 *Wan-tsai hsien su-fu cheng-shou nung-yeh lei-chin-shui chih i-i*), issued by the Wan-tsai County Soviet Government, western Kiangsi, December 28, 1930; reproduced in *A Collection of Red Bandit Secret Documents*, Vol. V, leaves 35–36, 008.2129/4074; SSC; mimeographed; approximately 600 words.

As its title indicates, this document sets forth the meaning of the collecting of the agricultural progressive tax, accompanied by a list of criteria of taxation.

SECTION 3. COMINTERN REPERCUSSIONS
DOCUMENT 7

RESOLUTION ON THE CHINESE PROBLEM, ADOPTED BY THE ECCI POLITICAL SECRETARIAT ON JULY 23, 1930 (中國問題決議案—共產國際執委政治秘書處一九三〇年七月二十三日通過 *Chung-kuo wen-t'i chüeh-i-an—kung-ch'an kuo-chi chih-wei cheng-chih pi-shu-ch'u i-chiu-san-ling nien ch'i yüeh erh-shih-san jih t'ung-kuo*), Chinese version printed in *Red Documents*, published by *Chiai-fang-she*, February, 1938, n.p., pp. 346–61, 008.2129/2703, SSC; reproduced in: *A Collection of Red Bandit Secret Documents*, Vol. III, leaves 3–12, 008.2129/4070, SSC; Hsiao Tso-liang, *Power Relations within the Chinese Communist Movement, 1930–1934: Vol. II, The Chinese Documents;* mimeographed; approximately 7,800 words.

This Comintern directive has been discussed at length in my study *Power Relations within the Chinese Communist Movement, 1930–34*, I, 28–31. For our present purposes it should be noted that sections 6 to 8 of this statement are exclusively concerned with the agrarian problems and that, as described previously, this was the first Comintern statement which called Li Li-san's land policy into question.

DOCUMENT 8

LETTER FROM THE ECCI TO THE CCP CENTRAL COMMITTEE, RECEIVED ON NOVEMBER 16, 1930 (共産國際執行委員會給中國共産黨中央委員會的信, 一九三〇年十一月十六日收到 *Kung-ch'an kuo-chi chih-hsing wei-yüan-hui chi chung-kuo kung-ch'an-tang chung-yang wei-yüan-hui ti hsin, i-chiu-san-ling nien shih-i yüeh shih-liu jih shou-tao*), Chinese version printed in *Red Documents,* published by *Chiai-fang-she,* February, 1938, n.p., pp. 362–75, 008.2129/2703, SSC; reproduced in: *A Collection of Red Bandit Reactionary Documents,* II, 433–47, 008.2129/4077, V.2, SSC; Hsiao Tso-liang, *Power Relations within the Chinese Communist Movement, 1930–1934: Vol. II, The Chinese Documents;* approximately 7,000 words.

This statement, as pointed out in my work *Power Relations within the Chinese Communist Movement, 1930–34,* I, 74–77, was a Comintern rejection of the CCP Third Plenum verdict that Li Li-san did not err in line but in tactics. The Comintern's criticisms of the land policy of Li Li-san were directed against collectivization and the like.

II

Land Policy of the Chu-Mao Group

SECTION 1. GENERAL PLAN

DOCUMENT 9
Translation on pages 130-35

LAND LAW (土地法 *T'u-ti fa*), promulgated by the Chinese Revolutionary Military Council, n.d., reprinted by the General Political Department of the First Army Corps of the Red Army, 1930; reproduced: (1931) *A Collection of Red Bandit Secret Documents*, Vol. V, leaves 1–4, 008.2129/4074, SSC; (1935) *A Collection of Red Bandit Reactionary Documents*, III, 912–18, 008.2129/4072,V.3, SSC; (1947) *A Collection of Important Documents of Communist Bandits' Land Policy*, pp. 33–37, 554.2821/ 804, BIC; Hsiao Tso-liang, *Power Relations within the Chinese Communist Movement, 1930–1934: Vol. II, The Chinese Documents;* approximately 2,000 words.

The reproductions of this law as listed above are identical except for a few typographical errors. Since the 1931 version is the earliest text available, it is used as the basis of our discussion here. With the exception of a small number of characters, the text of this document agrees entirely with that of the land law adopted by the Southwest Kiangsi Soviet Government in 1930 (Doc. 3), which is a genuine Communist document issued and reprinted by the Communists themselves.

Though it is not easy to determine precisely when the Chinese Revolutionary Military Council which promulgated this law was in existence, there seems to be little doubt that this land law was enacted by the Chu-Mao group.

The evidences are:

17

1. The principles of draw-on-the-plentiful-to-make-up-for-the-scarce and draw-on-the-fat-to-make-up-for-the-lean.

These twin principles are a special feature of this land law (art. 10). The land law of the Southwest Kiangsi Soviet Government provides only the principle of draw-on-the-plentiful-to-make-up-for-the-scarce but not the principle of draw-on-the-fat-to-make-up-for-the-lean (art. 10). According to an official CCP statement, it was Mao who introduced these twin principles.[1] Another official CCP source says that these twin principles were introduced in the February 7 Conference of 1930,[2] which, according to still another source, was a conference sponsored by Mao and his group.[3] It must, however, be remembered that the February 7, 1930, conference which discussed the land question at length apparently did not pass a land law. It is not clear when this law was adopted. Could this be a survival of the land law which was recommended by Ch'en Yi, foreign minister of the present Communist regime? That law was decided upon by the West River Joint Meeting in the summer of 1930, but was defeated at the last moment through the effort of a member of the Southwest Kiangsi group, the same group that was behind the Fut'ien incident toward the end of that year.[4]

It should be noted that the twin principles in question reappear in article 6 of the land law adopted by the CCP national land conference on September 13, 1947, and that they are again provided in article 11 of the land reform law of June 28, 1950, abbreviated into the two characters *ch'ou pu*, standing for *draw-on* and *make-up*. Both these land laws were sponsored by Mao shortly before and after the Communist conquest of the Chinese mainland in 1949.

2. Land redistribution according to the number of persons.

Communists in China, as in Russia, have followed two criteria in land redistribution: (1) labor power or working capacity of individuals, and (2) the number of persons or, rather, the mouths to be fed. They

---

[1] "Resolution on Some Historical Problems," adopted by the CCP Central Committee on April 20, 1945, in Mao Tse-tung, *Selected Works of Mao Tse-tung*, Chinese ed., III, 974; English ed., IV, 191; pamphlet form of this resolution, p. 25; *Power Relations*, II; cf. Lu Ch'iang, *The "Hero" on the Ching-kang-shan*, p. 25.

[2] "Political Resolution Adopted by the First Party Congress of the [Central] Soviet Area" (printed by Central Bureau, Soviet Areas, November, 1931), leaf 3, side 1; reprinted in *Power Relations*, II.

[3] "A Reply of the General Front Committee," in *A Collection of Reactionary Documents* (compiled by KMT Headquarters, Fourteenth Division of the Army, March 1, 1932), Vol. III, leaf 14, side 2; reprinted in *Power Relations*, II; see also *Power Relations*, I, 7, 8, 21, 99, 106, 107, 109, 165; cf. Snow, *Red Star over China*, pp. 174–75.

[4] Mao, *Investigations of the Rural Districts*, p. 77.

have sometimes adopted one or the other (e.g., Li Li-san's land law), sometimes mixed them together (e.g., the land law of the Chinese Soviet Republic). Mao has persistently advocated land redistribution on the basis of the number of persons in preference to labor power. This land law confirms Mao's position by providing in article 8 that land shall be equally redistributed according to the number of persons in the villages, irrespective of sex or age, and that the method of using labor power as the criterion for land redistribution shall not be adopted.

Mao stood for the equal redistribution of land among all people, without respect to sex or age, at Ching-kang-shan (see Appendix), though he for some time also adopted labor power as a criterion of redistribution in accordance with instructions of the party leadership.[5] He later made it clear that redistributing land according to labor power was wrong and that equal land redistribution according to the number of persons had generally been followed throughout the long years in the Red areas.[6] During the Fu-t'ien incident in December, 1930, Mao and his group reaffirmed the principle of equal land redistribution as opposed to the criterion of labor power.[7]

The criterion of the number of persons was again adopted in the land law of 1947 (art. 6) and the land reform law of 1950 (art. 11, with supplementary provisions in art. 13).

According to William Henry Chamberlin, in the allotment of land to peasant households during the Russian revolution, the usual rule was for each household to receive land in proportion to the number of its members, and this practice remained in force until the introduction of state and collective farming.[8]

Prior to this land law, Mao had worked out two land laws, the one at Ching-kang-shan in December, 1928, and the other at Hsing-kuo in April, 1929. Thirteen years later, in 1941, Mao admitted that he and his fellow Communists had no experience in land struggle before Ching-kang-shan and that there were a number of errors of principle in the Ching-kang-shan land law, namely: (1) confiscation of all land rather than the land of the landlord alone, (2) landownership in the hands of the state rather than the peasants, who could only use the land, and (3) ban on the purchase and sale of land. This law also introduced common cultivation[9] and labor power as alternative measures for land

[5] Mao, *Selected Works*, Chinese ed., I, 73; English ed., I, 90.

[6] *Ibid.*, Chinese ed., I, 86, n. 21; English ed., I, 307–8, n. 21.

[7] *Power Relations*, I, 99, 101, 106.

[8] Chamberlin, *The Russian Revolution, 1917–1921*, I, 256.

[9] The term *collective cultivation* was not used.

redistribution, but these, as Mao said, were neither his own ideas nor his principal policies.[10]

In April, 1929, Mao adopted the land law at Hsing-kuo, in southern Kiangsi, after he and his troops had been driven from Ching-kang-shan. In this land law there was an important policy shift in that confiscation was restricted to the land of the landlord and what was known as public land, that is, land belonging to organizations, as distinguished from individuals. Mao did not explain why this policy shift was necessary at the time. He said only that this was a change of principle and that the other points were changed in 1930.[11]

One cannot fail to note how the policy shift in the Hsing-kuo land law harmonized with the land program of the CCP Sixth National Congress held in the summer of 1928. This land program prescribed: (1) confiscation of only the land of landlords, organizations, and so on, (2) redistribution of the confiscated land only to peasants for their use, and (3) no ban on the purchase and sale of the peasant land.[12] In addition, the idea of confiscating all land, as embodied in the 1928 Ching-kang-shan land law, was practically equivalent to land nationalization (Doc. 25), and the CCP Sixth National Congress, held in Moscow in July, 1928, prescribed land nationalization as a mere slogan for the moment in China, only to be carried out after the consolidation of the Soviet regime.[13]

On April 12, 1944, Mao commented on the land policy of the Russian Returned Student leadership of 1931–34:

> The errors of that time consisted in the ultraleftist policies of allotting no land to the landlords and only poor land to the rich peasants. But in confiscating the land of the landlords and redistributing it to the peasants who had no or little land, [they] were all at one with us.[14]

About a year later, on April 20, 1945, Mao reaffirmed his position by stating through his party machine that in Kiangsi and western

[10] See Appendix A: Mao's comments on the Ching-kang-shan land law of December, 1928.

[11] See Appendix B: the Hsing-kuo land law and Mao's comment on it.

[12] "Resolution of the Sixth National Congress on the Land Problem," July 9, 1928, chap. v, sec. 20, in *Red Documents*, pp. 196–222.

[13] "Resolution on the Chinese Problem," adopted by the Seventh Enlarged Session of the ECCI, November, 1926, chap. iv, sec. xi, in *Red Documents*, pp. 245–66; *International Line*, III, 1–21; "Resolution of the Sixth National Congress on the Land Problem," July 9, 1928, chap. v, sec. 21, in *Red Documents*, pp. 196–222; Document 25.

[14] Mao, *Selected Works*, Chinese ed., III, 943; English ed., IV, 158–59.

Fukien it had been necessary to provide the rich peasants with certain economic opportunities and to enable the ordinary landlords to make a living.[15]

Thus, Mao has given us to understand that he was in favor of allotting land to landlords and treating rich peasants on an equal footing with other peasants in land redistribution during the Kiangsi period. These views of Mao are not confirmed in the present land law. Even making a liberal allowance for Mao's claim and translating article 2 of this law in two different ways, it is still impossible to clarify the status of the landlords. Therefore, we must examine other sources.

Other sources show that Mao's position on the status of the landlords after confiscation of their land was not clear before the proclamation of the Chinese Soviet Republic in November, 1931. On the one hand, he advocated the division of the total land of a township by its total population.[16] Since he did not exclude landlords from the total population, the implication was that they were included. This implication was strengthened by the charge brought by the local party leadership against him that, as a result of equal land redistribution, landlords and their dependents had received equal land allotments with the peasants (Doc. 32). On the other hand, available documents suggest that Mao was not in favor of redistributing land to landlords whose land had been confiscated. The land laws of Ching-kang-shan (1928) and Hsing-kuo (1929) (see Appendix) did not provide redistribution of land to landlords and subsequent documents took the same position.[17]

It seems clear that most landlords fled before the Communists and that those who stayed behind were executed or otherwise maltreated.[18] There were few cases in which landlords were allotted land in strongly Communist-controlled areas.[19] Accordingly, the real problem left behind by the landlords was those of their dependents who remained in their home villages. According to Mao's policy, these dependents of the landlords received land allotments in redistribution.[20]

After the establishment of the Chinese Soviet Republic in November, 1931, Mao's attitude toward landlords whose land had been confiscated was clear. Like the Russian Returned Students, he denied landlords the

---

[15] *Ibid.*, Chinese ed., III, 974; English ed., IV, 191.

[16] Mao, *Investigations of the Rural Districts*, pp. 81–82.

[17] **Document 12**, sec. V, art. 16; **Document 13**; *The Red Flag Weekly*, No. 24, November 27, 1931, p. 45.

[18] Mao, *Investigations of the Rural Districts*, pp. 27–28.

[19] *Ibid.*, p. 27.

[20] *Ibid.*, p. 81.

right to land allotments in redistribution. Not only did he, as chief executive and premier, administer the land law of the Chinese Soviet Republic, which kept landlords from regaining expropriated land, but, more pertinently, he sponsored the important statement, *Decisions concerning Some Problems Arising from the Agrarian Struggle* (**Doc. 101**), in October, 1933. In that statement, landlords were denied all land allotments (sec. 1, expl. nn., item 6; secs. 14, 15, 16).

The position of the rich peasants in land redistribution was not an issue at Ching-kang-shan in December, 1928, nor at Hsing-kuo in April, 1929. After the arrival of the Comintern directive of June 7, 1929 (Doc. 26), ordering the liquidation of the rich peasants in China, the situation changed abruptly. The land of rich peasants was all confiscated[21] under the regime of Mao, during the period under review.

As to the allotment of land in redistribution to rich peasants whose land had been confiscated, the situation before the creation of the Chinese Soviet Government in 1931 was different from that after it. Before 1931, Mao and his group treated the rich peasants in the same manner as other peasants.[22] After 1931, Mao, like the Russian Returned Students, allotted only poor land to rich peasants according to article 3 of the land law of the Chinese Soviet Republic (**Doc. 34**), a law which was drafted, so far as the status of the rich peasants in redistribution is concerned, on the basis of the Comintern directive of July, 1931 (Doc. 36). In various authoritative documents for which Mao was responsible, the rich peasants were allotted only poor land without exception.[23]

DOCUMENT 10

THE LAND PROGRAM OF THE CHINESE COMMUNIST PARTY (中國共產黨 土地政綱 *Chung-kuo kung-ch'an-tang t'u-ti cheng-kang*), an official proclamation issued under the name of the Political Department of the First Army Corps of the Chinese Workers' and Peasants' Red Army, n.d. (probably July 9, 1928), 008.743/4041, SSC; reproduced with slight textual discrepancies in: *A Collection of Red Bandit Secret Documents,* Vol. V, leaves 6–7, 008.2129/4074, SSC; *A Collection of Red Bandit*

---

[21] See this land law (**Document 9**), arts. 1, 11; **Document 21**, secs. 2, 3, 4; Mao, *Investigations of the Rural Districts,* pp. 19, 28, 70; **Document 60**, secs. 6, 7; **Document 96**, sec. 2.

[22] Mao, *Investigations of the Rural Districts,* p. 28; **Document 12**, sec. 5, par. 15; cf. Document 32 (008.743/4047–3, SSC), leaf 2, side 2.

[23] **Document 60**, sec. 6; **Document 62**, par. 3; **Document 96**, sec. 2; **Document 101**: latter part of sec. 1; sec. 3, illus. 1 and 2; sec. 6, expl. nn. 1 and 2.

Reactionary Documents, III, 910–12, 008.2129/4072, V.3, SSC; and *A Collection of Red Bandit Documents,* I, 10–11, 008.2129/4070, V.1, SSC; approximately 360 words.

This document is an official Communist proclamation captured by Nationalist troops in the Kiangsi-Fukien area in late 1930 or early 1931. It was issued under the name of the political department of the First Army Corps of the Chinese Red Army, of which Chu Teh was commander and Mao apparently political commissar. As Volume V of the *Collection of Red Bandit Secret Documents,* in which a reproduction of this document is included, was printed on September 1, 1931, it is obvious that this proclamation was issued in the Kiangsi-Fukien area before that date.

This statement consists of eight articles dealing with (*1*) replacement of the old regime by a peasant regime in the rural districts, (*2*) confiscation of the land of landlords, gentry, and village bosses, and redistribution of it to the peasants for their use, (*3*) redistribution of the land of temples, churches, and so on, to the peasants for their use, (*4*) appropriation of a part of public land for reclamation and for the use of the Red Army personnel, (*5*) nullification of usurious loans, (*6*) burning of the title deeds of the landlords, and so on, (*7*) state assistance in the peasant economy, and (*8*) replacement of all exorbitant taxes by a uniform agricultural progressive tax.

Though not indicated, this statement is taken almost verbatim from chapter 5, section 20, of the resolution on the land problem adopted by the CCP Sixth National Congress held at Moscow in July, 1928.[24] Commenting on the resolutions of the CCP Sixth National Congress on April 12, 1944, Mao declared that the line of that congress was basically correct despite some shortcomings.[25]

DOCUMENT 11

PROCLAMATION OF THE NAN-FENG COUNTY SOVIET GOVERNMENT ON LAND REDISTRIBUTION (南豐縣蘇維埃政府為重分土地之佈告 *Nan-feng hsien su-wei-ai cheng-fu wei ch'ung-fen t'u-ti chih pu-kao*), December 4, 1930; reproduced in *A Collection of Red Bandit Secret Documents,* Vol. V, leaves 18–19, 008.2129/4074, SSC; mimeographed; approximately 250 words.

Land redistribution was not carried out in Kiangsi once, but a number of times. Finding the past record unsatisfactory, this proclamation

[24] "Resolution of the Sixth National Congress on the Land Problem," July 9, 1928, *Red Documents,* pp. 196–222.

[25] Mao, *Selected Works,* Chinese ed., III, 943; English ed., IV, 159.

decrees another round of redistribution in the county of Nan-feng by December 12, 1930.

There seems to be no doubt that this document is based on Mao's ideas. This is evident from, *inter alia,* the adoption of the twin principles of draw-on-the-plentiful-to-make-up-for-the-scarce and draw-on-the-fat-to-make-up-for-the-lean.

Ho Kan-chih, a Communist historian, states that these twin principles of land redistribution were carried out in two phases. The first of the two principles, which sought to solve the problem of land redistribution quantitively, was put into effect first. Under it, those who had more land should give some of their holdings to those who had less land so that each one in the community might receive an equal share of land. That done, however, there was still the danger of inequality in respect to the quality of the land allotments. Therefore, a second redistribution of land was necessary, whereby those who had more fertile land must set aside part of it to help those who had less fertile land. In this way, the redistribution of land was made equal among all the people not only in quantity but in quality as well.[26] Ho's statement on this score has support in another Communist source, an article entitled "The Central Soviet Area in Kiangsi," printed in *Red Flag Weekly* of November 27, 1931, page 45.

DOCUMENT 12
Translation on pages 136-42

AN OUTLINE OF THE LAND PROBLEM (土地問題提綱 *T'u-ti wen-t'i t'i-kang*), adopted by the Joint Meeting of the Chairmen of County and District Soviet Governments, Kiangsi, sometime before September 1, 1931; reproduced in *A Collection of Red Bandit Secret Documents,* Vol. V, leaves 7–11, 008.2129/4074, SSC; mimeographed; approximately 2,000 words.

This paper itemizes in outline form the theory and practice of the land revolution in the early Kiangsi period. It falls into seven sections, dealing with (*1*) aggression of imperialism and the bankruptcy of rural economy, (*2*) land distribution and class relations in old China, (*3*) land revolution as the main content of the Chinese revolution, (*4*) equal land redistribution, (*5*) methods of equal redistribution, (*6*) land problem after redistribution, and (*7*) the problem of debts. Each section is subdivided into a number of items.

---

[26] Ho Kan-chih, *History of the Contemporary Chinese Revolution,* p. 143.

The basic ideas of this paper agree essentially with those of the land law of the Chu-Mao group (**Doc. 9**); some of the key words and phrases are identical. Points of similarity follow:

1. Land should be redistributed equally on a per capita basis. The total amount of land in a township should be divided by the total population of that township, irrespective of sex or age (sec. 5, par. 2).

2. Equal land redistribution should be carried out according to the principles of draw-on-the-plentiful-to-make-up-for-the-scarce and draw-on-the-fat-to-make-up-for-the-lean (sec. 4, par. 5).

3. Among the beneficiaries of land redistribution were hired farm hands, jobless persons, artisans, poor people, and so on (sec. 5, pars. 12–18).

However, this paper also has features which cannot be found in the land law of the Chu-Mao group—for example, approval of private landownership (sec. 6, par. 1).

It may be of interest to note that the figures of the composition of the rural population, as given in section 2 of this paper—10 per cent landlords and rich peasants, 20 per cent middle peasants, and 70 per cent poor peasants—agree with those given in Mao's 1927 statement, *Report on the Investigation of the Peasant Movement in Hunan.*[27] Curiously, this 1927 statement of Mao, described as a revolutionary classic on page 77 of *A Documentary History of Chinese Communism,*[28] cannot be found in the Ch'en Ch'eng collection in Taiwan, nor is it cited or mentioned in any of the documents in that collection, including the statements made by Mao himself.

With regard to land distribution among the different classes in China, it was estimated that approximately 30 per cent of the land belonged to landlords, 20 per cent to rich peasants, 20 per cent to landlords and rich peasants under the name of public land, 15 per cent to middle peasants, and 10 to 15 per cent to poor peasants. These figures are important in that they probably provided a guide for the Chinese Communists in the practical redistribution of land. It is likely that they were obtained in much the same manner that Mao outlines in Document 15.

---

[27] *Guide Weekly*, No. 191, March 12, 1927, pp. 2063–68; Mao, *Selected Works*, Chinese ed., I, 22; English ed., I, 31.

[28] By Conrad Brandt, Benjamin Schwartz, and John K. Fairbank.

DOCUMENT 13

Translation on pages 142-45

PROCLAMATION OF THE KIANGSI PROVINCIAL GOVERNMENT ON THE LAND PROBLEM (江西省府關於土地問題的佈告 *Chiang-hsi sheng-fu kuan-yü t'u-ti wen-t'i ti pu-kao*), 1931; reproduced in *A Collection of Reactionary Documents,* Vol. I, book 4, leaves 8–10, 008.2129/7120/V.1, Nos. 3–4, SSC; mimeographed; approximately 1,100 words.

In attempting to elaborate Mao's views, Ho Kan-chih declares that the ownership of confiscated land passed to the government, not to the peasantry, under the land laws enacted at Ching-kang-shan in December, 1928, and at Hsing-kuo in April, 1929. It followed that land could not be purchased and sold, and that the peasantry had the right of using the land only, not owning it. However, he says, all such things underwent a change in 1930 when the peasantry was allowed to own land and sell it at will.[29]

This document confirms the change reported by Ho Kan-chih. But the date of such a change as recorded in this proclamation and other available documents is 1931, rather than 1930. There can be little doubt that this change took place under the impact of Moscow.[30]

This Kiangsi Proclamation consists of eight clauses, the first of which provides that land should be redistributed according to the number of persons on the basis of the principles of draw-on-the-plentiful-to-make-up-for-the-scarce and draw-on-the-fat-to-make-up-for-the-lean, and that the land, thus redistributed, belonged to the peasantry who could lease, purchase, or sell it at will. In this connection, it should be noted that the 1930 land law of the Chu-Mao group stood for public ownership of all confiscated land (**Doc. 9,** arts. 1, 10, 12, 13), that Li Li-san prohibited the purchase, sale, lease, or mortgage of land (**Doc. 1,** art. IV) and advocated the carrying out of land nationalization (art. IV of the Chinese Soviet Political Program adopted at the National Conference of Delegates from the Soviet Areas, May, 1930)[31] and that the

[29] Ho Kan-chih, *History of the Contemporary Chinese Revolution,* p. 144.

[30] Document 7, "Resolution on the Chinese Problem," July, 1930, sec. 6, in *Red Documents,* pp. 346–61; Document 35, Draft Resolution on the Land and Peasant Problems in Soviet Areas, basic task No. 4, par. 3, in *A Collection of Red Bandit Secret Documents,* Vol. III, leaves 38–45; Document 36, Letter of the ECCI Presidium to the CCP, sec. 27, par. 1, in *Red Documents,* pp. 376–404.

[31] *The Chinese Soviet Political Program,* reprinted in *A Collection of Red Bandit Secret Documents,* Vol. II, leaves 1–2, in *A Collection of Red Bandit Reactionary Documents,* III, 655–56, and in *Power Relations,* II.

Russian Returned Students championed peasant landownership (**Doc. 34,** arts. 1, 2, 3, 6, 12).

Examination of this proclamation to determine the status of landlords before 1931 leaves a strong impression that landlords were not assigned land in Kiangsi in 1931 nor before.

DOCUMENT 14

PROCLAMATION OF THE KIANGSI PROVINCIAL SOVIET GOVERNMENT, URGING LAND REDISTRIBUTION AND ANNOUNCING LAND OWNERSHIP (江西省蘇維埃政府為督促分配土地及宣佈土地所有權之佈告 *Chiang-hsi-sheng su-wei-ai cheng-fu wei tu-ts'u fen-p'ei t'u-ti chi hsüan-pu t'u-ti so-yu ch'üan chih pu-kao*), reprinted at Shui-nan District, Kiangsi, December, 1931; reproduced in *A Collection of Red Bandit Secret Documents*, Vol. V, leaves 17–18, 008.2129/4074, SSC; mimeographed; approximately 1,000 words.

This statement agrees in spirit with Document 13. It denounces the past mistakes of making the government own the land, banning its free purchase and sale, and allowing the peasantry to use it only. New decisions are announced. As from that date, the redistribution of land was to be considered settled if it was carried out through the process of draw-on-the-plentiful-to-make-up-for-the-scarce and draw-on-the-fat-to-make-up-for-the-lean. The land thus redistributed belonged to the peasant who received it. He was to enjoy all the rights of using, leasing, selling, or otherwise disposing of the land at will.

It is made clear that it would take a long time to realize socialism, that private landownership was necessary for the moment, and that premature ideas like collectivization would not do.

SECTION 2. MAO'S RURAL INVESTIGATIONS
DOCUMENT 15

AN INVESTIGATION OF HSING-KUO (興國調查 *Hsing-kuo tiao-ch'a*), by Mao Tse-tung, late October, 1930; completed in article form on January 26, 1931; published at Yenan in 1941; printed in Mao Tse-tung, *Investigations of the Rural Districts*, Hsinhua Bookstore, Shantung, 1946, pp. 5–57, and in Mao Tse-tung, *Selected Works*, Northeast Bookstore, n.p., 1948, pp. 51–108; approximately 35,300 words.

During the period of land revolution from 1927 to 1934, Mao made a number of investigations into the rural conditions in Hunan and Kiangsi. He drafted a variety of papers, reports, and regulations on the basis of those investigations and managed to preserve about a dozen of them through the Long March of 1934–1935. In 1941 at Yenan he published these materials in a collection of documents entitled *Investigations of the Rural Districts*.[32] The present document is the first piece in that collection.

This document is important in that it was typical of the kind of rural investigation from which Mao derived his knowledge of the conditions in the Chinese countryside. He stated that the investigation of Hsing-kuo made in October, 1930, as described in this document, was more intensive than all previous investigations,[33] including those made in Hunan in the spring of 1927 and in Ching-kang-shan in the spring of 1928, the records of both of which were missing.[34]

Mao showed great pride in his methods of investigation, without which, he said, it would be impossible for the Communists to understand the true conditions in Chinese society. He insisted on his type of investigation despite the fact that it had been branded by other Chinese Communists as "narrow empiricism."[35]

In order to understand Mao's work of investigation, the following two points should be considered:

1. Mao stated that the investigations were made on the basis of class analysis.[36] This traditional Communist starting point imposes obvious strictures.

In Hsing-kuo, in particular, Mao divided the rural population into different classes: landlords, rich peasants, middle peasants, poor peasants, and hired farm hands, plus other kinds of people such as handicraftsmen and businessmen.[37] Mao first used this classification of the rural population in his 1927 *Hunan Report*, whose basic ideas were in turn derived from Lenin and the Comintern.[38] In accordance with Lenin's analysis of the Russian peasantry, Mao declared in his *Hunan Report* that the attitudes of the peasants toward the revolution are different: the rich peasants are inactive, the middle peasants vacillating,

---

[32] Mao, *Investigations of the Rural Districts*, pp. 1, 2–4, 144.

[33] *Ibid.*, p. 5.

[34] *Ibid.*, pp. 1, 2.

[35] *Ibid.*, pp. 2–4.

[36] *Ibid.*, p. 2.

[37] *Ibid.*, pp. 27–43.

[38] V. I. Lenin, "Preliminary Draft of Theses on the Agrarian Question," *Selected Works*, X, 218–30; "Theses on the Peasant Question," adopted by the Enlarged ECCI Meeting, April, 1925, *International Press Correspondence* (hereafter referred to as *Inprecorr*), Vol. V, No. 47 (June 4, 1925); Mao's *Hunan Report, Selected Works,* I.

and the poor peasants (including the landless farm hands) are the revolutionary vanguard or main force in the countryside.[39]

Just as Lenin made no mention of proletarian hegemony in his 1920 "Preliminary Theses on the National and Colonial Questions,"[40] Mao did not discuss this question in his *Hunan Report*. Mao never deviated from the Comintern line concerning proletarian hegemony.[41] An examination of Comintern statements on China from the beginning shows that when the Comintern directive of November, 1926,[42] referred to the proletariat as the only class capable of carrying on a radical agrarian policy, the word *proletariat* was used here as the antonym of the word *bourgeoisie* rather than as an antonym of *peasantry*. Since a Comintern-prescribed Communist revolution could be carried out in a country in which there was almost no industrial proletariat,[43] Mao was by no means generous to the peasants when he, in the original version of the *Hunan Report*, gave them only 70 per cent of the credit of the democratic revolution, while allotting 30 per cent of the credit to the city dwellers and the military. Later, Mao removed the 30–70 per cent formula from his *Hunan Report*.

2. Despite the title of this document, Mao's investigation did not cover the whole county of Hsing-kuo, but only the county's Tenth, or Yung-feng, district. The investigation was not conducted on the spot, but in another county, where Mao called in eight persons who had just arrived from the Tenth district of Hsing-kuo. The eight persons did not represent the different social strata of their home district; they were all peasants, some of them Communists, sent by the Hsing-kuo authorities to join the Red Army. Mao's procedure of investigation was to prepare a questionnaire first. Item by item he asked the participants questions and discussed them. He wrote down the conclusions reached at his suggestion and with the others' consent. Where no conclusions were reached, only their answers were recorded. The discussions took place two or three times a day during a week toward the end of October, 1930.[44]

[39] E. H. Carr, *The Bolshevik Revolution, 1917–1925*, II, 160–61.

[40] Lenin, "Preliminary Draft of Theses on the National and Colonial Questions," *Selected Works*, X, 231–38.

[41] See, for example, his two statements immediately preceding and following his *Hunan Report* in the official edition of his *Selected Works*, I.

[42] "Resolution on the Chinese Problem," adopted by the Seventh Enlarged Session of the ECCI, November, 1926, *Red Documents*, pp. 245–66.

[43] Lenin, *Selected Works*, X, 242.

[44] Mao, *Investigations of the Rural Districts*, pp. 5–6.

As a result of the investigations conducted in this manner, Mao drew up some interesting conclusions. He found that 40 per cent of the land of the Tenth district of Hsing-kuo belonged to landlords, 10 per cent to local welfare organizations known as public bodies (controlled by landlords and rich peasants), 30 per cent to rich peasants, 15 per cent to middle peasants, and 5 per cent to poor peasants. In contrast, landlords constituted only 1 per cent of the total population, rich peasants 5 per cent, middle peasants 20 per cent, poor peasants 60 per cent, hired farm hands 1 per cent, handicraftsmen 7 per cent, small businessmen 3 per cent, and idlers 2 per cent. Accordingly, Mao decided that the real exploiters were landlords and rich peasants who, put together, constituted only 6 per cent of the population but owned 80 per cent of the land.[45]

Mao pointed out that as the rich peasants not only owned 30 per cent of the land but controlled much of the land of the public bodies, it would be difficult to solve the land problem if their landholdings were not subjected to equal redistribution. However, as the middle peasants constituted 20 per cent of the population but owned only 15 per cent of the land, they favored equal redistribution because this would increase, rather than decrease, their landholdings. Mao refuted the thesis that equal redistribution would injure the middle peasants.[46]

It should be noted that the Comintern directive to the Chinese Communists of June 7, 1929 (Doc. 26) urged the liquidation of the rich peasants in China. The policy of not injuring the middle peasants was formulated by Lenin during the October Revolution.[47] This policy was scrupulously followed by the Chinese Communists throughout the period under study.

Document 16

Investigations of Tung-t'ang and Other Places (東塘等處調查 *Tung-t'ang teng-ch'u tiao-ch'a*), by Mao Tse-tung, November 7–8, 1930; published at Yenan in 1941; printed in Mao Tse-tung, *Investigations of the Rural Districts,* Hsinhua Bookstore, Shantung, 1946, pp. 58–65; approximately 3,900 words.

This is the text of Mao's report on the conditions in the four villages near Chi-an which he investigated early in November, 1930. Like his

[45] *Ibid.,* pp. 18–19.
[46] *Ibid.*
[47] Carr, *The Bolshevik Revolution,* II, 161.

other reports of rural investigation, this paper gives detailed figures regarding the local conditions.

Mao declared that not until his investigation of Li-chia-fang, one of the four villages about thirteen miles northeast of Chi-an, was he clear about the organization and work of the Soviets at the village and township levels during the land struggle in those places. He admitted that he had only hazy ideas about those localities before.

Land redistribution, according to Mao, had been under way in a large number of counties in southwestern Kiangsi. Not only did the land law of the higher level government prescribe the township as the unit of land distribution, but the members of the government generally assumed that the township had been used. To his surprise, he found that the village had generally been substituted for the township as the unit of redistribution in this area. This practice should be changed, Mao suggested, since it served the interests of the rich peasants rather than the middle peasants.

DOCUMENT 17

THE POSITION OF LAND REDISTRIBUTION IN WESTERN KIANGSI (贛西土地分配情形 Kan-hsi t'u-ti fen-p'ei ch'ing-hsing), by Mao Tse-tung, November 12 and 15, 1930; published at Yenan in 1941; printed in Mao Tse-tung, *Investigations of the Rural Districts,* Hsinhua Bookstore, Shantung, 1946, pp. 69–74; approximately 2,700 words.

Here are Mao's notes of the speeches made by delegates to the meeting of the Western Kiangsi Action Committee on November 12, 1930, and the enlarged meeting of the Kiangsi Provincial Action Committee held three days later. The two meetings took place at Chi-an,[48] which the First Front Army to which Mao belonged occupied from early October until November 18, 1930, after it had retreated from the abortive second attack on Changsha under the Li Li-san leadership.[49] Mao jotted down from those speeches what he believed to be important facts about land redistribution in the area surrounded by Tung-ku, Wan-an, and Yung-hsin in western Kiangsi. The major points of his notes may be summed up as follows:

1. Beginning in 1929, land had been redistributed three times in most cases, twice in some places, and only once in still fewer places. The principle of draw-on-the-plentiful-to-make-up-for-the-scarce was

[48] Mao, *Investigations of the Rural Districts,* p. 79.
[49] *Ibid.,* pp. 5, 66.

applied in the first redistribution. It was then followed by the principle of draw-on-the-fat-to-make-up-for-the-lean.

2. The village had more commonly been used as the unit of redistribution than the township.

3. Different criteria of redistribution had been in use: labor power, productive power, and productive output.

4. The position of workers in land redistribution had varied from place to place. They had either met with resistance from the peasants, or got less wages after receiving land allotments, or lost their opportunities for land allotments if they had been workers for more than six months. It should be noted that Mao, during the period of the Chinese Soviet Republic in Kiangsi, defined the workers to include the hired farm hands (see **Doc. 96,** item 5).

DOCUMENT 18

MISTAKES IN THE LAND STRUGGLE IN KIANGSI (江西土地鬪爭中的錯誤 *Chiang-hsi t'u-ti tou-cheng chung ti ts'o-wu*), by Mao Tse-tung, November 14, 1930; published at Yenan in 1941; printed in Mao Tse-tung, *Investigations of the Rural Districts*, Hsinhua Bookstore, Shantung, 1946, pp. 75–78; approximately 1,400 words.

Mao, as representative of the General Front Committee, attended the meeting of the Kiangsi Provincial Committee at Chi-an on November 14, 1930. Having heard reports by others, including Ch'en Yi, foreign minister of the present Chinese Communist regime, Mao pointed out that the Southwest Kiangsi Party had persistently followed a policy line of abandoning the land revolution. After a discussion of this question at the meeting, Mao stated, it was unanimously agreed that a resolute struggle must be waged against that erroneous line. The following are some of his random notes of the speeches made by others at the meeting:

The rich peasants controlled the economy in the Red areas. . . . The instructions of the central and regional leaderships could not reach the low echelons. . . . Land redistribution had not been satisfactorily carried out in vast areas. . . . Most of the Communists in southern Kiangsi were landlords and rich peasants. . . . The Second Plenum abandoned both the peasantry and the land revolution.

DOCUMENT 19
Translation on pages 145-52
QUESTIONS CONCERNING THE REDISTRIBUTION OF UNRIPE RICE AND THE

LEASE OF LAND (分青和出租問題 *Fen-ch'ing han ch'u-tsu wen-t'i*), by Mao Tse-tung, November 15, 1930; published at Yenan in 1941; printed in Mao Tse-tung, *Investigations of the Rural Districts*, Hsinhua Bookstore, Shantung, 1946, pp. 79–83; approximately 3,400 words.

As described previously, the Kiangsi Provincial Action Committee met in enlarged session on November 15, 1930. It is made clear in this document that Mao attended that meeting at Chi-an as representative of the General Front Committee. According to him, that meeting was characterized by discussions of two major questions: the redistribution of unripe rice and the lease of land. Mao declared that he called for support for the mass basis of the redistribution of the unripe rice still in the fields. As regards the lease of land, he said, the meeting repudiated the theory that "no land rent should be collected in the Soviet areas."

In addition, the meeting dealt with a number of other questions concerning land redistribution, such as labor power as the criterion of redistribution, the village as the unit of redistribution, and the status of the workers.

The question of the unripe rice was two-sided. It arose when land redistribution took place after the seeds of rice had been sown in the fields. On the one hand, the landowner understandably wanted to delay the actual transfer of that part of his holdings which had been assigned to others. When land was redistributed after the sowing of seeds, the landowner ordinarily sought to postpone its transfer until after harvest on the grounds that the products of the land in that year should belong to the original cultivator as provided for in article 14 of the land law of the Southwest Kiangsi Soviet Government (Doc. 3). On the other, there were real difficulties on the part of some beneficiaries of land redistribution in tilling the land assigned to them. For example, the disabled, the aged, and so on, simply could not cultivate the land they had received in land redistribution.

Mao and his group were in favor of the redistribution of land together with the unripe rice. Faced with the question of the lease of land, they could not resist the conclusion that those who were allotted land but were not able to till it themselves had no alternative but to lease the land to others and collect rentals from them.

This document is important in that it embodies Mao's views on a variety of questions that arose in the first phase of land redistribution in Kiangsi.

DOCUMENT 20

AN INVESTIGATION OF MU-K'OU-TS'UN (木口村調査 *Mu-k'ou-ts'un tiao-ch'a*), by Mao Tse-tung, November 21, 1930; published at Yenan in 1941; printed in Mao Tse-tung, *Investigations of the Rural Districts*, Hsinhua Bookstore, Shantung, 1946, pp. 66–68; approximately 1,400 words.

Mao made this investigation of the village of Mu-k'ou-ts'un at lunch time on November 21, 1930, when he was retreating from Chi-an under the attack of KMT troops.

He found that the middle peasants had nothing to lose but something to get from the equal redistribution of land and that the rich peasants and small landlords would join the counterrevolutionary camps in the face of the vehement struggle of the peasants.

SECTION 3. THE RICH-PEASANT QUESTION
DOCUMENT 21
Translation on pages 152-70

THE RICH-PEASANT PROBLEM (富農問題 *Fu-nung wen-t'i*), Resolution No. 2 adopted by a Joint Meeting of the Front Committee and the Western Fukien Special Committee; printed and distributed by the General Political Department of the First Front Army of the Red Army, June, 1930; leaf 6 missing; 008.75101/3057, SSC; approximately 7,400 words.

In harmony with the liquidation of the kulaks as a class in the Soviet Union, the Comintern issued a directive to the CCP on June 7, 1929 (Doc. 26), urging a similar movement against the rich peasants in China. Although this directive did not have as much support from Li Li-san as Moscow should like, it apparently caught the fancy of Mao who had no liking for the rich peasants from the very beginning.[50] In point of time, Mao began to liquidate the rich peasants at least a year earlier than equivalent action by the Russian Returned Student group.

It seems clear that the present statement represented the rich-peasant policy of the Chu-Mao group. That it was drafted under their sponsorship is apparent from the following:

1. As the heading of this entry indicates, the resolution was adopted by the Joint Meeting of the Front Committee and the Western Fukien Special Committee and was printed and distributed by the General

[50] Mao, "Report on the Investigation of the Peasant Movement in Hunan," sec. x, "Vanguard of the Revolution," in *Selected Works,* Chinese ed., I, 20–21; English ed., I, 29–30.

Political Department of the First Front Army of the Red Army. As I noted in *Power Relations*, I,[51] the Front Committee was under the control of Mao, and it is well known that western Fukien was the sphere of influence of his group. Furthermore, the General Political Department of the First Front Army, formed in June, 1930, was doubtless headed by Mao, with Chu Teh as military commander.

2. This document stands for land redistribution according to the number of persons in contradistinction to labor power (sec. 12).

3. This statement is in favor of the principles of draw-on-the-plentiful-to-make-up-for-the-scarce and draw-on-the-fat-to-make-up-for-the-lean (sec. 17).

4. The provisions governing the land tax in section 20 of this resolution agree with the provisions of chapter III of the Chu-Mao group land law.

5. This resolution objects to collective and Soviet farming for the moment and stands for redistribution of land to all those who need it (sec. 13). This agrees with the land law of the Chu-Mao group (**Doc. 9,** art. 19, part 1) in contradistinction to Li Li-san's land law (**Doc. 1,** art. V, expl. nn. 10 and 15).

6. This statement agrees with article 14 of the land law of the Chu-Mao group in that a peasant is entitled to the harvest of a field which is assigned to him at a time when the seeds have already been sown in it (sec. 14).

There can be little doubt that this resolution was drafted under the impact of the Comintern directive of June 7, 1929. Some of its basic ideas (even their phraseology) echo that directive. Using the resolutions of the CCP Sixth National Congress and papers of the party leadership as targets of attack, the Comintern directive (see discussion, **Doc. 1**), cites a letter from the CCP Central Committee to Mao as evidence of its pro-rich-peasant policy. It is not improbable that this Comintern attitude might also have given Mao the fillip he needed to adopt a tough policy toward the rich peasants.

As pointed out in the discussion of Document 1, the resolutions of the Sixth National Congress are relatively moderate in relation to the rich peasants, though understandably harsh to the landlords. This statement appears almost as harsh to the rich peasants as to the landlords. It takes the position that rich peasants and landlords alike were arch enemies of the peasant masses in the rural districts and that the rich peasants, who

[51] pp. 6, 99–108, *passim.*

were counterrevolutionary by nature, exploited people more ruthlessly than the landlords.

Rich peasants are divided into three groups, each subject to liquidation without distinction: rich peasants of a semilandlord character, rich peasants of a capitalistic character, and rich peasants of an initial-stage character. The rich peasants of a semilandlord character are those who till land themselves but who have surplus land for rent. The rich peasants of a capitalistic character have no land for rent and in some cases even lease land from others, but they hire laborers to help in the cultivation of land. The rich peasants of an initial-stage character have no land for rent and do not hire laborers, but they till land with their own labor and have surplus foodstuffs for sale or for loan.

It is pointed out in this statement that the first two categories of rich peasants had long been recognized by the Chinese Communists. In the Comintern directive of June 7, 1929 (Doc. 26), the rich peasants of a semilandlord character were stressed as comprising the main segment of the Chinese rich peasants, while those of a capitalistic character were said to be rather few. Both kinds of rich peasants, according to the directive, should be attacked. It contains no stipulations regarding the so-called rich peasants of an initial-stage character, who were an invention of the Chu-Mao group. It must be remembered that those now being described as rich peasants of an initial-stage character were traditionally known as well-to-do middle peasants in Chinese Communist circles and as such would not be subject to expropriation.

About a month after the adoption of the present statement, the Comintern passed a resolution on the Chinese problem on July 23, 1930 (Doc. 7), in which it was made clear that "the principle of confiscation should not apply to the land of the well-to-do peasants (referring to well-to-do middle peasants here)."[52] After that time, rich peasants of an initial-stage character were no longer heard of as a section of the rich peasantry subject to expropriation, except where they were cited as a target of attack as in the circular of the Central Bureau of the Soviet Areas of February 8, 1931 (Doc. 25). Throughout the period of the Chinese Soviet Republic, the well-to-do middle peasants were protected in the same way as the ordinary middle peasants. This was also true of Mao's own policy toward the well-to-do middle peasants during that period (see **Doc. 69,** sec. 2, par. 1; **Doc. 101,** sec. 2).

Ch'en Shao-yü claimed that the parenthetical note, "referring to

[52] The cited passage, including the parenthetical comment, is contained in sec. VI of the text of the resolution, as printed in *Red Documents,* pp. 346–61.

well-to-do middle peasants here," was not originally embodied in the
Comintern directive in question but was subsequently supplied by Li
Li-san and Ch'ü Ch'iu-pai in the Third Plenum of September, 1930.[53]

DOCUMENT 22
THE RICH-PEASANT QUESTION AFTER LAND REDISTRIBUTION (分田後的
富農問題 *Fen-t'ien hou ti fu-nung wen-t'i*), by Mao Tse-tung, October,
1930; published at Yenan in 1941; printed in Mao Tse-tung, *Investigations of Rural Districts*, Hsinhua Bookstore, Shantung, 1946, pp. 84–85;
approximately 670 words.

This short paper contains brief notes taken by Mao from reports of
two other local Communist leaders. One of them declared that there
were two different kinds of exploitation by rich peasants in the Red
areas in Yung-hsin county: (*1*) hoarding of foodstuffs, and (*2*) sale of
industrial products. The other stated that this was also true of the
North Route Red areas where rich peasants even sold rice to the
Kuomintang region.

DOCUMENT 23
THE QUESTION OF OPPOSING THE RICH PEASANTRY (反富農問題 *Fan fu-
nung wen-t'i*), issued by the Northeastern Kiangsi Special Committee,
n.d., probably late 1930, n.p.; reproduced in *A Collection of Red Bandit
Secret Documents*, Vol. V, leaves 28–31, 008.2129/4074, SSC; mimeographed; approximately 1,400 words.

Like Document 21, this document divides the rich peasantry into
three different categories. But unlike that joint resolution, this statement does not decree confiscation of all the land of the rich peasant of
a (semi)landlord character—it condemns only that part of his land
which he rents out. The other two kinds of rich peasants (of a capitalistic
character and of an initial-stage character) were not subject to confiscation at all—they were only to be restricted politically and economically.

After admitting past errors in Right and Left deviations, this document announces the decision that the tactics of opposing the rich peasantry required the setting up of the Hired-Farm-Hand Union and the
Poor-Peasant Corps, in addition to cooperating with the middle
peasantry.

It is interesting that this statement seems to contain traits of both

[53] Ch'en Shao-yü, *Struggle for the More Complete Bolshevization of the Chinese Communist
Party*, postscript I-B-1.

Li Li-sanism and the agrarian policy of the Chu-Mao group. The former lies in the confiscation of only that part of a rich peasant's land which he rents out, while the latter finds expression in the tripartite classification of the rich peasantry.

DOCUMENT 24

THE QUESTION OF OPPOSING THE RICH PEASANTRY—PROCLAMATION No. 2 OF THE CHINESE SOVIET CENTRAL REVOLUTIONARY MILITARY COUNCIL (反富農問題—中華蘇維埃中央革命軍事委員會佈告第二號 *Fan fu-nung wen-t'i—chung-hua su-wei-ai chung-yang ko-ming chün-shih wei-yüan-hui pu-kao ti-erh-hao*), dated 1931; reproduced in *A Collection of Red Bandit Secret Documents*, Vol. V, leaves 31–33, 008.2129/4074, SSC; mimeographed; approximately 1,600 words.

This statement was apparently the work of Mao and his group, for it was issued under the name of the Chinese Soviet Central Revolutionary Military Council with Hsiang Ying as chairman, and Mao Tse-tung and Chu Teh as vice-chairmen. It deals with the fight against the rich peasantry from various aspects: reasons for the fight, past mistakes, correct methods, and the prevention of possible future errors. It was charged that though the principle of draw-on-the-plentiful-to-make-up-for-the-scarce had been implemented in many places, such was not the case with the principle of draw-on-the-fat-to-make-up-for-the-lean.

It is not clear whether the military council which issued this document was the same agency that promulgated the land law of the Chu-Mao group (**Doc. 9**). The titles of the two agencies bear a very close resemblance but are not exactly the same.

DOCUMENT 25

THE LAND PROBLEM AND THE ANTI-RICH-PEASANT TACTICS (土地問題與反富農策略 *T'u-ti wen-t'i yü fan fu-nung t'se-lüeh*), Circular No. 9 of the Central Bureau of the Soviet Areas, February 8, 1931, 008.741022/4047-3, SSC; reproduced in *A Collection of Red Bandit Secret Documents*, Vol. V, leaves 19–28, 008.2129/4074, SSC; mimeographed; approximately 6,600 words.

This comprehensive document attacks the salient features of the land policies of Mao and Li Li-san alike in an effort to find solutions to the various problems arising from the agrarian revolution. As described on pages 109 and 150 in *Power Relations*, I, the Central Bureau of the Soviet Areas was set up in an effort to check Mao, but he managed to continue to hold power for some time. The present document seems to outline the relations between Mao and the Central Bureau along the lines suggested.

It is not surprising that Li Li-san's policy of collective and Soviet farming was condemned in this statement, for Li Li-san had already been removed from power. That policy was branded premature on the ground that collectivization in the Soviet Union was delayed until more than ten years after the outbreak of the Bolshevik revolution.

It is interesting to note that Mao's favorite program of land redistribution on a per capita basis was also repudiated in unmistakable terms. It was charged that this program was devoid of a class stand. To allot land to all the people, irrespective of age or other concerns, would tend to obscure class consciousness and impede the progress of the class struggle in the rural districts. In addition, it was contended, a rich peasant usually had a bigger family than a middle or poor peasant. It followed that a rich peasant could get more land if it was redistributed according to the number of persons. Consequently, this document adopts labor power as the criterion of land redistribution, using the number of persons as an auxiliary method.

Furthermore, this paper stresses the importance of opposition to the rich peasants, but makes it unmistakably clear that opposition to the rich peasants was meant to curb their political influence and economic exploitation, but not to annihilate them. It was argued that not until twelve years after the Bolshevik revolution was the slogan of annihilating the kulaks raised in the Soviet Union. The most effective way of opposing the rich peasants, as recommended in this paper, was to organize the poor-peasant corps and the hired-farm-hand union.

In addition, this paper discusses a number of other problems such as confiscation of all land, equal redistribution, and so on. Confiscation of all land was recognized as equivalent to land nationalization, having no basis in CCP Sixth National Congress resolutions. Equal redistribution of land was desirable on the ground that it had the emotional power to attract the masses, apart from its avowed aim to eradicate the feudal legacy and private property. Interestingly, this paper does not recognize the existence of the so-called rich peasants of an initial-stage character, who were actually the well-to-do middle peasants.

DOCUMENT 26
LETTER FROM THE ECCI TO THE CHINESE COMMUNIST PARTY—REGARDING THE PEASANT PROBLEM (共產國際執行委員會與中國共產黨書—關於農民

問題 *Kung-ch'an kuo-chi chih-hsing wei-yüan-hui yü chung-kuo kung-ch'an-tang shu—kuan-yü nung-min wen-t'i)*, dated June 7, 1929; Chinese version printed in *Red Documents,* pp. 319–33, 008.2129/2703, SSC; approximately 7,800 words.

In this directive the ECCI Political Secretariat ordered the CCP to liquidate the rich peasants. As the main points in this statement have been discussed (**Doc. 1, Doc. 21**) it is not necessary to recapitulate them here.

It should be noted that Pavel Mif endorsed this statement by saying that it corrected the ambiguous position of the CCP Sixth National Congress on the rich peasant problem.[54]

A debate between Ts'ai Ho-shen and Li Li-san over the peasant problem was cited in this document as an example of the misconceptions of CCP leaders about the problem. This seems to give a clue to an article by Ts'ai Ho-shen which, according to Chang Kuo-t'ao, began to estrange Li Li-san from Moscow in June, 1929.[55]

SECTION 4. ORGANIZING THE POOR PEASANTS

DOCUMENT 27

Translation on pages 170-75

PROVISIONAL REGULATIONS FOR THE HIRED-FARM-HAND UNION (僱農工會暫行章程 *Ku-nung kung-hui chan-hsing chang-ch'eng*), printed by the General Political Department of the Chinese Soviet Areas Central Revolutionary Military Council, February, 1931; reproduced in *A Collection of Red Bandit Secret Documents,* Vol. II, leaves 31–35, 008.2129/4074, SSC; mimeographed; approximately 1,000 words.

Communists in China, as in Russia, look upon the poor peasants as the main revolutionary force in the countryside. While they are supposed to be the peasants who possess too little land to maintain even a bare subsistence, the poor peasants, broadly speaking, often include among themselves the farm hands who are literally landless and have to hire out to others to keep alive. To the Communists, the hired farm hands are the workers of the rural districts. They must organize their own labor unions in order to achieve the success of the bourgeois-democratic revolution so as to speed up the transition to a socialist revolution.

---

[54] Mif, *Heroic China: Fifteen Years of the Communist Party of China* (Chinese version, 1936), p. 81.

[55] *Power Relations,* I, 27.

Up until 1930, however, few labor unions of the hired farm hands had been established in China. Ch'en Shao-yü, leader of the Russian Returned Students who had come back from Moscow in May, 1930, or thereabouts, deplored this situation and called for a remedy for it.[56]

On July 23, 1930, the Comintern passed a resolution calling upon the Chinese Communist Party to organize hired-farm-hand unions as well as poor-peasant corps. Moscow attached so much importance to this new move that it was considered inseparably linked to the task of the land revolution in the Soviet areas.[57] According to the Comintern resolution, hired farm hands and poor peasants were the two classes of people who generated the power for the carrying out of the land revolution. They should get the middle peasantry to ally with them and operate under the leadership of the working class.[58]

The Eastern Department of the Communist International, in its draft resolution on the land and peasant problems in the Soviet areas, received in the middle of November, 1930 (Doc. 35), also called upon the CCP to organize hired farm hands and coolies into labor unions, in addition to setting up poor-peasant corps (see the part of this draft resolution dealing with CCP basic tasks 1 and 2).[59] The ECCI in its directive to the CCP, received on November 16, 1930 (Doc. 8), charged that the hired-farm-hand union as well as the poor-peasant corps had not been established in China (par. 10).

It was against this background that the present organic law of the hired-farm-hand union was drafted. It consists of twenty-three articles, dealing with the organization and functions of the union at great length. The purposes of the union were to unite all the hired farm hands and strengthen their leadership in the class struggle in the rural districts. The union should gather the poor and middle peasants around it for the prosecution of the struggle to expand and strengthen the Soviet movement.

According to this law, every three or more hired farm hands were to form a small group, every three or more small groups a branch, every three or more branches a district union, every three or more district unions a county union, and every three or more county unions a provincial or special-area union which was the apogee of the hired-farm-hand hierarchy. It was made clear that only hired farm hands could

[56] *Red Flag*, May 17, 1930, p. 3.

[57] Document 7, "Resolution on the Chinese Problem," July, 1930, sec. 7, in *Red Documents*, pp. 346–61.

[58] *Ibid.*, sec. 6.

[59] *Red Bandit Secret Documents*, Vol. III, leaves 38–45.

become members of the union. Hired farm hands were defined as the workers who lived on selling their manual labor for production in the villages.

The agency responsible for the printing indicates that this document was probably sponsored by Mao and his group. It is not improbable that it was Mao who headed that agency himself.

DOCUMENT 28

Translation on pages 175-81

REGULATIONS FOR THE POOR-PEASANT ASSOCIATION (貧農會章程 *P'in-nung-hui chang-ch'eng*), by the General Political Department, Central Revolutionary Military Council, Chinese Soviet Areas; reprinted by the Ning-tu County Soviet Government, February, 1931; reproduced in *A Collection of Reactionary Documents*, Vol. I, book 4, leaves 10–15, 008.2129/7120/V.1, Nos. 3–4, SSC; mimeographed; approximately 2,300 words.

Judged by its letter and spirit, this law appears to have been drafted as a companion document to Document 27. Says the Comintern directive of July 23, 1930:

> The task of the agrarian revolution in the Soviet areas is inseparably linked to the organization of the hired-farm-hand union, [i.e.,] the union of the proletarians of the rural districts, and to the organization of the poor-peasant corps. The purpose of the poor-peasant corps was to gather the middle peasants around it and bring all the measures of the Soviet agencies in harmony with the interests of the poor and middle peasants.[60]

The organization of poor peasants was also urged in the Comintern Eastern Department's draft resolution on the land and peasant problems (Doc. 35) a few months before these regulations were formulated.

In the Comintern directive received on November 16, 1930 (Doc. 8), it was charged that the organization of the poor peasants had not even been started and that the poor-peasant corps had not yet been set up.[61]

It seems clear that the present law was drafted under this Comintern impact. But the work of organizing the poor-peasant corps did not seem quick enough. In the Comintern directive of July, 1931, it was urged

[60] *Red Documents*, pp. 346–61.

[61] Document 8, Letter from the ECCI to the CCP Central Committee, par. 10, in *Red Documents*, pp. 362–75.

that the organization of the poor-peasant corps should not be further delayed in the townships.[62]

The present law consists of twenty-four articles. The membership of the poor-peasant association includes poor peasants, hired farm hands, manual workers, coolies, and artisans. It should be noted that the poor-peasant association included hired farm hands while the hired farm-hand union did not include the poor peasants.

According to this law, the poor-peasant association was a three-level organization, ranging from the village through the township to the district. Every three corps of a lower level could combine to form a group of a higher level.

The agency which had this law printed was the same that was responsible for the printing of Document 27. As the date of the printing of both documents is the same, this document was also, in all likelihood, sponsored by Mao and his group.

It should be remembered that in his 1927 *Report on the Investigation of the Peasant Movement in Hunan,* Mao sees the poor peasantry as the revolutionary vanguard without whom there would be no revolution at all.[63]

DOCUMENT 29

Translation on pages 181-86

ORGANIC LAW OF THE POOR-PEASANT ASSOCIATION AND ITS TASKS (貧農會組織法及其任務 *P'in-nung-hui tsu-chih-fa chi ch'i jen-wu*), Circular No. 20 of the CCP Southwest Kiangsi Special Area Committee; n.d., probably 1931; reproduced in *A Collection of Red Bandit Secret Documents,* Vol. II, leaves 35–38, 008.2129/4074, SSC; mimeographed; approximately 1,700 words.

This party circular concerns the organization of the poor-peasant association in southwestern Kiangsi. It consists of three sections dealing with the significance, organization, and functions of the poor-peasant association. The following five points are worthy of note:

1. It was pointed out that according to regulations promulgated by the defunct Provincial Action Committee, the poor-peasant association was an organization ranging from the provincial level to the township. This was considered a sort of dual leadership to the detriment of the

[62] Document 36, Letter of the ECCI Presidium to the CCP, sec. 25, in *Bolshevik* (Kiangsi), No. 1 (July, 1934), pp. 1–41.

[63] See section of this report entitled "Vanguard of the Revolution," *Selected Works,* Chinese ed., I, 2–33; English ed., I, 29–33.

exclusive leadership of the working class. Accordingly, the poor-peasant association was made an organization of the township level only. Under the township were branches of the association and hired-farm-hand cells.

2. The membership of the poor-peasant association included: (*a*) hired farm hands; (*b*) those who had no or little land, nor sufficient foodstuffs to live on; (*c*) coolies and poor women.

3. The main tasks of the poor-peasant association were: (*a*) opposition to the rich peasants; (*b*) thorough redistribution of land; (*c*) objection to all new types of exploitation such as cooperatives sponsored by rich peasants; (*d*) supervising the Soviets; and (*e*) strengthening alliance with the middle peasants.

4. It would appear that the Southwest Kiangsi Special Area Committee which adopted this document was not controlled by the group of people who staged the Fu-t'ien incident against Mao late in 1930.[64] In contrast to the policy of the Fu-t'ien rebels, this document was directed primarily against the rich peasantry. In unmistakable terms it follows Mao's favorite principles of draw-on-the-plentiful-to-make-up-for-the-scarce and draw-on-the-fat-to-make-up-for-the-lean. It begins with a denunciation of the peasant policy of the Southwest Kiangsi party leadership of the past. Accordingly, there is good reason to believe that the Southwest Kiangsi Special Committee which was responsible for the Fu-t'ien incident had been reorganized into the agency which issued the present statement and was, in all probability, controlled by the Mao group.

5. The basic ideas of this document can be traced to a number of Comintern directives such as those dated June 7, 1929 (Doc. 26), July 23, 1930 (Doc. 7), November 16, 1930 (Doc. 8), the draft resolution on the land and peasant problems, received in November, 1930 (Doc. 35), and the resolution on the peasant problem, reprinted on February 18, 1931 (Doc. 30).

DOCUMENT 30

[COMINTERN] RESOLUTION ON THE CHINESE PEASANT PROBLEM ([國際] 對於中國農民問題決議案 [*Kuo-chi*] *tui-yü chung-kuo nung-min wen-t'i chüeh-i-an*), n.d.; reprinted by the North Route Subcommittee, February 18, 1931; reproduced in *A Collection of Red Bandit Secret Documents*, Vol. III, leaves 33–38, 008.2129/4074, SSC, and in Hsiao Tso-liang, *Power Rela-*

---

[64] *Power Relations*, I, 99, 101–9, *passim*.

tions within the Chinese Communist Movement, 1930–1934: Vol. II, The Chinese Documents; mimeographed; approximately 3,400 words.

This Comintern statement has been discussed in my study *Power Relations*, I, 71. It was one of the Comintern authorizations for the organization of the poor peasants and the hired farm hands in China, and it should be examined along with the "Resolution on the Peasant Problem" adopted by the CCP Sixth National Congress in 1928.[65]

---

[65] Reprinted in *The International Line,* pp. 145–55, and in *Red Documents,* pp. 228–34.

III

The Land Law of the Chinese Soviet Republic

SECTION 1. THE LAND LAW

DOCUMENT 31

DRAFT LAND LAW (土地法草案 *T'u-ti fa ts'ao-an*), prepared by CCP Central Committee in 1931; printed in *Draft Resolutions Introduced by the CCP Central Committee to the First National Soviet Congress*, reproduced by the Political Department, Third Army Corps, First Route Army, Chinese Workers' and Peasants' Red Army, pp. 9–14, n.d., 008.631/8064-2, SSC, and in Hsiao Tso-liang, *Power Relations within the Chinese Communist Movement, 1930–1934: Vol. II, The Chinese Documents;* approximately 2,400 words.

This is the draft land law introduced by the CCP Central Committee to the First National Soviet Congress opening at Jui-chin on November 7, 1931. Since the CCP Central Committee was then controlled by the Russian Returned Student group set up in party leadership by Pavel Mif in January, 1931, this draft law was actually the work of that group.

According to *Räte-China*,[1] the text of this draft law was published in the Chinese Communist organ *Red Flag* in March, 1931.

As I pointed out in *Power Relations*, I,[2] there are slight verbal discrepancies between this draft law and the final text adopted. On examination, the only significant discrepancies are the following:

1. The unemployed and independent laborer in the village is added in the final text to the list of persons entitled to land allotments as provided in the draft (art. 1).

2. In the equal redistribution of land, the final text contains an

[1] P. 610.
[2] P. 179.

additional provision that the middle peasants may not take part in equal redistribution if the majority of them do not want it (art. 5).

3. The rich peasant is more ruthlessly discriminated against in the final text than in the draft. This is evident in two respects. First, over and above the mixture of toiling and consuming norms in land redistribution, an alternative provision is added in the final text: land could be redistributed on a per capita basis in the case of the village poor ranging from the middle peasant downward, but in the case of a rich peasant, labor power is the principal consideration. That means, as explained in a parenthetical note, that where land is redistributed on an equal basis according to the number of persons, a rich peasant can receive an equal allotment of land only if he has labor power (art. 7). Second, in this draft law only surplus farm implements and livestock of a rich peasant are subject to confiscation. In the final text, however, surplus houses, grain-husking water mills, oil-pressing mills, and so forth, of a rich peasant are to be confiscated in addition to surplus farm implements and livestock (art. 8).

A German version of this draft land law appears on pages 619–23 of *Räte-China*, a collection of German translations of official Chinese documents of the Kiangsi period, published at Moscow in 1934, presumably under the sponsorship of the Comintern. Some of the errors in translation are grievous. For example, the adverbial phrase *nach der Arbeitsnorm* (meaning "according to the labor norm") in article 3 should be converted into a noun phrase "labor land allotment." The term *Arbeitsnorm,* meaning labor norm, is one of the two different criteria of land redistribution in Communist China as in Soviet Russia, the other being the consuming norm. The term "labor land allotment" is employed to denote the plot of poor land assigned to a rich peasant who was required to till it with his own labor. The two terms stand for two different things and cannot be used interchangeably.

In addition, the expression *die Organisierung der ersten landwirtschaftlichen Kollektiven* in article 8 of this draft land law should be changed to "the organization of rudimentary cooperatives."

DOCUMENT 32

RESOLUTION ON THE LAND PROBLEM (關於土地問題的決議案 *Kuan-yü t'u-ti wen-t'i ti chüeh-i-an*), adopted by the CCP Central Bureau of the Soviet Areas, August 21 (1931); reprinted by the Shui-tung District Committee, September 7, 1931, 008.743/4047–3, SSC; mimeographed; approximately 3,600 words.

After receiving the draft land law prepared by the CCP Central Committee, the Central Bureau of the Soviet Areas adopted this resolution to give support and effect to the draft land law in the Soviet areas. In writing this resolution, the Central Bureau admitted its scrupulous deference to the draft land law as well as to the Comintern directive of July, 1931 (Doc. 36).

As has been noted previously, the Central Soviet Area in Kiangsi and western Fukien had been the scene of struggle between the agrarian ideas of Mao and Li Li-san. Now that the draft land law of the Russian Returned Student leadership began to penetrate that area, it portended a conflict between the agrarian policies of Mao and his other opponents there. As they were standing on the vantage ground of the Central Committee, the Russian Returned Students were bound to emerge victorious from the struggle. No wonder that the Communist historian, Ho Kan-chih, declares that the land policy of the Chinese Communist Party was formulated under Mao's sponsorship during the period of 1928–31.[3] Ho's statement must, of course, be accepted with the qualification that Li Li-san adopted a land law in May, 1930.

Against this background, it is not surprising that Mao's land policy was called in question when this resolution was drafted. Mao's favorite principles of draw-on-the-plentiful-to-make-up-for-the-scarce and draw-on-the-fat-to-make-up-for-the-lean were attacked as lacking a class line and obscuring class consciousness. In commenting on land redistribution in Kiangsi and western Fukien, this resolution says:

> In the course of equal land redistribution, land has been allotted to all men and women in the villages. Village bosses, gentry, landlords, and their dependents, as well as rich peasants, and so forth, have enjoyed equal rights with poor peasants and middle peasants and received equal land allotments in quantity and quality.
> Such a principle of land redistribution is not correct. It is nonclass [in character]. . . . It has been putting into effect the nonclass program of draw-on-the-plentiful-to-make-up-for-the-scarce and draw-on-the-fat-to-make-up-for-the-lean.[4]

In the same breath, however, this resolution stands for land redistribution on a per capita basis, as advocated by Mao. It is contended that overpopulation in the rural districts calls for a swift redistribution of land and that, to that end, the number of persons should be the proper

[3] Ho, *History of the Contemporary Chinese Revolution,* p. 143.
[4] Leaf 2, side 2.

line of approach. Labor power, it is stated, might be a proper criterion in redistribution if the population is sparse and the land plentiful.[5]

It will be recalled that when the Central Bureau of the Soviet Areas, which adopted this resolution, was created in January, 1931, it was believed to be a device to hold Mao, who had become increasingly insubordinate in the Kiangsi-Fukien area, in check. Chou En-lai, who stood at the head of a list of a nine-man membership of the bureau, must have played a leading role in the new setup, especially because the secretary, Hsiang Ying, was not a capable, strong man.[6] Such being the case, it is likely that this document more or less represented the standpoint of Chou En-lai who, as shown in the Third Plenum of the CCP Central Committee, was given to compromise.[7]

DOCUMENT 33

LETTER FROM THE CENTRAL [COMMITTEE] TO THE CENTRAL BUREAU OF THE SOVIET AREAS ON THE LAND PROBLEM (中央為土地問題致中央蘇區中央局信 *Chung-yang wei t'u-ti wen-t'i chih chung-yang su-ch'ü chung-yang chü hsin*), dated November 10, 1931; printed in *Red Flag Weekly*, No. 26 (December 11[?], 1931), pp. 31–42, 052.1/809, BIC; approximately 5,700 words.

This statement represented the official reaction of the party central leadership to the resolution on the land problem (Doc. 32). Though recognizing that resolution as marking the beginning of the end of the nonclass line, it was nevertheless charged that the resolution contained many standpoints of a nonclass nature which had to be changed to make certain that the land revolution would not play into the hands of the rich peasants. Accordingly, the Central Bureau of the Soviet Areas was requested to correct its errors so that the land law being adopted by the First National Soviet Congress then in session might be carried out without deviation.

The errors of the Central Bureau resolution as listed in this document included: (*1*) misconceptions about the rich peasantry, (*2*) confiscation and equal redistribution of all land, (*3*) protection of the interests of the middle peasantry at the expense of the poor peasantry and hired farm hands, and (*4*) the number of persons rather than labor power adopted as the criterion of land redistribution.

It was pointed out that landlords, along with their dependents,

[5] Leaf 2, side 1.
[6] *Power Relations*, I, 150–52.
[7] *Ibid.*, pp. 63–66.

though not receiving land allotments after expropriation, were allowed to reclaim waste land under the Central Bureau resolution in question. This, it was charged, would bring them all to the *status quo ante* in land relations.

As to the rich peasants, the Central Bureau resolution decreed confiscation of the land of those of a semilandlord character who engaged in semifeudal exploitation, and then assigned them poor land instead. This was taken to mean that the rich peasants who were neither semilandlords nor usurers, but who constantly had the aid of the hired farm hands, were not subject to expropriation. Besides, it was added, no mention was made of the confiscation of the surplus farm implements and draft cattle owned by the rich peasants.

It was maintained that to refrain from violating the interests of the middle peasantry could only mean that the middle peasants should not be affected by land redistribution. It did not mean, as laid down in the Central Bureau resolution, that the middle peasants, poor peasants, and hired farm hands were entitled to absolute equality in land allotments, since such absolute equality was not only impossible but also likely to do poor peasants and hired farm hands harm in practice. Special protection, it was said, should be accorded to these two classes of toiling people.

Above all, it was charged, the Central Bureau had made the mistake of adopting the number of persons as the criterion of land redistribution at the sacrifice of labor power or a mixed principle. It was explained that the July, 1931, Comintern resolution (Doc. 36) and the CCP Central Committee's draft land law (Doc. 31) avoided fixing a definite criterion for land redistribution, but spoke in general terms of the mixture of labor power and the number of persons as the desired criterion. The guiding principle of equal land redistribution was to give rich peasants poor land, poor peasants and hired farm hands good land, and middle peasants due protection of their interests. A proper criterion of land redistribution should be the one which would give effect to that guiding principle according to local conditions. Accordingly, the letter continues, the Central Bureau was wrong in taking the position that the number of persons should be the criterion in the case of overpopulation while labor power should prevail where the population was sparse and the land plentiful. When the Comintern and the CCP Central Committee put forward labor power and the number of persons as the mixed criterion of land redistribution, they all had overpopulation in mind. The hard fact was that the rich peasants had, in general, relatively big families and that therefore they would benefit by the number of persons, but not by labor power. On the other hand, the mixed criterion was generally advantageous to poor peasants and hired farm hands, and only in special cases would the number of persons do them good.

Finally, Mao's favorite twin principles of draw-on-the-plentiful-to-make-up-for-the-scarce and draw-on-the-fat-to-make-up-for-the-lean were also condemned.

Beyond a doubt, this document sheds considerable light on the land law of the Chinese Soviet Republic, which will be discussed in the next entry.

DOCUMENT 34
Translation on pages 186-91

LAND LAW OF THE CHINESE SOVIET REPUBLIC (中華蘇維埃共和國土地法 *Chung-hua su-wei-ai kung-ho-kuo t'u-ti fa*), adopted by the First National Soviet Congress in November, 1931; an original copy of the law issued as a proclamation by the Presidium of the First National Soviet Congress and the Central Executive Committee of the Chinese Soviet Government on December 1, 1931, 008.742/4043, SSC; reproduced in (*1*) *The Soviet Code*, II, 41–47, 008.542/4424/V.2, SSC; (*2*) *The Red Flag Weekly*, No. 29 (January 15, 1932), pp. 67–72, on file in the Hoover Library; (*3*) *A Collection of Red Bandit Documents*, I, 2–9, 008.2129/4070/V.1, SSC; (*4*) *A Collection of Red Bandit Reactionary Documents*, III, 922–27, 008.2129/2977/V.3, SSC; (*5*) Hsiao Tso-liang, *Power Relations within the Chinese Communist Movement, 1930–1934: Vol. II, The Chinese Documents;* approximately 2,500 words.

This is the original text of the land law of the Chinese Soviet Republic of 1931–1934. It bears the official seal of the Central Soviet Government and retains almost all the earmarks of its original condition as it was issued as an official proclamation on December 1, 1931. The reproductions of this law, as listed above, can be found in both Taiwan and the West, including the Chinese collection of the Hoover Library.

As noted earlier, the draft of this law was prepared by the CCP Central Committee, which was then controlled by the Russian Returned Students. The final text of the law, as passed by the First National Soviet Congress, is the same as the draft except for a few slight changes which, as outlined in the preceding entry, were also introduced by the Russian Returned Student leadership. Accordingly, we have good reason to refer to this law as the land law of the Russian Returned Students.

However, this was the land law of the Chinese Soviet Republic, enforced in all the Soviet areas during the 1931–34 period. Mao, as chief executive and prime minister, was entrusted with the task of putting this law into practice. The record shows that he undertook that task without signs of deviation.

The major differences between this law and the land laws sponsored by the Chu-Mao group and Li Li-san have been too often discussed to need wholesale repetition. Suffice it to say that this land law has these outstanding characteristics *inter alia:* peasant ownership of land; no land allotments to the landlords; poor land to the rich peasants; land redistribution according to the mixed criterion of labor power and the number of persons; permission for the lease, purchase, or sale of land; no collectivization; and no nationalization for the moment.

This land law consists of a total of fourteen articles, but only the first seven articles have, until now, appeared in English translation, and those were not done with complete fidelity.[8] For this and for other reasons, there have been confusions about this land law which should be clarified. First, it must be remembered that this land law, like the whole Communist agrarian program in the period under study, was *revolutionary* rather than *reformist* in nature. But some observers have looked upon the land revolution in Kiangsi as an agrarian reform.[9]

Second, the omission of the last seven articles of this law coupled with errors of translation has led to serious misconceptions about the agrarian movement in Kiangsi. In fact, rich peasants whose land had been confiscated rather than *t'u-hao* (village bosses) could be allotted land of poorer quality if they tilled it by their own labor (art. 3). Nationalization remained an ultimate objective in article 12, while collectivization, which had been eliminated during the liquidation of the Li-san line, could not possibly revive in the drafting of this law. Rudimentary cooperatives rather than collectives were actually introduced (art. 8).[10]

Third, as pointed out above, this law was drafted and adopted under the sponsorship of the Russian Returned Student leadership. Mao, as chief executive and prime minister, carried it into effect. The due

[8] See Victor A. Yakhontoff, *The Chinese Soviets*, pp. 221–23; Brandt, Schwartz, and Fairbank, *A Documentary History of Chinese Communism*, pp. 224–26.

[9] Nathaniel Peffer, "Chinese Idea of Communism," *Current History*, XXXVI (July, 1932), 400–404; J. O. P. Bland, *China: The Pity of It*, pp. 273–84.

[10] Cf. Brandt, Schwartz, and Fairbank, *op. cit.*, pp. 218–19; Yakhontoff, *op. cit.*, pp. 137, 222; *Räte-China*, p. 621.

regard shown for the property interests of the middle peasantry and the concern for the religious feelings of the peasantry at large in redistribution (arts. 5, 6) did not originate with Mao but in Comintern instructions. To make the case clear, a comparison between this land law and the relevant Comintern sources is made in Table 1.

TABLE 1

COMPARISON OF THE LAND LAW OF THE CHINESE SOVIET REPUBLIC
AND COMINTERN DIRECTIVES

Land Law	Comintern Source
Preamble	July, 1931, directive (Doc. 36): section 23[a]
Article 1	July 23, 1930, directive (Doc. 7): section 6[b]; Eastern Department draft resolution (Doc. 35): basic tasks No. 4, par. 3[c]; July, 1931, directive: section 27, par. 1[d]
Article 2	November 16, 1930, directive (Doc. 8): item 4[e]; Eastern Department draft resolution: basic tasks No. 11[f]; July, 1931, directive: sections 1–7[g]
Article 3	June 7, 1929, directive (Doc. 26): par. 10[h]; July, 1931, directive: section 27, par. 2[i]
Article 4	July 23, 1930, directive: section 26, par. 2[j]
Article 5	November 16, 1930, directive: item 4[k]; Eastern Department draft resolution[l]; July, 1931, directive: section 27, par. 3[m]
Article 6	Eastern Department draft resolution[n]; July, 1931, directive: section 27, par. 4[o]
Article 7	July 23, 1930, directive: section 6[p]; Eastern Department draft resolution[q]; July, 1931, directive: section 27, par. 4[r]
Article 8	Eastern Department draft resolution[s]
Article 9	Eastern Department draft resolution[t]; July, 1931, directive: section 28, par. 2[u]
Article 10	Eastern Department draft resolution[v]
Article 11	July 23, 1930, directive: section 7[w]; Eastern Department draft resolution[x]
Article 12	November, 1926, resolution: section (11), par. 1[y]; July 23, 1930, directive: end of section 6, section 8, section 26, par. 2[z]; July, 1931, directive: section 26, par. 5[aa]; Eastern Department draft resolution[bb]
Article 13	Eastern Department draft resolution[cc]
Article 14	July, 1931, directive: section 5[dd]

[a] *Red Documents*, pp. 392–93.
[b] *Ibid.*, p. 349, lines 9–15.
[c] Lead-type printed copy, leaf 52, side 1.
[d] *Red Documents*, p. 396.
[e] *Ibid.*, p. 368, lines 7–8.
[f] Lead-type printed copy, leaf 53, side 2.
[g] *Red Documents*, p. 376, lines 5–6; p. 396, line 7.
[h] *Ibid.*, p. 325, lines 4–12; *International Line*, pp. 48–49.

[i] *Red Documents,* p. 396, lines 8–11.

[j] *Ibid.,* p. 359, lines 3–4.

[k] *Ibid.,* p. 368, lines 3–5.

[l] Lead-type printed copy, leaf 52, side 1, lines 2–3; also from line 18 to side 2, line 4.

[m] *Red Documents,* pp. 396–97.

[n] Lead-type printed copy, leaf 52, side 1, line 5; side 2, lines 4–6.

[o] *Red Documents,* p. 397, lines 9–10.

[p] *Ibid.,* p. 349, lines 9–13.

[q] Lead-type printed copy, leaf 52, side 1, lines 14–17.

[r] *Red Documents,* p. 397, lines 10–13.

[s] Lead-type printed copy, leaf 51, side 2, lines 10–15; leaf 53, side 2, lines 14–16.

[t] *Ibid.,* leaf 51, side 2, lines 16–17.

[u] *Red Documents,* p. 398, lines 2–3.

[v] Lead-type printed copy, leaf 53, side 1, line 8.

[w] *Red Documents,* p. 350, lines 2–3.

[x] Lead-type printed copy, leaf 51, side 1, lines 7–8, 14–17.

[y] "Resolution on the Chinese Problem," November, 1926 (*Red Documents,* pp. 255–56; *International Line,* III, 12, lines 1–2).

[z] *Red Documents,* pp. 349–50; 259, lines 4–5.

[aa] *Ibid.,* p. 397, lines 14–15; p. 401, lines 14–15.

[bb] Lead-type printed copy, leaf 52, side 2, lines 6–12; leaf 50, side 1, line 18—side 2, line 1.

[cc] *Ibid.,* leaf 54, lines 6–10.

[dd] *Red Documents,* p. 380, lines 2–9; p. 391, line 12; p. 392, line 1.

Incidentally, it may be mentioned that while the agrarian program of the Russian Returned Students was evidently based on Comintern instructions, their urban policy was not so clear. On one hand, it was the Comintern position that capitalism would continue to develop in China for a long time.[11] On the other, Ch'en Shao-yü, leader of the Russian Student group, maintained that capitalists were as much a target of attack at the time as imperialists and feudal remnants.[12] Furthermore, the Russian Returned Students did use the term *key cities* (*chung-hsin ch'eng-shih*) as the targets of their attacks. But in fact, those key cities, as announced by them, were limited to the cities and towns in Kiangsi, such as Nan-ch'ang, Chi-an, and Fu-chou.[13] For caution's sake, this writer would think it advisable to remove the words "the revival, to a lesser degree, of the Li Li-san policy of taking urban centers" from page 200 of his book, *Power Relations within the Chinese Communist Movement: A Study of Documents,* when a revised edition is prepared.

[11] Document 7, "Resolution on the Chinese Problem," July, 1930, sec. 7, in *Red Documents,* pp. 346–61; Document 36, Letter of the ECCI Presidium to the CCP, sec. 31, in *Bolshevik* (Kiangsi), No. 1 (July 1, 1934), pp. 1–41.

[12] *Power Relations,* I, 203–4.

[13] *Ibid.,* p. 201.

DOCUMENT 35

[COMINTERN] DRAFT RESOLUTION ON THE LAND AND PEASANT PROBLEMS IN SOVIET AREAS (蘇維埃區域土地農民問題議決案草案 *Su-wei-ai ch'ü-yü t'u-ti nung-min wen-t'i i-chüeh-an ts'ao-an*), issued by the Comintern Eastern Department; reprinted and distributed by the CCP Central Secretariat, November 20, 1930, five days after it had been received; a pamphlet printed in lead type, 008.751/4424/C.1, SSC; reprinted by the CCP Wan-t'ai Ho-tung Committee, April 22, 1931, mimeographed, 008.751/4424/C.2, SSC; reproduced in *A Collection of Red Bandit Secret Documents,* Vol. III, leaves 38–45, in *A Collection of Reactionary Documents,* Vol. IV, leaves 1–8; in Hsiao Tso-liang, *Power Relations within the Chinese Communist Movement, 1930–1934: Vol. II, The Chinese Documents;* mimeographed, 008.2129/7120, SSC; approximately 5,200 words.

This document is referred to in this volume as the Comintern Eastern Department draft resolution on the land and peasant problems in the Soviet areas, received in the middle of November, 1930. The question of "November 20, 1930" as the date of the reprinting of this document, as recorded in my earlier study *Power Relations,* I, 71–72, should be removed, since the date is clear enough in the text of this document as printed in *A Collection of Reactionary Documents.* An editorial note reads: "This document was received five days ago," so it follows that the document was received in the middle of November, 1930. It is indicated that this was Document No. 5 released after the Third Plenum.

In this document the Eastern Department of the Comintern assigned the following tasks to the Chinese Communist Party in the Soviet areas:

1. The organization of the hired farm hands and the coolies.

2. The organization of the poor peasants.

3. The indiscriminate punishment of counterrevolutionaries like village bosses, gentry, and so on, without trying to distinguish between "good" and "bad"; confiscation of not only the land but also other properties; nullification of all usurious loans, title deeds, and slave contracts.

4. The equal redistribution of all land, including the land of the peasants, with labor power as the preferred criterion in redistribution; rich peasants, coolies, and hired farm hands to share in the redistribution of land.

5. The equal redistribution of land as applicable to the middle peasants also.

6. The nationalization of land and waters in due course.

7. The organization of Red Guards, Red Army, and so on.

8. The exercise of regard for the interests of the middle peasants, religious habits, and peasant prejudices.

9. The transformation of clan land into peasant land.

10. The conversion of temple land into public land.

11. The allotment of land to Red Army men, their dependents, and others engaged in revolutionary work.

12. The dismissal of collectivization as a premature idea.

13. The creation of credit cooperatives under the leadership of the poor peasants.

14. The storing up of goods in the villages on a public basis; improving irrigation, and so forth.

15. The carrying out of a unified progressive agricultural tax.

It is important to remember that this statement was one of the most direct Comintern sources of the land law of the Chinese Soviet Republic.

DOCUMENT 36

LETTER OF THE ECCI PRESIDIUM TO THE CCP (共產國際執委主席團給中國共產黨的信 *Kung-ch'an kuo-chi chih-wei chu-hsi-t'uan chi chung-kuo kung-ch'an-tang ti hsin*), dated July, 1931; Chinese version printed in *Bolshevik* (Kiangsi), No. 1 (July, 1934), pp. 1–41, 008.105/4013, SSC; also printed in *Red Documents,* pp. 376–404, 008.2129/2703, SSC, and in Hsiao Tso-liang, *Power Relations within the Chinese Communist Movement, 1930–1934: Vol. II, The Chinese Documents;* approximately 15,000 words.

This was the last of the long series of available Comintern directives to the CCP during the era of land revolution. As I pointed out in *Power Relations,* I, 155–57, it was the most immediate Comintern authorization for the proclamation of the Chinese Soviet Government in 1931. It included, primarily in section 27, a fairly detailed land program which was written almost verbatim into the land law of that government. A comparison between this Comintern directive and the land law was made in the discussion of Document 34.

SECTION 2. RESPONSES IN SOVIET AREAS

DOCUMENT 37
Translation on pages 191-98

REGULATIONS OF THE KIANGSI PROVINCIAL GOVERNMENT FOR THE CONFISCATION AND REDISTRIBUTION OF LAND—APPROVED BY THE PROVI-

SIONAL CENTRAL GOVERNMENT (江西省政府對於沒收和分配土地的條例——臨時中央政府批准 *Chiang-hsi sheng cheng-fu tui-yü mo-shou han fen-p'ei t'u-ti ti t'iao-li—Lin-shih chung-yang cheng-fu p'i-chun*), probably adopted sometime between December 1, 1931, and April 1, 1932; reproduced in: *The Land Problem—Manual of Political Instruction in Camp Schools*, April 1, 1932, leaves 3–6, 008.741022/4047–2, SSC; *A Collection of Red Bandit Documents*, I, 17–27, 008.2129/4070/V.1, SSC; *A Collection of Red Bandit Reactionary Documents*, III, 927–34, 008.2129/4072/V.3, SSC; approximately 2,600 words.

To give effect to the land law passed by the First National Soviet Congress, immediate steps were taken to carry out the confiscation and redistribution of land and other properties in the various Soviet areas. To that end, a number of regulations and resolutions were adopted by the various local Soviet regimes as guides to action. The work of preparing those regulations and resolutions did not necessarily wait until after the formal passage of the land law, since the draft of the law had long been prepared and made available to the several Red regimes. The document under study is a set of regulations governing the detailed procedures of land revolution in Kiangsi province. As the numbering of the articles of this document in the three sources cited is different, the text in *The Land Problem,* which is the only available text printed by the Communists, is used as the basis of our discussion.

All non-Communist sources give the date of this document as December 1, 1932. This is certainly not true, because the full text of this document was included in *The Land Problem—Manual of Political Instruction in Camp Schools,* which was printed as early as April 1, 1932, and because the text of section II, article 6, of this document was invoked several times and printed in full as article 10 in the newspaper *Red China* for June 23, 1932, page 8.

The importance of this document cannot be overestimated. If the land law was a statement of objectives, this document was a set of detailed rules for the carrying out of those objectives. The scope of this document can be seen from its contents: (*1*) Whose land shall be confiscated? (sec. I, arts. 1–4); (*2*) Who shall be allotted land? (sec. II, arts. 1–14); (*3*) How shall land be redistributed? (sec. III, arts. 1–8); (*4*) How shall land be redistributed to the Red Army? (sec. IV, arts. 1–2); (*5*) Lease, purchase, sale, succession, and other matters (sec. V, arts. 1–18).

Despite its title, this document deals with the confiscation and redistribution of not only land, but also houses, farm implements, and so forth.

As this document is based on the land law of the Chinese Soviet Republic, it is naturally different from the land laws of the Chu-Mao group and Li Li-san in important respects. It differs from Li Li-san's land policy, for instance, in that it permits the lease, purchase, or sale of land. As distinct from Chu-Mao's ideas, it adopts the mixed principle of labor power and the number of persons as the criterion of land redistribution. But this does not mean that this document reflects precisely the land law of the Chinese Soviet Republic. There are quite a few important additions, which can be seen in Table 2. The corresponding clauses of the two documents are given side by side, while the new provisions of the regulations are placed in a separate column:

TABLE 2

Comparison of the Land Law of the Chinese
Soviet Republic and the Regulations of the
Kiangsi Provincial Government for the
Confiscation and Redistribution of Land

Land Law (Articles)	Regulations (Sections)	New Provisions of Regulations
1, 8	I, article 1	
6	I, article 2	
4	I, article 3	A rich peasant who had participated in a counterrevolutionary organization might be allotted a poorer house to live in.
3	I, article 4	
1, 5	II, article 1	A minority of the middle peasants might participate in equal redistribution, if they so desired.
1	II, article 2	
1	II, article 3	Unemployed physicians and teachers in the villages might be allotted land.
	II, article 4	Shop proprietors in the villages and their dependents might not be allotted land.
3, 7	II, article 5	A rich peasant who had no labor power might be allotted poor land not exceeding two thirds of the amount of land allotted to an ordinary person.
1	II, article 6	The female dependents of landlords and other counterrevolutionaries might not be allotted land, even if they had been married to workers, hired farm hands, poor peasants, or middle peasants.
	II, article 7	In the event that workers, hired farm hands, poor peasants, or middle peasants joined the families of landlords and other counterrevolu-

Land Law (Articles)	Regulations (Sections)	New Provisions of Regulations
		tionaries through marriage with their daughters and former wives, thereby succeeding to their properties, such properties must be confiscated.
	II, article 8	Foster children of landlords and other counter-revolutionaries might not be allotted land.
	II, article 9	Monks, Taoist priests, and so on might not be allotted land.
	II, article 10	Children of landlords and other counterrevolutionaries who had been admitted to the families of workers and peasants might not be allotted land.
1	II, article 11	All families of rich peasants who had led revolts might not be allotted land.
	II, article 12	Small businessmen in the villages might not be allotted land.
	II, article 13	Unemployed paupers in small market towns might be allotted land.
	II, article 14	When women married, their land should be disposed of by themselves.
	III, article 1	The township should be the unit for land redistribution. The village might become a unit if the majority of poor peasants and middle peasants so desired.
5, 7	III, article 2	
10	III, article 3	Rich peasants could receive only barren hills.
	III, article 4	Mountains should be managed publicly. They might be rented out for the purpose of exploitation according to the decision of the government.
10	III, article 5	The fish, not the water, in ponds should be distributed.
8	III, article 6	
4	III, article 7	
	III, article 8	Persons working in government and revolutionary organizations might not be allotted land.
2	IV, article 1	Red Army men should receive land close to their lodgings.
	IV, article 2	Public lands should be reserved for Red Army men.
12	V, article 1	
12	V, article 2	
	V, article 3	Land acquired by redistribution could be inherited.
14	V, article 4	
	V, article 5	The masses who had once been forced to flee or revolt might be allotted land.
	V, article 6	Former White Army men might be allotted land.

Land Law (Articles)	Regulations (Sections)	New Provisions of Regulations
	V, article 7	Workers, hired farm hands, poor peasants, or middle peasants who were misled into joining counterrevolutionary organizations, might be allotted land. Land should be reserved for those who were still detained pending a decision of their cases.
	V, article 8	Waste land might be leased to dependents of landlords and other counterrevolutionaries for cultivation or reclamation.

DOCUMENT 38

QUESTION AND ANSWER, No. 2 (問題與答覆 *Wen-t'i yü ta-fu*), issued by the Central People's Commissariat of Land; printed in *Red China*, No. 24 (June 23, 1932), p. 8, 008.1052/2125/V.1, SSC; approximately 1,000 words.

This is an official interpretation of article 10 (or sec. II, art. 6 as given in the preceding entry) of the *Regulations of the Kiangsi Provincial Government for the Confiscation and Redistribution of Land* (**Doc. 37**). The article provides, in effect, that the wife, daughter-in-law, or daughter of a village boss, a member of the gentry, a landlord, a counterrevolutionary rich peasant, and so forth, might not be allotted land, even if she had been married (or remarried) to a worker, a hired farm hand, a poor peasant, or a middle peasant.

DOCUMENT 39

HOW TO REDISTRIBUTE LAND (怎樣分配土地 *Tsen-yang fen-p'ei t'u-ti*), released by the General Political Department of the Military Council of the Oyuwan Soviet Area; reprinted by the General Political Department of the Fourth Front Army of the Chinese Workers' and Peasants' Red Army, on the anniversary of the October Revolution (i.e., November 7), 1931; reproduced in *A Collection of Red Bandit Documents*, I, 38–56, 008.2129/4070/V.1, SSC, and *A Collection of Red Bandit Reactionary Documents*, III, 934–46, 008.2129/4072/V.3, SSC; approximately 5,000 words.

This enactment concerns the confiscation and redistribution of land under the Oyuwan Soviet. As indicated in the discussion of Document 1, it was adopted by the Second Soviet Conference of the Oyuwan

Soviet Area opening on November 7, 1931, the same day that the First National Soviet Congress was inaugurated at Jui-chin.[14]

This document is divided into five major sections: (*1*) Why should land be redistributed? (*2*) Why should land be redistributed in the Oyuwan Soviet Area? (*3*) Errors and shortcomings in land redistribution in the past. (*4*) How should redistribution be carried out? (*5*) An explanation of the rural classes. In addition, a list of questions and answers on land redistribution is included as an appendix.

It is disclosed that a provisional land law was promulgated as a result of the First Conference of Delegates of the Oyuwan Soviet. Though the circumstances of that conference remain a mystery,[15] it is likely that the provisional land law referred to was enacted under the influence of Li Li-san's land law, which bears the same title. It is, therefore, not surprising to learn from this document that Oyuwan was greatly influenced by Li Li-sanism, which found expression in a number of aspects of its agrarian revolution. For instance, the rich peasant was deprived of his surplus landholdings only, so that he could manage to retain fertile land for himself (secs. I, art. 3; II). Second, landholdings of the peasants were pulled together to create (collective) farms (sec. II). Third, Red Army men were denied land allotments (secs. II, III).

As this statement was predominantly based on the land law of December 1, 1931 (**Doc. 34**), the documents agree with each other in general spirit, if not in letter. Nevertheless, this statement contains something new. For example, landlords and rich peasants who had long betrayed their own classes and surrendered to the proletariat unflinchingly might be allotted land like ordinary peasants. Again, widows of landlords might not be allotted land, while widows of rich peasants might be allotted poor land.

Of interest is an explanatory note on the rural classes, whose differentiation lies at the basis of the Communist revolution. The rural population was divided into five different classes: hired farm hands, poor peasants, middle peasants, rich peasants, and landlords.

DOCUMENT 40

RESOLUTION CONCERNING THE LAND PROBLEM ADOPTED BY THE THIRD PLENARY SESSION OF THE YANG-HSIN COUNTY SOVIET EXECUTIVE COMMITTEE (陽新縣蘇第三次全體執行委員會議土地問題決議 *Yang-hsin hsien-su ti-*

---

[14] For information concerning the Second Soviet Conference of Oyuwan, see *Power Relations*, I, 192, 193.

[15] *Ibid.*, p. 193.

san-tz'u ch'üan-t'i chih-hsing wei-yüan hui-i t'u-ti wen-t'i chüeh-i), dated December 5, 1931; reproduced in *A Collection of Red Bandit Documents*, I, 56–97, 008.2129/4070/V.1, SSC; approximately 10,000 words.

Situated in southeastern Hupeh, the county of Yang-hsin must have belonged to the Hsiangokan Soviet Area. From this lengthy and comprehensive statement one can have a fairly clear picture of what was going on during the agrarian revolution in that county.

Though not stated, this resolution was in all probability designed to carry out the land law of the Chinese Soviet Republic. This can be seen from a comparison of some of the key provisions of both documents in Table 3.

TABLE 3

COMPARISON OF THE LAND LAW OF THE CHINESE
SOVIET REPUBLIC AND THE YANG-HSIN
COUNTY SOVIET RESOLUTION

Yang-hsin Resolution (Paragraph)	Land Law of the Chinese Soviet Republic (Article)
8, 37	2
4, 6	3
22, 23	7
27	8
33	10
40	12

This resolution is divided into six major sections dealing with (*1*) land confiscation and redistribution, (*2*) procedure of redistribution, (*3*) the fight against the rich peasantry, (*4*) deportation of the dependents of reactionaries from their native places, (*5*) the progressive tax, and (*6*) miscellaneous matters. By far the most detailed section is the one on the confiscation and redistribution of land, which contains a quite complete enumeration of the general principles and policies. That section is followed by a list of specific directives to the several districts of the county, which may be summed up into three main points:

1. The rich peasants should be allotted poor land according to their labor power. The land they had received according to the number of people in their families should be surrendered.

2. If a middle peasant received more land than a poor peasant according to the number of persons, the excess land received by the middle peasant should be surrendered.

3. Those who were not entitled to land allotments, such as profes-

sional superstitious persons, reactionary ringleaders, physicians, teachers, *et al.*, must surrender the land they had received in the past.

SECTION 3. QUESTIONS IN ENFORCEMENT OF THE LAND LAW

DOCUMENT 41

RESOLUTION OF THE CENTRAL [POLITBURO] ON THE SLOGAN OF THE "EQUAL REDISTRIBUTION OF ALL LAND" (中央關於 "平分一切土地" 的口號 的決議 *Chung-yang kuan-yü "p'ing-fen i-ch'ieh t'u-ti" ti k'ou-hao ti chüeh-i*), adopted by the CCP Central [Politburo], December 24, 1931; printed in *Red Flag Weekly*, No. 28 (January 18, 1932), pp. 24–29, 052.1/809, BIC; approximately 1,900 words.

After the land law of the Chinese Soviet Republic (**Doc. 34**) went into effect, the Chinese Communists were confronted with a multitude of problems arising from the practice of confiscation and redistribution in the various localities. What did the equal redistribution of all land mean? How should the rural population be divided into different classes, and which classes should be liquidated and which ones protected? How was it possible to make the land law intelligible to the cadres and the masses at large? How could one make sure that the procedure of confiscation and redistribution would not go wrong? All these and related questions could not, of course, be answered in a vacuum, but on the basis of what had been learned from the practical experience of the land revolution. Accordingly, in the first year and a half after the promulgation of the land law, a variety of documents, papers, and articles relating to the above questions were issued or published in response to the requirements of the time. This statement, as its title indicates, concerns itself with the slogan of the equal redistribution of all land.

This resolution indicates that the slogan "equal redistribution of all land" was understood and implemented differently and confusedly in the various Soviet areas. For that reason, the various areas were condemned on charges ranging from adherence to the rich-peasant line to violation of the interests of the basic masses.

It was with a view to unifying the different interpretations of the slogan that the present resolution was adopted, emphasizing the protection of the interests of the middle peasantry.

The Comintern directive of July 23, 1930 (Doc. 7), was cited as the authority on which this resolution was based. In urging the allotment of the confiscated lands to the poor and middle peasantry according to the principle of equal distribution, that directive cautioned in section 6 that "the principle of confiscation should not apply to the land of the well-to-do peasants (referring to the well-to-do middle peasants here)." Acting on this Comintern injunction, the present resolution takes the position that the land of a middle peasant must not be confiscated anyway, not even if he had more land than a poor peasant or a hired farm hand could receive during land redistribution. Any infringement on the interests of a middle peasant under the pretext of the equal redistribution of all land was not allowed. The active support of the basic masses of the peasantry (including the middle peasant) was considered a precondition of the equal redistribution of all land.

The gist of the foregoing was already contained in a letter from the Central Committee to the Central Bureau of the Soviet Areas under date of November 10, 1931 (Doc. 33).

It is interesting to note that this resolution includes the middle peasants in the basic masses of the peasantry; ordinarily only the poor peasants and hired farm hands were understood as the basic masses of the peasantry.

DOCUMENT 42
DEFINITIONS OF THE RICH PEASANTS, MIDDLE PEASANTS, POOR PEASANTS, HIRED FARM HANDS, SHOP PROPRIETORS, MASTER WORKMEN, FOREMEN, INDEPENDENT LABORERS, AND WORKERS, AS WELL AS TACTICS TO OPPOSE THE RICH PEASANTS, SHOP PROPRIETORS, MASTER WORKMEN, AND FOREMEN, AND TO ALLY WITH THE MIDDLE PEASANTS AND INDEPENDENT LABORERS (富農, 中農, 貧農, 雇農, 與老板, 師父, 工頭, 獨立勞働者, 工人之解釋, 以及反對富農, 老板, 師父, 工頭與聯合中農, 獨立勞働者之策略 *Fu-nung, chung-nung, p'in-nung, ku-nung, yü lao-pan, shih-fu, kung-t'ou, tu-li lao-tung-che, kung-jen chih chieh-shih, i chi fan-tui fu-nung, lao-pan, shih-fu, kung-t'ou, yü lien-ho chung-nung, tu-li lao-tung-che chih ts'e-lüeh*), compiled and mimeographed by the CCP Ning-tu County Committee, January 18, 1932; 008.2122/2715, SSC; approximately 1,400 words.

This statement brings together the definitions of the different classes, presenting them with a listing of tactics on how to deal with them.

The 1933 statement, *How to Analyze the Classes* (**Doc. 96**), and this paper differ on these points:

1. The number of classes listed here is much greater than the 1933 statement, which listed only landlord, rich peasant, middle peasant, poor peasant, and worker (including hired farm hand).

2. The 1933 statement, confining itself to rural groups only, used land as the yardstick to distinguish one class from another, while this paper determined the class status by the amounts of food one had to eat and money one had to spend.

3. The treatment of the rich and middle peasants was different in the two statements. So, too, was the concept of the poor peasants.

DOCUMENT 43

THE RICH PEASANTRY IN THE AGRARIAN REVOLUTION (土地革命中的富農 *T'u-ti ko-ming chung ti fu-nung*), by Hui Wen; printed in *Red China*, No. 15 (March 23, 1932), p. 8, 008.1052/2125/V.1, SSC; approximately 450 words.

This short article contains the following two points:

1. The land-to-everybody program as manifested in "draw-on-the-plentiful-to-make-up-for-the-scarce and draw-on-the-fat-to-make-up-for-the-lean" was branded as representing a nonclass line.

2. The rich peasants were demanding rice seedbeds now that they had been allotted poor land. This was thought to be another way for the rich peasants to keep fertile land for themselves and was denounced accordingly.

DOCUMENT 44

A LETTER FROM THE COUNCIL OF PEOPLE'S COMMISSARS TO WESTERN FUKIEN [SOVIET GOVERNMENT] ON WORK IN SHANG-HANG AND WU-P'ING (人民委員會為杭武工作給閩西的一封信 *Jen-min wei-yüan-hui wei hang wu kung-tso chi min-hsi ti i-feng hsin*), March 9, 1932; printed in *Red China*, No. 13 (March 9, 1932), pp. 7–8, 008.1052/2125/V.1, SSC; approximately 3,700 words.

After the capture of the two counties of Shang-hang and Wu-p'ing in western Fukien, the Central Government sent this letter to the local authorities, telling them how to redistribute land there. About one third of the space of this letter is devoted to discussion of the land problem, though this problem covers only two of the ten points discussed.

In substance, this letter is based on the land law of the Chinese Soviet Republic (**Doc. 34**). In procedure, it gives a succinct account of how land should be redistributed in the newly occupied areas. Above all, it is stressed, the class stand should be strictly followed so that the fruits of the agrarian revolution might not fall into the hands of the rich peasants. Mass work was basic to the procedure, it is stated.

DOCUMENT 45

THE LAND PROBLEM (土地問題 *T'u-ti wen-t'i*), compiled by the Propaganda Department of the Central Bureau of the Soviet Areas; Lenin Bookstore edition, Western Fukien, lithographed, March, 1932, 12 leaves, 008.741022/4047/C.1, SSC; Red Army School edition, n.p. or d., 14 leaves, 008.741022/4047/C.2, SSC; reproduced in *A Collection of Red Bandit Reactionary Documents*, III, 890–910, 008.2129/4072/V.3, SSC; approximately 5,000 words.

Though described in *A Collection of Red Bandit Reactionary Documents* as the theoretical basis of the land revolution in China, this document was actually an explanatory statement of the land law of the Chinese Soviet Republic (**Doc. 34**). This is evident from the fact that the document was compiled by the Propaganda Department of the Central Bureau of the Soviet Areas, but not by a higher authority like the central party leadership. Nevertheless, this statement is extremely helpful to an understanding of the issues involved in the Chinese land revolution.

DOCUMENT 46

NOT TO INJURE THE MIDDLE PEASANT (反對侵犯中農 *Fan-tui ch'in-fan chung-nung*), by Po Chao; printed in *Red China*, No. 14 (March 16, 1932), p. 7, 008.1052/2125/V.1, SSC; approximately 1,300 words.

According to this article, it was discovered that leftist excesses had been committed in a number of places in the county of Jui-chin during the agrarian revolution. An investigation conducted by the Central Soviet Government revealed that the excesses had taken three different forms: (*1*) assigning medium land to the middle peasant; (*2*) attacking the middle peasant as a rich peasant; and (*3*) disenfranchising the middle peasant. The responsibility lay with the local Communist cadres who did not understand that the middle peasant was an integral part of the basic masses and an indispensable ally in the agrarian revolution. The middle peasant, the writer emphasizes, should be carefully distinguished from the rich peasant, who was not to be allowed to seize the fruits of the revolution. The following steps should be taken in the treatment of the rich peasant: (*1*) he should be assigned poor land according to the criterion of labor power; (*2*) his surplus farm implements should be confiscated; (*3*) he should be disenfranchised; (*4*) taxes on his land and foodstuffs should be increased; and (*5*) he should be barred from Soviet agencies, mass organizations, and so forth.

It seems almost superfluous to point out that the policy of not injuring the middle peasant was a strategy decided by Lenin during the October revolution.[16]

DOCUMENT 47

SOME OF MY VIEWS ON LAND REDISTRIBUTION (我對分田中幾點意見 *Wo tui fen-t'ien chung chi-tien i-chien*), by Han Wen; printed in *Red China*, No. 15 (March 23, 1932), p. 8, 008.1052/2125/V.1, SSC; approximately 1,800 words.

The writer points out that the work of land redistribution had not been well done, primarily because people looked upon it as an ordinary mass movement rather than a class struggle. He cites some facts to support this view, and makes a number of recommendations, the more important of which are as follows:

1. Before land redistribution, personal properties seized from landlords, reactionaries, *et al.*, should be allotted, in the first instance, to the masses so as to stir up their enmity against those persons. The property should in no way be misappropriated by those who were responsible for the redistribution of land.

2. A realistic working program of redistribution should be formulated according to the wishes of the basic masses of the peasantry, with due regard to the manpower and time required.

3. A thorough investigation of facts in connection with redistribution should be undertaken.

In conclusion, some details of procedure are suggested to carry out the work of land redistribution. From these one can get some idea of what the actual prosecution of the work was like at that time.

DOCUMENT 48

THE LAND PROBLEM (土地問題 *T'u-ti wen-t'i*)—MANUAL OF POLITICAL INSTRUCTION IN CAMP SCHOOLS, compiled by the Political Department of the 12th Army of the Chinese Workers' and Peasants' Red Army, April, 1932, 7 leaves, 008.741022/4047-2, SSC; lithographed; approximately 3,800 words.

Prepared for the political training of all those attached to the army in the field, this pamphlet is based on the official statement *The Land*

[16] Carr, *The Bolshevik Revolution*, II, 161.

Problem, compiled by the Propaganda Department of the CCP Central Bureau of the Soviet Areas and reprinted in 1932 (Doc. 45). On leaves 3–6 is the text of the *Regulations of the Kiangsi Provincial Government for the Confiscation and Redistribution of Land,* approved by the Provisional Central Government (**Doc. 37**).

DOCUMENT 49

QUESTION AND ANSWER, No. 1 (問題與答覆 *Wen-t'i yü ta-fu*) issued by the Central People's Commissariat of Land; printed in *Red China,* No. 24 (June 23, 1932), pp. 7–8, 008.1052/2125/V.1, SSC; approximately 1,600 words.

In reply to a questionnaire submitted by a cadre, the Communist leadership in this statement made an important distinction between the rich peasantry and the well-to-do middle peasantry, between the landlord and the rich peasantry—a distinction which was accepted by the well-known 1933 document *Decisions concerning Some Problems Arising from the Agrarian Struggle* (**Doc. 101**). Exploitation of others marked the rich peasant as opposed to the well-to-do peasant; land relations distinguished the landlord from the rich peasant.

DOCUMENT 50

A GENERAL SURVEY OF LAND REDISTRIBUTION—REPORT OF THE KIANGSI PROVINCIAL SOVIET (土地分配概況—江西省蘇報告 *T'u-ti fen-p'ei kaik'uang—chiang-hsi sheng-su pao-kao*), printed in *Red China,* No. 41 (November 21, 1932), p. 5, 008.1052/2125/V.2, SSC; approximately 2,500 words.

This is part of an official report of the Kiangsi Provincial Soviet, giving the result of land redistribution in nine counties in Kiangsi up to November, 1932. Allowing for the inaccuracies present in any official Communist statement, this report cited facts, supported by statistics and figures, about land redistribution. What was the average amount of land one received under the land redistribution program? What was the maximum or minimum amount of land one received? How about the masses who had fled? Did the rich peasants receive land of good quality? How much public land for the Red Army men? How much land for their dependents? These and other questions were answered at great length. For the sake of clarity Table 4 is constructed from the data contained in this document.

TABLE 4

REPORT OF THE KIANGSI PROVINCIAL SOVIET ON THE PROGRESS OF LAND REDISTRIBUTION, NOVEMBER, 1932

	Hsing-kuo	Kung-lüeh	An-yüan	Yung-feng	Ning-tu	Kan-hsien	Hsün-wu	Wan-t'ai	Yü-tu
Redistribution complete?	Yes	Greater part	Not quite	Greater part	In a few districts	Greater part	Greater part	Greater part	
Average amount of land per person	8[a]	7	7	6	1.5?	7	4 (+)	6?	?
Minimum amount of land per person	4.25	3.5	1	3	1.5?	3	2 (+)	4	?
Maximum amount of land per person	11	15	7	10	20	11	5 (+)	12	?
Redistribution unit: township or village?	Township, usually	Village, usually	Township, usually	Both	Township, usually	Township, usually	Both	Village, usually	
Did masses who had deserted to the enemy receive land?	Yes	Yes	Yes	Yes	Yes	Yes	Yes	Yes	
Amount of public land for Red Army men	2,401.1	317.6	861.6	2,410.1	8,072	1,673	803.5	825	
Amount of land for Red Army dependents	132,614.3	No statistics	Not investigated	Not investigated	Not investigated	Not investigated	Not investigated	33,029.5	
Were any middle peasants mistaken for rich peasants and given poor land?	Some in every district	Some	No	Very few	Not investigated	Unknown	Some	Very few	Very many

TABLE 4 (continued)

	Hsing-kuo	Kung-lüeh	An-yüan	Yung-feng	Ning-tu	Kan-hsien	Hsün-wu	Wan-t'ai	Yü-tu
Did landlords receive land?	1 (but now expropriated)								Very many
Did rich peasants receive good land?	3	Some, but now corrected	Some	Very few	Not investigated	Some	Some	Some	Very many
Were forests, houses, and ponds redistributed?	Yes	Yes	In some districts	Yes	Yes	No	In progress	In most cases	
Number of absentees[b]	134,256	Unknown yet	Unknown yet	Very few	Unknown yet	Unknown yet	Not investigated	1,000	
Amount of uncultivated rice fields	6,596.75	6,604.3	10,430	Not investigated			9,819	27,488.5	
Amount of uncultivated dry fields	191	517	Not investigated	Not investigated			Unknown	Unknown	

a The unit of the figures given is a picul, standing for the potential yield of a plot of land.
b The masses who had deserted to the enemy and not yet returned home.

DOCUMENT 51

INSTRUCTION NO. 1 OF THE CENTRAL PEOPLE'S COMMISSARIAT OF LAND—
ON INTENSIFYING LAND STRUGGLE AND CONFISCATING COMPLETELY THE
PROPERTY OF THE LANDLORD CLASS (中央土地人民委員部訓令第一號—為
深入土地鬥爭, 澈底沒收地主階級財產 *Chung-yang t'u-ti jen-min wei-yüan-pu
hsün-ling ti-i hao—wei shen-ju t'u-ti tou-cheng, ch'e-ti mo-shou ti-chu chieh-chi
ts'ai-ch'an*), issued December 28, 1932; printed in *Red China*, No. 47
(January 14, 1933), pp. 5–6, 008.1052/2125/V.5, SSC; approximately
2,500 words.

This is an important document regarding the procedure, as distinguished from the substance, of the agrarian struggle. The instruction is
simple: to confiscate not only the land of a landlord, but all his property
as well. But the implication of the document has been far-reaching, in
that the procedure described has been extensively readopted for the
liquidation of landlords on the Chinese mainland after the inauguration
of the present Peiping regime in 1949. To sum up the five major points:

1. All hidden or disguised landlords must be detected in strict accordance with the class line, and all their movable and immovable
properties must be confiscated.

2. The more important of their confiscated properties, such as
money, gold, and other valuables, should go to the government, while
the less important things, such as rice, clothes, and farm implements,
should be distributed among the poor masses so as to push them to
struggle against the landlords. The latter point was stressed so much
that failure to do so was regarded as alienating the masses.

3. Confiscated articles must be distributed on the spot so as to pay
due regard to the self-interest and provincialism of the peasantry, which
was admittedly difficult to remove. The masses of one locality should
not be allowed to receive confiscated articles of another.

4. The confiscation of property must pass through the following
steps: (*a*) investigation, (*b*) decision by the government, (*c*) convocation
of a mass meeting to excite public agitation, (*d*) implementation through
the Poor-Peasant Corps and the Hired-Farm-Hand Union.

5. Mass action alone would not do. It must be supplemented by
action of the poor-peasant and hired-farm-hand organizations. This
applied to the redistribution of land also.

In addition, it is pointed out that fines on landlords could reduce or
eliminate some of their distant or unknown holdings.

DOCUMENT 52

CIRCULAR, SERIES *Chih*, No. 15, OF THE HSIANGKAN PROVINCIAL SOVIET EXECUTIVE COMMITTEE—REGARDING DISPOSAL OF ARTICLES CONFISCATED DURING LAND INVESTIGATION (湘贛省蘇維埃執行委員會通令執字第十五號—關於查田中没收的東西的處理 *Hsiang-kan sheng su-wei-ai chih-hsing wei-yüan-hui t'ung-ling chih-tzu ti shih-wu hao—kuan-yü ch'a-t'ien chung mo-shou ti tung-hsi ti ch'u-li*), issued December 29, 1932, Yung-hsin, Kiangsi; reproduced in *A Collection of Red Bandit Documents*, I, 111–14, 008.2129/4070/V.1, SSC; approximately 600 words.

Since the confiscation of property had not been carried out satisfactorily, the Soviet Government of Hsiangkan Province (bordering Hunan and Kiangsi), issued the present order.

1. All land and other properties confiscated must be handed over to the Department of Finance. No private individuals were allowed to divide confiscated articles among themselves, nor were the responsible officials permitted to buy them at reduced prices.

2. All draft cattle and farm implements confiscated must be handed over to the Poor-Peasant Corps for redistribution among the poor peasants and hired farm hands who needed them.

3. All confiscated poultry should be handed over to the wounded or disabled Red Army men.

4. All wadded coverlets confiscated should also be distributed to wounded or disabled Red Army men.

DOCUMENT 53

RESOLUTION ON THE LAND, ECONOMIC, AND FINANCIAL PROBLEMS (關於土地經濟財政問題決議案 *Kuan-yü t'u-ti ching-chi ts'ai-cheng wen-t'i chüeh-i-an*), adopted by the Fourth Congress of the CCP Hsiangosi (Western Hunan-Hupeh) Branch; approved by the CCP Hsiangosi Central Subbureau, n.d.; reproduced in *A Collection of Red Bandit Documents*, I, 27–38, 008.2129/4070/V.1, SSC; approximately 2,600 words.

As its title indicates, this document is a blending of land, economic, and financial policies of the Hsiangosi Soviet Area, situated on the borderland of northern Hunan and western Hupeh. Its land policy was apparently based on the land law of the Chinese Soviet Republic and was designed to put that law into effect under the Hsiangosi Soviet.

It was probable that this document was drafted under the influence

of the Comintern Eastern Department directive on the economic policies in the Soviet areas (Doc. 59).

DOCUMENT 54
COLLECTING CONTRIBUTIONS FROM THE RICH PEASANTRY TO SUPPORT
THE REVOLUTIONARY WAR AND MOBILIZING THE MASSES TO HELP TILL
LAND FOR GOVERNMENT EMPLOYEES (向富農募集一次革命戰爭捐款, 發動群
眾幫助政府工作人員耕田 *Hsiang fu-nung mu-chi i-tz'u ko-ming chan-cheng
chüan-k'uan, fa-tung ch'ün-ch'ung pang-chu cheng-fu kung-tso jen-yüan keng
t'ien*), n.p. or d.; reproduced in *A Collection of Red Bandit Documents*, I,
120–23, 008.2129/4070/V.1, SSC; approximately 1,000 words.

This statement seems to have been issued by a provincial government
sometime after April 14, 1933, when the Central Soviet Government
ordered the mobilization of the masses to help till the land of government officials. It begins with a reference to two previous government
orders to collect tributes from the rich peasantry for purposes of war
and to mobilize villagers to help till land for government employees.
It makes clear that the rich peasants should be made to pay contributions either by persuasion or by compulsion. It should be pointed out
to rich peasants that they were required only to contribute money in
times of war while landlords were deprived of all their property. Continuing, the statement comments that although competent workers and
peasants were often not willing to serve in the government on the ground
that they were indispensable in their homes, undesirable elements
wormed their way into government agencies. With this background,
the statement stresses two points:

1. Rich peasants must be made to pay contributions to support the
war against the Nationalists. The masses must be stirred up to oppose
the rich peasants, and past errors in the determination of the class status
of the rich peasants must be corrected so that those who pretended to
be middle peasants might not be able to evade war levies.

2. Each government employee whose help was indispensable in his
home should be given a certificate, by virtue of which he could get aid
from the masses in the cultivation of his land. People who were really
indispensable to work in their homes should not be picked to do routine
business in government agencies.

DOCUMENT 55
THE CLASS STRUGGLE UNDER THE SOVIET REGIME (蘇維埃政權下的階級
鬥爭 *Su-wei-ai cheng-ch'üan hsia ti chieh-chi tou-cheng*), by Lo Fu (Chang

Wen-t'ien), May 26, 1933; printed in *Struggle* (Kiangsi), No. 15 (June 15, 1933), pp. 9–14, 008.2105/4420/V.1, Nos. 1–15, SSC; approximately 1,800 words.

This is a fairly clear account of the use of class analysis for the purpose of class struggle in the rural districts. The author, one of the leading Russian Returned Students, declares in no uncertain terms that the correct class line was to represent the hired farm hands, rely on the poor peasants, ally with the middle peasants, oppose the rich peasants, and annihilate the landlords. In the initial stage, he goes on, the task of revolution was to be undertaken by the general body of the toiling and miserable peasants against the landlords and rich peasants. After that, the classes must be sharply differentiated from one another and the class line must be closely followed. Above all, he adds, care must be taken to strengthen the alliance with the middle peasantry, as was taught by Lenin.

This is the second part of an article, the first of which is missing.

DOCUMENT 56

GENERAL PRINCIPLES OF ORGANIZATION AND FUNCTIONS OF THE LAND-REGISTRATION COMMITTEE (土地登記委員會組織與工作綱要 *T'u-ti teng-chi wei-yüan-hui tsu-chih yü kung-tso kang-yao*), n.p. or d., reproduced in *A Collection of Red Bandit Reactionary Documents*, III, 1011–14, 008.2129/4072/V.3, SSC; approximately 600 words.

This document was probably enacted by the Central Commissariat of Land for the registration of land in Kiangsi. Its sixteen articles may be divided into three parts as follows:

1. Terms of reference—investigation, registration, estimation, and verification of land (art. 1).

2. Structure—establishment of committees on the county, district, and township levels and their membership (arts. 2, 3, and 4).

3. Procedure and guiding principles of work—details of work of all concerned, including both the government and people (arts. 5–16).

DOCUMENT 57

REGULATIONS FOR LAND REGISTRATION (土地登記規則 *T'u-ti teng-chi kuei-tse*), issued by the Central Commissariat of Land and approved by the Council of Commissars, n.d.; reproduced in *A Collection of Red Bandit Reactionary Documents*, III, 1014–16, 008.2129/4072/V.3, SSC; approximately 450 words.

The essentials of the sixteen articles of these detailed rules for the registration of land are:

1. The purpose of land registration is to establish the ownership of land by the peasants so as to increase production and encourage the economic development of the nation.

2. Registration is to be carried out in all places where land has been redistributed. It applies also to forests, ponds, and dry fields.

3. Land is to be registered again if it is sold, leased, or otherwise transferred to others after the initial registration.

4. In cases where landlords and rich peasants have disguised themselves as middle or poor peasants and have received land, such land must be taken back when discovered. A fresh registration should take place if the majority of peasants, on the ground that mistakes have been made, so request.

DOCUMENT 58

LAND REGISTRATION FORMS (土地登記表格 *T'u-ti teng-chi piao-ko*), n.d., reproduced in *A Collection of Red Bandit Reactionary Documents*, III, 1017–23, 008.2129/4072/V.3, SSC.

A set of forms useful for reference in any serious study of the agrarian problem under the Kiangsi Soviet. In addition to one duplicate, there are six different kinds of registration forms:

1. Relating to landlords and rich peasants.
2. Relating to old and new landlords in a district.
3. Relating to dry fields, ponds, and so forth.
4. Relating to forests.
5. Relating to land registration in Chang-sheng county, Kiangsi.
6. Relating to public land for Red Army men.

DOCUMENT 59

COMINTERN EASTERN DEPARTMENT ECONOMIC POLICIES IN THE SOVIET AREAS (國際東方部對蘇區的經濟政策 *Kuo-chi tung-fang-pu tui su-ch'ü ti ching-chi cheng-t'se*), n.d.; reproduced by a Chinese Communist branch in Kiangsi on April 18, 1931; contained in *A Collection of Red Bandit Secret Documents*, Vol. III, leaves 52–55, 008.2129/4074, SSC; mimeographed; approximately 2,700 words.

This Comintern directive related to CCP economic policies in the Soviet Areas. As it touches upon the land problem only briefly, it has not been studied before, and was not included in my earlier work,

Power Relations within the Chinese Communist Movement, 1930–34: A Study of Documents (Power Relations, I).

An editorial note attached to the end of the draft resolution on the land and peasant problems in Soviet areas (Doc. 35) indicates that this document was received with that draft resolution five days before they were reprinted on November 20, 1930. That means that this Comintern directive was also received in the middle of November, 1930.

IV

The Land Investigation Drive

SECTION 1. OPENING THE DRIVE

DOCUMENT 60

Translation on pages 198-202

INSTRUCTION NO. 11 OF THE COUNCIL OF PEOPLE'S COMMISSARS OF THE PROVISIONAL CENTRAL GOVERNMENT OF THE CHINESE SOVIET REPUBLIC —LAUNCHING AN EXTENSIVE AND INTENSIVE LAND INVESTIGATION DRIVE (中華蘇維埃共和國臨時中央政府人民委員會訓令，第十一號—實行廣泛深入的查田運動 *Chung-hua su-wei-ai kung-ho-kuo lin-shih chung-yang cheng-fu jen-min wei-yüan-hui hsün-ling, ti shih-i hao—shih-hsing kuang-fan shen-ju ti ch'a-t'ien yün-tung*), issued June 1, 1933; printed in *Red China*, No. 87 (June 20, 1933), p. 5, 008.1052/2125/V.3, SSC; also in *A Guide to the Land Investigation Drive*, pp. 7–10, 008.743/4063–3/C.1,2, SSC; approximately 1,800 words.

In the summer and early fall of 1933, a general land investigation drive took place in the Central Soviet Area. The purpose of the drive, as announced by the Communists themselves, was to ferret out hidden landlords and rich peasants in a ruthless class struggle, but not to investigate conditions of land ownership and redistribution as such.[1]

According to Mao, who was responsible for the prosecution of the land investigation drive, the class struggle in the agrarian revolution would roughly go through three phases: (*1*) land confiscation and redistribution, (*2*) land investigation, and (*3*) land reconstruction.

When an area first fell into Communist hands, Mao states, it was termed a *newly developed area,* in which the Communist task was to confiscate and redistribute land. In an area where the Communist political power had already been consolidated, land redistribution completed, and counterrevolutionary resistance smashed, the important thing to

[1] C. Martin Wilbur (ed.), *Chinese Sources on the History of the Chinese Communist Movement,* p. 19.

79

do was to carry out land reform in order to increase its production in an over-all program of land reconstruction. An area reaching this stage of development was called an *advanced struggle area*. Between the two extremes there was an intermediate area in which, though the task of land confiscation and redistribution had been completed, some landlords and rich peasants might have managed to slide into the toiling masses, seeking to sabotage the revolutionary cause. In an area of this intermediate phase, the main thing to do was to search out the hidden counterrevolutionaries and deal them a fatal blow. Such an area was known as a *comparatively retarded struggle area,* where the important task facing the Communists was to launch a land investigation drive.

As Mao points out, the greater part of the Central Soviet Area remained in this intermediate stage when the present order for the land investigation drive was issued on June 1, 1933 (see **Doc. 62**).

The land investigation drive began with this cabinet order issued over the signatures of Chairman Mao and his two deputies. The order begins with the statement that the land problem had not been solved in almost 80 per cent of the Central Soviet Area, an area with a population of more than 2,000,000. With a view to the solution of this problem, the land investigation drive was being launched. This order sets forth twelve points, the gist of which follows:

1. The whole government machine, particularly the departments of land, prosecution, justice, and state political security, should be made to lead and direct the drive.

2. Eight counties bordering Kiangsi and Fukien were to hold two conferences to start the drive: (*1*) a conference of responsible government officials, and (*2*) a conference of delegates of poor-peasant corps. The eight counties named were Jui-chin, Hui-ch'ang, Yü-tu, Sheng-li, Po-sheng, Shih-ch'eng, Ning-hua, and Ch'ang-t'ing.

3. In attempting to ferret out and eradicate hidden landlords and rich peasants, the class line should be strictly followed to ensure the leadership of rural workers, the reliance on poor peasants, and the alliance with middle peasants.

It seems clear that the land investigation drive was initiated and organized by Mao. There is evidence to support this thesis. (*1*) The present order was issued by the Council of People's Commissars, of which Mao was chairman at this time. (*2*) As will be seen later, the CCP Central Bureau of the Soviet Areas, which was then under the control of the Russian Returned Students, adopted a resolution in support of the land investigation drive the day following a report made by

Mao before it. (*3*) In the course of the drive a number of important relevant statements were made by Mao but none was made by other top-ranking Communist leaders. (*4*) The first paragraph of this document was adopted almost verbatim as the conclusion of Mao's article, "The Land Investigation Drive Is the Central Task of Great Magnitude in Vast Areas" (**Doc. 62**). (*5*) The first four tasks concerning the land investigation drive listed in this order constitute the main contents of a statement made by Mao on June 18, "The First Step of the Land Investigation Drive—A Large-Scale Mobilization of the Organization" (**Doc. 63**). (*6*) Item 9 and to a lesser degree item 4 of the list of tasks were incorporated in another statement made by Mao during the land investigation drive, "Unfold the Land Investigation Drive According to the Disparity of the Condition of the Development of the Class Struggle in the Rural Districts" (**Doc. 65**).

However, it is interesting to note that the basic ideas of this order reflect the land law of the Chinese Soviet Republic (**Doc. 34**), but not the land law of the Chu-Mao group (**Doc. 9**). The rich peasants, for instance, were allotted poor land under this order, as they were under the land law of the Chinese Soviet Republic.

Chang Kuo-t'ao, one of the CCP leaders who was defeated and ousted by Mao in 1938, answered in the affirmative, when this writer asked him during an interview in Hongkong late in October, 1959, whether the land investigation drive had been shaped in Moscow. He said that similar movements were also afoot in other Soviet areas, but were called by different names. In retrospect, it seems reasonable to suppose that what Chang had in mind was not the actual drive but probably the basic idea of the liquidation of the landlords and rich peasants, which culminated in the land investigation drive. There is no evidence that Moscow had ever issued any special directive to set the land investigation drive in motion in the hinterland of China.

DOCUMENT 61

RESOLUTION OF THE CENTRAL BUREAU ON THE LAND INVESTIGATION DRIVE (中央局關於查田運動的決議 *Chung-yang-chü kuan-yü ch'a-t'ien yün-tung ti chüeh-i*), dated June 2, 1933; printed in *Red China*, No. 87 (June 20, 1933), p. 2, 008.1052/2125/V.3, SSC; also in *A Guide to the Land Investigation Drive*, pp. 1–5, 008.743/4063-3/C.1,2, SSC; approximately 2,400 words.

This was the first statement of the party, as distinct from the government, in regard to the land investigation drive. Though similar in outline to the government instruction (**Doc. 60**), it has its own characteristics:

1. This resolution was adopted one day after Document 60, and after the Central Bureau had heard a report made by Mao and his associate, Hu Hai, on the position of the individual cases of land investigation which had been going on here and there before the start of the general land investigation drive.

2. This statement makes no mention of the two conferences of the eight counties referred to in the government instruction.

3. The government instruction was distributed to government organs; this statement was addressed to the party headquarters at various levels, asking them to give support to the land investigation drive decreed by this resolution as well as by the government instruction.

4. In contradistinction to the government instruction, this statement of the party attributes the past failure of a complete solution to the land problem to, *inter alia*, the incorrect lines of (*1*) draw-on-the-plentiful-to-make-up-for-the-scarce and draw-on-the-fat-to-make-up-for-the-lean, and (*2*) no confiscation of the land of small landlords.

Obviously, the specific reference to the first as an incorrect line gave Mao a slap in the face.

DOCUMENT 62

Translation on pages 202-5

THE LAND INVESTIGATION DRIVE IS THE CENTRAL TASK OF GREAT MAGNITUDE IN VAST AREAS (查田運動是廣大區域的中心重大任務 *Ch'a-t'ien yün-tung shih kuang-ta ch'ü-yü ti chung-hsin chung-ta jen-wu*), by Mao Tse-tung; printed in *Red China,* No. 86 (June 17, 1933), p. 3, 008.1051/2125/ V.3, SSC; approximately 2,100 words.

This statement of Mao was published on June 17 when the eight-county conference on the land investigation drive opened in Jui-chin. It was also his first speech to the gathering the next day.[2]

The significance of this statement lies in the division of the agrarian revolution into three phases, and the fitting of the land investigation drive into the second phase. In so doing, Mao gave, in effect, the *raison d'être* of the land investigation drive.

The gist of this statement has already been outlined in the discussion of Document 60, but it cannot be too often reiterated that the agrarian revolution, according to Mao, could be divided into three stages: (*1*) land confiscation and redistribution, (*2*) land investigation, and (*3*)

[2] *Red China,* June 23, 1933, p. 3.

land reconstruction. These three stages fitted into three different kinds of Communist areas: (*1*) the newly developed area, (*2*) the comparatively retarded struggle area, and (*3*) the advanced struggle area.

The first stage of the agrarian revolution in a newly developed area, Mao points out, covered the whole period from the beginning of the revolution until the defeat of the counterrevolutionaries and the disposal of their properties. Confiscation and redistribution of land were the features of this period.

The third and last stage was reached in an advanced struggle area where counterrevolution had been subdued and the revolutionary struggle had entered into a phase of land reform, with an anticipation of increase of land productivity. The crucial problem of this period was one of land reconstruction.

Between these two extremes lay the second stage of the land revolution in which the landlords and rich peasants, though subdued and offering no more open resistance, had in many cases slid into the poor and toiling masses of the peasantry. There they claimed a share in land redistribution, and sought to sabotage the revolution by any means possible. The task of the revolution in this stage was particularly difficult as the landlords and rich peasants had shifted from open to underground resistance. The effective way of combating counterrevolution during this period lay, therefore, in the land investigation drive, which was indeed the central task of great magnitude in vast areas.

As pointed out previously, Mao used the prologue of Document 60, which launched the land investigation drive, as the epilogue of this statement.

DOCUMENT 63

Translation on pages 205-8

THE FIRST STEP OF THE LAND INVESTIGATION DRIVE—A LARGE-SCALE MOBILIZATION OF THE ORGANIZATION (查田運動的第一步—組織上的大規模動員 *Ch'a-t'ien yün-tung ti ti-i pu—tsu-chih shang ti ta-kuei-mu tung-yüan*), by Mao Tse-tung; printed in *Red China*, No. 87 (June 20, 1933), p. 3, 008.1052/2125/V.3, SSC; approximately 1,300 words.

This was the second speech delivered by Mao before the eight-county conference on the land investigation drive on June 18, 1933.[3] Mao stresses that the drive must be a concerted effort of the party, the government, and mass organizations. Since it was a ruthless class strug-

[3] *Red China,* June 20, 1933, p. 3.

gle as well as a great revolution, the drive could not be brought to a successful conclusion without the cooperation of them all. It would therefore be wrong, according to Mao, to look upon the drive as the responsibility of the land department of the government alone; it was rather the concern of all government branches and mass organizations under the leadership of the party.

The basic ideas of this statement were already embodied in Document 60.

DOCUMENT 64

USE OUR HAMMER (用我們的鉄錘 *Yung wo-men ti t'ieh-ch'ui*), by Chih Ying; printed in *Red China*, No. 87 (June 20, 1933), p. 5, 008.1052/2125/V.3, SSC; 154 words.

This song, dedicated to the land investigation drive, is a Communist literary gem. It is divided into three sections dealing with the plot of the landlords and rich peasants to undermine the agrarian revolution, their attempt to seize upon the fruits of the revolution, and the necessity to detect their remnants and hammer them.

DOCUMENT 65
Translation on pages 208-10

UNFOLD THE LAND INVESTIGATION DRIVE ACCORDING TO THE DISPARITY OF THE CONDITION OF THE DEVELOPMENT OF THE CLASS STRUGGLE IN THE RURAL DISTRICTS (依據農村中階級闘爭的發展狀態的差別去開展查田運動 *I-chü nung-ts'un chung chieh-chi tou-cheng ti fa-chan chuang-t'ai ti ch'a-pieh ch'ü k'ai-chan ch'a-t'ien yün-tung*), by Mao Tse-tung; printed in *Red China*, No. 88 (June 23, 1933), p. 3, 008.1052/2125/V.3, SSC; approximately 700 words.

Judged by its wording and content, this short statement was one of a series of speeches delivered by Mao before the eight-county conference on the land investigation drive. Referring to another of the series, Mao dwells on the importance of the division of Communist districts into (*1*) the advanced struggle area, (*2*) the retarded struggle area, (*3*) the newly developed area. He says this tripartite division applied not only to a province, but to a county, a district, a township, or even a village. In other words, any geographical unit under Communist control could be divided into the same three categories according to the degree of progress of the class struggle.

Only by taking the uneven development of these three different kinds of areas into account, Mao continued, could the land investigation drive be carried out effectively. The greatest possible effort must be concentrated on the retarded areas where it was most difficult to set the mass struggle in motion. Communist cadres of the advanced areas should be transferred to the retarded areas to help work.

This statement was a follow-up to another important statement by Mao (**Doc. 62**). It was also an amplification of item 9 and to a lesser degree of item 4 of the government order of June 1 (**Doc. 60**) which set the land investigation drive in motion.

SECTION 2. EIGHT-COUNTY CONFERENCE

DOCUMENT 66
Translation on pages 210-15
CIRCULAR OF THE CENTRAL GOVERNMENT—CALLING A CONFERENCE OF RESPONSIBLE SOVIET AUTHORITIES OF EIGHT COUNTIES ON AND ABOVE THE DISTRICT LEVEL AND A CONFERENCE OF DELEGATES OF THE POOR-PEASANT CORPS OF EIGHT COUNTIES (中央政府通告—召集八縣區以上蘇維埃負責人員會議及八縣貧農團代表大會 *Chung-yang cheng-fu t'ung-kao—chao-chi pa-hsien chü i-shang su-wei-ai fu-tse jen-yüan hui-i chi pa-hsien p'in-nung-t'uan tai-piao ta-hui*), dated June 1, 1933; printed in *Red China*, No. 85 (June 14, 1933), p. 3, 008.1052/2125/V.3, SSC; approximately 2,000 words.

This circular announces the calling of two eight-county conferences for the promotion of the land investigation drive decreed by government order (**Doc. 60**). The two conferences were: (*1*) a conference of responsible government officials scheduled for June 17–20, and (*2*) a conference of delegates of poor-peasant corps scheduled for June 25–July 1. Both gatherings were to be held at the town of Yeh-p'ing in the suburbs of Jui-chin, a town which, rather than Jui-chin proper, was in fact the seat of the Chinese Soviet Government.

It is made clear that the drive was designed to precede the proposed Second National Soviet Congress and that it was not meant to be another round of land redistribution but a campaign to eliminate landlords and rich peasants who had managed to slide into the masses of the toiling peasants. Participants in the eight-county conference of responsible government officials were to be drawn from the district, county, and provincial levels, viz., chairmen of the district and county governments, vice-chairman of the provincial government, together with land commissars, chief workers' and peasants' procurators, and leading security officers at all three levels.

The conference of the poor-peasant corps, which were in existence only at the township level at that time, was designed to arouse the interest of the masses for the sake of propaganda and agitation so that an atmosphere favorable to the drive might be created in the nine hundred townships of the eight counties.

Apart from its political significance, this paper gives details of the procedure for calling a conference. It has served as a prototype for the procedure of calling a meeting on the Chinese mainland since 1949. Every delegate was, for instance, requested to bring with him a rice bowl, a pair of chopsticks, and so forth. Such small things must not be dismissed as insignificant; they constitute an essential part of the Communist way of doing things.

DOCUMENT 67

SLOGANS AND WATCHWORDS FOR THE LAND INVESTIGATION DRIVE (查田 運動的口號標語 *Ch'a-t'ien yün-tung ti k'ou-hao piao-yü*), printed in *Red China*, No. 87 (June 20, 1933), p. 6, 008.1052/2125/V.3, SSC; also in *A Guide to the Land Investigation Drive*, pp. 51–54, 008.743/4063/C.1,2, SSC; approximately 1,100 words.

This is a list of sixty-five slogans and watchwords for the land investigation drive. While the words "eight counties" were employed to qualify these slogans and watchwords when they were printed in *Red China*, they were dropped altogether in the text reproduced in *A Guide to the Land Investigation Drive*. This seems to suggest that the slogans and watchwords applied to all Soviet areas. However simple they may be, they reflect appropriately the multifarious objectives of the land investigation drive and provide a bird's-eye view of the movement.

DOCUMENT 68

THE CONFERENCE OF RESPONSIBLE SOVIET AUTHORITIES OF EIGHT COUNTIES ON AND ABOVE THE DISTRICT LEVEL ON THE LAND INVESTIGATION DRIVE HAS BEEN A SUCCESS (八縣區以上蘇維埃負責人查田運動大會 成功了 *Pa-hsien ch'ü i-shang su-wei-ai fu-tse-jen ch'a-t'ien yün-tung ta-hui ch'eng-kung liao*), printed in *Red China*, No. 88 (June 23, 1933), p. 3, 008.1052/2125/V.3, SSC; approximately 2,300 words.

This was a news report on the eight-county conference on the land investigation drive held during June 17–21, 1933.

A previous report on the inauguration of the conference appeared in the newspaper *Red China*, No. 87, June 20, p. 3, in which it was disclosed that Mao and a number of other appropriate government authorities addressed the gathering but that no one spoke for the party except the first speaker, a representative of the CY. It was further reported that the conference was preceded by more than a month of preparatory work following the decision of the Council of People's Commissars to call it. Though not complete, the present news report contains some items not otherwise available.

The conference was held in the auditorium of the central government situated at the town of Yeh-p'ing in the suburbs of Jui-chin. More than four hundred delegates were present. Mao gave a series of speeches before the conference on the afternoon of the 18th, during the whole day of the 19th, and on the morning of the 21st. His speeches that marked the occasion were on the following topics:

1. The land investigation drive is the central task of great magnitude in vast areas (**Doc. 62**).

2. The first step of the land investigation drive—a large-scale mobilization of the organization (**Doc. 63**).

3. Follow the class line steadfastly during the land investigation drive.

4. Struggle for the winning over of the great majority of the masses for the annihilation of the feudal remnants.

5. Reform the Soviets during the land investigation drive.

6. The task of combating counterrevolution during the land investigation drive.

7. Conclusions reached by the conference (**Doc. 69**).

The texts of some of the above-mentioned speeches cannot be found; the available ones are noted above.

It was reported that Lo Mai, representative of the Department of Organization of the CCP Central Bureau of the Soviet Areas, made a speech to party members among the delegates present. He stressed that a total of 80,000 new party members should be recruited during the land investigation drive in the eight counties represented at the conference.

The closing speech in the conference was delivered by Teng Fa, chief of the State Political Security Bureau. A number of other government officials including Hsiang Ying, vice-chairman of the central government, also addressed the conference before it closed. A land investigation contest contract was to be signed on July 22, which provided that from July through September another 80,000 Red Army men should be recruited and a total of 800,000 Chinese dollars should be collected from landlords and rich peasants. In addition, the central government was urged to float another loan for 3,000,000 Chinese dollars for the promotion of the cooperatives.

DOCUMENT 69

Translation on pages 215-30

CONCLUSIONS REACHED BY THE CONFERENCE OF RESPONSIBLE SOVIET AUTHORITIES OF EIGHT COUNTIES ON AND ABOVE THE DISTRICT LEVEL ON THE LAND INVESTIGATION DRIVE (八縣區以上蘇維埃負責人員查田運動

大會所通過的結論 *Pa-hsien ch'ü i-shang su-wei-ai fu-tse jen-yüan ch'a-t'ien yün-tung ta-hui so t'ung-kuo ti chieh-lun),* dated June 21, 1933; printed in *Red China,* No. 89 (June 29, 1933), pp. 5–7, 008.1052/2125/V.3, SSC; also in *A Guide to the Land Investigation Drive,* pp. 11–26, 008.743/4063–3/ C.1,2, SSC; approximately 8,600 words.

This paper was a summing up of the decisions made by the eight-county conference on the land investigation drive. It must have been the text of a speech delivered by Mao on June 21 as described on p. 87.

Based on the government instruction of June 1, which set the land investigation drive afoot, this statement delineates the nature and procedure of the projected land investigation drive in relatively clear and definite terms. The scope of its content can be judged from the subjects discussed: (*1*) mobilization of the organization; (*2*) correct application of the class line; (*3*) winning over the great bulk of the masses; (*4*) consolidating the Soviets; (*5*) combating counterrevolution; (*6*) attacking landlords and rich peasants by means of fines; (*7*) war mobilization plus economic and cultural reconstruction; (*8*) facing the offensive of the [KMT] enemy; (*9*) supporting the projected Second National Soviet Congress; and (*10*) punishing saboteurs.

Though almost entirely a repetition of the old arguments, this summing up of the decisions of the eight-county conference is a useful document for a study of the land investigation drive.

DOCUMENT 70

RESOLUTION OF THE CONFERENCE OF DELEGATES OF THE POOR-PEASANT CORPS OF EIGHT COUNTIES ON THE LAND INVESTIGATION DRIVE (八縣貧

農團代表查田運動大會的決議 *Pa-hsien p'in-nung-t'uan tai-piao ch'a-t'ien yün-tung ta-hui ti chüeh-i),* printed in *A Guide to the Land Investigation Drive,* pp. 31–33, 008.743/4063–3/C.1,2, SSC; approximately 1,400 words.

In accordance with instructions of the central government, a conference of delegates of the poor-peasant corps of the same eight counties was held at Yeh-p'ing, Jui-chin, from June 25 to July 1, 1933. The occasion was marked by a speech of Chairman Mao.

This statement is the text of the resolution adopted by that conference. It contains eight points reaffirming the conclusions reached by the eight-county conference of responsible Soviet authorities on the land investigation drive. Attention was called to pertinent official documents such as the central government instruction of June 1 (**Doc. 60**), Mao's speeches on the land investigation drive, and the statement *How to Analyze the Classes* (**Doc. 96**). No mention was, however, made of the June 2 resolution of the CCP Central Bureau (Doc. 61).

SECTION 3. AGENCIES OF THE DRIVE
DOCUMENT 71
ON THE LAND INVESTIGATION DRIVE (關於查田運動 *Kuan-yü ch'a-t'ien yün-tung*), by [Wang] Hsiu, June 11, 1933; printed in *True Words of Youth*, II, No. 20 (June 25, 1933), 9–12, 008.2105/5083, SSC; approximately 1,900 words.

This was a brief discussion of the part to be played by the CY in the land investigation drive. The CY was called upon to carry out accurately and resolutely the general tactics laid down by the Party, to lead the youth to participate in the class struggle, and to absorb activists who might emerge in the course of the movement.

DOCUMENT 72
ORGANIZATION AND TASKS OF THE LAND INVESTIGATION COMMITTEE ON THE COUNTY, DISTRICT, AND TOWNSHIP LEVELS (縣區鄉三級查田委員會的組織與任務 *Hsien-ch'ü-hsiang san-chi ch'a-t'ien wei-yüan-hui ti tsu-chih yü jen-wu*), printed in *Red China*, No. 89 (June 29, 1933), p. 8, 008.1052/2125/V.3, SSC; also in *A Guide to the Land Investigation Drive*, p. 49, 008.743/4063/C.1,2, SSC; approximately 400 words.

For the purpose of carrying out the land investigation drive, a land investigation committee was established in every county, district, or township. This document is the organic law of that setup, providing for its organization and functions. It is composed of four articles, stipulating, *inter alia,* that the committee was responsible for the prosecution of the land investigation drive, and, to that end, should undertake to draw up the plan, educate the cadres, determine the class status, and so forth.

DOCUMENT 73

THE ROLE OF THE COUNTERREVOLUTION-COMBATING AGENCIES IN THE
LAND INVESTIGATION DRIVE (查田運動中肅反機關的任務 *Ch'a-t'ien yün-tung
chung su-fan chi-kuan ti jen-wu*), printed in *Provincial Committee Correspondence,* No. 13 (July 12, 1933), pp. 1–3, 008.2105/9023/Nos. 11–88, SSC;
mimeographed; approximately 1,100 words.

Issued shortly after the start of the land investigation drive and based
on the practical experience gained in the county of Yü-tu, this statement was apparently a directive of the Kiangsi Provincial Political
Security Bureau to its agents on the county and district levels throughout the province, telling them how to work effectively to smash landlords and rich peasants. In view of the fact that many landlords, rich
peasants, and members of the gentry attempted to escape by disguising
themselves in one way or another, all the political security men on the
county and district levels were called upon to stay alert. The major
points:

1. The blacklist of the gentry, landlords, and rich peasants should be
made available to the appropriate Land Investigation Committees as
a guide to action.

2. The political security men on the district level were authorized to
arrest and to try the above-mentioned class of men and hand them
over to the district judiciary department for a second, public trial
during which the political security men should expose the guilt of the
culprits to the fullest possible extent.

3. The work of the Surprise Inspection Posts should be stepped up
to prevent the escape of landlords and others.

DOCUMENT 74

THE TASK OF COMBATING COUNTERREVOLUTION IN THE LAND INVESTIGA-
TION DRIVE (查田運動中的肅反工作 *Ch'a-t'ien yün-tung chung ti su-fan kung-
tso*), by Jan Chih; printed in *Red China,* No. 94 (July 14, 1933), p. 6,
008.1052/2125/V.4, SSC; approximately 1,100 words.

The last part of this signed article contains some specific measures
against counterrevolutionaries such as the establishment of sentry posts
in the countryside, the blockade of outlets, the search of mountains, the
roundup and detainment of the gentry and landlords, and so forth.
These measures have been revived following the Communist conquest
of the Chinese mainland in 1949.

DOCUMENT 75

GENERAL PRINCIPLES OF ORGANIZATION AND FUNCTIONS OF THE POOR-PEASANT CORPS (貧農團組織與工作大綱 *P'in-nung-t'uan tsu-chih yü kung-tso ta-kang*), issued by the Central Government, July 15, 1933; printed in: *A Guide to the Land Investigation Drive*, pp. 35–40, 008.743/4063–3/C.1,2, SSC; and in *A Collection of Red Bandit Reactionary Documents*, II, 625–28, 008.2129/4072/V.2, SSC; approximately 4,000 words.

As its title indicates, this is a delineation of the guiding principles of the organization and functions of the Poor-Peasant Corps, which was the instrument for the carrying out of the land investigation drive. The document consists of an introduction and eleven sections. The main points:

1. The Poor-Peasant Corps was not an organization of one class alone, but of the general body of the poor masses including the rural workers who were to play a leading role.

2. The responsibility of the Corps was to help the government carry out laws and ordinances, but not to supplant its work.

3. The Corps was required to follow the leadership of the CCP and the Soviets.

4. The Corps was an organization on the township level.

DOCUMENT 76

A REVIEW OF THE LAND INVESTIGATION DRIVE (關於查田運動中的檢查 *Kuan-yü ch'a-t'ien yün-tung chung ti chien-ch'a*), by [Wang] Hsiu; printed in *True Words of Youth*, II, No. 24 (August 13, 1933), 3–5, 008.2105/4083/V.2, Nos. 21–31, SSC; approximately 900 words.

This article called upon the Communist Youth Corps to recognize the significance of the land investigation drive and participate in the work of investigation earnestly. It was pointed out that the Youth Corps had generally overlooked the drive.

DOCUMENT 77

Translation on pages 230-34

INSTRUCTION NO. 7 OF THE STATE POLITICAL SECURITY BUREAU [SPSB] —THE RESPONSIBILITY AND WORK OF THE SPSB AND ITS SPECIAL COMMISSIONERS IN THE LAND INVESTIGATION DRIVE (國家政治保衛局訓令第七號 —查田運動中保衛局及其特派員之任務與工作 *Kuo-chia cheng-chih pao-wei-chü hsün-ling ti-ch'i hao—ch'a-t'ien yün-tung chung pao-wei-chü chi ch'i t'e-p'ai-*

yüan chih jen-wu yü kung-tso), issued probably in July, 1933; reproduced by the SPSB Branch in Minkan Province, [January] 23, 1934, 008.237/ 4063, SSC; mimeographed; approximately 1,800 words.

In every sense this order sounded like a death warrant for landlords, village bosses, gentry, rich peasants, and other counterrevolutionaries. The terms of reference of the SPSB during the land investigation drive, as set forth in this statement, were as follows:

1. To get rid of landlords, village bosses, gentry, rich peasants ruthlessly and completely;

2. To put down all sabotage and resistance against the land investigation drive on the part of landlords, gentry, rich peasants, and other counterrevolutionaries;

3. To step up the curfew and the surprise investigation;

4. To strengthen the work of the net of secret service;

5. To empower SPSB special commissioners on the district level to arrest and try the landlords, gentry, rich peasants, *et al.* (ordinarily the SPSB had powers solely to detect and investigate those outlaws);

6. When landlords, village bosses, gentry, and rich peasants were found guilty of undermining the drive, they could be arrested on the spot and tried in any manner considered appropriate.

Document 78
Translation on pages 234-36
Instruction No. 9 of the State Political Security Bureau (國家 政治保衛局訓令第九號 *Kuo-chia cheng-chih pao-wei-chü hsün-ling ti-chiu hao*), July 12, [1933]; reproduced by the SPSB Branch in Minkan Province, January 23, 1934; 008.237/4063, SSC; mimeographed; approximately 600 words.

As distinguished from SPSB Instruction No. 7 (**Doc. 77**), which was virtually designed to eliminate the landlords, village bosses, gentry, rich peasants, and other counterrevolutionaries, this document was meant to exact gold, silver, and other valuables from them. Specifically, the responsibility of the SPSB men was:

1. To prevent the hiding or throwing away of valuables;

2. To prevent escape with valuables;

3. To detain the able-bodied of the above-mentioned classes of people and to subject them to hard labor;

4. To prevent members of these groups from joining secret societies like the Big Swords, all of which were banned.

SECTION 4. NINE-COUNTY CONFERENCE
DOCUMENT 79
THE SUCCESS OF THE CONFERENCE OF NINE-COUNTY SOVIET OFFICIALS ON AND ABOVE THE DISTRICT LEVEL ON THE LAND INVESTIGATION DRIVE! (九縣區以上蘇維埃工作人員查田運動大會的成功! *Chiu-hsien ch'ü i-shang su-wei-ai kung-tso jen-yüan ch'a-t'ien yün-tung ta-hui ti ch'eng-kung*), issued by the Kiangsi Provincial Committee; printed in *Provincial Committee Correspondence*, No. 18 (July 27, 1933), pp. 1–3, 008.2105/9023/Nos. 11–88, SSC; mimeographed; approximately 1,300 words.

Following the eight-county conference on the land investigation drive held under the auspices of the central government, the Kiangsi provincial government called another conference. Nine counties from the northern border of the Communist region in Kiangsi province met from July 21 to July 25, 1933. Since the task of this conference was based upon the conclusions reached by the first, there was little difference in the sphere of policy between the two parleys. However, the nine-county conference had its own characteristics as follows:

1. As the nine counties were situated along the northern border of the Soviet region, there was a need for not only land investigation, but land redistribution as well.

2. Since the border areas were under the constant threat of an armed attack, the agrarian revolution called for the support of both the army and the guerrilla forces.

3. Efforts in the economic field were essential to improve the lot of the people and to increase supplies for the troops.

4. Armed protection of the autumn harvest was indispensable to the land investigation drive.

5. A contest for the collecting of additional recruits and contributions was to be held between the counties concerned.

DOCUMENT 80
A CONTEST AGREEMENT REACHED AT THE NINE-COUNTY CONFERENCE ON THE LAND INVESTIGATION DRIVE (九縣查田運動大會中的競賽條約 *Chiu-hsien ch'a-t'ien yün-tung ta-hui chung ti ching-sai t'iao-yüeh*), printed in *Red China*, No. 104 (August 22), p. 3, and No. 106 (August 31), p. 6, 1933, 008.1052/2125/V.4, SSC; approximately 800 words.

The present contest agreement was entered into by the delegates to the nine-county conference on the land investigation drive which took place July 21–25, 1933. The contest agreement was so called because it was intended to give the impression that the parties took the matter so seriously that they wanted to compete with one another for the honor of success. The agreement was couched in familiar Communist terms patterned after the provisions of laws and ordinances concerning the investigation of land at the time.

SECTION 5. SUCCESSES AND FAILURES
DOCUMENT 81
UNFOLD THE LAND INVESTIGATION DRIVE VEHEMENTLY (猛烈的開展查田 運動 *Meng-lieh ti k'ai-chan ch'a-t'ien yün-tung*), printed in *Provincial Committee Correspondence*, No. 12 (July 9, 1933), pp. 1–3, 008.2105/9023/Nos. 11–88, SSC; mimeographed; approximately 1,100 words.

Acting on the resolution of the CCP Central Bureau of the Soviet Areas on the land investigation drive dated June 2, 1933, this statement, presumably representing the views of the CCP Kiangsi Provincial Committee, lashed out at bureaucratism and formalism which had developed in various counties during the prosecution of the land investigation drive. Accordingly, mass action was called for as a necessary procedure for the accomplishment of the task of land investigation.

DOCUMENT 82
INITIAL RESULTS OF THE STRUGGLE IN THE INVESTIGATION OF LANDS AND CLASSES IN PO-SHENG COUNTY (博生縣查田查階級鬥爭的初步成績 *Po-sheng hsien ch'a-t'ien ch'a-chieh-chi tou-cheng ti ch'u-pu ch'eng-chi*), printed in *Provincial Committee Correspondence*, No. 13 (July 12, 1933), pp. 3–4, 008.2105/9023/Nos. 11–88, SSC; mimeographed; approximately 900 words.

This was a balance sheet of the initial stage of the land investigation drive in three different districts of the county of Po-sheng. Although the drive was considered successful in detecting a large number of disguised landlords and rich peasants, several weak points were disclosed:

1. There had been no prior plan of concentrating the struggle upon one or two of the worst villages and then applying the experience gained to the rest of the district.

2. There had been a failure to properly redistribute confiscated lands and other properties to the masses on the spot through mass meetings attended by members of the organizations of the poor peasantry and of the hired farm hands.

3. There had been no due regard for the treatment of the detected landlords and rich peasants as well as disposal of their lands.

DOCUMENT 83
THE LESSON LEARNED FROM THE LAND INVESTIGATION DRIVE IN THE COUNTY OF SHENG-LI IS ALSO A LESSON FOR THE WHOLE PROVINCE (勝利縣查田運動的教訓也就是全省的教訓 *Sheng-li hsien ch'a-t'ien yün-tung ti chiao-hsün yeh chiu-shih ch'üan-sheng ti chiao-hsün*), printed in *Provincial Committee Correspondence*, No. 12 (July 9, 1933), pp. 3–5, 008.2105/9023/ Nos. 11–88, SSC; mimeographed; approximately 1,400 words.

Apparently representing the views of the CCP Kiangsi Provincial Committee, this statement points out the defects of the land investigation drive in the county of Sheng-li with a view to improvement. The following are given as the principal reasons for many disheartening things that happened:

1. People did not understand that the drive was directed against the landlords and rich peasants and was not just another round of land redistribution.

2. It had not been made unmistakably clear that the drive should be carried out by mass action.

3. No timely action had been taken to meet the resistance of the landlords and rich peasants.

4. Imposition rather than persuasion was the order of the day, resulting in the alienation of the masses.

This paper cites the above points to vindicate three basic assumptions: (*1*) Land investigation was in fact an investigation of class status. (*2*) To that end, there must be violent mass action to carry it out. (*3*) Everything in the struggle to detect landlords and rich peasants must be done through the instrumentality of the masses.

DOCUMENT 84
Translation on pages 236-54
PRELIMINARY CONCLUSIONS DRAWN FROM THE LAND INVESTIGATION DRIVE (查田運動的初步總結 *Ch'a-t'ien yün-tung ti ch'u-pu tsung-chieh*), by Mao Tse-tung; printed in *Struggle* (Kiangsi), No. 24 (August 29, 1933), pp. 4–12, 008.2105/7720/V.2, SSC; reproduced in *A Collection of Red Bandit Reactionary Documents*, III, 970–88, 008.2129/4072/V.3, SSC; approximately 9,500 words.

Reviewing the land investigation drive for the month of July, Mao points out a whole host of errors of omission and commission during the drive with a view to correcting them in time. He also acknowledges some successes made by both the party and the government. That he pays a tribute to the party as well as the government may help to explain why, in the official collection of documents, *A Guide to the Land Investigation Drive*, the resolution of the Central Bureau of the Soviet Areas on the land investigation drive, dated June 2 (Doc. 61), is placed before the instruction of the Central Government, dated June 1 (**Doc. 60**).

The present statement falls into nine sections: (*1*) the successes made; (*2*) failures in the leadership; (*3*) concessions made to landlords and rich peasants; (*4*) injuries done to the middle peasants; (*5*) closed-door policy of the Poor-Peasant Corps and disregard for the leading role of the hired farm hands; (*6*) incorrect ideas on the rich-peasant problem; (*7*) dereliction of duty on the part of the prosecution department; (*8*) the art of leadership; and (*9*) unfolding a two-front struggle.

Mao singles out Jui-chin and Po-sheng as the two successful counties in the land investigation drive in July, since a total of more than two thousand households of landlord and rich-peasant status were uncovered there. He makes it clear that the investigation of land was in fact an investigation of the classes, or rather an effort to ferret out hidden landlords and rich peasants.

The mistakes made during the drive, according to Mao, were as follows: Some of the committees for land investigation, created to organize and direct the drive, never met in session. Some of the chairmen of the district and township Soviet governments refused to head those committees on the pretext of the pressure of business. In addition, some party units simply ignored the drive. Mao complains that there were even cases in which Communist cadres yielded to landlords and rich peasants.

As always, Mao warns against the violation of the interests of the middle peasants. He urges the return of the landholdings taken from them.

Since the Poor-Peasant Corps was the main instrument for the carrying out of the land investigation drive, it should of course be open to all poor peasants. But according to Mao, this was not the case in many places. He also charges that the leading role of the hired farm hands did not receive due attention.

Although theoretically the rich peasant was not to be annihilated, in practice he often was. In many instances, complains Mao, the land of rich peasants was completely expropriated, as though they were land-lords. This error was attributed to the lack of a clear conception about the rich peasantry.

He felt that bureaucratism and formalism were common in the Workers' and Peasants' Prosecution Department.

Mao attaches great importance to the mass line which he calls the Bolshevik art of leadership. But in practice, according to him, this art of leadership was not followed.

In keeping with the party line of the time, Mao concludes with a call for a two-front struggle against both Right and Left deviations.

DOCUMENT 85

PROCLAMATION NO. 27 OF THE PROVISIONAL CENTRAL GOVERNMENT OF THE CHINESE SOVIET REPUBLIC—FOR UNFOLDING THE LAND INVESTIGA-TION DRIVE (中華蘇維埃共和國臨時中央政府佈告第二十七號—為開展查田運動 *Chung-hua su-wei-ai kung-ho-kuo lin-shih chung-yang cheng-fu pu-kao ti erh-shih-ch'i hao—wei k'ai-chan ch'a-t'ien yün-tung*), September 1, 1933, Jui-chin; 008.743/7774, SSC; lithographed; approximately 1,100 words.

This proclamation reaffirms the policies of land investigation as laid down in the government instruction of June 1. With the exception of a routine reference to the successes scored, the proclamation is concerned with the failings of the drive: injuring the middle peasants, giving shelter to landlords and rich peasants, and what not. Proceeding on these premises, the paper sets forth ten points in reaffirmation of the guiding principles of class struggle for the drive. It is, for instance, made clear that land investigation did not mean a redistribution of land but an investigation of classes, which should result in the detection of landlords and rich peasants.

DOCUMENT 86

RESOLUTION NO. 2 OF THE CENTRAL [BUREAU] CONCERNING THE LAND INVESTIGATION DRIVE (中央關於查田運動的第二次決議 *Chung-yang kuan-yü ch'a-t'ien yün-tung ti ti-erh-tz'u chüeh-i*), September 8, 1933; 008.743/4063-2, SSC; mimeographed; approximately 1,700 words.

Being a sequel in order rather than in logic to the Central Bureau Resolution (Doc. 61) decreeing the land investigation drive on June 2, this paper reviews the progress of the work with particular reference to the mistakes made. The principal mistakes included: (*1*) apathy and inertness in far-off areas owing to ignorance of local cadres; (*2*) widespread injuries done to the middle peasantry and excesses committed in regard to the rich peasantry; (*3*) failure to allot confiscated properties speedily to the hired farm hands and the poor and middle peasants; (*4*) bureaucratism in the form of working over the heads of the masses.

DOCUMENT 87

PROCLAMATION NO. ——— OF THE KUAN-CH'ANG COUNTY SOVIET GOVERNMENT—THE PROPER WAY OF THE LAND INVESTIGATION DRIVE (廣昌縣蘇維埃政府佈告第　號—查田運動的正當辦法 *Kuang-ch'ang hsien su-wei-ai cheng-fu pu-kao ti ——— hao—ch'a-t'ien yün-tung ti cheng-tang pan-fa*), September 20, 1933; 008.743/4033, SSC; approximately 340 words.

This proclamation points out that the purpose of the drive was to detect landlords and rich peasants only. Accordingly, the logic of class struggle ruled out clan disagreements or other irrelevant tussles. As an ally, the middle peasantry should attend all meetings held to determine class status, to confiscate and redistribute land, and so forth. As this proclamation was issued for the benefit of the general public, it presented the complicated land problem in condensed, popular terms.

DOCUMENT 88

A GENERAL SURVEY OF THE LAND INVESTIGATION DRIVE (查田運動的概況 *Ch'a-t'ien yün-tung ti kai-k'uang*), issued by CCP Kiangsi Provincial Committee, September, 1933; 008.741026/4463, SSC; mimeographed; approximately 4,300 words.

This review of the implementation of the land investigation drive in Kiangsi during the months of June–July, 1933, was classified as reference material for the Kiangsi Provincial Conference of the CCP then in session. The drive was emphasized as a device of ruthless class struggle. The two counties of Jui-chin and Po-sheng were portrayed as having made the greatest achievements in the movement. In general, however, the drive was not considered a success for a number of reasons: (*1*) lack of a proper understanding of the issues involved; (*2*) inadequate effort in combating counterrevolution; (*3*) inadequate ideological struggle against family and other feudal ties; (*4*) failure to rely on the poor peasants and unite with the middle peasants.

DOCUMENT 89

EXPERIENCE OF LAND INVESTIGATION IN THE AREA OF THE PO-SHENG COUNTY SEAT (博生城區的查田經驗 *Po-sheng ch'eng-ch'ü ti ch'a-t'ien ching-*

yen), by Chung Ping; printed in *Red China*, Nos. 115 and 116 (October 3 and 6, 1933), pp. 3; 008.1052/2125/V.4, SSC; approximately 1,000 words.

This is a brief account of the fight against Right and Left deviations in the course of land investigation in the area of the seat of Po-sheng county in the fall of 1933. The first part of the article is devoted to the fight against rightism, singling out a chairman of the local Soviet government as a target for attack. It describes how this man was compromising with landlords and rich peasants and how he was removed from office on that account. The second part is an expression of concern with the leftist excesses committed by the Children's Corps, the Youth Vanguard, and the Poor-Peasant Corps. The Children's Corps, for example, beat, detained, and imprisoned men and confiscated their property at will. Responsibility for these malpractices lay with (*1*) refusal of mass organizations to follow the Soviet leadership, and (*2*) juvenile discontent with the powerful Poor-Peasant Corps.

DOCUMENT 90

SOME SERIOUS MISTAKES IN PROPAGANDA LITERATURE DURING THE LAND INVESTIGATION DRIVE (查田運動中宣傳材料幾個嚴重的錯誤 *Ch'a-t'ien yün-tung chung hsüan-ch'uan ts'ai-liao chi-ko yen-chung ti ts'o-wu*), by San Hsiang; printed in *Red China*, Nos. 118, 119, 120 (October 12, 15, 18, 1933); 008.1052/2125/V.4, SSC; approximately 1,800 words.

This article falls into four sections: (*1*) inadequate understanding of the leadership and the achievements of the agrarian revolution, (*2*) lack of a clear-cut conception about class analysis, (*3*) mistakes in looking upon propaganda literature as ordinance and upon the land investigation drive as the task of a few government officials, and (*4*) separation of the drive from the over-all struggle of the revolution.

DOCUMENT 91

INSTRUCTION NO. 5 OF THE LAND DEPARTMENT OF THE KIANGSI PROVINCIAL SOVIET GOVERNMENT (江西省蘇維埃政府土地部訓令第五號 *Chiang-hsi sheng su-wei-ai cheng-fu t'u-ti-pu hsün-ling ti-wu hao*), November 21, 1933; 008.743/4013, SSC; mimeographed; approximately 2,100 words.

Issued five months after the inauguration of the land investigation drive in June, 1933, this paper points out the failings of the drive as a lesson for the future. The failings summed up show traditional Communist bifurcation: Right and Left opportunism. The principal charge is estrangement from the masses so as to play into the hands of the land-lords and rich peasants. Violation of the interests of the middle peasantry is condemned.

DOCUMENT 92

RESOLUTION ON THE LAND PROBLEM (土地問題決議案 *T'u-ti wen-t'i chüeh-i-an*), n.p., or d.; 008.743/4947–2, SSC; approximately 2,700 words.

Judging from the wording of its introduction, this resolution may have been adopted by the Second Conference of Delegates of the Kiangsi Provincial Soviet, which was held December 21–29, 1933.[4] The resolution falls into two major sections: (*1*) a review of land distribution in the past, and (*2*) a working program for the future. The first section deals with the nonclass line in the agrarian revolution and its manifestation in the confiscation and redistribution of land. The second section lists nine points as guides to future work, all of which are within the general framework of the land law of the Chinese Soviet Republic.

DOCUMENT 93

SOVIET WORK IN CH'ANG-KANG TOWNSHIP, HSING-KUO (興國長岡鄉的蘇維埃工作 *Hsing-kuo ch'ang-kang-hsiang ti su-wei-ai kung-tso*), by Mao Tse-tung, December 15, 1933; published in *Struggle* (Kiangsi), No. 42 (January 12), pp. 10–16, No. 43 (January 19), pp. 15–20, No. 44 (January 26), p. 16, 1934; 008.2105/4420/V.4, SSC; and in Mao Tse-tung, *Investigations of the Rural Districts*, published at Yenan in 1941, reissued by the Hsinhua Bookstore, Shantung, 1946, pp. 91–125; approximately 14,000 words.

Around the turn of 1933/34, Mao published reports on two model townships, the Ch'ang-kang township in Hsing-kuo county in southern Kiangsi and the Ts'ai-hsi township in Shang-hang county in western Fukien. Both reports, according to Mao, are accounts of the advanced stage as distinguished from the initial stage of the land revolution.[5]

The present account is a report on the Ch'ang-kang township in Hsing-kuo county in Kiangsi. It is a fairly detailed listing of the major aspects of the Soviet work of that township, based extensively on statistical data. Mao had no doubt about the reliability of the data and praised Ch'ang-kang as a "model" township on that account.

Mao says in the introductory statement that all Soviet work was done

---

[4] *Red China*, January 1 and 4, 1934.
[5] Mao, *Investigations of the Rural Districts*, p. 1.

in townships and municipalities but that many people simply did not know just how Soviet work had actually been accomplished. In consequence, Mao complains, Soviet authorities on a higher level issued numerous orders and instructions which did not square with the local conditions. He calls this bureaucratism.

In order to carry out Soviet work effectively, says Mao, there was no alternative but to rely on mass work and learn from practical experience. Problems could not be solved in a vacuum. Sloppiness and commandism would not do. To make Soviet work successful, emphasizes Mao, it was essential to gather material on what had actually been going on in lower Soviets through mass work and to find models for others to follow. The Ch'ang-kang township had been picked for a model because it fulfilled practically all the major requirements of Soviet work.

Being a general survey of Soviet work in the advanced stage of land revolution, this article seldom touches upon the investigation and redistribution of land, which was probably thought to have been brought to a successful conclusion. In broad outline, it concerns itself with the general work of what a free world observer would legitimately call a local government. The following are the more important items listed in this report:

(*1*) The assembly of popular delegates and their election, (*2*) mass organizations, (*3*) local militia and civil defense, (*4*) regulation of labor power, (*5*) cooperatives, (*6*) cultural movement, (*7*) social relief, (*8*) women, (*9*) children, (*10*) workers, (*11*) poor-peasant corps.

DOCUMENT 94

SOVIET WORK IN TS'AI-HSI TOWNSHIP, SHANG-HANG (上杭才溪鄉的蘇維埃工作 *Shang-hang ts'ai-hsi-hsiang ti su-wei-ai kung-tso*), by Mao Tse-tung; published in *Struggle* (Kiangsi), No. 45 (February 2), pp. 15–16, No. 46 (February 9), pp. 15–16, No. 48 (February 23), pp. 18–20, 1934; 008.2105/7720/V.4, SSC; and in Mao Tse-tung, *Investigations of the Rural Districts,* published at Yenan in 1941, reissued by Hsinhua Bookstore, Shantung, 1946, pp. 126–142; approximately 7,000 words.

This report on the Ts'ai-hsi township was of the same nature as that on the Ch'ang-kang township. The titles, subtitles, organization, and subject matter of both articles are similar except for some necessary changes of names.

Accordingly, Mao's brief introductory statement attached to the other article applies to this one also. That means that Ts'ai-hsi as well as Ch'ang-kang served as a model township in the Soviet movement in the hinterland of China in the early thirties. The content of this article can be judged from the major items listed in it: (*1*) the assembly of popular delegates and their election, (*2*) committees under the township Soviet, (*3*) expansion of the Red Army, (*4*) economic life, (*5*) culture and education.

In this article, as in the other, Mao does not claim that the Soviet work done was perfect.

DOCUMENT 95

NOTICE No. 25 FROM THE YUNG-FENG COUNTY COMMITTEE TO ALL DISTRICT COMMITTEES AND CELLS—CONCERNING REVIEW OF THE TASK OF LAND REDISTRIBUTION (永豐縣委給各區委支部通知第廿五號—關於檢查分配土地工作 *Yung-feng hsien-wei chi ko chü-wei chih-pu t'ung-chih ti nien-wu hao—kuan-yü chien-ch'a fen-p'ei t'u-ti kung-tso*), February 14, (1934?); 008.744/4848, SSC; mimeographed; approximately 900 words.

This paper calls for a review of land redistribution with emphasis on the prosecution of the work from bottom to top. Noteworthy is a questionnaire at the end of the paper, giving the nature and object of the move.

V

Class Analysis

SECTION 1. GENERAL PRINCIPLES

DOCUMENT 96
Translation on pages 254-57
HOW TO ANALYZE THE CLASSES (怎樣分析階級 *Tsen-yang fen-hsi chieh-chi*),
adopted by the Eight-County Conference on the Land Investigation
Drive, June 17–21, 1933; printed in: *Red China*, No. 89 (June 29, 1933),
p. 8, 008.1052/2125/V.3, SSC; *A Guide to the Land Investigation Drive*,
pp. 27–30, 008.743/4963–3/C.1–2, SSC; appendix to *Decisions concerning
Some Problems Arising from the Agrarian Struggle*, 008.743/4047, SSC;
Selected Works of Mao Tse-tung, I, 121–24; *A Collection of Red Bandit
Reactionary Documents*, III, 946–49, 008.2129/4972/V.3, SSC; approximately 1,300 words.

Since the land investigation drive was designed primarily as an investigation of the classes, a clear conception of the classes was, of course,
a prerequisite. Though the notion of class underlay all the Communist
documentations of the period under study, and in some cases, as described previously (**Doc. 21**; Doc. 42), attempts had already been made
to define the different classes, the meaning of class analysis was nevertheless vague, particularly when applied to individual cases. What kind
of man was a landlord or rich peasant, who was to be searched out and
liquidated? Who was a middle peasant, whose interests should not be
violated? What about a poor peasant or a hired farm hand? All these
and related questions were closely bound up with the practical work of
land investigation, which could not easily be performed without satisfactory definitions. To meet the requirements of the land investigation
drive, the eight-county conference, held from June 17 to June 21,
adopted the present statement as a guide to action. In it the rural
population was divided into five different classes—landlord, rich peasant, middle peasant, poor peasant, and worker (including hired farm

hand). The definition of each class was coupled with an outlining of the official policy toward that class at the time.

This document was soon found inadequate to meet the complex situation during the land investigation drive and was supplemented about four months later by another statement entitled *Decisions concerning Some Problems Arising from the Agrarian Struggle* (**Doc. 101**). Both documents were reissued with modifications in 1948 and 1950 for "land reform" on the Chinese mainland.

It is interesting that when this document was picked for inclusion in Mao's *Selected Works* in 1953, twenty years after the event, it was given a wrong date, October, 1933.[1] As a matter of fact, as pointed out above, this statement was adopted at the eight-county conference on the land investigation drive, held during June 17–21, 1933. In the "conclusions" reached by that conference on June 21, *How to Analyze the Classes* was cited as a guide to the solution to all problems concerning the class status.[2] In addition, the full text of this statement was printed on page 8 of the newspaper *Red China,* No. 89, June 29, 1933.

Perhaps the anachronism of the editors of the *Selected Works,* attributable also to Mao, who had personally checked all writings printed in his *Selected Works,* was due to the fact that this document was approved by the central government on October 10, 1933 (see note to its text when it was printed as an appendix to *Decisions concerning Some Problems Arising from the Agrarian Struggle* [**Doc. 101**]). There is no sign that *How To Analyze the Classes* was ever approved by the party.

In shaping policies toward the different classes, Mao in this statement followed the party line as embodied in the land law of the Chinese Soviet Republic (**Doc. 34**). The policy toward the rich peasants, for instance, was to confiscate their land as well as their surplus draft cattle, farm implements, and houses, and to give them poor land instead. No mention was, however, made of denying former landowners land allotments, as provided in article 1 of the land law.

It is interesting that the stipulations on policies toward the several classes disappear altogether from the text of this document as printed in Mao's *Selected Works*. And Mao and his editors fail to indicate this change. Thus, *How to Analyze the Classes* in Mao's *Selected Works* retains only the definitions of the several classes, but not the policies toward

---

[1] Mao, *Selected Works,* Chinese ed., I, 121, 122; English ed., I, 138, 140.
[2] See *A Guide to the Land Investigation Drive,* p. 15; also *Red China,* No. 88, June 29, 1933, p. 5, bottom column, II, 2.

them, as originally embodied in the 1933 text. The following stipulations were deleted:

1. Landlord:
The landlord class is the principal enemy of the land revolution. The policy of the Soviets toward the landlords is to confiscate all their land and [other] properties and to annihilate the landlord class.

2. Rich peasant:
The policy of the Soviets toward the rich peasants is to confiscate their land. But only the surplus part of their draft cattle, farm implements, and houses are to be confiscated. They are still to be assigned labor land allotments of a poorer quality.

3. Middle peasant:
The policy of the Soviets toward the middle peasants is to enter into a solid alliance with them. Without their consent, the land of the middle peasants shall not be subject to equal redistribution. Those middle peasants who do not own enough land shall be allotted the same amount of land as the poor peasants and hired farm hands.

4. Poor peasant:
In land redistribution, the poor peasants should obtain the same benefits as the middle peasants and hired farm hands. The small amount of land and the few farm implements they have originally owned shall not be confiscated.

5. Worker:
In the course of the land revolution, all workers in the rural districts should be allotted the same amount of land, and the few farm implements which some of the workers may originally own shall not be confiscated.

A number of minor discrepancies between the original and revised texts of the present statement follow:

1. The two words *rural areas* which do not appear in the original are added to the title of the revised text.

2. The words *what is meant by* as embodied in each subtitle in the original are left out in the revised text.

3. The parenthetical note *irrespective of the amount* which appears in the first sentence in the passage on the landlord in the original is omitted in the revised text.

4. In the same paragraph, the word *peasantry* has been added as an object of the word *exploit* in the revised text.

5. In the third paragraph, this sentence is omitted in the revised text: "Among landlords, small landlords exploit more ruthlessly."

6. The phrase "Their living conditions are better than those of the average middle peasants" is added in the revised text to modify the bankrupt landlords and those who help landlords in collecting land rent and managing their households.

7. The sentence "Often there are also smaller village bosses and bad gentry among the rich peasants" is added to the revised text in the passage on the landlord.

8. Toward the end of the passage on the rich peasant in the revised text, this phrase is added: "Some of the rich peasants possess a considerable amount of good land." Immediately thereafter, the phrase "the Chinese rich peasantry," which appears in the original, is omitted.

SECTION 2. SPECIFIC CASES

DOCUMENT 97

A LETTER TO THE SOVIET OF THE HUANG-PAI DISTRICT, JUI-CHIN, ON THE LAND INVESTIGATION DRIVE (為查田運動給瑞金黃柏區蘇的一封信 *Wei ch'a-t'ien yün-tung chi jui-chin huang-pai ch'ü-su ti i-feng hsin*), addressed by the Central Commissariat of Land, July 13, 1933; printed in *Red China*, No. 95 (July 23, 1933), p. 6, 008.1052/2125/V.4, SSC; and in *A Guide to the Land Investigation Drive*, pp. 41–47, 008.743/4063–3/C.1,2, SSC; reproduced in *A Collection of Red Bandit Reactionary Documents*, III, 961–70, 008.2129/4072/V.3, SSC; approximately 3,300 words.

Listing a total of ten different cases in which landlords and rich peasants were mistaken for members of other classes in the district of Huang-pai, the Central Commissariat of Land makes an effort to correct the mistakes in order to provide an example for the determination of class status. In this letter, the abstract and often ambiguous class concepts which underlie the whole Communist ideology were subjected to a case study. It foreshadowed the thought pattern of the more detailed statement *Decisions concerning Some Problems Arising from the Agrarian Struggle* (**Doc. 101**), which was to be promulgated some three months later.

Among the ten cases in question, it is pointed out, seven households should be changed from the status of rich or middle peasants to that of landlords, one household from middle peasant to rich peasant, and two households from usurers or landlords to rich peasants.

The first of the ten cases provides an illustration: A certain Chou Tsung-jen had a household of three persons. None was engaged in labor, though Chou himself had been a hired laborer for twelve years about two decades before. The household owned a plot of land which yielded fifty piculs of rice a year. All the land was rented out. They collected twenty-five piculs of rice as land rent annually and they did so for seven years. In addition, they owned two hills, which earned them an interest of several hundred *mao* (a *mao* was equal to ten cents) a year. They also earned four piculs of rice as interest on a plot of land given in security for a loan made by them to the amount of a hundred Chinese dollars. This Chou family had been accorded the status of a middle-peasant household during the land redistribution. The Central Commissariat of Land considered this case to be a mistake. It was decided that the Chou household should be changed to the status of the landlord class on the ground that they were not engaged in labor, but lived on land rent.

DOCUMENT 98

STRENGTHEN THE ALLIANCE WITH THE MIDDLE PEASANTRY!—FIRST OF ALL, DO NOT VIOLATE THE INTERESTS OF THE MIDDLE PEASANTRY! (鞏固與中農的聯盟!—首先就要不侵犯中農的利益! *Kung-ku yü chung-nung ti lien-meng—shou-hsien chiu yao pu ch'in-fan chung-nung ti li-i!*), printed in *Provincial Committee Correspondence*, No. 18 (July 27, 1933), pp. 5–7, 008.2105/9023/Nos. 11–88, SSC; mimeographed; approximately 1,300 words.

As its title indicates, this statement's purpose was the protection of the interests of the middle peasantry. Referring to the CCP policy of allying with the middle peasantry, it emphasizes that even if the middle peasants received more land than others, their land should not be cut down under the pretext of egalitarian redistribution. As a point of fact, it comments, the violation of their interests was common. Examples of such violation are given with the admonition that, because of their number, the middle peasants were indispensable to the revolution in the rural districts.

It cannot be too often emphasized that the policy of allying with the middle peasantry was formulated by Lenin as a check to the poor peasants, who had gone so far in the Russian revolution as to promote the tendency to identify middle peasants as *kulaks*.[3]

DOCUMENT 99

TWO QUESTIONS ABOUT HOW TO ANALYZE THE CLASSES (怎樣分析階級

[3] E. H. Carr, *The Bolshevik Revolution*, II, 161 ff.

兩點疑問 *Tsen-yang fen-hsi chieh-chi liang-tien i-wen*), released by the Secretariat of the Central Government, August 14, 1933; printed in *Red China*, No. 110 (September 18, 1933), p. 8, 008.1052/2125/V.4, SSC; approximately 950 words.

During the course of land investigation a leading Communist cadre in Yung-feng county raised two questions:

1. Since the rich peasantry was supposed to differ from the middle peasantry in that the former exploited others regularly while the latter exploited others, but not regularly, just how many years were required to make the sense of *regularly*?

2. Since the registration forms relating to class status that were used in land investigation indicated that one's class status should be determined by one's living conditions before the insurrection, just how many years were to be included by the word *before*?

In reply, the Secretariat of the Central Government was rather noncommittal on the first point, stating that a period of, say, three to seven years would be adequate to make up the meaning of the word *regularly*, depending upon the circumstances of the individual case. In addition, it was pointed out, a fairly important part of a person's means of subsistence must come from exploitation for him to be identified as a rich peasant.

As to the second question, the answer was simple, saying that the word *before* was understood in its generally accepted sense. For instance, if a Communist insurrection took place in January, 1931, anything that had happened prior to that date should belong in the category of *before*.

DOCUMENT 100

A REPLY TO WAN-T'AI [COUNTY SOVIET] (答覆萬泰的一封信 *Ta-fu wan-t'ai ti i-feng hsin*), by Secretariat of the Kiangsi Provincial Soviet, September 26 (1933), 008.74122/7123, SSC; mimeographed; approximately 1,300 words.

During the course of land investigation it was the Communist policy to expropriate the land of the reactionary rich peasant and all those who were directly connected with his counterrevolutionary action. It was also made clear that a rich peasant who had perpetrated a serious counterrevolutionary action should be called a reactionary rich peasant.

Now two questions were put to the Kiangsi Provincial Soviet authorities:

1. Just what did the word *serious* in the phrase *a serious counterrevolutionary action* mean?

2. What was meant by *those who are directly connected with his counter-revolutionary action?*

In reply to the first question, the Kiangsi provincial authorities stated that the word *serious* denoted a leading or active part played by a rich peasant in a counterrevolutionary action. That meant that only a ringleader or an active wrongdoer was called a reactionary rich peasant who was subject to expropriation. An ordinary rich peasant was entitled to his share of poor land even if he joined a reactionary organization.

With regard to the second question, the Kiangsi provincial authorities actually had the accomplices in a counterrevolutionary action in mind. Accordingly, they made it clear that the relatives of a rich peasant who were not accomplices in his counterrevolutionary action should be treated as ordinary rich peasants.

It should be noted that this communication foreshadowed the provisions of section 4 of the October 10, 1933, statement *Decisions concerning Some Problems Arising from the Agrarian Struggle.*

DOCUMENT 101

Translation on pages 257-82

DECISIONS CONCERNING SOME PROBLEMS ARISING FROM THE AGRARIAN STRUGGLE (關於土地鬥爭中一些問題的決定 *Kuan-yü t'u-ti tou-cheng chung i-hsieh wen-t'i ti chüeh-ting*), adopted by the Council of People's Commissars of the Central Government, October 10, 1933, mimeographed, 008.743/4047, SSC; reproduced in *A Collection of Red Bandit Reactionary Documents*, III, 989–1010, 008.2129/4072/V.3, SSC; approximately 11,000 words.

In the course of the redistribution and investigation of land, a whole host of practical problems arose in regard to the determination of the class status of the rural population. They flowed partly from the lack or ambiguity of the official documents which could be invoked and partly from the misinterpretations of the pertinent documents by Communist cadres. In order to solve all these problems, the Council of People's Commissars of the Central Government issued the present statement, listing a total of twenty specific problems illustrated with sample cases. Since Document 96, *How to Analyze the Classes*, was a statement of general principles, this paper was a detailed supplementary document introducing an elaborate system of mathematical percentages for the determination of the class status. The mathematical percentages were necessarily mechanical and tedious. But they were perhaps inevitable when the abstract and vague idea of class status was applied to individual cases.

The scope of the treatment of this statement can be seen from its table of contents: (1) labor and supplementary labor; (2) well-to-do middle peasant; (3) rich-peasant exploitation—its duration and degree; (4) reactionary rich peasant; (5) rich peasant contributions; (6) land, houses, draft cattle, and farm implements rightfully owned by a rich peasant; (7) compulsory labor of the rich peasant; (8) bankrupt landlord; (9) poor people; (10) intellectual; (11) idler-proletarian; (12) religious practitioner; (13) the Red Army man of landlord or rich-peasant origin and the land; (14) worker from a rich-peasant or landlord family; (15) the class status of landlords, rich peasants, or capitalists after marrying workers, peasants, or poor people, and vice versa; (16) landlord or rich peasant who is concurrently merchant; (17) management of landholdings of public bodies; (18) the problem of livelihood of some functionaries; (19) land for public enterprises; and (20) the problem of debts.

It should be noted that this statement, like its companion paper, *How to Analyze the Classes,* was issued by cabinet order over the signatures of Mao and his deputies, but not by order of the party, then controlled by the Russian Returned Students. Less than half a year later, on March 15, 1934, this document was castigated by another cabinet order, a month after Chang Wen-t'ien, a leading member of the Russian Returned Student clique, had replaced Mao as premier. The principal charge brought against this document was that it had reduced the political move of class struggle to a mechanical calculation of class status. Consequently the land investigation drive had come to a standstill in many places, the charge continued, and had been replaced by a campaign to correct past mistakes in the determination of class status by applying the mechanical percentages. This had, in turn, been exploited by landlords and rich peasants to their advantage.[4]

In drafting this statement, Mao and his associates in the cabinet certainly followed the land law of the Chinese Soviet Republic (**Doc. 34**). Details were supplied where the land law fell short. Of particular interest is the case of the landlord, whose position in Mao's land redistribution program has been doubtful. In accordance with article 1 of the land law, this document provides in unmistakable terms that a landlord was not allowed to receive a land allotment in redistribution

[4] For the text of this cabinet order, see *Red China,* No. 164, March 20, 1934, p. 1.

(sec. 1, expl. nn., item 6; secs. 14, 15, 16). However, there were the following exceptions to this rule, in which a landlord was treated as a peasant or rich peasant:

1. A landlord ceased to be a landlord but should be treated as a rich peasant if some of his household were engaged in essential labor and if he had a very big family to support at immense expense (sec. 1, expl. nn., *special circumstances*).

2. A rich peasant or middle peasant who lost his physical capacity to work several years before the Communist takeover and who therefore had to lead a landlord's life by renting out all his land or hiring labor to till it, retained his original class status and should not be treated as a landlord (*ibid.*).

3. A person who, though a landlord in name, had lost his landed property to others, and who was engaging in supplementary labor, exploiting others very little, and leading a life even worse off than a peasant, should be treated as a rich peasant or, with the consent of the masses, as a peasant (*ibid.*).

4. A person who was originally a peasant but who became a landlord two years before the Communist takeover should be treated as a rich peasant with the consent of the masses, provided that his land was confiscated (*ibid.*).

5. Red Army men and their dependents were all entitled to land allotments in redistribution, even though they had a landlord or rich-peasant status (sec. 13).

Indeed, the importance of this document in Chinese Communist annals cannot be overestimated. With *How to Analyze the Classes,* as has already been noted, this statement was reissued with modifications in 1948 and 1950 for "land reform" on the mainland of China. The modifications reflected the changed policies toward the landlords and rich peasants under changed circumstances. A comparison of the present text and the 1950 version is as follows:

1. As against twenty sections of the present text, the 1950 version consists of fifteen sections with some textual alterations and additions. Sections 5, 7, 18, 19, and 20 of the original were removed.

2. The present text is much more severe to the landlord than the 1950 version. This is natural in view of the fact that the landlord was assigned land under the land reform law of 1950 (art. 10) but not under the land law of 1931 (art. 3). Accordingly, the present text provides that the landlord should not be allotted land, while the 1950 version contains no such restrictions.

Moreover, under the 1950 version the workers, peasants, and poor people were not allowed to exchange for the land, houses, draft cattle, and farm implements of the landlords (see sec. 5, supplementary decision adopted by the Government Administration Council). But landlords had no such protection in 1933. In addition, bankrupt landlords were not allowed to receive land in 1933, while they were allowed to do so in 1950. Another difference is that the class status of the landlord could not be changed in 1933, while it could be changed under certain conditions in 1950.[5]

3. The original is considerably more ruthless to the rich peasant than the 1950 version. This lies in the different positions of the rich peasant in the land law of 1931 (arts. 3, 7, and 8) and the land reform law of 1950 (art. 6). Thus:

(a) The present text provides that the rich peasant should be allotted only poor land and that he should be deprived of surplus houses, draft cattle, and farm implements (sec. 1, toward its end; sec. 3, illus. 1, 2; sec. 6, expl. nns. 1, 2). Such provisions are not contained in the 1950 text.

(b) Contributions, exorbitant progressive taxes, and compulsory labor, imposed on the rich peasants by the present text, disappear from the 1950 text.

(c) The demarcation line between the rich peasant and the well-to-do middle peasant was narrower in 1933 than in 1950. For example, while 15 per cent of the income from exploitation of others was the demarcation line in 1933, it was 25 per cent in 1950.

(d) The present text provides, in section 6, that the houses of a rich peasant were subject to exchange with poor peasants if the exchange was made for the benefit of production and with his consent. This provision is not embodied in the 1950 text.

(e) The class status of a rich peasant could not be changed in 1933, whereas it could be changed under certain conditions in 1950 (see the end of the 1950 text).

4. Provisions for the class status of landlords, rich peasants, or capitalists after their marriage with workers, peasants, or poor people and vice versa were more liberal in 1950 than in 1933.

---

[5] See "Some New Decisions Adopted by the Government Administration Council," item 11, embodied as the last part of the 1950 version, in Mao, *Selected Works,* Chinese ed., Vol. I; English ed., Vol. I.

Document 102

Notice No. 3 of the Hsin-hsia County Committee of the CCP (中共新峽縣委通知第三號 *Chung-kung hsin-hsia hsien-wei t'ung-chih ti-san hao*), October 24, 1933(?); reproduced in *A Collection of Red Bandit Documents*, I, 117–20, 008.2129/4070/V.1, SSC; approximately 650 words.

A series of disputes arose when the middle peasants in the county of Hsin-hsia insisted on the return of the land removed from them, while the poor peasants and hired farm hands objected. The county branch of the CCP stepped forward to try to settle the matter and issued the present statement to reaffirm party policies. Two major points emerged:

1. The loss of the property of a middle peasant could only be made up by what came from a landlord, rich peasant, and the like.

2. The land taken from a middle peasant could not be returned to him unless the majority of poor peasants and hired farm hands agreed.

Document 103

A Few Special Cases in Class Analysis—[extract from] a Letter of the Central Commissariat of the Interior to the Hsing-kuo County Soviet (分析階級中幾個特殊例子—中央內務部給興國縣蘇的信 *Fen-hsi chieh-chi chung chi-ko t'e-shu li-tzu—chung-yang nei-wu-pu chi hsing-kuo hsien-su ti hsin*), printed in *Red China*, No. 128 (November 23, 1933), p. 3, 008.1052/2125/V.5, SSC; approximately 1,000 words.

This communication contains five different cases of class status which were difficult to decide in the course of class differentiation. Outstanding among them was the case of the *liu meng* or vagabond, whose status was always a matter of dispute. According to this communication, it was the policy of the CCP to win over the rank and file of the *liu meng*, but to get rid of their ringleaders. Accordingly, the rank and file were to be assigned land and jobs.

Document 104

Registration Forms Relating to the Class Status (階級成份調查表 *Chieh-chi ch'eng-fen t'iao-ch'a-piao*), issued by the Central Commissariat of Land, n.p. or d.; 008.51027/7125, SSC.

This is a blank form for the investigation of the class status. The items to be filled out are many and varied, with particular reference to the economic status of the person investigated before the (Communist) insurrection. They include a listing of real and personal estate; whether he was a hirer or hireling, a creditor or debtor. Among the other questions are: Has the man under investigation oppressed others? Does he have influence among the villagers?

VI

End of an Epoch

SECTION 1. REOPENING THE LAND INVESTIGATION DRIVE

DOCUMENT 105

THE PHENOMENA THAT MUST BE OVERCOME IN THE LAND INVESTIGA-
TION DRIVE (查田運動中必須克服的現象 *Ch'a-t'ien yün-tung chung pi-hsü k'o-
fu ti hsien-hsiang*), by Pang Hua, February 19 (1934); printed in *True
Words of Youth*, III, No. 17 (April 1, 1934), 5–6, 008.2105/5083/V.5,
SSC; approximately 800 words.

As a result of the Second National Soviet Congress held from January
22 to February 1, 1934, Chang Wen-t'ien, a leading member of the
Russian Returned Student group, replaced Mao as chairman of the
Council of People's Commissars or premier who had charge of the
executive duties of the Soviet regime including the carrying out of the
agrarian revolution.[1] This article from a local cadre was the first one
published under the new cabinet in connection with land investigation.
As it contains a statement to the effect that "we want now to reopen
the land investigation drive," it apparently gave a hint to another land
investigation drive which was soon to be launched by Premier Chang
Wen-t'ien in denunciation of Mao's policies as set forth in the statement
Decisions concerning Some Problems Arising from the Agrarian Struggle (**Doc.
101**) adopted on October 10, 1933.

This signed article frankly admits the failure of the land investigation
drive in Pu-ch'ien in Minkan province. The failure was attributed to
the following causes:

1. Members of the Surprise Attack Teams specially appointed for
the work of land investigation had paid more attention to the collection
of grain than to the investigation of land since they had not understood
the tasks assigned to them.

[1] For the cabinet change, see *Power Relations*, I, 280–81.

115

2. Class heretical elements had infiltrated into the said teams.

3. Opportunism of the local party leadership.

4. Failure to mobilize the basic masses.

In conclusion, the article calls upon the younger generation in the rural districts to do a good job in the renewed campaign for land investigation.

DOCUMENT 106

Translation on pages 282-85

ON THE QUESTION OF REOPENING THE LAND INVESTIGATION DRIVE— INSTRUCTION, SERIAL CHARACTER *Chung,* No. 1, OF THE COUNCIL OF PEOPLE'S COMMISSARS (關於繼續開展查田運動的問題—人民委員會訓令, 中字 第一號 *Kuan-yü chi-hsü k'ai-chan ch'a-t'ien yün-tung ti wen-t'i—jen-min wei-yüan-hui hsün-ling chung-tzu ti-i hao*), dated March 15, 1934; printed in *Red China,* No. 164 (March 20, 1934), p. 1, 008.1052/2125/V.6, SSC; approximately 1,300 words.

By this order the Chang Wen-t'ien cabinet reopened the land investigation drive, repudiating Mao's policies as manifested in the 1933 statement *Decisions concerning Some Problems Arising from the Agrarian Struggle* (**Doc. 101**).

As a result of the 1933 statement, says this order, a multitude of serious problems had arisen in the land investigation drive. Many people had actually abandoned the task of land investigation and devoted themselves to what was called the "correction" of the leftist excesses made in the past. Still worse, landlords and rich peasants had sought to restore their lost landholdings by taking advantage of some provisions of the 1933 statement, particularly sections 1, 2, and 3, in an effort to "calculate" instead of investigating the class status. In other words, the political move of class struggle had degenerated into a technical game of playing on the figures and percentages prescribed in the 1933 statement.

In the light of the foregoing, the present document decrees a fresh land investigation drive and sets forth eight points as guides to work. The more important of the eight points follow:

1. The status of the landlords and rich peasants which had been established before the land investigation drive could not be changed.

2. Errors in the determination of the class status of the landlords and rich peasants during the land investigation drive could not be corrected without the active support of the masses.

3. It was not allowed to replace the investigation of classes by the "calculation of classes," or, in other words, to replace the class struggle by the mechanical application of percentage formulas.

Incidentally, it is interesting to note that only important labor in agricultural production was regarded by this order as the principal criterion for distinguishing between peasants and landlords, but not other kinds of labor such as cooking, laundry, bookkeeping, and so forth. Though a departure from the 1933 statement, this point was adopted by Mao when he reissued the 1933 statement with modifications for "land reform" on the Chinese mainland in 1950.

DOCUMENT 107

REOPENING THE LAND INVESTIGATION DRIVE AND SUPPRESSING RUTH-LESSLY THE COUNTERATTACK OF LANDLORDS AND RICH PEASANTS (繼續開展查田運動與無情的鎮壓地主富農的反攻 *Chi-hsü k'ai-chan ch'a-t'ien yün-tung yü wu-ch'ing ti chen-ya ti-chu fu-nung ti fan-kung*), by Wang Kuan-lan; printed in *Red China*, No. 164 (March 20, 1934), p. 1, 008.1052/2125/ V.6, SSC; approximately 2,000 words.

This leading article was intended to give support and publicity to the cabinet order of March 15 (**Doc. 106**), reopening the land investigation drive. Though its basic arguments are the same as the cabinet order, this article contains some interesting and illuminating details. It is pointed out, for instance, that there had originally been a total of 1,576 landlord and rich-peasant households in the county of Sheng-li and that 536 more households of that kind were uncovered during the land investigation drive in 1933. But following the application of the formulas provided in the 1933 statement in question (**Doc. 101**), as many as 941 households had managed to clear themselves from the landlord and rich-peasant status. That is to say, not only did the result of the land investigation drive become nil, but an additional number of 405 households which had been decided as belonging to the landlord and rich-peasant class before the drive were acquitted and rehabilitated.

According to Edgar Snow, the writer of this article became editor of the newspaper *Red China* in 1932 and vice-chairman of the Land Commission in 1933.[2] This man is still active in the field of agrarian administration on the Chinese mainland since the Communist takeover in 1949.

---

[2] Edgar Snow, *Random Notes on Red China (1936–1945)*, p. 34.

DOCUMENT 108

INTENSIFYING THE CLASS STRUGGLE IN VILLAGES, REOPENING THE LAND
INVESTIGATION DRIVE (加深農村中階級鬪爭, 繼續開展查田運動 *Chia-shen
nung-ts'un chung chieh-chi tou-cheng, chi-hsü k'ai-chan ch'a-t'ien yün-tung*), by
Ah Wei, April 1, 1934; printed in *True Words of Youth*, III, No. 17
(April 1, 1934), 2–5, 008.2105/5083/V.5, SSC; approximately 1,200
words.

Written to support the reopened land investigation drive, this article
begins with a complaint that some people belittled the class struggle
under the Soviet regime and that they applied the 1933 statement in
question (**Doc. 101**) as though the classes should not be investigated
along the class line but calculated mathematically. Warning that an
attempt by landlords and rich peasants to take advantage of the 1933
statement was doomed to failure, this article concludes by calling upon
the younger generation of the peasantry to do what they could to fight
the class enemies.

DOCUMENT 109

TASKS OF THE LAND DEPARTMENTS OF ALL LEVELS DURING THE RE-
OPENED LAND INVESTIGATION DRIVE (在繼續開展查田運動中各級土地部的
任務 *Tsai chi-hsü k'ai-chan ch'a-t'ien yün-tung chung ko-chi t'u-ti-pu ti jen-wu*),
by Kao Tzu-li; printed in *Red China*, No. 175 (April 14, 1934), p. 3,
008.1052/2125/V.6, SSC; approximately 1,500 words.

This article outlines a six-point program for the land departments of
the government at all levels to follow. The author was apparently the
head of the land department of the Central Soviet Government. As
distinguished from the cabinet order of March 15 (**Doc. 106**), this
article emphasizes that in order to bring the renewed land investigation
drive to a successful conclusion by the end of June it was important to
refute the idea that the land investigation drive had been all too Left-
oriented in the past. The six-point program follows:

1. Emphasis should be placed on the border or retarded areas.
2. The party line should be strictly followed in land redistribution.
3. Land investigation committees on the district and township levels
should be well organized.
4. The drive should be coordinated with the task of combating
counterrevolutionaries.
5. The drive should be intimately associated with war mobilization.

6. The work of the land departments on all levels should be strengthened.

DOCUMENT 110

RESULTS OF THE LAND INVESTIGATION SURPRISE ATTACK DRIVE IN MINKAN PROVINCE (閩贛省查田突擊運動的總結 *Min-kan-sheng ch'a-t'ien t'u-chi yün-tung ti tsung-chieh*), by Shao Shih-ping, printed in *Red China*, No. 181 (April 28, 1934), p. 3, 008.1052/2125/V.7, SSC; approximately 2,200 words.

This is a general survey of the land investigation surprise attack drive in Minkan province, which was going on for fifty days in the spring of 1934. It was pointed out that the agrarian struggle had stepped up mobilization on all sides—such as the expansion of guerrilla forces, the assembling of foodstuffs, and so forth. The success of the drive, as outlined in this article, was made possible by the following:

1. Errors in the Left deviation of the past had been corrected, and a number of class heretical elements had been purged from government agencies.

2. The spread of the campaign against the landlords and rich peasants had greatly encouraged the activism of the masses.

3. The leading role of the Surprise Attack Teams had helped strengthen the unity of the local activists.

DOCUMENT 111

A PRELIMINARY REVIEW OF THE REOPENED LAND INVESTIGATION DRIVE (繼續查田運動的初步檢查 *Chi-hsü ch'a-t'ien yün-tung ti ch'u-pu chien-ch'a*), by Kao Tzu-li, May 3, 1934; printed in *Red China*, No. 185 (May 7, 1934), p. 2, 008.1052/2125/V.7, SSC; approximately 2,600 words.

The reopened land investigation drive, announced on March 15, was to last from April to June, 1934, inclusive. When it entered upon the second month, a review of the campaign was undertaken, apparently by the head of the land department of the central government. The review begins with a tribute to the record of the county of Sheng-li in the drive, saying that a total of 89 landlord and rich-peasant households had been detected among 1,512 households which managed to clear themselves from their landlord and rich-peasant status by virtue of the 1933 statement, *Decisions concerning Some Problems Arising from the Agrarian Struggle* (**Doc. 101**). In this connection, it should be noted that the figure 1,512 does not agree with the one given in the leading article by Wang Kuan-lan in the March 20, 1934, issue of *Red China* (**Doc. 107**).

The present article then proceeds to single out more than ten counties for criticism, charging that the local authorities had not given due attention to the drive. Accordingly, the following four major points are given as guides to future action:

1. A ruthless fight against Right opportunism.
2. A strict adherence to the class line and mass work.
3. Placement of emphasis on border districts.
4. Mobilization of Youth Corps for the fighting on the front.

DOCUMENT 112

THE PROBLEM OF DISPOSING OF LANDLORDS AND RICH PEASANTS IN THE WAR ZONE (戰區內處置地主富農問題 *Chan-ch'ü nei ch'u-chih ti-chu fu-nung wen-t'i*), by Sheng Yung; printed in *True Words of Youth,* III, No. 23 (May 13, 1934), 2–4, 008.2105/5083, SSC; approximately 900 words.

This leading article reaffirms a war policy of evacuating to the rear all landlords, rich peasants, and other suspected persons. It was pointed out that the wisdom of this policy had been borne out by facts. Accordingly, it was suggested that the able-bodied of those people be sent to the rear for forced labor, while the aged and children should be simply expelled from the war zone.

DOCUMENT 113

EXPERIENCE OF THE REOPENED LAND INVESTIGATION DRIVE IN SHENG-LI COUNTY (勝利縣繼續開展查田運動經驗 *Sheng-li-hsien chi-hsü k'ai-chan ch'a-t'ien yün-tung ching-yen*), by Wang Kuan-lan, May 18, 1934; printed in *Struggle* (Kiangsi), No. 61 (May 26, 1934), pp. 9–14, 008.2105/7720/V.6, Nos. 61–83, SSC; approximately 1,400 words.

In attempting to justify the renewed land investigation drive unleashed by the government order of March 15, 1934, this article singles out the situation in the county of Sheng-li to show the danger of the revival of landlords and rich peasants since November, 1933. It is pointed out that there was originally a total of 3,124 landlord and rich-peasant households in Sheng-li, including the 670 households uncovered during the land investigation drive in 1933. As a result of the statement *Decisions concerning Some Problems Arising from the Agrarian Struggle,* 1,512 households, among them mostly landlords and rich peasants, had managed to change their class status. Interestingly, these figures do not agree with those cited by the same writer in the March 20, 1934, issue of *Red China* (Doc. 107).

According to this writer, there were four different maneuvers on the part of landlords and rich peasants, namely, (*1*) attempting to restore their lost possessions; (*2*) spreading rumors to undermine the revolution; (*3*) infiltrating into Soviet agencies; and (*4*) deceiving or intimidating activities, and so forth.

From the experience gained in Sheng-li, this writer suggests three courses of action: (*1*) continued vigilance against landlords, rich peasants, *et al.*; (*2*) organized mobilization and adequate mass action as opposed to commandism; (*3*) combination of land investigation with the tasks of counterrevolution-suppression and war mobilization.

DOCUMENT 114

FOR OUR CLASS ENEMIES, ONLY HATRED, BUT NO FORGIVENESS! (對於我們的階級敵人, 只有仇恨, 沒有寬恕! *Tui-yü wo-men ti chieh-chi ti-jen, chih-yu ch'ou-hen, mei-yu k'uan-shu*), by Chang Wen-t'ien, May 22, 1934; published in *Red China*, No. 193 (May 25, 1934), pp. 1–2, 008.1052/2125/V.7, SSC; approximately 3,500 words.

In face of the serious military situation at the time, Premier Chang Wen-t'ien calls for a Reign of Red Terror against all counterrevolutionaries. Though a stern war measure against class enemies as a whole, this leading article singles out landlords and rich peasants for attack and devotes the last part of its space to the imposition of extra financial contributions and labor service on them. Landlords should be organized into permanent labor corps while rich peasants should be formed into temporary labor corps. In addition, the dependents of the landlords should be removed from the war zone without exception but those of the rich peasants only in case of need.

It is stated that in the critical moment of military action some changes must be allowed for in the application of the 1933 statement *Decisions concerning Some Problems Arising from the Agrarian Struggle.*

DOCUMENT 115

ORDER NO. 9 OF THE MINKAN PROVINCIAL SOVIET GOVERNMENT OF THE CHINESE SOVIET REPUBLIC (中華蘇維埃共和國閩贛省蘇維埃政府命令第九號 *Chung-hua su-wei-ai kung-ho-kuo min-kan-sheng su-wei-ai cheng-fu ming-ling ti-chiu hao*), n.d., probably in late spring of 1934, 008.743/4038, SSC; mimeographed; approximately 1,200 words.

Part of this government order is missing; the remainder calls for a Red pacification campaign in the countryside in Minkan province during the land investigation drive. The main points:

1. The masses should be given to understand that the campaign against landlords, rich peasants, and other counterrevolutionaries is absolutely necessary.

2. All past errors, such as commandism, which contributed to the alienation of the masses should be corrected through self-criticism.

3. A mobilization of the masses for the campaign as well as the [civil] war should be started at once.

SECTION 2. A TURN TO THE RIGHT

DOCUMENT 116

OPPOSING PETTY BOURGEOIS ULTRALEFTISM (反對小資産階級的極左主義 *Fan-tui hsiao tzu-ch'an chieh-chi ti chi-tso chu-i*), by Chang Wen-t'ien, June 24, 1934; published in *Struggle* (Kiangsi), No. 67 (July 10, 1934), pp. 2–6, 008.2105/7720/V.6, SSC; approximately 1,600 words.

By the time of this statement, the military situation had become so desperate to the Communists that a general retreat from the Kiangsi-Fukien area must have been decided upon.[3] Accordingly, the reopened land investigation drive which had been announced on March 15 and scheduled to last to the end of June was no longer heard of. On the contrary, Premier Chang Wen-t'ien published two articles on two consecutive days in late June calling a halt to the excesses in treatment of the landlords and rich peasants. These excesses, the articles state, had actually strengthened their will to resist. Besides, it was recognized that the leftist trend had created a panic among the masses.

In this first article Chang Wen-t'ien points out that the struggle against the Right deviation in the past few months had been carried to such extremes that it had to be brought to a stop for the moment and that a movement against the Left deviation must be introduced instead. He complains that the general feeling was that "Left deviation is better than Right deviation, anyway," and that Left opportunists were in practice better treated than Right opportunists, and sometimes no attempts at all were made even to bring the former under control.

According to the premier, ultraleftism, which was the reflection of the petty bourgeois and peasant ideology in a proletarian party, manifested itself in a variety of ways: (*1*) intraparty ideological struggle, (*2*) the campaign to ferret out counterrevolutionaries, (*3*) the fight against the landlords and rich peasants, and (*4*) economic policies and the land investigation drive.

[3] *Power Relations*, I, 286 ff.

Obviously, the last two points apply to a study of the agrarian problem.

DOCUMENT 117
Translation on pages 285-90
SHOULD WE STAND FIRM IN SUPPRESSING THE COUNTERREVOLUTIONARIES OR GET MAD AND CONFUSED IN FACE OF THEM? (是堅決的鎮壓反革命還是在反革命前面的狂亂 *Shih chien-chüeh ti chen-ya fan-ko-ming, hai-shih tsai fan-ko-ming ch'ien-mien ti k'uang-luan*), by Chang Wen-t'ien, June 25, 1934; published as editorial of *Red China*, No. 208 (June 28, 1934), pp. 1-2, 008.1052/2125/V.7, SSC; approximately 2,200 words.

This was the second article published by Premier Chang Wen-t'ien in June, 1934, on the subject of the agrarian revolution. It was also the last available statement of its kind ever published by the Chinese Communist leadership in the Kiangsi period. Thus, it is significant that the epoch of the agrarian revolution in the history of the Chinese Communist movement ended with a call for a turn from the Left to the Right.

The target of attack as a symbol of the ultraleftist trend was an order issued by the State Political Security Bureau on May 23, 1934, which was described as exceedingly radical and ruthless to the landlords and rich peasants. Unfortunately, no text of that order is available.

Proceeding on the assumption that although basic policies toward the landlords and rich peasants were immutable, tactics had to change in times of military emergency, Chang Wen-t'ien charges that many government policies had actually been violated. He says the Red Terror, originally aimed at the counterrevolutionary landlords and rich peasants, had been applied to the landlords and rich peasants who had not been engaged in counterrevolutionary activities at all. The policy of annihilating landlords as an exploiting class had degenerated into massacre. Finally, the policy of opposing the rich peasants had been perverted to the extent that many of them had been annihilated economically or even physically.

The leftist trend, according to the writer, had driven the landlords and rich peasants to the wall and strengthened their will to resist. Besides, it had created a panic among the masses. In consequence, ultraleftism had actually operated in the interests of the landlords and rich peasants.

After giving some other illustrations of the excesses committed,

Chang Wen-t'ien concludes with a reaffirmation of the two-front struggle, but with particular reference to the danger of ultraleftism—a departure from Comintern policy followed since 1928.

THE BASIC DOCUMENTS

DOCUMENT 1

PROVISIONAL LAND LAW

Adopted by the National Conference of
Delegates from the Soviet Areas, May, 1930.
(As printed in *The Red Flag*, No. 107, June 4, 1930, pp. 2–3)

I. ALL LAND BELONGING TO LANDLORDS SHALL BE CONFISCATED WITH-
OUT COMPENSATION.

Explanatory notes:

1. Any person who possesses land and cannot cultivate it himself but makes use of it to exact rent [from others] is a landlord. All the land of such a landlord shall be confiscated.
2. A rich peasant possesses land and, aside from that which he tills himself, rents out a part of it to others for cultivation. The part of the land he rents out shall be confiscated altogether.

II. ALL LAND IN THE POSSESSION OF ANCESTRAL SHRINES, TEMPLES,
CHURCHES, [AGENCIES IN CHARGE OF] PUBLIC PROPERTY . . . SHALL BE
CONFISCATED WITHOUT COMPENSATION.

Explanatory note:

3. Most of the land in the possession of such ancestral shrines, temples, churches, [agencies in charge of] public property, and so forth, is privately owned by village bosses, gentry, monks, nuns, clergymen, and clan chiefs. Even if such land may appear to be jointly owned by members of a clan or by the local peasants, it is, in fact, monopolized by clan chiefs, heads of associations, village bosses, and the gentry, and used by them for exploitation of the peasants. Hence all such land must be confiscated without exception.

III. ALL LAND BELONGING TO THOSE WHO HAVE TAKEN ACTIVE PARTS IN
COUNTERREVOLUTIONARY ACTIVITIES SHALL BE CONFISCATED.

Explanatory notes:

4. All land belonging to the counterrevolutionaries and to those who have violated Soviet laws and decrees shall be confiscated.
5. All land belonging to the rich peasants who have opposed the revolution shall be confiscated. As to the masses of the middle and poor peasants who have been deceived or influenced by the

landlords and rich peasants, the method of propaganda and education should be applied to them as far as possible; they should not be treated in the same way as the rich peasants.

IV. ALL CONFISCATED LAND SHALL BE REDISTRIBUTED BY THE SOVIET GOVERNMENT TO PEASANTS WITH LITTLE OR NO LAND OF THEIR OWN FOR THEIR USE. ALL PURCHASES, SALES, LEASES, MORTGAGES, AND SO FORTH, OF LAND SHALL BE FORBIDDEN. ALL PREVIOUS TITLE DEEDS, LEASE CONTRACTS, MORTGAGE PAPERS, AND SO FORTH, SHALL BECOME NULL AND VOID.

Explanatory notes:

6. The abolition of the institutions of the purchase, sale, lease, and mortgage of land is intended to prevent the rise of new landlords, village bosses, and gentry.

7. The redistribution of land to peasants for their use means that any person who does not cultivate land himself shall have no right to use it.

V. THE METHODS OF LAND REDISTRIBUTION SHALL BE DETERMINED BY THE TOWNSHIP CONGRESS OF SOVIET DELEGATES.

Explanatory notes:

8. The township shall be the unit for the redistribution of land. As the [land] relations and the conditions of land distribution in various localities are extremely complicated, it is impossible to have uniform methods [of redistribution]. The methods [of redistribution] can only be determined in the light of the actual circumstances in each township.

9. There are two methods for the redistribution of land: (*i*) equal redistribution of all land; (*ii*) redistribution of only the confiscated land without making any change in [the land] originally cultivated by the peasants. There are also two criteria for the redistribution of land: (*i*) redistribution according to the number of persons; (*ii*) redistribution according to labor power. Each township Soviet may decide upon a suitable method in the light of the actual circumstances in that township.

10. Large-scale farms may not be divided into small pieces; they shall be organized into collective farms, producers' cooperatives, and so forth, in order to carry out collective production so that the productive power may not be diminished or weakened.

11. In case the township Soviet confronts an [insurmountable] difficulty in the redistribution of land, the matter shall be referred to the district Soviet government for a decision.

12. Farm implements and houses seized from landlords or reactionary rich peasants shall be redistributed for their use to the peasants who lack farm implements and houses, and may not be destroyed without cause.

13. If the township Soviet congress has, in the meantime, to decide on practical methods to maintain the livelihood of the families which lack labor power to cultivate land (such as orphans, widows, and so on), the best method would be that of social relief.

14. Soldiers of the Red Army who have already been allotted land shall hold it as before. Those who have not yet been allotted land shall have to wait for the establishment of the National Soviet Government which will decide on the redistribution of land to them.

15. As hired farm hands enjoy special protection under the labor law of the Soviet government, they need not be allotted land. But if the Soviet congress decides to allot land to them as well, it must allot them draft cattle and farm implements at the same time and let them combine to form collective farms.

16. After land redistribution, [the beneficiaries] must go to the county Soviet government to receive their certificates for the use of the land.

VI. LARGE-SCALE FORESTS, WATERWAYS, LAKES, SALT FIELDS, FARMS, AND MULBERRY GROVES WHICH WERE ORIGINALLY OPERATED BY THE GOVERNMENT SHALL ALL BE MANAGED AND OPERATED BY THE SOVIET GOVERNMENT.

VII. ALL LAND TAXES, TITLE-DEED DUTIES, AND OTHER LEVIES, WHICH WARLORDS, VILLAGE BOSSES, AND THE GENTRY EMPLOYED TO EXPLOIT THE PEASANTS, SHALL BE ABOLISHED. THE PEASANTS WHO HAVE BEEN ALLOTTED LAND SHALL PAY A SUITABLE PUBLIC WELFARE FEE, THE AMOUNT OF WHICH WILL BE FIXED BY THE LOCAL SOVIET GOVERNMENT ACCORDING TO THE PRINCIPLE OF PROGRESSIVE TAXATION.

Explanatory notes:

17. Since warlords, village bosses, and the gentry used to exploit the peasants by means of various kinds of taxes and levies which were sometimes even more cruel than the exploitation of the peasants by the landlords, all such taxes and levies must be abolished.

18. As the Soviet government is called upon to undertake all sorts of public welfare work such as the establishment of peasants' banks, the organization of producers' and consumers' cooperatives, the

running of educational institutions, the support of orphans and widows, and so on, and especially in view of the urgent need of the Red Army for military expenses during the course of the relentless revolutionary war, the peasants should pay a suitable public welfare fee out of their farm products.

19. The principle of progressive taxation is that the rate of the payment of the public welfare fee increases with the amount of the income earned and that particularly the rate of the public welfare fee paid by the rich peasants who employ hired farm hands to cultivate [land] must be higher than that paid by the peasants who are engaged in independent labor.

VIII. SHOULD THERE BE SPECIAL CIRCUMSTANCES IN VARIOUS COUNTIES WHICH ARE NOT COVERED BY THE PROVISIONS OF THE PRESENT LAW, THEY SHALL BE DEALT WITH ACCORDING TO ENACTMENTS ADOPTED BY THE COUNTY CONGRESS OF SOVIET DELEGATES.

IX. THE PRESENT PROVISIONAL LAW WILL BE ANNULLED WHEN THE NATIONAL SOVIET GOVERNMENT COMES INTO BEING AND PROMULGATES A FORMAL LAND LAW.

DOCUMENT 9

LAND LAW

Promulgated by the Chinese Revolutionary Military Council, n.d.
(As reprinted by the General Political Department of the First Army Corps of the Red Army, 1930; reproduced in *A Collection of Red Bandit Secret Documents,* Vol. V, leaves 1–4, 1931)

CHAPTER I. CONFISCATION AND REDISTRIBUTION OF LAND

Article 1: After the overthrow by uprising of the regime of the class of village bosses, gentry, and landlords, all the lands, forests, ponds, and houses belonging to individuals and organizations—village bosses, gentry, landlords, ancestral shrines, temples, associations, rich peasants— shall be immediately confiscated and turned over to the public ownership of the Soviet government. They shall be redistributed for use to the peasants who have no or little land and to other poor people who need them. In places where there are only peasant associations and no

Soviets yet established, the peasant associations may also carry out confiscation and redistribution.

Article 2: [Owing to the ambiguous structure of the Chinese original, this article may be translated in two different ways.]

Either (preferred version): The dependents of village bosses, gentry, landlords, and reactionaries, who, after being examined by the Soviets, are allowed to [continue to] live in their townships but have no other means of subsistence, may be given suitable allotments of land.

Or: Village bosses, gentry, landlords, and the dependents of reactionaries, who, after being examined by the Soviets, are allowed to [continue to] live in their townships but have no other means of subsistence, may be given suitable allotments of land.

Article 3: Officers, soldiers, and coolies in active service in the Red Army and persons engaged in revolutionary work shall be allotted land as well. The Soviets shall designate persons to help their dependents in cultivation.

Article 4: Persons engaged in the occupations of industry or handicraft,[1] commerce, and studies in the villages who can maintain their livelihood shall not be allotted land, while those who cannot make an adequate living may be given suitable allotments of land to the extent that [the inadequacies of] their[2] livelihood are supplied.

Article 5: Hired farm hands and jobless idlers who wish to share in land redistribution shall be allotted land. But a jobless idler who receives a land allotment shall be required to rid himself of his bad habits such as opium-smoking, gambling, and so on; otherwise the Soviet shall take back the land allotted to him.

Article 6: Absentees shall not be allotted land.

Article 7: The township shall be the unit for land redistribution. The peasants of a given township shall pool for common redistribution all the land they are tilling in their own township and neighboring townships. If three or four townships adjoin one another and some of them have a large acreage and others a small acreage, and if the townships with a small acreage cannot support themselves in the event that each township should be taken as a unit for redistribution, nor do they have other products to maintain their livelihood, then the three or four

---

[1] The Chinese character *kung* may be translated as *industry* or *handicraft*. These two English words actually reflect two different schools of thought among the Chinese Communists in the period under study as to whether there were industrial workers in the Soviet areas in the hinterland of China. For lack of an English equivalent, both words are given here.

[2] The Chinese original is a little involved here.

townships shall combine to form a unit for redistribution. But this can be done only at the request of the township Soviets concerned and with the approval of the district Soviets.

Article 8: In order to satisfy the demands of the majority of people and to enable the peasants to obtain land quickly, land shall be equally redistributed according to the number of persons in the villages, irrespective of sex or age. The method of using labor power as the criterion for redistribution shall not be adopted.

Article 9: Merchants and workers in cities shall not be allotted land as a rule. But if unemployed workers and the poor people in cities demand a share in land redistribution, they may be given suitable allotments in so far as circumstances permit.

Article 10: In order to destroy the feudal forces and to deal a blow to the rich peasants quickly, land redistribution shall be carried out according to the principles of draw-on-the-plentiful-to-make-up-for-the-scarce and draw-on-the-fat-to-make-up-for-the-lean. The landlords and rich peasants are not allowed to conceal land by not declaring it, nor to keep fertile land for themselves. After land redistribution, the Soviet shall have a wooden board made and erected in the field, indicating the amount of production of this field and the name of the person who is to cultivate it.

Article 11: All title deeds of village bosses, gentry, landlords, and rich peasants as well as those of ancestral shrines, temples, and [other] public lands shall be surrendered within a prescribed time to the township Soviets or the township or district peasant associations to be publicly destroyed by burning.

Article 12: After land redistribution the county Soviets or the district Soviets shall issue cultivation permits.

Article 13: If a person in a township has died, or changed his occupation, or lived away from home, the land allotted to him shall be taken back by the Soviet for redistribution. If a person has moved in from another place or was newly born, the Soviet shall make arrangements to allot land to him, but this can be done only after harvest.

Article 14: If land redistribution following an uprising takes place at a time when the peasants have already sown seeds [in the field], the products of the field shall be harvested by that peasant to whom the land has been allotted, and the original cultivator shall not be allowed to hold them.

Article 15: Vegetable gardens, river banks, and waste land (capable of producing nonstaple grains)[3] shall be subject to redistribution. Large ponds which are not convenient for distribution shall be managed and operated or leased out at a fixed charge by the Soviets.

Article 16: Forests of bamboo and tea-oil plants[4] shall be converted into equivalent amounts of land according to their yields to be redistributed together with land. But if such forests partake of the nature of industrial capital by reason of the fact that labor has been employed and workshops have been set up to make [finished products], they may be leased out altogether by the Soviets and need not be redistributed.

Article 17: Forests of pines, firs, and so on, shall be operated or leased out by the Soviet government. But if the people of the township concerned need timbers for the construction of ditches,[5] for the making of articles and houses for public use, or for the repair of houses burned by reactionaries, such forests may be exploited with the approval of the district Soviet government.

Article 18: Firewood forests shall be opened or closed to the public for exploitation by order of the Soviet government.

Article 19: In order to satisfy the demands of the poor and miserable peasants, all the confiscated land shall be redistributed to them, and the Soviets need not reserve [any part of the land] for themselves. Under certain circumstances, however, any part of the land in excess of the amount required for redistribution may be used for the establishment of model farms or leased out on a temporary basis. Meanwhile, a part of those houses shall be [reserved] for use by public enterprises.

CHAPTER II. CANCELLATION OF DEBTS

Article 20: All debts owed by workers, peasants, and poor people to village bosses, gentry, landlords, and rich peasants shall not be repaid. The IOUs shall be surrendered within a prescribed time to the Soviets or the peasant associations to be destroyed by burning.

Article 21: All debts, both old and new, owed by village bosses, gentry, landlords, and merchants to the public, or to workers, peasants, and poor people shall be repaid.

Article 22: All old debts owed by workers, peasants, and poor people

[3] Nonstaple grains mean the various grains other than the chief foodstuff of rice in South China.

[4] *Thea oleosa,* Lour. Here the Chinese character *t'ing* which means *top* is left untranslated because it makes no sense. It might be a typographic error through confusion with the sound of another character, *teng,* which means *et cetera.*

[5] The Chinese character *p'o,* meaning a *slope,* is left untranslated here since it makes no sense.

to business firms before the uprising, irrespective of whether such debts have been incurred as a result of business transactions at usurious rates of interest or in the form of personal debts, shall not be repaid.

Article 23: All debts owed by workers, peasants, and poor people to one another and incurred before the uprising shall, as a rule, not be repaid. Only the kind of debt which has been incurred for the purpose of friendly assistance free of interest and which the debtor himself is willing to repay is an exception.

Article 24: Workers, peasants, and poor people who have mortgaged or pawned articles and houses to village bosses, gentry, landlords, rich peasants, and pawnbrokers shall get back their securities unconditionally.

Article 25: All money associations and grain associations[6] shall be abolished.

Article 26: Under the Soviet regime, loans at usurious rates of interest shall be forbidden. The county Soviets shall fix a suitable rate of interest according to the local financial situation, provided that the rate does not exceed what ordinary capital will fetch under the general economic condition of the locality.

CHAPTER III. THE LAND TAX

Article 27: In order to meet the needs for suppressing counterrevolution (e.g., for expanding the Red Army and the Red Guards, making supplies available to agencies of political power, and so forth) and promoting the interests of the masses (e.g., establishing schools and clinics; providing relief to the disabled, the old and the young; repairing roads, ditches,[7] etc.), the Soviets may ask the peasants to pay the land tax.

Article 28: The land tax is based on the principle of protecting the poor peasants, winning over the middle peasants, and dealing a blow to the rich peasants. It shall be levied only after the Soviets have been

---

[6] Money associations and grain associations are literal translations from *chien hui* and *ku hui*, which were widely prevalent in southern Kiangsi. It is said that they were voluntary and exclusive associations of a few, usually seven, individuals who banded together for the sole purpose of making loans to each other, in cash in the case of *chien hui* and in kind in that of *ku hui*. A *hui* of this nature was formed upon the signing of a written contract, under which the members took turns collecting the contributions (either in cash or in kind, as the case might be) made by fellow members, on a yearly basis. The recipients of earlier contributions had to pay specific amounts of interest to those whose turns came later. The rights and obligations of membership in such a *hui* might be handed down from father to son.

[7] See note 5.

set up, the masses have obtained real benefits, and the Soviets at a higher level have approved it.

Article 29: The land tax shall be levied in different grades according to the annual amount of rice a peasant harvests from the land allotted to him:

1. Every person who harvests less than 5 piculs of rice from the land allotted to him shall be exempt from the land tax.

2. Every person who harvests less than 6 piculs of rice from the land allotted to him shall pay 1 per cent of them as land tax.

3. Every person who harvests 7 piculs of rice from the land allotted to him shall pay $1\frac{1}{2}$ per cent of them as land tax.

4. Every person who harvests 8 piculs of rice from the land allotted to him shall pay $2\frac{1}{2}$ per cent of them as land tax.

5. Every person who harvests 9 piculs of rice from the land allotted to him shall pay 4 per cent of them as land tax.

6. Every person who harvests 10 piculs of rice from the land allotted to him shall pay $5\frac{1}{2}$ per cent of them as land tax.

7. Every person who harvests 11 piculs of rice from the land allotted to him shall pay 7 per cent of them as land tax.

8. Every person who harvests 12 piculs of rice from the land allotted to him shall pay 8 per cent of them as land tax.

Thereafter, for every additional picul of rice harvested, an additional $1\frac{1}{2}$ per cent of it shall be levied as land tax.

Article 30: The levying and disbursement of the land tax shall be the sole responsibility of the Soviet government at a higher level, and the government at a lower level may not levy and disburse it at discretion. The criterion of disbursement shall be determined by the government at a higher level according to the amount of taxes collected and the urgency or importance of the needs of governments at all levels.

CHAPTER IV. WAGES

Article 31: Where the wages of handicraft workers and hired farm hands in the villages have been too low in the past, they shall be raised. The amount of wages in the future shall be determined by the Soviets according to two criteria: the rise or fall of the prices of daily necessities, and the amount of the peasant's income derived from a rich or poor harvest. When the township and district Soviets fix the wages, they must have the approval of the county or provincial Soviets.

DOCUMENT 12

AN OUTLINE OF THE LAND PROBLEM

Adopted by the Joint Meeting of the Chairmen of
County and District [Soviet Governments], Kiangsi
Province, sometime before September 1, 1931.
(As reproduced in *A Collection of Red Bandit*
Secret Documents, Vol. V, leaves 7–11)

I. THE AGGRESSION OF THE IMPERIALISTS AND THE BANKRUPTCY OF THE RURAL ECONOMY

1. The inroad of foreign goods and the decline of domestic goods have led to the breakdown of the self-sufficient rural economy.
2. The increasing demand of the landlords has aggravated their exploitation of the poor and miserable peasants.
3. The increasing demand for money amidst destruction and exploitation of the internecine strifes of warlords has added to the poverty of the peasants.
4. The number of the unemployed in the rural districts is increasing, while the demand for land is pressing.

II. LAND DISTRIBUTION AND CLASS RELATIONS IN OLD CHINA

A. Land distribution
1. Land was largely in the hands of the landlord class, constituting about 30 per cent.
2. The land occupied by the rich peasants was second only to that of the landlords in size, constituting about 20 per cent.
3. Public land, controlled as it was by the landlords and rich peasants, constituted about 20 per cent.
4. The land owned by the middle peasants was about 15 per cent.
5. The land owned by the poor peasants was about 10 to 15 per cent.

B. Ratio of the Chinese population
1. Ten per cent of the population was made up of the landlords and rich peasants.
2. Twenty per cent of the population was made up of the middle peasants.

    3. Seventy per cent of the population was made up of the poor peasants, independent laborers, hired farm hands, and other poor people.

C. Methods of exploitation

    1. Land rental reached from 50 to 80 per cent.

    2. [Loan] interest ranged from 30 to 40 per cent per annum.

    3. Levies and taxes were too many to be enumerated.

    4. Commercial capital [was lent] to the peasants at high [rates of interest], while the farm produce was bought at low prices.

III. LAND REVOLUTION AS THE MAIN CONTENT OF THE CHINESE REVOLUTION

    1. Down with feudal forces.

    2. Down with imperialism.

    3. Satisfy the demand of the peasants for land and liberate the broad masses of the poor and miserable peasants.

    4. Remove the curse of [civil] war waged by soldiers and bandits, and prevent natural calamities.

    5. Step up production so as to solve China's problem of poverty.

IV. A FIRM LEADING ROLE IN EQUAL REDISTRIBUTION

    1. Confiscate all the land belonging to the landlord class, organizations, rich peasants, and other private owners, and carry out the equal redistribution of all land.

    2. The equal redistribution of land is a necessary bridge across which to get to the destruction of feudal forces and to the thorough completion of the democratic revolution for transition to socialism.

    3. The equal redistribution of all [land] is an important principle in the land revolution.

    4. The redistribution of land should not only be fair but fast. The masses can be won over very fast only if an equal redistribution of land is carried out very fast.

    5. Equal redistribution lies in the carrying out of the [principles of] draw-on-the-plentiful-to-make-up-for-the-scarce and draw-on-the-fat-to-make-up-for-the-lean. Where land differs in quality, it should be divided into three different grades of top, medium, and poor [quality] for equal redistribution.

V. METHODS OF EQUAL REDISTRIBUTION

    1. The township shall be the unit for land redistribution. But in a township where there are more mountains than fields within the bounds of its vast area, and where in some villages the fields are inadequate for the crowded population, one or more villages may

become a unit for redistribution, provided that the masses themselves demand one or more villages to form a unit for redistribution and that the district government approves it.

In demarcating the boundaries of the townships, attention
should be given to an even distribution of land among themselves
as far as possible, so that land may not be found to be too much
in one township while too little in another. In townships where
boundaries are not well demarcated and land is distributed with
great disparity among themselves [Chinese original not clear],
the lines of demarcation may be drawn all over again with a view
to another redistribution, provided that the majority of the masses
in the townships with smaller acreages request a fresh demarcation.

2. The number of persons shall be used as the criterion for equal
   redistribution in which the total amount of land in a township is
   divided by the township's total population, irrespective of sex or
   age.

3. [Six Chinese characters not clear here]. Land cultivated by people
   in their own and neighboring townships shall be pooled for equal
   redistribution. If necessary, several neighboring townships may
   hold joint meetings in order to readjust or redemarcate their
   boundaries so that the people of each township may be able to till
   the land in their own township.

4. The question of reserving public land:
   a. In places where land is inadequate for the teeming population,
      no public land should be reserved so that the needs of the
      masses may be satisfied.
   b. In places where land is abundant for the sparse population,
      a part of the land may be reserved for public ownership, aside
      from [the part of the land] equally redistributed to meet the
      needs of the people. The land thus reserved may be used for
      the purpose of immigration under the auspices of the state.
      Prior to the arrival of the immigrants, the land may be
      assigned or leased for cultivation to those peasants who have
      sufficient labor power for it. It must, however, be made clear
      that the land [thus assigned or leased] may be withdrawn in
      case of need.
   c. In case there are odd amounts of land left over from redistribu-
      tion, they should be turned into public land, either to be
      assigned to hired farm hands or leased to other peasants for

cultivation. Upon the arrival of immigrants, such land must be redistributed to them.

5. When land is redistributed, the uncut rice on it should go with it. Its cost, including fertilizers, may not be reimbursed.

6. The question of distributing the rice: The rice should be distributed upon the arrival of the guerrillas so as to stir up the masses. Once the masses start a struggle, a drive for an equal distribution of the rice will inevitably arise. Thereupon, the rice of the landlords and rich peasants should be equally redistributed in order to satisfy the needs of the masses. This is a necessary struggle in a newly developed area as distinguished from an [old] Red area.

7. The question of distributing the forests:

   a. Forests of tea-oil plants shall be converted into equivalent amounts of rice fields for redistribution. (In Hsing-kuo, for example, a forest producing two and a half piculs of tea-oil nuts is equal to a field producing a picul of rice.) Only the forests which are not convenient for division and which the masses are willing to operate in common may be operated jointly and consumed individually with permission of the district government.

   b. Bamboo forests: (1) Ordinary bamboo forests shall all be handed over to the peasants for equal redistribution among themselves. The government may reserve a suitable portion of bamboo in the forest allotment of each person for purposes of public repair and construction. (2) Large-scale bamboo forests shall be managed, leased, or operated by the government except that a part of them shall be assigned to the local inhabitants for their use according to their requirements.

   c. Hillside lands producing nonstaple grains or fruits are to be converted into equivalent amounts of rice fields for equal redistribution.

   d. Firewood forests are handled with the village as the unit. Bamboos and trees are opened or closed to the public for exploitation [at designated times] while weeds and twigs are gathered freely.

   e. Barren hills are to be redistributed equally and the planting of trees should be encouraged there.

   f. Hills with mineral deposits are to be administered and leased out by the government. They may either be operated by the government itself or exploited by the public [Chinese original not clear].

8. The redistribution of ponds:
   a. All ponds are to be used primarily for irrigation and secondarily for raising fish.
   b. Methods of redistribution: (*1*) If circumstances permit, a number of households may be organized into a group for raising fish. (*2*) [Ponds] may be converted into equivalent amounts of land for redistribution.

9. The redistribution of houses:
   a. Houses in the countryside: Aside from those reserved for public use by the government or mass organizations, the houses of the landlord class and the surplus houses of the rich peasants shall all be redistributed to those who have no or inadequate houses of their own.
   b. Houses in the cities: Houses owned by the capitalist class may not be confiscated. Houses owned by the landlord class and counterrevolutionaries shall be confiscated and, aside from those reserved for public use, redistributed to the poor people and workers to live in.

10. Oil-pressing mills and grain-husking water mills: The oil-pressing mills and grain-husking water mills of the rich peasants and landlords are to be confiscated and administered by the township government, while those of the middle and poor peasants may not be confiscated.

11. Draft cattle and farm implements: The draft cattle of the landlord class and the surplus draft cattle of the rich peasants shall be confiscated and redistributed to those who have no or few draft cattle of their own but who should divide themselves into groups to use them. The surplus farm implements of the rich peasants shall be redistributed to those who lack such implements but who need not divide themselves into groups [to use them].

12. Land allotments to hired farm hands: Hired farm hands are to be allotted land [Chinese original not clear].

13. Poor handicraftsmen and other independent laborers in the rural districts, as well as poor people and dependents of the professionals in small towns, are to be allotted land as well. As to the professionals themselves, they shall each receive half an allotment of land if they are half unemployed, a full allotment of land if full unemployed, and no allotment of land if not unemployed.

14. Poor petty merchants in the countryside or small towns are not to be allotted any land if their business is good enough to support themselves and their families; those who cannot make a living may receive suitable subsidiary allotments according to the number of persons [in their households].

15. The rich peasants shall be treated in land redistribution in the same way as the middle and poor peasants. They must not be permitted to keep good land for themselves, nor are they to be allotted poor land purposely.

16. Those dependents of the landlords who obey the Soviet laws and refrain from opposing the revolution shall all be allotted land and compelled to engage in labor.

17. [Former] soldiers of the White Army shall be allotted land, but their officers may not be given any land.

18. [Former] members of the local [KMT] Pacification Corps who are of poor-worker and peasant origin shall be allotted land, but in case they fail to return home after half a year, the land assigned them must be withdrawn.

VI. THE LAND PROBLEM AFTER LAND REDISTRIBUTION IN THE DEMO-
CRATIC STAGE

1. Land shall be reaffirmed as belonging to the peasants in private ownership so as to develop both the struggle and production.

2. No land shall be assigned to a newborn child; land allotted to a person may not be taken back [from his family] after his death.

3. Land may be leased out freely [Chinese original not clear], bought and sold. The rental [in case of a lease] may be agreed upon freely between the parties concerned. The purchase and sale of land should be registered with the government.

4. A landowner is free to have his landholdings disposed of after his death. They may be divided among his children or given to his relatives or donated to public welfare. In no case may the government interfere.

5. Women have the same right to land as men and are perfectly free to dispose of their land upon marriage or divorce.

6. The disparity between rich and poor is certainly inevitable so long as private landownership is established, free trade permitted, and production developed. Only by consolidating the broad masses of the poor and miserable peasants so as to form a solid alliance, by broadening the scope of the struggle in order to achieve a nationwide victory in the democratic revolution, by

passing through numerous transitional stages in an effort to win the financial support of the nation in order to enable the poor-peasant economy to move forward step by step, and by liberating [realizing] definitively the collective economy of the poor and middle peasants to achieve the success of socialism, [only then] the poor and miserable masses of the peasants can aspire to the private economy of the rich peasants.

VII. THE PROBLEM OF DEBTS
  A. Debts incurred before land redistribution:
    1. All exploiting debts incurred before the [Communist] uprising shall be abolished.
    2. All debts owed by village bosses, gentry, landlords, rich peasants, and businessmen to the poor and miserable workers and peasants shall be paid.
  B. The problem of loans after land redistribution:
    1. It is allowed to make loans, which will be reimbursed.
    2. The rate of interest will be fixed according to local conditions; it must not, as a rule, exceed 1 per cent per annum.

DOCUMENT 13

PROCLAMATION OF THE KIANGSI PROVINCIAL
GOVERNMENT ON THE LAND PROBLEM

1931
(As reproduced in *A Collection of Reactionary
Documents,* Vol. I, book 4, leaves 8–10)

The land problem is the main content of the bourgeois-democratic revolution in China at the present stage. The poor and miserable peasants in the various provinces in South China have already launched a general struggle for the acquisition of land and for the Soviet regime. But in southwest Kiangsi there are still not a few places where now, after several years of fierce struggle, the redistribution of land has not followed the principles of draw-on-the-plentiful-to-make-up-for-the-scarce and draw-on-the-fat-to-make-up-for-the-lean. Nor has it used the township as the unit, nor the number of persons as the criterion, nor the measure of a thorough equal redistribution.

On the one hand, this has been due to the fact that there have lurked in the various levels of the Soviet government in the past not a few younger members of the families of the rich peasants, vagabonds, village bosses, gentry, and landlords, in addition to counterrevolutionaries like members of the A-B League, who have occupied dominant positions and carried on disruptive activities. This has happened in the past in certain places where instances of sham redistribution (using a family branch as the unit of land redistribution), nonredistribution, and delayed redistribution of land have been discovered.

On the other hand, the various levels of government have not carried the struggle of land redistribution deeply enough among the masses of people. That is to say, they have not mobilized the hired farm hands and poor peasants to carry out equal land redistribution resolutely. They have only issued governmental orders once, twice, and even as many as five or six times to carry out one round of redistribution after another, thus causing the poor and miserable peasants much annoyance and trouble. All these have been bad enough to obstruct the deepening and development of the land revolution.

Meanwhile, land has all been redistributed in the past in equal terms, without distinction as to class status. In consequence, the dependents of village bosses, gentry, and landlords could likewise receive their land allotments. This has also impeded the progress of the land struggle in the rural districts.

Lately, as a result of the Second Campaign of the KMT warlords against the Soviet areas, the village bosses, gentry, and landlords took advantage of the opportunity to grab back the land from the hands of the peasants. Now the enemy has been defeated by our workers' and peasants' Red Army. So far as the land problem is concerned, it is likely that the reactionary elements will take advantage of the opportunity to destroy the principle of equal land redistribution which has throughout been followed.

At the same time, as the able-bodied poor and miserable peasants were all coping with the enemy during the [KMT] campaign, they have had no spare time for the cultivation of land. In addition, the lack of draft cattle, farming implements, and seeds has become all the more serious in the places devastated by the White Army. All these problems have to be solved right away.

Based on the spirit of the resolution on the land problem adopted at the Joint Meeting of the Chairmen of Southwest Kiangsi, this provincial government has made the following decisions on the current land problem:

1. Land redistribution should be based on the resolution adopted at the Joint Meeting of the Chairmen of Southwest Kiangsi by using the township as the unit and the number of persons as the criterion, following the principles of draw-on-the-plentiful-to-make-up-for-the-scarce and draw-on-the-fat-to-make-up-for-the-lean, and bringing about a thorough equal redistribution of land. All forests, houses, and ponds must be redistributed without exception. Once redistributed, the land should belong to the peasants, who shall be free to lease or sell it. Those who were born after the redistribution shall receive no land. The land of those who died after the redistribution may not be returned.

2. Once thoroughly redistributed, the land shall not be redistributed afresh. But if the land has not been thoroughly redistributed according to the above-mentioned principles, or if it has been redistributed with a family branch as the unit of redistribution (such as happened in . . . places), the poor and miserable workers and peasants should come forward at once to ask the government to carry out a thorough equal redistribution. Where the rice sprouts have been planted, the uncut rice may be redistributed.

3. The dependents of village bosses, gentry, and landlords shall not be allotted land. Any land that has been assigned to them shall be taken back by the government. But such dependents may be permitted to lease land and the amount of rent for the land thus leased by them may be fixed according to the opinions of the local poor and miserable workers and peasants.

4. All land belonging to counterrevolutionary elements who have been executed or have escaped, to members of the A-B League, the Liquidationists, and so forth, shall be confiscated by the government. If their dependents are all found to have committed counterrevolutionary acts, the land of the entire family shall be confiscated. The land thus confiscated by the government may be leased to the poor and miserable workers and peasants for cultivation.

5. All land that has been grabbed from the hands of the poor and miserable workers and peasants by village bosses, gentry, landlords, and rich peasants at the time of the [KMT] militarists' attack on the revolutionary forces shall be taken back from them by the poor and miserable workers and peasants under the guidance of the government. The land thus taken back shall be cultivated according to its original apportionment without fail.

6. Forests, ponds, the houses of village bosses, gentry, and landlords, and the surplus houses of the rich peasants shall be redistributed accord-

ing to the resolution of the Joint Meeting of the Chairmen of Southwest Kiangsi, and the redistribution shall be completed by the various levels of government in the shortest possible time.

7. All the draft cattle, farming implements, seeds, and fertilizers in the homes of absentee reactionaries shall be confiscated by the government for redistribution to the poor and miserable workers and peasants.

8. The land of the poor and miserable workers and peasants who have died for the revolutionary cause, whether it has not been cultivated by them or it has been their original land, should be cultivated on the basis of mutual help (lending draft cattle and farming implements and offering physical labor) by the masses of the neighboring villages. Such idle land should be cultivated very quickly indeed, whether it is to be used for planting rice or nonstaple grains.

The provincial government hereby calls upon the broad masses of the poor and miserable workers and peasants in southwest Kiangsi to come forward and see to it that the various levels of government carry out these eight items of work. If any responsible government authorities are found to be negligent in such work, they may be removed by the local congress of delegates of the workers, peasants, and soldiers. Only in this way the poor and miserable workers and peasants can gain benefits and the Soviets can really become the organs of political authority of the workers, peasants, and soldiers. Such is this proclamation.

TSENG SHAN
Chairman

1931

DOCUMENT 19

QUESTIONS CONCERNING THE REDISTRIBUTION OF UNRIPE RICE AND THE LEASE OF LAND

Mao Tse-tung, November 15, 1930
(As printed in Mao Tse-tung, *Investigations of the Rural Districts,* published at Yenan in 1941, reissued by Hsinhua Bookstore, Shantung, 1946, pp. 79–83)

The Kiangsi Provincial Action Committee met in enlarged session at Chi-an on November 15, 1930. Besides the members of the standing committee of the provincial committee, the participants included the chairmen of the county Soviets of Yung-hsin, Chi-an, T'ai-ho, Wan-an, Chi-shui, Fu-an, Fen-i, and Hsia-chiang, and Comrade Ch'en Yi of the 22nd Army. I attended the meeting as representative of the General Front Committee. The outstanding features of this meeting were discussions of two questions: the "redistribution of unripe rice" and the "lease of land."

Regarding the question of redistributing unripe rice, I called for support for the mass basis of the redistribution of unripe rice. As to the question of leasing land, I refuted the leftist, but actually rich-peasant, theory that "no rent should be collected in the Soviet areas." In addition, we objected to the Chiang Han-po type of redistribution based on labor power, pointing out that his mistake lay in serving the interests of the rich peasants at the expense of the poor peasants. This meeting adjourned before the completion of its work, on the ground that the enemy had already reached Hsia-chiang, and that the responsible authorities of the various counties must go back to take steps to deal with the enemy. In consequence, we had not discussed the questions of "mountains and forests," "ponds," "houses," "waste land," "unemployment," "debts," and so on, which we had originally planned to discuss.

Hardly had the meeting adjourned when we were facing the serious enemy attacks and the Fu-t'ien incident. Consequently, the provincial committee has thus far not released the resolutions of this meeting. The following are some brief notes I jotted down myself in the meeting on that day. I have preserved them since they contain some important materials.

1. District as Unit of Land Redistribution in Shun-hua

The third redistribution of land (October, 1930) in the district of Shun-hua entered upon the stage in which the district was used as the unit. The first step was to figure out the size of the population and the output of production in order to see how much land each person could receive. Then the redistribution was carried out in the scope of a township. "Move the land if the land can be moved; move the people if the land cannot be moved." There are now more than thirty thousand people in the district of Shun-hua. Everyone has received an equal amount of land. (Everyone receives a plot of land capable of yielding eleven piculs of unhusked rice. A picul weighs forty-four catties.)

2. Weaknesses in Using the Village as Unit of Land Redistribution

The weaknesses of using the village as the unit of land redistribution are: (*1*) The large villages are unwilling to give land to the small ones. (*2*) If there are too many units, it would not be easy for the district government to supervise work. Many irregularities could follow in secret. (*3*) It is in the village that the landlords and rich peasants would easily use clan ties to mislead the masses into rejection of a thorough division of land and a deadly blow to village bosses. This idea is worthy of note.

3. Land Struggle Cannot Go Deep Overnight

No matter how many times land may be redistributed, the rich peasants would conceal good land, at least on the first occasion, thus making it impossible to investigate land satisfactorily by dividing it into three different grades. The first time, the rich peasants and middle peasants would inevitably play the leading role, while the poor peasants had no power. "When the insurrection has been in force a little longer, the proletariat will rise." This idea is right.

4. Yang Ch'eng-fu's Plan on "Agricultural Socialization"

Yang Ch'eng-fu, chairman of Chi-an county government (formerly secretary of the Shun-hua District Committee, and concurrently chairman), has advocated common cultivation and common consumption and proposed three different steps to attain it: (*1*) using the district as the unit of land redistribution; (*2*) organizing the cooperatives; (*3*) common cultivation and common consumption. This is entirely wrong.

5. The Chiang Han-po Type of Redistribution by Labor Power

The trouble with labor power as the unit of land redistribution is that orphans, widows, the aged, the young, women with bound feet, and all those who are not capable of tilling land will not have enough to eat. Even those poor peasants who have plenty of labor power cannot compete with the rich peasants because poor peasants are inferior to rich peasants in draft cattle, farm implements, and capital. Besides, the rich peasants can lease land from orphans, widows, the aged, the young, women with bound feet, and so on, to cultivate. Hence, using labor power as the unit would only serve the interests of the rich peasants.

The "Chiang Han-po plan" of the labor power unit has been carried out in the "border area" between An-fu, Chi-an, and Fen-i, and in Chi-an's Yen-fu township. It has been carried out so strictly that whoever has labor power gets his land allotment and whoever has no labor power gets no land allotment, regardless of age. The vagabonds receive land allotments. Those who have no labor power are fed by those who have labor power to till land. A political commissar of the Third Army Corps has come to Chi-an, telling Wang Huai that the method of land redistribution in the border area between Hunan, Hupeh, and Kiangsi is the use of labor power as the unit, and that whoever has no labor power receives half an allotment, and makes up his deficiency through government aid.

If labor power is used as the unit of redistribution, the rich peasants who have more land will keep their draft cattle and farm implements for their own use and will not lend them to the poor peasants. Only in equal redistribution can the poor peasants borrow the spare farm implements from the rich peasants. That is why the poor peasants demand equal redistribution.

6. *The Question of Redistributing Unripe Rice*

The peasants of Jui-chin and Yü-tu are divided. Some of them give support to the slogan "unconditional redistribution of unripe rice," as adopted at the T'ing-chou Conference, while others support the slogan, "no redistribution of unripe rice," as adopted at the P'i-t'ou Conference. The latter have brought the excuse that "It is not allowed to violate the land law."

This happened in various counties in the northern route on February 8: Six hundred cash were paid to compensate the original cultivator for his cost in producing a picul of unhusked rice. In Fu-t'ien [not the place where the Fu-t'ien incident of December, 1930, occurred] no compensation has been made for the land of the rich peasants, while two hundred cash have been paid for a picul of unhusked rice from the land of the poor peasants.

When land was redistributed in Shun-hua in March, the rice sprouts had not been transplanted. The land has been plowed only once, and in some cases, just seeded and fertilized. Accordingly, no compensation for the cost of the rice has been made after land redistribution.

Six hundred or one thousand cash have been paid in compensation of the cost of a picul of unhusked rice in the northern route. As the official price of a picul of unhusked rice was given by the county authorities at four thousand cash before May, the compensation has been only one-sixth to one-fourth of that price. Since the land redistribution had not been carried out by them and since it was a time of dearth, the policy of fixing the price of unhusked rice at four thousand per picul was indeed meant to hold down the rice price in the interests of the poor peasants. However, the price of unhusked rice remained fixed at four thousand cash per picul after harvest. "This is certainly wrong."

The Fifth District government of the Northwest Special Area of Yung-hsin made some decisions in the fifth month of the last lunar year. There are the fields which yield an earlier crop in the year. In this case, if land was redistributed at a time when rice was nearly ripe, the person who received the land should pay a Chinese dollar for a picul of unhusked rice (two hundred catties, that is per *tan* of land), to the person who gave away the land. There are also the fields which yield only one crop a year. In this case, one thousand cash were paid for a *tan* of land (two piculs of unhusked rice) to the person who gave away the land in the fifth month of the lunar calendar when the rice sprouts had just been transplanted and were not yet ripe. The county committee, on their part, had decided that land must be obtained without compensation. But since the Fifth District had not received instructions from the county committee owing to transportation difficulties, it acted according to its own decisions.

The peasants in eastern Yü-tu and northwestern Kan-hsien demanded a compensation of two small Chinese dollars (worth four thousand cash) for each unit of land producing a picul of unhusked rice (actually only eight pecks). But the party disagreed, with the result that the land was obtained without compensation.

The proper policy should be "to obtain land without compensation and to redistribute both land and unripe rice." The landlords' dependents should be assigned land as well, in a spirit of nondiscrimination. Since the landlords have plenty of money, extra financial burdens should be imposed upon them. The vagabonds should be assigned land as well. They are hard-working and it would be incorrect for the rich peasants to keep them from receiving land allotments.

Since the middle peasants have no excess land to give away, they will not be affected. Though the "upper poor peasants" who till more than enough land would be affected, there are other kinds of advantages to satisfy them. The broad masses of lower poor peasants, handicraftsmen, and hired farm hands would give full support to this program. Those who are not capable of tilling land after the redistribution of unripe rice should be allowed to act according to the regulations governing the lease of land.

7. Equal Redistribution of the Originally Tilled Total Acreage

In the past, the "village" and "family" have been used as the units for equal redistribution on the basis of original cultivation. As a result, the interests of the rich peasants rather than the poor peasants have been served. The proper measure should be: to use the township as the unit and let the total population of a county divide the total acreage originally cultivated by the total population of the county (the total population of a county means the total number of those who have originally tilled land in their home county and those who have originally tilled land outside their home county); to draw on the plentiful to make up for the scarce and to draw on the fat to make up for the lean; to move the land if the land can be moved (the villages which have more land should give a part of it to the villages which have less land), and move the persons if the land cannot be moved (in case of a great distance, it would not be possible to move the land, but to move the persons). This measure is known as the "redistribution of the originally tilled total acreage."

8. The New Laboring Population and the New Land-Lease System

Those who have no labor power lease their land to those who have labor power. The tenants give unhusked rice to landowners as rent. This rent is 40 per cent at Shun-hua, Wan-an, and Hsing-yü, 50 per cent at Fen-i and Ning-tu, and one third at Yung-hsin. There are three different grades at Fu-t'ien (a district of Chi-an): 40 per cent for the first-class land, 30 per cent for medium land, and 20 per cent for poor land. This seems comparatively reasonable.

Those who have no labor power and have to lease out their land constitute 20 per cent of the population at Shun-hua, An-fu, T'ai-ho, Hsing-yü, Fen-i, and Hsia-chiang, respectively, and more than 20 per cent at Ning-tu. For most women in these places have bound feet. It is only 5 per cent at Yung-hsin, since the women there do not have bound feet. Those who lease out their land are generally orphans, widows, the disabled, the aged, the young, and the participants in the revolution.

What has been said above refers only to the cases in which a family has no labor power at all and must lease out its land. There are more cases in which some members of a family are without labor power, but others in the family can do the cultivating, and the family need not lease its land. Generally speaking, those who have no labor power constitute 75 per cent of the total population. In other words, out of every four persons, only one is able-bodied and has adequate strength to till land. This is a big problem in China.

However, when we say "no labor power" here, we refer to the proper work of cultivating the land. Half of the population have partial labor power for, say, tending cattle, collecting firewood, cooking, laundry, and so on. Statistics follow:

25 per cent with full labor power
37.5 per cent with partial or little labor power
37.5 per cent with no labor power at all.

"Lease land and pay rent in unhusked rice" in all the above-mentioned places has been going on under the so-called "new unhusked-rice system" with the exception of Shun-hua where the "rent-collecting system" is the order of the day. The weaknesses of the unhusked-rice-dividing system are: In tilling land, the tenant is apt to give his principal attention to his own land and to work and fertilize the land of his landowner half-heartedly. When the rice [in this latter land] is harvested, it is divided [between the tenant and landlord] at a 50–50, 40–60, or other, rate. This system is disadvantageous to the landowner. As to the rent-collecting system, it is based on a fixed rate of rent, regardless of the actual amount of the crop. Accordingly, the tenant will have to attend to his cultivation and fertilizing. This will be helpful, not only for the output of production, but also to the tenant himself.

The weaknesses of the rent-collecting system are: (1) The rent in cash in years of dearth would not be in the interests of the tenant. (2) It would also not be in the interests of the tenant if the Red Guards go out on business too frequently, and have to cut down their working days on the farm.

In brief, the unhusked-rice-dividing system is favorable to the rich peasants, while the rent-collecting system is favorable to the poor peasants.

The proper policy should be: (1) Some poor peasants, hired farm hands, and the unemployed receive land allotments, but lack cattle, farm implements, and capital. The government should confiscate the excess cattle, farm implements, and so on, of rich peasants and land-lords and give them to the hired farm hands, poor peasants, unemployed workers, and so on, for their private cultivation. Meanwhile, the collective use of these implements should be encouraged by placing some of the confiscated articles of rich peasants and landlords in the coopera-tives. There is another way: Private individuals may borrow cattle and farm implements from rich peasants as a temporary aid. The government should punish those rich peasants who deliberately refuse to lend their articles to help the poor peasants, hired farm hands, and the unemployed. (2) As to those who cannot till land at all, they may be allowed to lease their land to rich peasants and middle peasants for cultivation under the following conditions: (a) Abolish the unhusked-rice-dividing system and prescribe a fixed rate of rent, which will not be reduced in times of dearth. (b) Prescribe a minimum rate of rent (50 per cent), so that the rich peasant cannot exploit the poor peasants and hired farm hands too much. (c) Do not allow the rich peasants, under any pretext, to till only their own land but not the land of others. If the rich peasants are not willing to lease land from others, the township government should assign the land which is to be leased out in the township to the rich peasants and middle peasants of the township and compel them to till it.

9. The Question of Land Redistribution as Demanded by the Unemployed Workers in Cities

There are more than two hundred masons and carpenters in the city of T'ai-ho who have demanded the redistribution of land. But their demand has been turned down. Since they are people from other counties, the peasants in the city area do not permit them to receive their land allotments. In addition, those who make [?] sugar canes outside the south gate of the city demand land redistribution, too.

Hsing-kuo is also plagued with this question.

This question deserves serious consideration.

DOCUMENT 21

THE RICH-PEASANT PROBLEM

*Resolution No. 2 Adopted by a Joint Meeting of the Front
Committee and the Western Fukien Special Committee, June, 1930*
(As printed by the General Political Department of
the First Front Army of the Red Army, June, 1930)

1. Who are the rich peasants?

There are three kinds of rich peasants. The first kind consists of rich peasants of a semilandlord character, that is, the kind of persons who do the farming themselves and at the same time have surplus land to rent to others. The second kind consists of rich peasants of a capitalistic character, that is, the kind of persons who do not rent out their land and in some cases may even lease land from others and hire laborers to till it. The third kind consists of rich peasants of an initial-stage character, that is, the kind of persons who neither rent out land nor hire laborers, but till land with their own labor, and who, being adequate both in land and in labor, have surplus foodstuffs for sale or for loan every year.

All kinds of rich peasants have in common two ways of exploiting the poor and miserable masses, namely, loans at usurious rates of interest (interests on loans of money, grains, pigs, oxen, and vegetable oils), and the sale of foodstuffs and like commodities. Rich peasants of the first two kinds have each a special form of exploitation, viz., rich peasants of a semilandlord character exploit land rent while rich peasants of a capitalistic character exploit hired labor. Besides, many of the rich peasants are concurrently engaged in commerce—running small stores and peddling farm produce—thus exploiting the poor and miserable masses by means of commercial capital.

2. The counterrevolutionary nature of the rich peasants

The rich peasants are the bourgeoisie in the rural districts. But the exploitation carried on by the rich peasants in China generally partakes of semifeudal brutality. Whether in land rent, in usury, in hired labor, or in commercial capital, exploitation by the rich peasants appears more ruthless than that by the landlords. For this reason, there is a fundamental conflict between the interests of this class and those of the poor-peasant and hired-labor class. From beginning to end, this class is opposed to the revolution.

Although at the beginning of the revolution the rich-peasant class had the need to oppose the exorbitant levies and miscellaneous taxes imposed on them by the warlords, yet their own fundamental interests (land and capital) dictate that they would certainly stand on the side of the landlords in opposition to the poor peasants and the hired farm hands if the revolution comes only from the poor peasants and the hired farm hands.

At the upsurge of the revolutionary tide, the rich peasants, in a show of generosity, may well burn their title deeds, divide their land, wear red ribbons as signs of comrades, and even worm their way into the Communist Party. All these opportunist activities are for the purpose of winning them a social position, seizing the leadership of the poor peasants and hired farm hands, and attempting to tide over the crisis of the development of rural capitalism (moving from the protection of their present property to the development of capitalism). This is a most serious problem in the struggle in the villages, to which it is necessary to call the full attention of our comrades.

When the village struggle becomes intensified—that is, when the poor peasants and hired farm hands have firmly established their leadership, toppled the political position of the rich peasants, confiscated the land, forests, and draft cattle of the rich peasants, and abolished the debts owed to the rich peasants—the rich peasants act to spread rumors to confuse the public and resort to passive sabotage.

When the revolution is heading from crisis to failure, the rich peasants will waver, compromise, and even entirely betray it by standing on the side of the landlords and directing their attacks against the poor peasants and hired farm hands.

3. The controversy over the rich peasants of an initial-stage character

In the past, various quarters (especially the East River region) recognized only the rich peasants of a semilandlord character and of a capitalistic character as rich peasants. The rich peasants of an initial-stage character were not called rich peasants but "middle peasants." There were objections to the confiscation of their surplus land and even to the cancellation of debts owed to them. This has overlooked the fact that such initial-stage rich peasants are still an exploiting class. Though they do not collect land rent nor exploit hired labor, yet they make loans at usury and, in addition, sell their surplus foodstuffs at high prices whenever an opportunity offers. These two forms of exploitation agree completely with those practiced by rich peasants of a semilandlord character and of a capitalistic character. This category of rich peasants, by virtue of the above-mentioned two forms of exploitation, gradually accumulates its capital and moves in the direction of joining the ranks of the rich peasants of a capitalistic and a semilandlord character. The poor peasants and hired farm hands not only demand both the confiscation of the land of the rich peasants of a semilandlord and a capitalistic character and the cancellation of the debts owed to them, but also want to confiscate the land of the rich peasants of an initial-stage character and annul the debts owed to them. The poor peasants and hired farm hands have all acted this way in the intensified struggle areas.

However, this question still remains an undecided one of controversy within the Communist Party. In regard to this question, the present Joint Meeting takes the position that it supports the masses to confiscate the land of the rich peasants of an initial-stage character and annul the debts owed to them as firmly as it insists on the confiscation of the land of the other two kinds of rich peasants and the annulment of debts owed to them. Why is it that such a policy has been adopted? It is because only the confiscation of the land of the landlords of an initial-stage character can retaliate their ruthless exploitation through selling their surplus foodstuffs at high prices whenever an opportunity offers, and only the cancellation of the debts owed to them can retaliate their ruthless exploitation through usury. These two kinds of exploitation are all semifeudalistic in nature. Not until the thorough elimination of these two kinds of exploitation can the peasants be completely liberated from semifeudalistic relationships. It would not be enough to put an end to the exploitation of merely the landlords and the rich peasants of the first two categories [i.e., rich peasants of a semilandlord and a capitalistic character].

4. *The strength of the broad masses of poor peasants is enough to overcome the rich peasants, and only when the party adopts an anti-rich-peasant tactic can the broad masses of poor peasants be won over to thoroughly complete the task of the democratic revolution to head for the stage of a socialist revolution*

In the Yangtze River and the Pearl River valleys, generally speaking, the poor peasants and hired farm hands constitute more than 70 per cent [of the rural population], the middle peasants around 20 per cent and the rich peasants less than 10 per cent. In the struggle of the rural districts the main force of the struggle is the vast masses of poor peasants and hired farm hands. In addition, the middle peasants can be expected to become allies. As to the rich peasants, they are an extremely isolated small group of the masses. Though the rich peasants are necessarily counterrevolutionary in nature, they, in respect of class strength, will be overthrown by the broad masses of poor peasants.

Some people assert that there are provinces in South China where the rich peasants or owner-peasants constitute also the majority or quite a large number. (They assert, for example: "The majority of the peasants in Kiangsi province are owner-peasants"; "The land revolution cannot be enforced in Mei-hsien and Ta-pu because there are many owner-peasants there"; and "The rich peasants constitute 40 per cent [of the rural population] in Ch'ang-t'ing and Chien-ning in Fukien province," and so forth.) Those people are obviously exaggerating the numerical strength of the rich-peasant class. They feel that the first step should be confined to opposing the landlords and that it is still premature to oppose the rich peasants.

The foregoing assertions are not only objective mistakes at complete variance with social conditions. Some of them are even subjective intrigues of the counterrevolutionaries in an attempt to establish the leadership of the rich peasants in the party and among the masses, to confuse class consciousness in the party and among the masses, and to lessen and even stop the party's work of opposing the rich peasants.

To exaggerate the class strength of the rich peasants and to suggest that concessions should be made to them at the time of attacking the landlords represents a viewpoint of Right opportunism which is very dangerous. Meanwhile, merely recognizing that the rich peasants are "an extremely isolated small group of the masses" without recognizing their "extremely ruthless semifeudalistic exploitation" will also necessarily lessen and even stop the party's work of opposing the rich peasants. This is also very dangerous, indeed. The opportunist opposition represented by Ch'en Tu-hsiu and company asserts that the Chinese villages have already become capitalist in nature and that feudalistic exploitation is merely the residue of residues. Their conclusion is, of course, the abandonment of the democratic revolution and the cessation of the struggle against the landlords. But if we, in reply, do not view the question from the standpoint of the substance of exploitation but only from the standpoint of the form of exploitation, we shall have to concede that "the rich peasants are not the principal enemies, only the landlords are the principal enemies." If we do not recognize that the nature of the struggle against the landlords is that both are struggles against ruthless semifeudalistic exploitation, our conclusion will also necessarily be such as would lessen and even stop the important work of opposing the rich peasants. Once this work is abandoned, it will no longer be possible to win over the broad masses of poor peasants and thoroughly complete the democratic revolution to head for the stage of a socialist revolution.

On the contrary, if only we recognize that the struggle against the rich peasants and the struggle against the landlords alike are equally directed against ruthless semifeudalistic exploitation, we shall be able to formulate firm party tactics against the rich peasants, win over the broad masses of poor peasants, and complete thoroughly the democratic revolution to head for the stage of a socialist revolution. Only then, we shall also be able to topple the whole basis of the theory of Ch'en Tu-hsiu and company, keeping them from occupying an area of the "rich peasants" in which to talk a lot of nonsense.

5. *The failure of the struggle in Hai-lu-feng was due to blind actionism and Hai-lu-feng's localism but not to opposition to rich peasants*

Laboring under the illusion that the failure in Hai-lu-feng was due to the revolt of the rich peasants (rich peasants of an initial-stage character whom they called "middle peasants"), our comrades in the East River region called upon the various localities to refrain from attacking the rich peasants of an initial-stage character. In the meantime, a similar view prevailed in other places. This did not differ much from the outcry, "The peasant movement has gone too far," which our comrades in the two provinces of Hunan and Hupeh raised, following at the heels of Tang Sheng-chih and Hsü Ke-hsiang after the failure of the Great Revolution. Now we have all come to realize that the Great Revolution failed, not because it "went too far," but because it "did not go far enough" (opportunism). The failure in Hai-lu-feng and other places was due to blind actionism and narrow localism, in addition to the fact that the revolutionary situation in the whole country was then at a low ebb. The failure was not due to opposition to the rich peasants.

Anything done under the leadership of blind actionism and localism is bound to fail at any time. The failure cannot be avoided by stopping opposition to the rich peasants. In the meantime, the struggle against the rich peasants must not be identified with arson, massacre, and wholesale looting as instances of blind actionism to be guarded against in the future. Quite on the contrary, struggling resolutely against the rich peasants and establishing an absolute leadership of the poor peasants and hired farm hands in the villages will be an important condition for safeguarding the victory of the revolution.

6. *Nothing is more stupid than to keep the rich peasants' loans intact in order to maintain the circulation of money*

It would be quite wrong to keep the masses of poor peasants from unleashing a thorough struggle to repudiate their debts owed to rich peasants in order to maintain the "circulation of money," that is, to make rich peasants continue to lend money to poor peasants. It should not be surprising if such a slogan is raised by the rich peasants for the purpose of deception. But nothing can be more stupid from the standpoint of the poor peasants than this idea. For once the order of the rural society is upset, all moneylendings and credits will come to a stop immediately. How is it possible that the rich peasants will come forward to keep the circulation of money when the struggle reaches a point of the confiscation of land? To illustrate by example, events in the Red areas have long taught us that if the circulation of money is desired at all, the only way is for the poor peasants themselves to organize credit cooperatives and for the Soviets to compel the rich peasants to loan out their money at a low rate of interest. It is sheer fantasy to assume that the rich peasants can be charitable and helpful to the poor peasants if the latter do not attack the former.

7. Confiscate all land and write off all debts

"Confiscate all land" and "Write off all debts" are two immutable central slogans in the course of the land struggle in the various southern provinces. The masses in all places have generally been carrying out these two slogans. However, the party has become a tail, as it were, to the masses everywhere, simply waiting for the masses to carry those slogans out and then "recognizing them afterwards." In some cases the party even "withheld its recognition." Thus, the party has not only become a tail to the masses but become their opponent as well. If this grave situation is not corrected, the party cannot lead the land struggle in the various southern provinces.

There can be no doubt that the two slogans, "Confiscate the land of the landlord class" and "Write off usuries," are no longer suitable. For they have been used by the rich peasants and opportunistic Communists as tools to obstruct the struggle of the poor peasants in many places. Beyond a doubt, "Confiscate all land" and "Write off all debts" have to be put forth openly and positively at any time and at any place in various southern provinces. To "withhold recognition" is, indeed, absolutely wrong; to "recognize afterwards" is also "tailism." These two slogans should be used by the party to rouse the masses to action instead of waiting for the masses to start the struggle and then stepping forth to lead them. The tactic of "waiting for the masses to rise and then stepping forth to lead them" betrays an abysmal ignorance of the land situation in various southern provinces. It will degenerate into tactics of opportunistic vacillation. This tactic of vacillation is not equal to the task of leading the great struggle of thousands upon thousands of poor and miserable peasants, a struggle that is fast approaching.

8. The two slogans must be shouted at all times

There is a view that the party's tactics toward the rich peasants in the White areas should be different from those in the Red areas. It is suggested that in the Red areas the rich peasants may be attacked and the slogans of "Confiscating all land" and "Writing off all debts" may be put into effect, while in the White areas the slogans should still be "Confiscation of the land of the landlords" and "Cancellation of the debts owed to the landlords." The latter is intended to neutralize the rich peasants for the time being and to enable the poor peasants to win a victory in their struggle against the landlords at first. This view is erroneous.

We must recognize that the rich peasants (including those peasants who are actually rich peasants but are ordinarily regarded as middle peasants) are numerically a small group in the farming population (a big group as compared with the landlords). Yet this small group of rich peasants are exploiting the poor peasants and hired farm hands with the most ruthless semifeudalistic methods. They are necessarily opposed to the revolution. Accordingly, our tactics should be to make known the sins of the rich peasants from the very beginning and look upon the rich peasants in the same way as the landlords are looked upon. Under no circumstances should the boundaries of class status between the rich peasants and other peasants be confused, thereby giving the rich peasants a chance to take advantage of the situation. From the very beginning, the true nature of the rich peasants should be exposed, so that the masses will know that the rich peasants are opposed to the revolution.

Besides, the rich peasants can never become "neutral." The moment they see the outbreak of the struggle of the poor peasants and hired farm hands, they will take their stand on the side of the landlords. How can there be any neutrality? This kind of illusion of neutralizing the rich peasants will inevitably obstruct the work of the proletariat to start a fierce struggle of the poor peasants and hired farm hands and to win over the middle peasants to join them in an alliance.

If we fail to put forth the slogans against the rich peasants from the very beginning, the poor peasants will feel disappointed. This has already been proved to be the case in the struggle in western Fukien and various other places. The enemies of the poor peasants and hired farm hands are not only landlords, but also the rich peasants. The exploitation by the landlords is indeed serious, but the exploitation by the rich peasants is even worse.

9. The two slogans must be shouted in all places

There is another view which recognizes that concessions should be made to the rich peasants in some places. For instance, in certain counties in a province and in certain townships in a county where there are "a large number of rich peasants," the two questions of confiscating land and writing off debts may be different from those in the places where the poor peasants are large in number. In such cases, the local Soviets should adopt some measures which are different from the ordinary measures—such as the redistribution of land according to labor power, the refusal to write off debts of the petty bourgeoisie, and so on, subject to the approval of the superior Soviets.

This kind of view is dangerous on two counts. First, in those so-called "special places," the interests of the poor peasants and hired farm hands are completely sacrificed for the sake of the pleasure of the rich peasants. People holding this view fail to understand that in places where there are a large number of rich peasants, there must be still more poor peasants and hired farm hands. To accommodate the interests of the rich peasants at the expense of the poor peasants and hired farm hands is the policy of the Kuomintang. The Communist Party should not. . . . [One whole leaf of the Chinese original including sections 10 and 11 of this text is missing here.]

12. Equal redistribution according to the number of persons would not only not reduce production but constitute a condition for the increase of production

As pointed out above, only the equal redistribution of land according to the number of persons can win over the broad masses of poor peasants when the struggle goes on intensely. Even in respect to the promotion of production, it would also be more advantageous to implement equal redistribution according to the number of persons than unequal redistribution according to labor power. Western Fukien provides good evidence. In western Fukien, land is redistributed equally according to the number of persons. The rice promises a fine crop this year. It is expected that the crop will probably be 20 per cent more than last year, when land was not yet redistributed. Some comrades in western Fukien used to worry that "land would be divided into too small pieces," and that "those who never did any farming before would not know how to farm if they are allotted land, and consequently the land that may be allotted them would become waste." Behind these and other worries was the danger of reduction in production. Now the facts have shown that all the worries are unwarranted. On the contrary, [production] has not only been not decreased, but increased. Why? Because the poor peasants and the jobless masses have devoted all their manpower to the land they have received. All former nonproductive parasites in the villages, like landlords and idlers, are obliged to farm now or else they will have nothing to eat. The labor power of some of the poor peasants which was formerly left unused for lack of land is being put to use, now that land has been assigned them. For this reason, production has been on the increase.

Moreover, agricultural production in China is still in the stage of manual farming, manual irrigation, and manual application of fertilizers (human manure, animal manure, and so on). During the period of exploitation by landlords, the poor peasants, knowing that the land did not belong to them, were not willing to do the so-called "deep plowing and frequent weeding" at all. Nor were they willing to do anything to improve irrigation, nor willing to use more fertilizers, or were simply too lazy to gather fertilizers. Consequently, more and more land has become neglected and production has been greatly reduced, with the result that a general agricultural crisis has befallen the whole country.

In contrast, the peasants in western Fukien in particular have now been allotted land, and each person gets his share on the basis of equal redistribution. Accordingly, they have given up all their sabotaging practices of the past and are now willing to do the deep plowing. They are spending a sizable portion of their manpower in repairing ponds and ditches, and this is totally different from the situation in the days of exploitation by the landlords and rich peasants when the ponds and ditches were not taken care of at all. Without equal redistribution, it would not be possible [for the peasants] to devote a sizable portion of manpower to repairing ponds and ditches. They are cutting weeds and putting them in pigsties and cowpens to make animal manure. They are digging up the grass and soaking it in water to make refuse and combining it with human night soil and urine, with the consequence that the problem of fertilizers has been solved. All these are the results of the equal redistribution of land and the mobilization of large-scale manpower. They have led to the increase of production.

If one says that without draft cattle they [the peasants] cannot farm even if they receive their land allotments, then [one must realize that] those who used to lease their draft cattle from the rich peasants will no longer have a problem since they can use the draft cattle seized from the rich peasants (they no longer need to pay rent for their use). As to those who formerly could not afford even to lease any draft cattle, they can now borrow or lease such cattle from their relatives and friends on occasion.

If one says that there are not enough farm implements available, then they [the peasants] may borrow the surplus implements from the rich peasants (if the surplus land of the rich peasants is confiscated, they will have surplus implements available), or even confiscate the surplus farm implements of the rich peasants.

If one says that the division of land into too-small pieces is not good for production, then [one must realize that] this phenomenon exists only in large-scale corporation agriculture. The fact is that there is little, if any, corporation agriculture in China. The prevailing picture is one of small peasants' production. Even the landholdings of big landlords are rented out to many peasants to cultivate, not to a single peasant household in a lump. Actually, there is not such a thing as dividing the land into too-small pieces so as to make them unfit for production. In addition, we in the sphere of agriculture must encourage the poor peasants to proceed from collective production to the road of socialism, but not encourage the rich peasants to head for capitalist production. Our objective is for the poor peasants to put their numerous small pieces of land together to set up a system of production so as to move in the direction of socialist agricultural production.

In revolutionary times, the prices of agricultural products are particularly low. There develops the phenomenon of the "scissors crisis."[1] scissors. The rich peasants have more than sufficient land. But as the farming brings them no profit, they are simply not enthusiastic about it In the end, this is damaging to production.

In case the number of the members of a family who can engage in labor is smaller than that of those who cannot, equal redistribution of land would not cause any decrease in production, either. For the minority of the members of the family who have labor power can usually bear the responsibility of providing food for the whole family. Moreover, those who cannot engage in labor are not entirely without labor power. They can still help in work of one kind or another. There are very few cases of big families in which those who cannot engage in labor are exceptionally more numerous than those who can (let us say, nine to one). In such cases, the land assigned to those families may be returned to the Soviets to be transferred to others for cultivation. Thus, the land will not lie waste, either.

---

[1] This name, given to the period 1922-23 in Russia, is from a diagram Trotsky used in a speech which showed the intersection of a falling rural price curve and a rising urban price curve, resembling a scissors.

13. The rich peasants ask for the retention of public land and take advantage of the slogan of joint production

The Soviet model farms and the collective production of the type of cooperatives are good methods to lead agriculture to socialization. But at the present stage of the struggle, the principal task of the Soviets is to direct the struggle, but not to develop production. For this reason, we cannot operate model farms just now. In order to win over the masses and expand the struggle, we must redistribute all the land to those who need it. It is not necessary for the Soviets to retain public land. Forests and surplus houses should also be redistributed, as a rule, if the masses need them.

Because the Soviets will need money or because they themselves are expecting babies next year, some people hold that land should not be redistributed wholesale but some public land should be retained and that forests and surplus houses should not be redistributed at all. There are others who outwardly stand on the Left and advocate the so-called "socialist joint production": (All land is to be operated by the Soviets under the direction of which the peasants will cultivate it with their own labor. The products will be apportioned according to the needs of the population. That which is left over will belong to the Soviets.) To this group of people belong Yüan Wen-tsai of Kiangsi, Fu Po-ts'ui of Fukien, *et al.*, who are all advocates of the rich-peasant line. They represent a subtle deceptive policy of the clever rich peasants to try to slow down the efforts of the poor peasants to redistribute land at a time of the revolutionary upsurge. For what really concerns the poor peasants is not whether they are going to have babies next year, but whether they will have anything to eat next year. For this reason, the demand of the poor peasants is for a quick redistribution of all land. To reserve some public land in anticipation of newborn babies next year is not necessary at all in the eyes of the poor peasants.

As to socialist production, it will have to be postponed until after land is redistributed and feudalistic relationships are thoroughly eradicated. Only then will the poor peasants form cooperatives to undertake collective farming. Only after the success of the revolution throughout the country will the Soviets select locations to operate farms themselves. All this will lead to socialism. To follow the policy of Soviet operation without first going through the process of redistribution and the process of cooperatives is entirely an illusion of the petty bourgeoisie. It will objectively obstruct the land struggle and lead the land revolution to failure. It will fundamentally destroy the future of socialism.

14. The uncut rice goes with the land when redistributed

It was formerly our policy to give the one crop of the land immediately following redistribution to those who had originally cultivated the land if land redistribution took place after the seeds had been sown. This policy would satisfy only the rich peasants, while it would greatly dissatisfy the poor peasants. Under this policy, where there was only one crop a year, the poor peasants and jobless masses, though nominally assigned land, would actually have to wait until the fall of the next year before they could reap their first rice crop. Where there were two crops a year, they had also to wait until the second crop. For this reason, the poor peasants and jobless masses were all dissatisfied.

What should be done is that when the land is redistributed, the crop of the land should, *ipso facto*, belong to those who have received the land. Though this may dissatisfy the rich peasants, it will have the support of the poor peasants and jobless masses.

Suppose a compensation is made to the rich peasants for the crop taken away from them: that is also a measure designed to protect the interests of the rich peasants. To meet the needs of the poor peasants, no compensation should be made to the rich peasants at all, because the poor peasants have no money to pay.

15. Grains may also be equally redistributed

As the struggle in the villages develops to the point of violent uprising, when the poor peasants, hired farm hands, and jobless masses are plunged in a struggle of beating village bosses and gentry and burning their title deeds, there will certainly be a struggle for an equal redistribution of the grains, which will be followed by a struggle for an equal redistribution of land. Accordingly, the equal redistribution of the grains is an important item in the struggle in the villages.

If the struggle for an equal redistribution of the grains is thorough enough, it will be necessary to apportion in equal terms not only the grains of the landlords but also the grains of the rich peasants. All the grains available in a township are to be divided by the total population of that township. Thus, the surplus grains of all households will be redistributed on an equal basis without compensation.

If we in this struggle take the point of view of the rich peasants and raise the slogan "Object to absolute egalitarianism," we are bound to lose the masses of the poor peasants. Obviously, this will not do. Beyond a doubt, we must take the point of view of the poor peasants, hired farm hands, and other poor and miserable masses and launch a struggle for an equal redistribution of the grains.

In times of guerrilla warfare, when our political power cannot possibly be secure even for a short moment in certain places, the method of "looting the grains" will have to be adopted. Though the principal aim is to loot the grains of the landlords, we must give full support to the action of the masses if they want to loot the grains of the rich peasants, too.

16. Raising funds from the rich peasants is not blind actionism

It would be all right for the guerrilla units of the Red Army and the Soviets to requisition money from the rich peasants. In the past the masses were stopped from raising funds from the rich peasants on the ground that this was a case of blind action. This has stemmed from the standpoint of winning over the rich peasants, and it is fundamentally wrong.

17. Draw-on-the-fat-to-make-up-for-the-lean

If the equal redistribution of land is carried out solely on the basis of "draw-on-the-plentiful-to-make-up-for-the-scarce," such as the occurrences last year in western Fukien, where official documents also told people "not to entertain any illusory hopes of equality," then the rich peasants are actually emboldened to give lean land to others and keep fat land for themselves. Certainly, this would cause great dissatisfaction to the poor peasants. As a matter of fact, this has happened not only in western Fukien, but also in almost all other places. This is really an important struggle in the course of the land struggle, and we must not overlook it. In addition to "draw-on-the-plentiful-to-make-up-for-the-scarce," we must lay down the principle of "draw-on-the-fat-to-make-up-for-the-lean." Besides, the phrase in official documents, "not to entertain any illusory hopes of equality," should be changed to read: "not to keep fat land for oneself."

18. Oppose the rich-peasant slogan for investigation and study; land must be redistributed quickly

Many members of the Communist Party who are of rich-peasant origin have tried to obstruct the land struggle by delaying land redistribution. Their excuse is that their investigation is not yet finished and their study is still under way. Following the uprising, there have been cases in which land has not yet been redistributed after three years of investigation and study. There have also been cases in which land has not been redistributed after one year of investigation and study. We must basically object to this sort of investigation and study, which is nothing but idle talk. So far as the question of the practical redistribution of land is concerned, we simply do not need the investigation and study of the superior organs. Land can be redistributed as soon as the township government has investigated it. Land must be redistributed very fast in order that a thorough mobilization of the masses may take place quickly and the influence of the revolution may spread quickly. Where the masses have risen in revolt, land redistribution must be completed in not more than two weeks.

19. *The land tax should be based on the principle of protecting the poor peasants, winning over the middle peasants, and attacking the rich peasants*

The objective of imposing a progressive agricultural tax on land is to supply the financial needs of the struggle. With this objective in view, the principle is to protect the poor peasants, win over the middle peasants, and attack the rich peasants. To meet the financial needs of the struggle, the poor peasants certainly must pay a certain amount of land tax, though it must be very low, and the extremely poor of them (who have not enough to eat every year) should be exempted from taxation. The middle peasants are required to pay a bit more than the poor peasants, but this should not run counter to the principle of winning over the middle peasants. That is to say, the middle peasants must not be called upon to pay too heavy a tax. As to the rich peasants, a land tax as high as 15 per cent may be collected from them. To meet the urgent needs of the struggle, the surplus food of the rich peasants may be requisitioned without compensation.

20. *There will still be rich peasants after land redistribution*

In attacking the rich peasants at present, our principal aim is not to annihilate them, but to win over the masses of poor peasants, to enlarge the struggle, and to win a victory for the revolution. In reality, the rich peasants will not cease to exist after they have been attacked. For the rich peasants have a variety of advantageous social and economic conditions. Even after their land has been redistributed, they will still have an advantage over the poor peasants. They will certainly grow more quickly than the poor peasants. The poor peasants and hired farm hands, on their part, will continue to suffer from the rich peasants' exploitation. (The principal forms of such exploitation will be commercial transactions such as buying when prices are low and selling when prices are high, and running small stores.)

In a very real sense, the rich peasants cannot be annihilated and the poor peasants and hired farm hands cannot be freed from the exploitation by rich peasants until after a nationwide success of the democratic revolution, plus a nationwide success of the socialist revolution that will follow. By then agriculture will have been socialized. It will have been socialized through the efforts of the poor peasants and hired farm hands themselves, with the assistance and direction of the urban workers. Then the capitalist production of the rich peasants will be replaced by socialized production. Then all peasants will become proletarians and no exploitation whatever will exist in the rural districts. This is the common goal toward which the industrial proletariat and their vanguard, the Communist Party, have wanted to lead the peasants.

21. Criticisms are meant to encourage the poor peasants to move forward, but not to throw cold water on them

When the masses rise up enthusiastically to carry out the equal redistribution of land, criticisms like "illusory hopes of equality" and "illusions of the petty bourgeoisie" are often utilized by those members of the Communist Party who are of rich-peasant origin to distort their meanings and to resist the poor peasants' struggle for an equal redistribution of land. Instances of this kind can be found almost everywhere. To the poor peasants who are enthusiastically engaging themselves in the struggle, this has the feel of a ladleful of cold water poured over them, and it necessarily causes disappointment. Criticisms which we have originally proposed to practice do not mean that the redistribution of land is no good. What they do mean is this: As far as the rural districts are concerned, a redistribution of land will mean that the system of private property has not yet been abolished and that the Communist system remains to be realized. Thus, the exploitation of the poor peasants by the rich peasants will continue to exist. For this reason, the poor peasants after land redistribution must go a step further to head for socialism so as to win a final victory.

[On the other hand,] as far as the whole country is concerned, a redistribution of land cannot bring in its train a combination of the strengths of the workers and peasants to overthrow the capitalists and imperialism. Capitalism will not only continue to exploit the peasants, but will do so more severely than before. The consequence will be a cruel phenomenon of "scissors crisis" in the villages. Though they have food to eat, the masses will have no clothes to wear and no goods to consume. All agricultural products will be terribly cheap, while all other goods, like cloth, terribly expensive. The living of the peasants will be as painful and miserable as ever.

If the peasants want to avert a "scissors crisis," they can only expand the Red Army and spread the struggle. They must help the working class to win a victory in overthrowing the capitalists and imperialism in the big cities all over the country. Then the Soviets will rule over the entire nation. At the same time the high tide of the global revolution will be stepped up and the capitalism of the whole world toppled. Not until then can the peasants secure the help of the working class in the whole country and even the whole world to put an end to the sufferings caused by the "scissors crisis."

Our comrades in every Red village should explain the (above-mentioned) political and economic conditions in the rural districts and indeed in the whole country to the peasants by all means and on all occasions that present themselves. The peasants must be encouraged to move a step forward, and must not be pulled back a step in conformity with the point of view of the rich peasants.

Criticisms should begin after the success of the struggle of land redistribution. If they are practiced amidst the desperate violence of the struggle of land redistribution, they would not only be easily distorted and exploited by the rich peasants, but also make it possible to let two different goals (democracy and socialism) appear in the eyes of the masses so as to confuse their minds. The masses can only understand the goal of the present stage, but not the goal of the next stage, before the goal of the present stage is reached. If we, before the attainment of the goal of the present stage, do not encourage the masses to do what they can to reach this goal, but let it go and encourage them to reach the goal of the next stage, the masses would have misgivings like this: "Now you say this is good. Now you say that is good. After all, which is good?" This danger can be avoided if criticisms begin after the success of the struggle of land redistribution on the part of the masses (the struggle of land redistribution can be completed in two weeks' time).

22. Suppress rich peasants in organizations

1. In order to safeguard the victory of the land revolution it is necessary, first of all, to suppress the rich-peasant elements in the party.

In order to win over the masses of poor peasants and hired farm hands for a resolute offensive against the rich peasants, to establish the leadership of the poor peasants and hired farm hands in the villages, and to safeguard the victory of the land revolution in the villages, it is necessary, first of all, to suppress the rich-peasant elements in the party, especially the party units in the villages. This task is extremely important. For the local party organizations, especially their directing organs, have been filled with rich-peasant elements everywhere, from the past to the present. This has resulted from the fact that before the struggle was launched in the villages, those who were sent by the higher level official organs to work in the villages were first met by intellectuals who, for the most part, started out as rich peasants and small landlords. As time went by, those intellectuals ushered in others who were, of course, all birds of a feather. As the struggle in the villages has been unfolded, those party members with rich-peasant and small-landlord backgrounds have become the cadres in the directing organs of various levels above the branches. The fact that the struggle has developed so slowly and superficially is all due to the mischiefs made by this group of people. Directives from the higher level directing organs have been stopped by them from reaching the masses. This has lasted until the mass struggle has reached the point of breaking through their opportunistic leadership, and the anti-rich-peasant policy of the higher level directing organs has brought pressure to bear on them. In this way the anti-rich-peasant policy of higher level directing organs has combined with the mass struggle to liquidate the rich-peasant line in the directing organs of all levels. This process of work has been gone through almost in every place.

Obviously, if the rich peasants (notably in the directing organs) are not purged, the mass struggle cannot possibly rise. The unconditional expulsion of the rich peasants and all the followers of the rich-peasant line from the party is a prior condition for winning over the masses to safeguard the success of the struggle in the villages. How should the rich peasants be purged? Whoever has been seen following the rich-peasant line in the course of various struggles should be purged immediately.

2. The rich peasants should not be allowed to join the Soviets.

In order to establish the leadership of the poor peasants and hired farm hands in the villages, and to prevent a possible leading role on the part of the rich peasants, there is another basic measure to be taken besides suppressing the rich peasants in the party: depriving the rich peasants of their right to vote. All former and present rich peasants must not be allowed to take part in Soviet elections, much less to be elected as Soviet representatives or officials of other political organs. This will be an important factor in assuring the transition from democ-

racy to socialism. If this important factor is overlooked, we are bound
to make serious mistakes.

23. Develop a theory for the struggle against rich peasants

Not only should the rich peasants be expelled from the organizations;
even more important is to develop a theory for the struggle against the
rich peasants. Either in the party or among the masses, this theory for
the struggle against the rich peasants should be developed as far as
possible. Only in this way can the rich-peasant line be basically overcome. In practice, it is not only necessary to overthrow the leadership
of the rich peasants at present, but also to make it impossible for them
to rise again in the future.

DOCUMENT 27

PROVISIONAL REGULATIONS FOR THE
HIRED-FARM-HAND UNION

Printed by the General Political Department,
Central Revolutionary Military Council,
Chinese Soviet Areas, February, 1931
(As reproduced in *A Collection of Red Bandit Secret*
Documents, Vol. II, leaves 31–35)

CHAPTER I. GENERAL PROVISIONS

Article 1: This union shall be known as "The . . . Hired-Farm-Hand
Union."

Article 2: The purposes of this union are:

1. To consolidate the strength of the hired farm hands in order to
set up organizations of class struggle.

2. To practice the class struggle, resist all oppression and exploitation, and fight for the liberation of the working class.

3. To strengthen leadership over the poor and miserable laboring
masses in the rural districts and participate in all struggles for the land
revolution and for the consolidation and expansion of the Soviets.

CHAPTER II. MEMBERSHIP

Article 3: All hired farm hands who accept the purposes, regulations,
and decisions of this union may be admitted to the membership of this

union. The hired farm hands are the workers who sell their labor only and do productive work in the rural districts. Only those hired farm hands who work on a long-term or temporary basis as the principal source of their livelihood may be admitted to the hired-farm-hand union. Those who used to work on a long-term basis but who have now been allotted land may not be admitted to it, while those who have been allotted land but who still work on a long-term basis may be admitted to it.

Article 4: Members of this union shall have the following duties:

1. To observe and execute all decisions and orders of this union absolutely.

2. To pay membership fees and extraordinary contributions in accordance with the present regulations.

3. To attend all meetings to be called by this union.

Article 5: Members of this union shall have the following rights:

1. The right to vote, the right to be elected, and the right to express opinions and make recommendations on the affairs of this union.

2. The right to enjoy the benefits of the educational, cultural, and mutual-aid enterprises sponsored by this union.

CHAPTER III. ORGANIZATION

Article 6: All the labor unions which fall under the jurisdiction of this union shall be organized in accordance with the regulations promulgated by this union. Every three or more members may form a small group of hired farm hands. Members of every three or more small groups of hired farm hands may form a branch of hired farm hands. Every three or more branches of hired farm hands may form a district hired-farm-hand union. Every three or more district hired-farm-hand unions may form a county hired-farm-hand union. Every three or more county hired-farm-hand unions may form a provincial hired-farm-hand-union or a Soviet special-area hired-farm-hand union.

Article 7: This union is based on the principle of democratic centralism. All important matters of this union shall be decided upon or passed by the congress of delegates or the all-member congress of this union. The organs of all levels (all executive committees, executive councils, chiefs of small groups) shall be elected by the delegates. When the congress of delegates is not in session, the executive committee shall be the organ of the highest authority.

Article 8: The organization of the agencies of this union at all levels shall be decided upon according to the actual number of the hired farm hands in the locality.

Article 9: The system of organization of this union shall be as follows: [The original chart, as its translation below indicates, is not clear.]

Special-area hired-farm-hand union	District hired-farm-hand union	[Name of place] branch of the hired-farm-hand union	Hired-farm-hand small group
Provincial hired-farm-hand union	[Not clear] hired-farm-hand union	[Name of place] branch of the hired-farm-hand union	Hired-farm-hand small group
County hired-farm-hand union	. . . .	. . . .	Hired-farm-hand small group

CHAPTER IV. THE CONGRESS OF DELEGATES

Article 10: The congress of delegates or the all-member congress shall be the organ of the highest authority of this union. Its functions and powers are as follows:

1. To decide on the regulations of this union and the principles and plans of the prosecution of its work.

2. To elect and recall members of the executive committee.

3. To adopt workers and to participate in the organization and struggle of the revolutionary workers in the rural areas, special areas, and, indeed, the whole country.

4. To adopt the budget, the financial statement, and the methods of raising funds.

Article 11: The congress of delegates of this union shall meet at least once every three months. In case of necessity, a special meeting may be convened by the executive committee. The all-member congress shall meet at least once every three months.

Article 12: The members of the congress of delegates of this union shall be elected once a year in proportion to the number of its members. Therefore, the tenure of office of a delegate is one year. In case a delegate is derelict in duty, he may be recalled by resolution of the congress of delegates of the labor union which has elected him.

CHAPTER V. EXECUTIVE COMMITTEE

Article 13: The executive committee of this union shall be appointed by the congress of delegates or the all-member congress. The executive committee shall in its plenary session elect———persons to organize a standing committee and elect a chairman. The executive committee shall be responsible to the congress of delegates. The branch shall establish an executive council to be composed of three to five members who shall be elected by the all-member congress. The small group shall establish a chief to be elected by its members in a plenary session. The tenure of office of a member of the executive committee on and above the county level shall be one year, that of a member of the district executive committee, six months, and that of the director of the branch or the chief of the small group, three months.

Article 14: There shall be established under the executive committee a department of organization, a department of propaganda, a secretariat, a committee on education, and a committee for financial safekeeping. [Some original Chinese characters missing here.] The directors of the various departments and the chairmen of the various committees shall be members of the executive committee concurrently. Under the executive council of the branch there shall be one officer in charge of organization and another in charge of propaganda, both of whom shall be members of the executive council concurrently.

Article 15: The executive committee shall meet at least once a month. In case of necessity, it may meet in special session to be convened by the standing committee. The executive committee of the district union shall meet at least once every two weeks. The standing committee or executive council at each of the various levels shall meet at least once every three days. The small group shall meet at least once every seven days.

CHAPTER VI. AFFAIRS OF THIS UNION

Article 16: The major affairs of this union are as follows:

1. To lead struggles: There shall be constant plans to lead and direct the labor unions at all levels, or to lead their members to wage all kinds of struggles; to resist all exploitation and oppression of the hired farm hands; to rally the poor peasants and middle peasants around this union; and to carry out all struggles for the consolidation and expansion of the Soviets.

2. Work of organization: To organize the hired-farm-hand unions at all levels, guide the subordinate labor unions at all levels to reform their work, and build up cadres of the hired-farm-hand unions.

3. Work of propaganda: To use oral or written propaganda such as leaflets, pamphlets, pictorials, and so forth to enlarge the scope of

revolutionary propaganda and to direct the work of propaganda at all levels.

4. Work of education: To run workers' schools, clubs, physical education associations, book and newspaper societies, and public speech meetings, so as to raise the political and cultural levels of the workers.

5. Work of the economic committee: To be responsible for the safe-keeping and management of the economic [*sic*] expenditures of this union.

CHAPTER VII. DISCIPLINE

Article 17: All labor unions at the various levels which violate the resolutions, regulations, and programs of struggle of this union shall be cautioned or warned by the executive committee of this union. If they remain intransigent, they may be reorganized by the congress of delegates or all-member congress of the hired-farm-hand union of the respective level at a meeting specially called for the purpose.

Article 18: Members of the executive committees, staff members, and members of all the subordinate hired-farm-hand unions of this union at various levels who violate the regulations and resolutions of this union and who act against the interests of the hired-farm-hand class may be removed from office or from membership of this union if they remain intransigent despite warning. Serious cases shall be dealt with severely.

Article 19: All work and activities of the subordinate labor unions of this union shall be reported to this union. Important matters may not be carried out until they have been approved.

CHAPTER VIII. FUNDS

Article 20: The incomes of this union shall come from the following sources:

1. All the subordinate levels of this union shall earmark a certain percentage of the income of each member to be sent to this union as membership fee.

2. In case of necessity, free contributions and extraordinary contributions may be solicited, with the approval of the congress of delegates or the all-member congress, from the members of this union.

Article 21: All incomes and expenses of this union shall be clearly accounted for and publicly announced every month.

Chapter IX. [blank]

Article 22: The provisions of the present regulations which may be found to be no longer applicable may be amended by resolution of the congress of delegates of this union.

Article 23: The present regulations shall be adopted by the congress of delegates of this union and come into force after its promulgation by the executive committee.

DOCUMENT 28

REGULATIONS FOR THE POOR-PEASANT ASSOCIATION

*By the General Political Department, Central Revolutionary Military Council, Chinese Soviet Areas;
reprinted by the Ning-tu County Soviet Government,
February, 1931*
(As reproduced in *A Collection of Reactionary Documents*, Vol. I, book 4, leaves 10–15)

Chapter I. General Provisions

Article 1: This association shall be known as "The . . . Poor-Peasant Association."

Article 2: The purposes of this association are:

1. To consolidate the strength of the poor and miserable laboring masses in the rural districts in order to fight for their interests and their liberation.

2. To carry out the land revolution thoroughly and deeply, practice the class struggle, and resist all oppression and exploitation.

3. To support the Soviets and fight for their victory in the whole country.

4. To ally with the middle peasants and support them in their opposition to all oppression and exploitation.

5. To participate in all revolutionary struggles and expand and intensify them in order to make it possible for the Chinese revolution to head for socialism.

Chapter II. Membership

Article 3: Qualifications for membership:

1. Poor peasants (who till land, suffer from an insufficient domestic economy, and are subject to exploitation), hired laborers (who only sell their labor and do productive work on a long-term or short-term basis in the rural districts), manual workers (who are willing to sell their labor directly to shop proprietors or contractors, such as paper-making workers in paper mills and woodworkers in big carpenters' shops), coolies (who sell their labor as burden carriers or cart pushers), and handicraftsmen (who have tools and employers but no assistants and apprentices, such as carpenters, tailors, and so forth), in the rural districts may all be admitted to this association as members.

2. All members of this association shall be required to observe the present regulations and all its decisions. A person may be admitted to this association as a full member only on the recommendation of a worker.

Article 4: Members of this association shall have the following duties:

1. To observe the regulations and orders of this association.

2. To pay membership fees and extraordinary contributions in accordance with the present regulations.

3. To attend meetings in accordance with the present regulations, carry out their resolutions, and perform all tasks assigned [to them] by this association.

Article 5: Members of this association shall have the following rights:

1. The right to vote, the right to be elected, and the right to express opinions and make recommendations on the affairs of this association.

2. The right to enjoy the benefits of the educational, cultural, and cooperative enterprises sponsored by this association.

CHAPTER III. ORGANIZATION

Article 6: The organization of this association is based on the principle of democratic centralism. All important matters of this association shall be decided upon or passed by the congress of delegates or the all-member congress of this association. The executive committee shall be elected by the congress of delegates or the all-member congress. When the congress of delegates is not in session, the executive committee shall be the highest directing body. The executive committee shall be responsible to the congress of delegates or the all-member congress.

Article 7: The system of organization of this association shall be as follows:

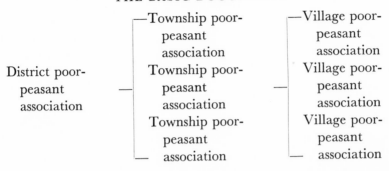

Article 8: This association shall have only three levels of organization: village, township, and district. Three village poor-peasant associations may form a township poor-peasant association, and three township poor-peasant associations may form a district poor-peasant association. There shall be no poor-peasant association from the county level on. All work [of the different associations] shall be carried out under the control and guidance of the Soviet Government.

CHAPTER IV. CONGRESS OF DELEGATES

Article 9: The township delegates of this association shall be elected by the village all-member congress in proportion to the number of its members. The district delegates shall be elected by the township congress of delegates. The tenure of office of all delegates shall be one year. In case of a dereliction of duty on the part of the district and township delegates, the village all-member congress may have them recalled.

Article 10: The congress of delegates is the highest authority of this association. Its functions are as follows:

1. To decide on the progress, planning, and so on of the work of this association.

2. To elect and recall members of the executive committee and representatives of this association.

3. To pass and examine the budget of this association and make arrangements for [the collection of] the general operating funds and special expenses.

4. To consider and propose programs of struggle for this association. (In special circumstances, the executive committee may exercise this function.)

5. When the congress of delegates is not in session, the executive committee shall be the highest authority [of this association].

Article 11: The congress of delegates of this association on the district and township levels shall meet once every two months, while the all-member congress on the village level shall meet twice a month. Small groups shall meet once every ten days. In case of necessity, special meetings may be convened by the [executive] committee.

Chapter V. Executive Committee

Article 12: There shall be seven to nine members of the district executive committee, to be elected by the district congress of delegates; five to seven members of the township executive committee, to be elected by the township congress of delegates; and three to five members of the village executive committee, to be elected by the village congress of the poor peasants. Chiefs of small groups shall be elected by [members of] the small groups.

Article 13: During the period when the congress of delegates of this association is not in session, the executive committee shall be the highest authority of this association. Its functions are as follows:

1. To carry out all resolutions, either of the congress of delegates of this association or of higher authorities, and to be responsible for the conduct of the affairs of this association.

2. To take part in all the revolutionary struggles under the leadership of the Soviet Government.

3. To execute all affairs of this association as prescribed by it.

Article 14: The district executive committee shall elect [from among themselves] three members to form a standing committee for the transaction of daily business. A chairman shall be elected to preside over meetings of the executive committee and the standing committee. On the township or village level, there shall be elected only a chairman rather than a standing committee.

Article 15: There shall be established under the district executive committee five sections in charge of organization, propaganda, youth affairs, finance, and women's affairs, respectively, and under the township or village executive committee three sections in charge of organization, propaganda, and finance, respectively. There shall be created an educational committee on the district or township level. The chiefs of sections and the chairman of the educational committee shall be chosen from among members of the executive committees. Under the village poor-peasant association there shall be organized small groups of hired laborers, manual workers, handicraft workers, and coolies, respectively. The poor peasants shall be organized into small groups according to their geographical location, and there shall be a chief for each small group.

A. *Organization of the district poor-peasant association*

District congress of delegates
↓
District executive committee
↓
Standing committee
↓
Chairman
—Organization section
Propaganda section
Youth-affairs section
→ Women's affairs section
Finance section
—Educational committee

B. *Organization of the township or village poor-peasant association*

Township congress of delegates (or village congress of delegates)
↓
Township or village executive committee
↓
Chairman
—Organization section
→ Propaganda section
—Finance section

Village poor-peasant association
Village executive committee
—Small group of hired laborers
Small group of handicraft workers
→ Small group of coolies
—Small group of poor peasants

Article 16: The district executive committee shall meet once a month. The standing committee shall have no fixed dates to meet, but shall meet at least once every five days. The township executive committee shall meet at least once every ten days and the village executive committee at least once every ten days [also]. As a general rule, there shall be no regular staff of personnel working in the offices of the executive committees on the various levels. In case of need, the district executive committee may have some regular personnel working in its office.

Article 17: The executive committee of this association and its subordinate associations shall work hard to further the affairs of this association in accordance with the decisions of the congress of delegates and of the all-member congress.

CHAPTER VI. AFFAIRS OF THIS ASSOCIATION

Article 18:

The major affairs of this association are as follows:

1. To support the Soviets and to take part, under Soviet leadership, in all struggles for the consolidation and expansion of the Soviets.

2. [To take part in] all kinds of struggles to carry out the land revolution thoroughly and deeply.

3. To practice the class struggle, oppose all oppression and exploitation (such as the exploitation by rich peasants in the hiring of poor and miserable laboring masses, usurious loans, and compulsory purchase and sale), and fight for the benefit and liberation of the poor and miserable laboring masses.

4. To organize various kinds of cooperatives in order to promote the welfare of the poor and miserable laboring masses.

5. To hold joint meetings with the middle peasants and ally with them in order to carry out all struggles against exploitation and oppression.

6. Work of organization: to develop and consolidate the organization of this association on various levels and to foster and train cadres of this association.

7. Work of propaganda: to edit and publish this association's bulletins, pictorials, wall papers, posters, and pamphlets; to train propaganda teams, and supervise the propaganda work of the various [subordinate] associations.

8. Youth work: to lead the masses of young workers and peasants to take part in revolutionary struggles, and pay attention to their special training.

9. Women's affairs: to arouse and lead the poor and miserable laboring women to take part, under Soviet laws and decrees, in various kinds of struggles in order to fight for the liberation of women.

10. Financial affairs: planning, safekeeping and [*sic*] financial matters of this association.

CHAPTER VII. DISCIPLINE

Article 19: Any member of this association who does not observe the present regulations, nor acts in the interests of the poor and miserable masses, nor carries out the decisions of this association, shall be punished, according to the seriousness of the cases, with warning, or being put under watch, or expulsion from this association.

Article 20: If a [member] of the committee on the various levels does not carry out his work in the interests of the poor peasants or violates the decisions of this association, he may be removed through re-election or dismissal by the executive committee of a higher level, by the congress of delegates, or by the all-member congress.

CHAPTER VIII. MEMBERSHIP FEES

Article 21: The incomes of this association shall come from the following sources:

1. Membership fees: every member shall pay two coppers per month as membership fee.

2. Extraordinary contributions: in case of necessity and with the approval of the congress of delegates, extraordinary contributions may be solicited from members according to their economic position, as well as from nonmembers.

3. Suitable amounts of subsidies from the government.

Article 22: All incomes and expenses of this association shall be clearly accounted for and publicly announced every month.

CHAPTER IX. SUPPLEMENTARY PROVISIONS

Article 23: The present regulations shall be adopted by the congress of delegates and come into force from the day of its promulgation by the executive committee.

Article 24: Any inadequacies which may be found in the present regulations may be examined and amended by the all-district congress of delegates.

DOCUMENT 29

ORGANIC LAW OF THE POOR-PEASANT ASSOCIATION AND ITS TASKS

Circular No. 20 of the CCP Southwest Kiangsi
Special Area Committee, n.d., probably 1931
(As reproduced in *A Collection of Red Bandit*
Secret Documents, Vol. II, leaves 35–38)

1. The Chief Significance of the Poor-Peasant Association

Never since the beginning of the revolution has the party in southwest Kiangsi made a very accurate analysis of the rural economy. Accordingly, our class concept regarding the peasantry has been extremely hazy. We have not been able to understand the serious economic and political exploitation and oppression suffered by the poor peasants, nor their urgent need for the revolution. We have not been able to understand the counterrevolutionary character of the rich peasants. Thus, it has been possible for the landlords and rich peasants to take advantage of this situation to infiltrate into the party, occupying positions of leadership. Once the landlords and rich peasants have occupied positions of leadership, it has been natural that they have not only been unwilling to see a class line of battle [unfolded] in the rural districts, but have also purposely intended to make the class concept regarding the peasantry all the more hazy.

However, the waves of revolution among the masses keep on surging. The landlords and rich peasants in the party not only cannot be expected to play a firm role of leadership by standing in front of the masses, but also they would inevitably display panic and fear, thus obstructing and hindering the progress of the revolution. Hence, the growth of the subjective strength of the party has not been able to keep pace with the development of the objective situation. [The party] has lagged behind the masses and become their tails [so to speak]. As is natural, the more thoroughgoing the struggle, the clearer the class differentiations. Also, the landlords and rich peasants in the party have become more dissatisfied. They have not only wanted to try to hinder the progress of the revolution but also to go a step further and destroy it. That is why the A-B League, the Liquidationists, and the Reorganizationists have grown in strength throughout southwest Kiangsi and posed a great danger to the future of the revolution.

In order to consolidate the proletarian basis of our party, to save the revolution from its [present] crisis, and to let the Soviet areas make solid strides and have a good foundation among the masses, it is necessary to have the hired farm hands, poor peasants, and coolies united and organized into the poor-peasant association and to rally the middle peasants around it so as to oppose the rich peasants. [Only in this way] can we draw up a clear-cut class line of battle in the rural districts and assure the party of a proletarian basis. Accordingly, the organization of the poor-peasant association is one of the party's central tasks at the present moment.

2. ORGANIC LAW OF THE POOR-PEASANT ASSOCIATION

The organizational system of the poor-peasant association is confined to the township. It is not needed from the district level on. Small groups are to be set up below the township level. Hired-farm-hand small groups are to be set up especially for the hired farm hands and will play a leading role [among] the poor peasants. The organic law of the poor-peasant commission promulgated by the former Provincial Action Committee provided for a systematic organization for the whole province. This was [mixing up] the classes. Obviously, it created two [rival] powers of leadership, one of the working class and the other of the peasant class. It basically denied the leadership of the working class in the Chinese revolution. This was a residue of the Kuomintang type. It was undoubtedly intended to obscure class consciousness and to soft-pedal the class struggle. There can be no doubt that that organic law should no longer be used.

Accordingly, a correct organic law is hereby announced as follows:

A. Organizational system:

$$\text{Township poor-peasant association ...} \begin{cases} \text{—Branch association} \\ \text{Hired-farm-hand} \\ \text{—small group} \end{cases}$$

B. Organic law:

1. The township poor-peasant association shall call a mass meeting of the poor peasants of the whole township, which shall elect seven to nine executive members who shall choose from among themselves three standing members. The standing members shall choose [from among themselves] a chairman, an officer in charge of organization, and another in charge of propaganda. In addition, a secretary-general shall be appointed [by the standing members].

2. A branch association of the poor-peasant association shall be organized with the village as the unit. The branch association shall call a meeting of the poor peasants of the whole village, which shall elect three to five executive members.

3. The hired-farm-hand [small] group shall call a mass meeting of the hired farm hands of the whole township, which shall elect a chairman of the small group and two executive officers. In a [larger] area there may be organized two or more small groups, but each small group shall consist of at least three persons.

    4. The chairman of the township poor-peasant association must be a hired farm hand.

C. *Qualifications for membership of the poor-peasant association:*
    1. Hired farm hands.
    2. Those who have had no or little land and not enough to eat. (Those who hire labor or lend money at usurious rates of interest are not qualified for membership.)
    3. Coolies and poor women.

3. The Chief Tasks of the Poor-Peasant Association

A. *Opposition to rich peasants:*

    Opposition to the rich peasants is the principal task of the poor-peasant association. In our past struggle against the rich peasants, it was considered that to seize their persons and demand money [from them] was the only method that could be used to oppose them. This has been a departure from the chief significance of the opposition to rich peasants. In opposing the rich peasants, we must oppose their economic exploitation, remove their political influence, unfold the class line of battle in the rural districts, and foment the class struggle there. Therefore, the poor-peasant association should resolutely carry out the correct tactics for opposing the rich peasants in order to rectify the mistakes committed in the past.

B. *Thorough redistribution of land:*

    Owing to the fact that the rich peasants have control of political power in many places, not only has the equal redistribution of land not been thoroughly carried out, but there have also been cases of false redistribution of land. For example, in Ku-kiang and An-fu, where there have been too many rounds of land redistribution but the peasants have not yet acquired landownership, the peasant masses openly let it be known that they do not care for any land or are unwilling to till more land. All this has been due to the machinations of the rich peasants. Hereafter the poor-peasant associations shall take up the responsibility of leading the poor and miserable peasants in carrying out land redistribution according to the methods of drawing-on-the-plentiful-to-make-up-for-the-scarce and drawing-on-the-fat-to-make-up-for-the-lean, and this must be done thoroughly and at one stroke. As soon as land is redistributed, its ownership shall be turned over to the peasants. Under Soviet laws and decrees, the institution of the purchase and sale [of land] is not forbidden.

C. *Opposition to all new systems of exploitation:*

We are opposed to exploitation by means of usurious rates of interest, which must be absolutely abolished. Therefore, all debts owed by hired farm hands, poor peasants, and middle peasants to village bosses, gentry, landlords, and rich peasants, as well as other debts of an exploitative character, must be abolished without exception. On the other hand, all debts owed by village bosses, gentry, landlords, and rich peasants to poor peasants, hired farm hands, and middle peasants must be all paid, including principal and interest. Generally speaking, this work has been carried out in the Soviet areas. But it has happened that rich peasants in the Soviet areas have nevertheless made use of the cooperatives to carry out new methods of exploitation. Therefore, it behooves the poor-peasant association to lead the broad peasant masses to combat [such practices] resolutely.

D. *Supervision of the Soviets:*

The agencies of political power in southwest Kiangsi are mostly controlled by rich peasants. Accordingly, they not only cannot work for the benefit of the broad masses of the poor and miserable workers and peasants, but, on the contrary, make the Soviets daily more corrupt, so much so that the Soviets have become new bureaucratic organs. This has been possible because the poor and miserable workers and peasants have not exercised a firm supervision [over the Soviets], but have allowed the wavering *petite bourgeoisie* like rich peasants and rascals to play their dirty tricks. Therefore, the poor-peasant associations should, in the future, call upon the broad masses of the poor and miserable workers and peasants to exercise a firm supervision over the work of the Soviet government. The poor-peasant associations must purge the political power agencies of all rich-peasant elements and choose, instead, active elements among the poor and miserable workers and peasants to work in those agencies.

E. *Alliance with middle peasants:*

The middle peasants are the allies of the proletariat, but whether they will remain unshaken is yet undecided [Chinese original not clear]. As political power has fallen into the hands of the rich peasants in the past, the struggle against the rich peasants has turned out to be directed against the middle peasants (for example, those who had only three silver dollars were taken as rich peasants and became objects of attack) and the rich peasants themselves have escaped unhurt. Such a situation would alienate our allies from the revolution and constitute a very serious danger to the future of the revolution. Therefore, the poor-peasant association should not only endeavor to win over the middle peasants to its side, but also protect their interests and select faithful and courageous representatives of the middle peasants to [work in] the Soviet government.

After receiving this circular, the party headquarters at various levels should discuss it at length and execute it with determination. This is a most important matter to be attended to.

CCP SOUTHWEST KIANGSI SPECIAL AREA COMMITTEE

DOCUMENT 34

LAND LAW OF THE CHINESE SOVIET REPUBLIC

*Adopted by the First National Congress
of the Delegates of the Soviets of the
Chinese Workers, Peasants, and Soldiers
in November, 1931*
(As issued as a proclamation of the Presidium of
the First National Soviet Congress and the
Central Executive Committee of the Chinese
Soviet Government on December 1, 1931)

The peasant struggle led by the proletariat continues to develop and rises to new heights every day. Despite the fanatic resistance offered by the imperialists and warlords, the Soviet movement still grows and expands, making the Chinese peasants more successful every day in arming themselves and organizing the Red Army. The peasants in one county after another have been liberated from oppression imposed on them by feudal landlords, village bosses, and the gentry for thousands of years. They have confiscated and redistributed the landholdings of these oppressors, put an end to the feudal order of society, destroyed the political power of the Kuomintang, and set up the Soviet regime of the workers and peasants—a regime which will be able to accomplish the task of the anti-imperialist and agrarian revolution in China.

The First National Congress of the Delegates of the Soviets of the Chinese Workers, Peasants, and Soldiers hereby approves the confiscation of the land of the landlords and other big private owners. In order to establish a uniform system of the confiscation and redistribution of land, the First [National Soviet] Congress, which rests on the basis of the interests of both the basic peasant masses and the further revolutionary development, has adopted the following land law as the best safeguard for a solution to the land problem.

Article 1: All the lands belonging to feudal landlords, village bosses, gentry, warlords, bureaucrats, and other big private landowners, irrespective of whether they work the lands themselves or rent them out on lease, shall all be confiscated without compensation. The confiscated lands shall be redistributed to the poor and middle peasants through the Soviets. The former owners of the confiscated lands shall not be entitled to receive any land allotments. Hired farm hands, coolies, and toiling peasants, irrespective of sex, shall have an equal right to land allotments. Unemployed independent laborers in the rural districts may likewise be assigned land, subject to the consent of the peasant masses. The aged, infirm, or disabled persons, as well as orphans and widows, who cannot work themselves and have no dependents to rely upon, shall be given social relief by the Soviet government, or be otherwise taken care of after land redistribution.

Article 2: The Red Army is the front-rank fighter in the defense of the Soviet regime and in the overthrow of imperialism. Whether their native places have witnessed the formation of Soviets or are still under the reactionary rule, [the Red Army men] shall all be allotted land, which the Soviet government will make arrangements to cultivate for them.

Article 3: The Chinese rich peasants have the characteristics of being at once semilandlords and usurers. Their land shall be confiscated as well. The land of the middle-peasant class shall not be confiscated. After the confiscation of their land, the rich peasants may be allotted "labor land allotments" of poorer quality on condition that they cultivate such land allotments with their own labor.

Article 4: All the property and lands belonging to organizers of counterrevolution, organizers of the armed forces of the White Army, and active participants in counterrevolution shall be confiscated. Exceptions to this rule shall, however, be made in the case of the poor and middle peasants who have unconsciously been enticed to oppose the Soviets and whose offenses are deemed pardonable by the local Soviets concerned. Their leaders shall unconditionally be dealt with according to the present law.

Article 5: The first [National Soviet] Congress recognizes that the equal redistribution of all land is the most thorough method of destroying all servile and feudal land relations and eliminating the landlords' private ownership. However, the local Soviet governments shall on no account carry out [this measure] by force or by order from above. They shall explain this measure to the peasants from all angles, a measure which can be put into operation only at the desire and with the direct support of the basic peasant masses. If the majority of the middle peasants do not desire it, they may not participate in the equal redistribution [of land].

Article 6: The Soviet government shall see to it that all the lands belonging to ancestral shrines and temples as well as other public lands be handed over to the peasants unconditionally. However, in carrying out and handling [the transfer of] these lands, it shall be essential to obtain the voluntary support of the peasants, so that their religious feelings may not be offended in principle.

Article 7: The better-off peasants seek to have the land redistributed according to the means of production. The First [National Soviet] Congress considers this to be a reactionary attempt on the part of the rich peasants to hinder the development of the land revolution and to further their own ends, and it must be strictly prohibited. In redistributing the land, the local Soviet governments shall, in the light of local conditions in the different townships and villages, choose such a principle for land redistribution as is most favorable to the interests of the poor and middle peasants: either they shall redistribute the land according to the number of persons having labor power in each household and at the same time according to the number of persons [in that household], i.e., they shall adopt a mixed principle; or they shall, in the case of middle and poor peasants and hired farm hands, redistribute the land equally according to the number of persons, and, in the case of rich peasants, adopt labor power as the unit (i.e., in localities where land is equally redistributed according to the number of persons, each rich peasant having labor power shall receive an amount of land equal to that received by each person in equal redistribution according to the number of persons). In redistributing the land, not only its area but also its quality (especially the amount of its harvest) shall be taken into consideration. Furthermore, in redistributing the land, there shall be introduced, as far as possible, suitable land reforms in order to prevent various sorts of feudal relics such as narrow, fragmentary, or excessively big landholdings.

Article 8: All movable and immovable properties, houses, storehouses, livestock, farm implements, and so forth, belonging to feudal lords, warlords, landlords, village bosses, and the gentry shall be confiscated. After rich peasants have been allotted land, their surplus houses, farm implements, livestock, grain-husking water mills, oil-pressing mills, and so on, shall also be confiscated. Acting through the local Soviets in the interests of the poor and middle peasants, the confiscated houses shall be allotted to the poor and middle peasants who have no dwellings of their own, a part of such houses being set aside for the use of schools, clubs, local Soviets, Party and Youth Corps headquarters, Red trade unions, poor-peasant corps and various [other] organs. Livestock and farm implements may be assigned to the poor and middle peasants by groups or by households. The various kinds of the confiscated farm implements may also be used to form rudimentary cooperatives according to the voluntarily expressed opinion of the peasants. They may also be used to establish livestock and farm-implement stations on the recommendation of the peasants with the approval of the Soviets, so that the poor and middle peasants may be able to use them in the cultivation of their land. Such stations will be managed by local Soviets, and the peasants may have to pay reasonable amounts of service fees as prescribed by regulations. A small percentage of the said fees may be used as subsidies for repairing farm implements, supporting workers in the stations, and purchasing new farm implements and livestock.

Article 9: Simultaneously with the confiscation of the property and lands of landlords, village bosses, and the gentry, all oral and written lease contracts shall be annulled, all obligations or debts incurred by the peasants in connection with such property and lands shall be abolished, and all usurious loans shall be declared null and void. All attempts on the part of former landowners and peasants to commit themselves to a voluntary payment of such debts shall be strictly prohibited by revolutionary laws. In addition, the peasants shall not be allowed to return any part of the lands to landlords, village bosses, and the gentry, nor to pay them any part of the debts incurred.

Article 10: All water facilities, rivers, lakes, creeks, forests, pastures, and big mountains shall be managed by the Soviets, which shall carry out construction work there for the sake of common use by the poor and middle peasants. Mulberry fields, bamboo forests, tea-oil plantations, fish ponds, and other assets like rice fields and wheat fields shall be apportioned to the local peasant masses for their use according to their own wishes.

Article 11: In order to make the benefits of the land revolution a tangible and thorough reality, the First National Congress of the Delegates of the Soviets of the Chinese Workers, Peasants, and Soldiers declares that the hired-farm-hand union, the coolie union, and the poor-peasant corps are indispensable bodies. It holds that these organizations are the solid pillars of the land revolution launched by the Soviets.

Article 12: The First National Congress of the Delegates of the Soviets recognizes that the nationalization of land and water facilities under the Soviet regime is a necessary step toward the thorough destruction of all feudal relations in the rural districts—indeed, in effect, toward the achievement of a high and rapid development of the rural economy. However, the carrying out of this measure will practically have to proceed on the precondition that the land revolution is crowned with success in important areas in China and that the basic peasant masses give support to nationalization. At the present stage of the revolution, the Soviets must explain to the peasants the benefits of the nationalization of land and water facilities. But the lease of land or the purchase and sale of land shall, nevertheless, not be forbidden at present. Meanwhile, the Soviet government must strictly stop rich peasants from speculation and landlords from buying back their original land.

Article 13: The local Soviets, if circumstances in the localities permit, shall carry out the following undertakings: (*1*) reclamation of waste land; (*2*) handling affairs of migration; (*3*) improvement of existing irrigation works and construction of new ones; (*4*) promotion of forestation; (*5*) stepping up efforts for the construction of roads, establishment of enterprises, and promotion of the rural economic development.

Article 14: The present law shall apply not only to the existing Soviet areas, but also to non-Soviet areas and areas where Soviet regimes are newly created. The land which has already been redistributed in the various Soviet areas need not be redistributed all over again if it is found to be in conformity with the principles of the present law, while it has to be redistributed afresh if it is not found to be in conformity with the principles of the present law.

> HSIANG YING, CHOU I-LI, TSENG SHAN, TENG FA,
> CHANG TING-CH'ENG, CH'EN CHENG-JEN, CHU TEH
> *Members of the Presidium of the First National*
> *Congress of the Delegates of the Soviets of*

the Chinese Workers, Peasants, and Soldiers

Mao Tse-tung
*Chairman of the Central Executive Committee
of the Chinese Soviet Republic*

Hsiang Ying
Chang Kuo-t'ao
Vice Chairmen

December 1, 1931

DOCUMENT 37

REGULATIONS OF THE KIANGSI PROVINCIAL GOVERNMENT FOR THE CONFISCATION AND REDISTRIBUTION OF LAND—APPROVED BY THE PROVISIONAL CENTRAL GOVERNMENT

*Adopted probably sometime between
December 1, 1931, and April 1, 1932*
(As reproduced in *The Land Problem—Manual of Political
Instruction in Camp Schools*, April 1, 1932, leaves 3–6)

I. Whose land shall be confiscated?

1. The land, houses, property, and implements belonging to village bosses, gentry, landlords and [other] big landowners, and all land rented out on lease shall be confiscated without exception.

2. The land, houses, property, and implements belonging to ancestral shrines, temples, public bodies,[1] and associations shall be confiscated without exception.

3. The land and means of production belonging to the rich peasants who are definitely found to have joined counterrevolutionary organizations (such as the A-B League, the Social Democratic Party, and so on), shall be confiscated on a whole-family basis. [These rich peasants] may be given poorer houses to live in, while their dependents, after having

[1] This is a literal translation from the Kiangsi dialect, *kung t'ang*, which denotes, in a narrow sense, an estate established for the performance of rites in memory of an ancestor and, in a broad sense, all estates of ancestral shrines, temples, and associations.

been investigated by the Soviet government and found to have taken no part in counterrevolutionary organizations or counterrevolutionary actions and after having sincerely declared to the government the severance of their relations with the counterrevolutionary members of their families, may have such portions of the land and means of production returned to them as the government sees fit, provided that the local masses have no objection. Those who have a rich-peasant status may get back the portions of land due to them under the land law.

4. The rice fields of rich peasants shall be confiscated.

II. Who shall be allotted land?

1. All hired farm hands and poor peasants shall be entitled to equal land redistribution without exception. Whether the middle peasants are going to share in equal land redistribution with hired farm hands and poor peasants shall be decided by the middle peasants according to their own wishes. If the majority of the masses of the middle peasants are willing to participate in equal redistribution, then equal redistribution shall be carried out for them all immediately even if the minority of them are unwilling to do so. If the majority of the masses of the middle peasants want to keep their original land and are unwilling to participate in equal redistribution, then no equal redistribution shall be carried out for them. However, the minority of them who are willing to participate in equal redistribution shall nevertheless have the right to equal redistribution. But there shall be no further change in the land of the middle peasants which has already been redistributed in equal terms in the various counties of this province prior to December 31, 1931.

2. Dependents of workers and coolies in the villages shall be entitled to equal land redistribution without exception. The workers and coolies themselves, if unemployed, shall also be similarly allotted a share of land. (*Unemployed* used here means unemployment for most of the time during a year. Unemployment for only a small part of the year is temporary unemployment, which does not come under this provision.)

3. Independent laborers (including those who hire no employees but have apprentices under them), physicians, and village schoolteachers who have been unemployed for more than half a year shall be allotted land. (If their dependents are poor or middle peasants, the dependents shall naturally be allotted land as poor or middle peasants. If the dependents are not poor or middle peasants, they may be given suitable subsidiary assistance according to their actual needs, but the amount

of this subsidiary assistance may not exceed two thirds of what each person gets in equal land redistribution.)

4. Shop proprietors in the rural districts and their dependents shall not be allotted land.

5. Rich peasants shall be assigned poor land in accordance with the mixed principle of both labor power and the number of persons. That is to say, those who have labor power shall be assigned poor land equal in size to the land assigned to each person in the locality. Those who have no labor power shall be given suitable subsidiary assistance in terms of poor land, but such subsidiary assistance may not exceed two thirds of the amount of land assigned to each person in the locality.

6. The wives, daughters-in-law, and daughters of village bosses, gentry, landlords, and the rich peasants who have joined counter-revolutionary organizations and have voluntarily led the masses in revolt shall not be allotted any land after the promulgation of the present regulations, even if those women are married [or remarried] to workers, hired farm hands, poor peasants, or middle peasants.

7. In case the wives and daughters of village bosses, gentry, landlords, or counterrevolutionary rich peasants are married [or remarried] to workers, hired farm hands, poor peasants, or middle peasants through the practice of adopting the son-in-law as the heir of the wife's family[2] in an attempt to keep their original property, the government shall still confiscate all their property and houses. During the redistribution of houses and property, however, such married workers, hired farm hands, poor peasants, and middle peasants shall each receive a share for themselves.

8. In case the village bosses, gentry, landlords, and those rich peasants who have joined counterrevolutionary organizations have adopted or bought children of others and the children have enjoyed the same kind of living and education as the village bosses, gentry, and landlords themselves, such children shall absolutely not be allowed to receive land allotments. If they have only served as slaves to the village bosses, gentry, and landlords, they may be allotted land for themselves as well.

[2] *Chao-lang,* in which the groom, through the act of marriage, becomes a member of the family of the bride with rights of inheritance since the family has produced no son as an heir. Ordinarily the groom adopts the name of the family of his wife as his family name. If the couple later produce only one son, that son automatically becomes the heir of that family for the succeeding generation. If they produce two or more sons, the children are usually divided between the two families of the couple, and in that case the husband ceases to be a member of his wife's family and reassumes his original family name. All matters concerning the legal status of the couple and offspring in such a marriage are agreed upon by the two parties beforehand.

9. Monks, Taoist priests, nuns, lay devotees,[3] fortunetellers, and geomancers, who are all feudal remnants, as well as Protestant pastors and Catholic priests, who live on religion as a profession, shall not be allotted any land. The land that has already been allotted to them in the past shall be taken back from them. Those whose principal occupation is farming and secondary occupation is religion may be allotted land with the approval of the masses. Their dependents who do not live on the above-mentioned occupation [i.e., religion] but who are workers, hired farm hands, poor peasants, middle peasants, or rich peasants themselves, shall still be allotted land by virtue of their status as workers, hired farm hands, poor peasants, middle peasants, or rich peasants.

10. The children of village bosses, gentry, and landlords who have been received and cared for by poor and miserable workers and peasants may not be allotted any land after the promulgation of the present regulations.

11. Village bosses, gentry, landlords, and their dependents, as well as all the members of the families of rich peasants who have voluntarily led the masses in revolt, shall not be allotted any land. The land which has already been allotted them in the past shall be taken back from them.

12. Small merchants in the villages who were primarily doing business before the revolution and were able to support themselves and their families shall not be allotted any land. The land which has been allotted them in the past shall be taken back from them. In case they become unemployed after the revolution, they may be allotted land in the same manner as independent laborers.

13. Unemployed poor people in small market towns shall be entitled to land allotments.

14. When women get married, their land shall be disposed of by themselves.

III. How shall land be redistributed?

1. The township shall be the unit for land redistribution. However, if the great majority of the poor and middle peasants wish to use the village as the unit for land redistribution, then the village may also become a unit for land redistribution.

[3] *Tsai-kung,* or one who chooses to live in mountains, usually in a temple, to practice abstinence as a token of grief. He ordinarily adopts this life at his middle age when he has suffered great spiritual pain and lost all hope in this world.

2. Hired farm hands, poor peasants, middle peasants, unemployed workers, and unemployed independent laborers shall receive their allotments on an equal basis according to the number of persons, as well as the quality and size of the land. In the case of the middle peasants in particular, however, the principle of their voluntary choice shall have to be followed.

3. Tea-oil plantations, bamboo forests, and hillside land for non-staple grains may be converted into equivalent amounts of farmland or assessed at fixed prices for the purpose of equal redistribution in the light of local conditions. The rich peasants shall be allotted only barren hills. Large forests shall be turned over to the Soviet government, which is to be responsible for their management.

4. Big mountains shall be managed by the state. It will be up to the government to decide whether to lease them out or organize producers' cooperatives for their exploitation. For the time being, however, lease should be the principal policy to be followed.

5. For purposes of redistribution, fish ponds may be converted into equivalent amounts of farmland or assessed at certain prices or used to raise fish on a cooperative basis. It is the fish, and not the water, that is subject to redistribution. Water in the ponds is to be used principally for the purpose of irrigation, and secondarily for raising fish.

6. The surplus draft cattle, houses, and farm implements of the rich peasants shall be confiscated and redistributed to the poor and miserable workers and peasants according to their needs (for they have either none or an inadequate amount of such things).

7. After the confiscation of the houses, property, farm implements, and [other] tools of village bosses, gentry, landlords, and those rich peasants who have voluntarily led the masses in revolt, a portion [of these things] shall be turned over to the Soviets and revolutionary organizations for their use, another portion shall be used for the relief of both the dependents of the Red Army men and the masses in distress, and the remainder shall be apportioned among the poor and miserable workers and peasants.

8. Persons who work in the government and various revolutionary organizations may not be allotted any land unless they are hired farm hands, poor peasants, middle peasants, unemployed workers, coolies, or independent laborers.

IV. How shall land be redistributed to the Red Army?

1. Land redistribution for the dependents of the Red Army men shall

be the same as that for the poor and middle peasants, but the land allotted them should be situated in places which are near to or not too far from [the homes of the dependents of the Red Army men].

2. The criteria for the reservation of public land for the Red Army shall be as follows: Every township where each person is allotted an amount of land capable of producing more than five piculs of rice shall reserve for the Red Army an amount of public land [for the Red Army], while places having less land (where each person is allotted an amount of land capable of producing less than five piculs of rice) shall at least reserve sufficient public land for redistribution to two persons. No forests or tea-oil plants need be reserved [for the Red Army]. The public land [reserved] for the Red Army is to be cultivated chiefly by mobilizing the masses. Draft cattle, fertilizers, and seeds will be supplied voluntarily by the masses; only in case of necessity will the government lend a helping hand. If the land [reserved for the Red Army] may be leased out under certain difficult conditions, the rental and the lessees shall be determined in consultation with the government.

V. Lease, purchase, sale, succession, and other matters
1. After redistribution, land may be leased out but must not be leased to the dependents of village bosses, gentry, and landlords. The amount of the rental in terms of rice is to be agreed upon by both parties.

2. After redistribution, land may be bought and sold but must not be sold to the dependents of village bosses, gentry, and landlords. The price of the land is to be agreed upon by both parties. The purchase and sale of land shall be reported to the local governments for registration.

3. After redistribution, land can be inherited from generation to generation. Newborn persons shall not be given additional land, and land handed down from deceased persons shall not be taken away [from their families]. In case the deceased has left no dependents, his land shall be taken back by the government.

4. In localities where land has already been equally redistributed and where hired farm hands, poor peasants, and middle peasants have actually been benefited by the land revolution, that is to say, where the majority of the local masses do not demand a new redistribution, there shall be no new redistribution of land. Should conditions in these local-ities disagree with any new decisions [of the government] and the land law, such disagreements shall be removed or adjusted in accordance with the new decisions and the land law. Only in localities where hired

farm hands, poor peasants, and middle peasants have not been benefited by the land revolution, and where the rich peasants have been benefited instead, shall the masses of the hired farm hands, poor peasants, and middle peasants be mobilized for a new redistribution of land.

5. Except for leaders in revolt, all the masses who were forced to take part in it shall be allotted land. If such masses are still absent from home at the time of planting, their dependents may do the planting for them. When they return, the land may be considered as having been leased to them. If they fail to return after one year, their land shall be taken back by the government.

6. The rank and file in the White Army's pacification corps or local militia shall all be allotted land. Their dependents shall all be allotted land also. But those who were originally village bosses, gentry, landlords, or rich peasants shall not be allotted any land. The rank and file in the said pacification corps, local militia, and police force shall be required to return home for cultivation by a prescribed date. The land assigned to those who fail to return within the time limit may be taken back by the government.

7. Workers, hired farm hands, poor peasants, and middle peasants who were misled to join counterrevolutionary organizations (such as the A-B League, the Reorganizationist Clique, the Social Democratic Party, and so forth) and who have since surrendered themselves to justice and are willing to reform, shall be allotted land as well. Land shall be reserved for those who are still being detained and whose cases have not yet been decided. But this does not apply to rich peasants.

8. Hired farm hands, poor peasants, and middle peasants shall be encouraged to reclaim existing waste land by giving them first priority, and the government may exempt them from paying land rent and land tax for a number of years. Waste land in excess of the amount leased to hired farm hands, poor peasants, and middle peasants may be leased out to the rich peasants with a suitable reduction or exemption of land rent or land tax. But the period for the exemption of land rent and tax [for the rich peasants] must be shorter than that for hired farm hands, poor peasants, and middle peasants. Only waste land in excess of the amount leased to all the above categories of persons as well as unreclaimed land may be leased to dependents of village bosses, gentry, and landlords for cultivation or reclamation, provided that there is no need to bring in immigrants from the neighboring districts, or the immigrants thus brought in cannot use all the land, that no objection is raised on the part of the local masses and that [such lease] is placed

under the close supervision of both the township government and the masses. However, there shall be no reduction or exemption of land rent and tax in the case of such a lease. Moreover, this kind of lease shall apply only to the heart of the Red areas but not to the border regions. The period of lease, the amount of land rent, and the amount of land tax in the case of waste land and barren hills shall be stipulated by the government.

DOCUMENT 60

INSTRUCTION NO. 11 OF THE COUNCIL OF PEOPLE'S COMMISSARS OF THE PROVISIONAL CENTRAL GOVERNMENT OF THE CHINESE SOVIET REPUBLIC—LAUNCHING AN EXTENSIVE AND INTENSIVE LAND INVESTIGATION DRIVE

Issued on June 1, 1933
(As printed in *Red China*, No. 87, June 20, 1933, p. 5)

At present there are still large regions in the various Soviet areas, especially the Central Soviet Area, in which the land problem has not yet been thoroughly solved. Regions of this sort constitute almost 80 per cent of the total area of the Central [Soviet] Area, with a total of more than two million masses. Such are the entire regions of the fifteen counties of Jui-chin (except Wu-yang District), Hui-ch'ang, Hsün-wu, An-yüan, Hsin-feng, Yü-tu (except Hsin-p'i District), Lo-an, I-huang, Kuang-ch'ang, Shih-ch'eng, Chien-ning, Li-ch'uan, Ning-hua, Ch'ang-t'ing, and Wu-p'ing; large parts of [the counties of] Po-sheng, Sheng-li, and Yung-feng; parts of [the counties of] Kung-lüeh, Wan-t'ai, Shang-hang, Yung-ting, and Hsin-ch'üan; and the two districts of Chün-ts'un and Huang-t'ang [in the county of] Hsing-kuo. All these are places where the land problem has not yet been thoroughly solved.

In these places, the peasant masses have not yet been mobilized to the largest possible extent. Feudal remnant forces have not been finally crushed. Not a few class heretical elements are still hiding and operating clandestinely in the Soviet regimes, mass organizations, and local armed units. Not a few counterrevolutionary secret organizations are still operating here and there to undermine the revolution. For this reason, these places in the spheres of war mobilization and cultural and economic reconstruction are lagging far behind the advanced areas (such as almost the entire county of Hsing-kuo; parts of [the counties of] Sheng-li, Kan-hsien, Wan-t'ai, Kung-lüeh, Yung-feng, and Shang-hang; the districts of Huang-p'i and An-fu [in the county of] Po-sheng; the district of Wu-yang [in the county of] Jui-chin; the district of Ch'i-nan [in the county of] Yung-ting, and so on). To carry out a general and thoroughgoing land investigation drive in these vast regions so as to unfold a class struggle to the highest degree among the more than two million masses and to make a final assault on the feudal forces and eliminate them completely is a most urgent task which cannot be delayed for one instant by the Soviets in various places.

With reference to the specific things to do in regard to the land investigation drive, the Council of People's Commissars hereby makes the following decisions:

1. Government chairmen at all levels shall be required to lead the entire land investigation drive with the greatest care and attention.

2. At all levels, the land departments, the workers' and peasants' prosecution departments, the judicial departments, the state political security bureaus, and their special commissioners shall be required to exert all their strength to direct the land investigation drive, to solve the land problem thoroughly, to reform the local Soviets, and to suppress the counterrevolutionaries in the rural districts. The central people's commissariat of land, the people's commissariat of workers' and peasants' prosecution, the people's commissariat of justice, and the state political security bureau shall exert all their strength to direct the various agencies at lower levels to carry out these tasks faithfully and effectively.

3. The central people's commissariat of finance shall be required to direct the finance departments of various levels to attack the feudal and semifeudal forces by imposing fines on landlords and levying contributions from rich peasants, which will increase the national revenues in the meantime. The central people's commissariat of military affairs shall be required during the land investigation drive to direct the military departments of various levels to reorganize and expand local armed units and mobilize the masses to join the Red Army. The central people's commissariat of national economy shall be required, during the land investigation drive, to direct the national economy departments

of various levels to bring about the restoration and development of agricultural and handicraft production, the development of cooperatives, and the adjustment of producers' goods and consumers' goods. The central people's commissariat of education shall be required to direct the educational departments of various levels to supply all land investigation cadres and masses with simple and popular manuals and pamphlets for the development of the land investigation drive, and to develop the culture and education of the masses in keeping with the progress of the land investigation drive.

4. The governments on the provincial and county levels shall open short-term training classes on the land investigation drive by drawing cadres from areas under land investigation and from all advanced and relatively advanced areas. For a review of the progress of land investigation, the county Soviet shall call a meeting of the responsible authorities of the district Soviets once every month, while the district Soviet shall call a meeting of the chairmen of the township Soviets and the chiefs of the poor-peasant corps once every ten days.

5. There shall, first of all, be convened a conference of the principal responsible Soviet authorities on and above the district level in the eight counties of Jui-chin, Hui-ch'ang, Po-sheng, Yü-tu, Sheng-li, Shih-ch'eng, Ning-hua, and Ch'ang-t'ing, and a conference of delegates of the poor-peasant corps of the same eight counties, both to be held at [the seat of] the central government for the purpose of launching a land investigation drive in the eight counties.

6. During the land investigation drive it is necessary to carry out the class line resolutely. It is necessary to follow the leadership of the working class in the rural districts, rely upon the poor peasants, and unite closely with the middle peasants so as to launch a determined assault on the feudal and semifeudal forces. All the landlords and rich peasants who have disguised themselves as "middle peasants" and "poor peasants" must be uncovered. All the land and [other] property of the landlord class as well as the land of rich peasants and their surplus draft cattle, farm implements, and houses must be confiscated for redistribution to the workers, poor peasants, and middle peasants who have been allotted inadequate land or no land at all in the past. The rich peasants shall be allotted labor land allotments of a poorer quality.

7. During the land investigation drive it is necessary to give all attention to rousing the great majority of the masses to struggle with the feudal remnants. First of all, it is necessary to make widespread propaganda and agitation. All attempts to investigate the status of

landlords and rich peasants, determine their status, and confiscate their land and [other] property according to such status must be made with the consent and participation of the majority of the masses as far as possible. All confiscated property and articles, with the exception of cash, must be distributed to the poorest and most miserable masses, especially to the poor and miserable dependents of the Red Army. A greater proportion of the same should be distributed to the masses of those villages from which the [confiscated] property and articles have come.

8. The poor-peasant corps is the most important mass organization in the land investigation drive. The district and township Soviets should make utmost efforts to direct it, to purge it of bad elements, and to absorb as many active elements into it as possible. The workers' small group in the poor-peasant corps should be the leading spirit of the corps.

9. During the land investigation drive it is necessary to concentrate great attention on all the backward, and particularly the most backward, districts, townships, and villages. It should be noted that in unfolding the land investigation drive in backward districts and townships, especially in large villages, it is necessary to arouse the poor and miserable masses of the respective villages to rise up themselves in a struggle against the landlords and rich peasants of those villages. All wrong actions likely to lead to clan or local conflicts should be avoided as far as possible.

10. All counterrevolutionary organizations and activities must be suppressed during the land investigation drive. The spreading of rumors by landlords and rich peasants as well as sabotage by them must be prevented and exposed.

11. The local Soviets should be reformed during the land investigation drive. All class heretical elements and other bad elements in local Soviets must be purged, while large numbers of revolutionary activities should be introduced into the Soviets.

12. All persons in the Soviets of various levels who stand directly or indirectly in the way of the land investigation drive shall receive severe or the severest punishments.

It is only by carrying out the above-mentioned decisions resolutely that the class struggle in the rural districts can be waged extensively and intensively, that the activism of the broad masses can be aroused, that all the feudal and semifeudal forces in the rural districts can be suppressed completely, and that the task of land investigation can be consummated. Such is this decree.

MAO TSE-TUNG
Chairman
HSIANG YING
Vice-Chairman
CHANG KUO-T'AO
Vice-Chairman

June 1, 1933

DOCUMENT 62

THE LAND INVESTIGATION DRIVE IS THE CENTRAL
TASK OF GREAT MAGNITUDE IN VAST AREAS

Mao Tse-tung
(As printed in *Red China*, No. 86, June 17, 1933, p. 3)

All past experience has proved that only through the correct solution of the land problem and only through the fanning to the highest degree the flames of class struggle in the rural districts under the resolute class slogan can the broad peasant masses be mobilized, under the leadership of the proletariat, to take part in the revolutionary war, participate in the various aspects of Soviet reconstruction, and build up a strong revolutionary base, so that the Soviet movement may gather greater momentum and achieve a greater development and success.

According to the experience of the development of the land revolution, the unfolding of the class struggle in the rural districts has its approximate stages to follow, namely: (*a*) the stage of land confiscation and redistribution; (*b*) the stage of land investigation; and (*c*) the stage of land reconstruction. According to the three stages of the development of the land struggle, there are approximately three different areas in any Soviet region: (*a*) the intensified struggle area; (*b*) the comparatively retarded struggle area; and (*c*) the newly developed area.

In the newly developed area, the unfolding of the land struggle is still in the stage of land confiscation and redistribution. Here the central problems are: the overthrow of the regime of the landlord class by armed force; the establishment of a revolutionary provisional regime (a revolutionary committee); the build-up of local armed forces of the workers and peasants; the formation of revolutionary mass organizations; the confiscation of the land and [other] property of the landlord class, and the redistribution of the land of the rich peasants to the hired farm hands, poor peasants, and middle peasants, while the rich peasants are allotted only poor land; the annulment of debts; and the burning of land deeds and promissory notes. The struggle of this stage covers the whole period from the initial fight between the revolutionaries and counterrevolutionaries to the defeat of the latter by the former, coupled with the disposal of the land and [other] property of the counterrevolutionaries.

In the intensified struggle area, solid Soviet regimes have been established, local armed forces and revolutionary mass organizations have been widely set up, the feudal and semifeudal forces of landlords and rich peasants have been completely crushed, land has been thoroughly redistributed, and the land struggle of the peasant masses has entered upon the stage for the reform of land and the development of its productivity. Accordingly, the central problem here is the problem of land reconstruction.

As to the retarded struggle area, its stage of development lies between the above-mentioned two stages. It is a transition from a provisional to a formal regime, but the power of the regime is not yet completely consolidated. Here the open counterrevolutionary struggle of the landlords and rich peasants has already been crushed by the revolutionary masses in the first stage. Since then, many of them [landlords and rich peasants] have been disguised. They have taken off their counterrevolutionary masks and put on revolutionary masks. Also, they have apparently been in favor of the revolution and the redistribution of land. They have called themselves poor and miserable peasants, claiming that they are entitled to land allotments as a matter of course. They have been in great activity: relying on their traditional superiority, "they monopolize the situation to say what they would like to say and write what they would like to write." In the first stage, therefore, they have already availed themselves of the opportunity to snatch the fruits of the revolution. In numerous places, facts have shown that they have been dominating the provisional regimes, worming their way into local armed forces, manipulating revolutionary organizations, and receiving more and better land allotments than the poor and miserable peasants.

In the second stage, owing to the supervision of governments on higher levels and the development of the mass struggle, the revolutionary committees have been transformed into Soviets, the mass organizations and local armed forces have gone through the first step of reformation and development, and those elements who have pretended to be revolutionaries have been partially eliminated. In many places there has been a second, or even a third, or fourth redistribution of land. Part of the land stolen by landlords and rich peasants has also been found out. However, in the Soviets, mass organizations, and local armed forces, there are still hidden numerous class heretical elements who "put on red ribbons and call each other comrades," spread rumors, hold secret meetings, scold the masses for their "Left opportunism," for their "indiscriminate blows at village bosses," and for their "revenge of personal grudges in the name of the public." Or they [the hidden class heretical elements] "speak vociferously in meetings, but take no actions at all after the meetings are over." When the struggle is in full swing, they form counterrevolutionary secret organizations such as the Kuomintang, the Social Democratic Party, the A-B League, the New Communist Party, and a variety of other organizations in order to undermine the revolution and attempt the life of revolutionary activists. In a word, the landlord and rich-peasant classes make use of various methods to suppress the mass struggle in an attempt to preserve their political rights, their rights in land and [other] property, and their remnant feudal power.

In areas like this, a fierce struggle is going on between the revolutionary masses and the landlords and rich peasants. But this struggle, unlike that of the first stage, is not an open struggle between the red flag and the white flag, but a struggle between the revolutionary peasant masses and the landlord and rich-peasant elements in disguise. Such a struggle is particularly difficult in that the hidden counterrevolutionaries, unlike counterrevolutionaries in the open, cannot be clearly recognized by the peasant masses at one glance. Moreover, owing to the various deep-rooted feudal relations in the rural districts such as clan relations, and so on, it is not easy to expect the general peasant masses to have such a degree of class consciousness as to realize the necessity of wiping out the feudal remnants once and for all. Such a situation requires the Communist Party and the Soviet government to give a patient explanation to the peasants, to perform many difficult tasks, and to have a correct class line and correct methods of mass work. The central problem here is the problem of land investigation and class investigation. If this problem is not solved, the revolutionary activism of the peasant masses cannot be fully developed, the feudal remnant forces cannot be completely crushed, the Soviets cannot be consolidated to the greatest possible extent, and the enormous tasks of expanding the Red Army, raising funds for the Red Army, expanding local armed forces, carrying out land reconstruction and economic reconstruction, promoting culture and education, and so on, cannot be crowned with the greatest possible success. Therefore, the land investigation drive is the most central task of the greatest magnitude in these regions.

In the Central Soviet Area, the comparatively retarded struggle area constitutes the larger part of the whole Soviet region. Such are the thirteen entire counties of Hui-ch'ang, Hsün-wu, An-yüan, Hsin-feng, Lo-an, I-huang, Kuang-ch'ang, Shih-ch'eng, Chien-ning, Li-ch'uan, Ning-hua, Ch'ang-t'ing, and Wu-p'ing; the larger parts of Jui-chin, Yü-tu, Po-sheng, Sheng-li, and Yung-feng; parts of Kung-lüeh, Wan-t'ai, Kan-hsien, Shang-hang, Yung-ting, and Hsin-ch'üan; and even the two districts of Chün-ts'un and Huang-t'ang in the county of Hsing-kuo. All these are places where the land problem has not yet been thoroughly solved.

In these places the peasant masses have not yet been mobilized to the largest possible extent, the feudal forces have not yet been finally crushed, not a few class heretical elements are still hiding and operating clandestinely in the Soviet regimes, mass organizations, and local armed units, and not a few counterrevolutionary secret organizations are still operating clandestinely here and there to undermine the revolution. For this reason, these places in the spheres of war mobilization and economic and cultural reconstruction are lagging far behind the advanced areas (such as almost the entire county of Hsing-kuo, parts of [the counties of] Sheng-li, Kan-hsien, Wan-t'ai, Kung-lüeh, Yung-feng, and Shang-hang, the district of Huang-p'i in [the county of] Po-sheng, the district of Wu-yang in [the county of] Jui-chin, the district of Hsin-p'i in [the county of] Yü-tu, the district of Ch'i-nan in [the county of] Yung-ting, etc.). Such places constitute almost 80 per cent of the total area of the Central [Soviet] Area, with a total of more than two million masses. To carry out a general and thoroughgoing land investigation drive in this vast region, to fan the flames of class struggle to the highest degree among the more than two million masses, and to wage a final war with feudal forces and knock them down completely—these are the most urgent tasks of the Communist Party and the Soviet government.

DOCUMENT 63

THE FIRST STEP OF THE LAND INVESTIGATION DRIVE—A LARGE-SCALE MOBILIZATION OF THE ORGANIZATION

Mao Tse-tung
(As printed in *Red China*, No. 87, June 20, 1933, p. 3)

How to prosecute the land investigation drive? First of all, there must be an organizational mobilization.

All experience of leading the mass struggle in the Soviet areas tells us that it is only through the concerted action of the Communist Party, the Soviets, and the revolutionary mass organizations under the leadership of the party that the tasks of each and every struggle can be satisfactorily accomplished. The land investigation drive is a ruthless and fierce class struggle. It is a great revolutionary movement of the masses. It is the basis for improving the work of the party, the Soviets, and the mass organizations. It is the most important link in [the chain] of [our] present work. This drive can be started, developed, and successfully concluded if only the entire party, all the Soviets, and the labor unions mobilize all their strength to be put into it.

In regard to the mobilization of the party, the Central Bureau has already issued correct instructions.

As to the mobilization of the Soviets, we should first of all refute the view which has been held in the past that the land investigation drive is the work of the land department alone. Not only the finance department, the military department, the national economy department, and the education department maintain that they have nothing to do with the land investigation drive, but also the workers' and peasants' prosecution department, the judicial department, and the political security bureau hold that they do not have much connection with it, either. Worst of all, even the presidiums [of the Soviets] do not care about the land investigation drive. This is entirely wrong.

It must be realized that no part of the entire Soviets can dissociate itself from the land investigation drive and leave it alone. First of all, the presidiums of the governments on all levels are required to lead the entire land investigation drive with the greatest care and attention. Secondly, the land departments, workers' and peasants' prosecution departments, the judicial departments, and the state political security bureaus of various levels, as well as the special commissioners of the state political security bureau, are the principal supervisory and working agencies of the various levels of government in the land investigation drive. These government agencies must do what they can in the land investigation drive to solve the land problem thoroughly, reform the Soviets at the three levels of the township, district, and county, and suppress the counterrevolutionaries in the rural districts. The finance department must take care to attack the feudal remnant forces by imposing fines on landlords and levying contributions from rich peasants. This step will also increase the national revenues in the meantime. The military department must take care, in the course of the land investigation drive, to reorganize and expand local armed units and to mobilize the active elements among the masses to join the Red Army. The national economy department must take care, in the course of the land investigation drive, to bring about the restoration and development of agricultural and handicraft production, the development of cooperatives, and the adjustment of producers' and consumers' goods. Not that there is no work for the educational department to do. It should supply all land investigation cadres and masses with simple and popular manuals and pamphlets for the development of the land investigation drive and develop the culture and education of the masses in keeping with the progress of the land investigation drive.

Since the overwhelming majority of the members of labor unions in the Soviet areas live in the rural districts and have close relations with land, and since the proletariat must be the most resolute leaders in such a great and fierce class struggle as the land investigation drive, all labor unions, whether agricultural, handicraft, or other, must, under the leadership of the all-party executive bureau, mobilize their best cadres and all their members in the rural districts to take part in the land investigation drive and, above all, to play an active and leading role in the poor-peasant corps and to put forward positive and firm proposals in regard to the land investigation, class investigation, and governmental reform. In fine, the land investigation drive is not an ordinary, trivial matter; it cannot be thoroughly completed in [blank] months, or even in half a year. Therefore, there must be a large-scale mobilization through the coordinated efforts of the party, the Youth Corps, the government, and labor unions.

Here I should like to say something about the problem of educating the cadres. First, responsible persons in the lower echelons [cadres] must be called together and given adequate explanations about several important problems of the land investigation drive. In the past, the Soviet personnel on various levels did not know, for the most part, that the land investigation drive is an urgent task. They did not know how to define class status in actual practice. They did not know the ways and methods to be adopted to win over the masses and stir up struggles. Therefore, it was impossible to give wide scope to the drive. Secondly, this kind of education should also be given to cadres drawn from local lower echelons and from all advanced areas, for whom short-term training classes on the land investigation drive should be opened. Governments on the provincial and county levels should, for the sake of the land investigation drive, open many such training classes lasting from one to two weeks, specially designed for the teaching of [subjects on] several main problems of the land investigation drive. The land departments, workers' and peasants' prosecution departments, and political security bureaus of the provincial, county, and district governments should each have its own working personnel (most of the personnel on the district level should not be separated from productive work) and give them adequate education on the task of land investigation. Thirdly, education should be carried out in practical action. That is to say, the provincial and county levels should dispatch personnel to make inspection tours, while on the district level there should be a meeting every five to seven days of [three kinds of people] the working personnel sent out by the district itself, of the township Soviet chairmen, and of the chiefs of the poor-peasant corps, for the purpose of reviewing the progress of their work. If we have only the first two methods and do not have the last method, we shall not be able to achieve the greatest possible success in our work.

DOCUMENT 65

UNFOLD THE LAND INVESTIGATION DRIVE ACCORDING TO THE DISPARITY OF THE CONDITION OF THE DEVELOPMENT OF THE CLASS STRUGGLE IN THE RURAL DISTRICTS

Mao Tse-tung
(As printed in *Red China*, No. 88, June 23, 1933, p. 3)

We have said in Chapter I [referring here to **Doc. 62**] that there are three different areas in the Soviet districts, namely: (*a*) the intensified struggle area, (*b*) the retarded struggle area, and (*c*) the newly developed area. This is true not only of a province, but also of some counties in border regions. Take, for example, [the county of] Yung-feng where the three kinds of areas are in existence at the same time. In most border regions, both the comparatively retarded and the newly developed areas are found in a county. In the heartland, though some counties are, generally speaking, still backward on the whole, yet they do not lack districts which are relatively advanced. In [the county of] Hui-ch'ang, for example, the district of Hsi-chiang is relatively advanced, while most of the other districts are backward. The case of [the county of] Jui-chin is again different: the district of Wu-yang may be said to be an intensified [struggle] area, while the eight districts of T'ao-huang, Huang-pai, Sha-hsin, Jui-lin, Chiu-pao, Yün-chi, Tu-t'ou, and Ch'eng-shih are relatively advanced areas, and the other six districts are backward areas.

In general, [therefore], both the relatively advanced townships and the relatively retarded townships can be found in any district of any county where the Soviets have been established and where the land has gone through confiscation and redistribution. In a township there are also the relatively advanced villages and the relatively retarded villages alike.

Is this situation of uneven development in existence in a village? It is so in many places. There are many places where the small villages (or small hamlets) are generally advanced while the big villages (or big hamlets) are backward. [On the other hand], owing to different historical conditions, there are also certain places where individual big villages are advanced while individual small villages are backward.

Such a state of things determines the direction of our work. In carrying out the land investigation drive in a county, district, township, or even village, we have to concentrate our greatest attention on the backward localities and to devote our greatest efforts to them. It would be wrong to treat different places in the same manner and make equal efforts in them. It would be all the more wrong if one says the backward localities are "impossible of penetration" because it is difficult to win over the masses and launch the struggle there, and if one therefore shifts one's direction of work to the places where it would be easier to work and leave alone the places where things are difficult to handle.

Of course, in the process of our work in, say, a township, we may and should start work in the villages or hamlets where [the masses] can easily be roused to action. But the focus of our working plan is still on the backward villages and hamlets. In order to eliminate the particular backwardness of a certain village or hamlet (which is "momentarily impossible of penetration"), it would be perfectly right to start work in a village or hamlet where work can be more easily done, thereby influencing the backward village or hamlet so that a struggle in that backward village or hamlet can be launched.

In the case of a county or district, however, our work should be different. In planning the land investigation drive in a county or district, we should begin by using our major efforts to make a surprise attack on the backward districts and townships and devoting only our minor efforts to the relatively advanced districts and townships.

The condition of uneven development tells us to use another method, that of mobilizing cadres in the advanced areas to go to the backward areas to lead the land investigation drive. It is important, of course, to mobilize cadres from the most advanced areas like [the county of] Hsing-kuo, etc., to go to backward areas. It is equally urgent that cadres be mobilized from all relatively advanced areas in all places to go to backward areas. All advanced and relatively advanced areas should bear the responsibility of leading the backward areas, while all backward areas should learn from the advanced areas. Only in this way can the land investigation drive be carried out quickly.

DOCUMENT 66

CIRCULAR OF THE CENTRAL GOVERNMENT— CALLING A CONFERENCE OF RESPONSIBLE SOVIET AUTHORITIES OF EIGHT COUNTIES ON AND ABOVE THE DISTRICT LEVEL AND A CONFERENCE OF DELEGATES OF THE POOR-PEASANT CORPS OF EIGHT COUNTIES

Issued on June 1, 1933
(As printed in *Red China*, No. 85, June 14, 1933, p. 3)

Comrades—[members of] the presidiums of the county Soviets and district Soviets and chairmen of the township Soviets in the eight counties of Jui-chin, Hui-ch'ang, Yü-tu, Sheng-li, Po-sheng, Shih-ch'eng, Ning-hua, and Ch'ang-t'ing:

The land problem is still a very serious problem in many retarded struggle areas. In order to unfold an extensive and intensive land investigation drive prior to the Second National Soviet Congress and in order, during the land investigation drive, to solve the land problem thoroughly, suppress the counterrevolutionaries, and reform the Soviets and mass organizations, the central government has decided, first of all, to call a "Conference of Responsible Soviet Authorities of Eight Counties on and above the District Level" and a "Conference of Delegates of the Poor-Peasant Corps of Eight Counties" to be represented by the eight counties of Jui-chin, Hui-ch'ang, Yü-tu, Sheng-li, Po-sheng, Shih-ch'eng, Ning-hua, and Ch'ang-t'ing.

I. Conference of Responsible Soviet Authorities of Eight Counties on and above the District Level

1. Place of the conference: Yeh-p'ing, Yün-chi District, Jui-chin [County].

2. Time of the conference: All conferees to arrive by June 16; the conference opens on June 17 and closes on June 20.

3. Attendance at the conference:

> On the district level: chairman [of the district Soviet], chief of the land department, chief of the workers' and peasants' prosecution department, and special commissioner of the security bureau.

> On the county level: chairman [of the county Soviet], chief of the land department, chief of the workers' and peasants' prosecution department, and chief of the security bureau.

> On the provincial level: vice-chairman [of the provincial Soviet], chief of the land department, chief of the workers' and peasants' prosecution department, and chief of the security bureau.

4. The original official duties of those who attend the conference should be taken care of by their proxies for the time being.

5. Those who are designated to attend the conference may not be absent on some pretext or other.

6. Those who attend the conference must prepare and bring with them the following items of reports.

[Items are omitted.]

> In order to obtain materials for the reports in question, the district Soviet shall, upon the receipt of this circular, immediately call a meeting of all the chairmen of the township [Soviets] and the chiefs of the poor-peasant corps in the entire district so as to collect all the materials available. The county Soviet need not call a meeting of the district Soviets, but need only to ask for materials from the various departments and mass organizations on the county level. The provincial Soviet shall ask for materials from the various departments and mass organizations on the provincial level. All those who attend the conference must bring with them the above-mentioned reports. Those who bring no reports with

them shall be regarded as having committed sabotage. The reports must be faithful and may not be fabricated. Anyone who is found to have fabricated reports in order to save face shall be punished.

7. The traveling expenses for the round trips of the conferees will be taken care of by the respective finance departments on various levels, while meals for the duration of the conference will be taken care of by the central government.

8. Conferees should bring with them rice bowls, chopsticks, and unwadded coverlets.

II. Conference of Delegates of the Poor-Peasant Corps of Eight Counties

1. Place of the conference: Yeh-p'ing, Yün-chi District, Jui-chin [County].

2. Time of the conference: All conferees to arrive by June 24; the conference opens on June 25 and closes on July 1.

3. Attendance at the conference: One delegate is to be elected by the poor-peasant corps of each township, but two delegates should be elected if the number of the members of the peasant corps exceeds 300.

4. Election of delegates and their procedure for the trip:

   (a) When this circular reaches the various districts, each of the district Soviets should immediately call a meeting of the chairmen of the township Soviets and the chiefs of the poor-peasant corps of the entire district. The meeting should be informed about the great revolutionary significance of the convocation by the central government of the conference of the delegates of the poor-peasant corps of the eight counties and about the methods of electing the delegates and carrying out propaganda among the masses.

   (b) Then all the chairmen of the township [Soviets] and the chiefs of the poor-peasant corps should go back quickly to their respective townships and call an all-member meeting of the poor-peasant corps at which the significance of the convocation by the central government of the conference of the delegates of the poor-peasant corps should be explained. Thereupon the delegates [to the conference] should be elected immediately.

   (c) Only those poor peasants and hired farm hands who are activists, and usually carry on resolute struggles against landlords and rich peasants, are qualified to be delegates. If the chief or executive secretary of the poor-peasant corps is qualified in this sense, he may be elected as delegate. But if neither the chief nor the executive secretary is qualified, the delegate must be elected from among the ordinary members [of the poor-peasant corps]. The delegate must be elected at an all-member meeting and may not be appointed. No passivists shall be elected, much less [class] heretical elements.

(d) After the various delegates of the township level are elected, they shall be assembled at the district Soviet, where the district Soviet will act as the chairman to call a meeting of those delegates. A delegation must be organized and the best one of the delegates should be designated as chief of the delegation. Meanwhile, the significance of the projected conference convened by the central government should be explained and the traveling expenses [for the delegates] paid accordingly. Then the delegation departs under the leadership of the chief and should arrive at Jui-chin not later than June 24.

5. Each delegate must bring with him a brief but clear report in which the following particulars should be given:

(a) The size of the population of his township.

(b) The number of members of the poor-peasant corps and their class status.

(c) The time of the formation of the poor-peasant corps.

(d) Whether or not there are the poor-peasant corps established at the village level.

(f) The number of small groups into which the poor-peasant corps is divided. [Either this item is misnumbered or Item (e) is skipped.]

6. The traveling expenses of the delegates will be taken care of by the district Soviets. Meals for the duration of the conference will be taken care of by the central government.

7. The delegates should bring with them rice bowls, chopsticks, and unwadded coverlets.

8. Propaganda after the departure of the delegates: The township Soviet shall pick five revolutionary activists from either the township congress of delegates or the poor-peasant corps to organize a "land investigation drive propaganda team." After the departure of the delegates of the poor-peasant corps, this propaganda team should go to the various villages and hamlets to call mass meetings there. It should be brought home to the mass meetings that in order to launch a big drive for the investigation of land and of class status, the central gov-

ernment is calling a conference of delegates of the poor-peasant corps of eight counties, to which this township has elected such and such persons as delegates and all other townships and districts of this county have also sent their delegates. The masses should be urged to get ready and keep an eye on those landlord and rich-peasant elements who have received land allotments under the disguise of middle peasants and poor peasants. As soon as the delegates come back [from the conference], a very big investigation will be started. The feudal forces must be completely wiped out before the poor masses can obtain the greatest possible benefits. However, the investigation of land is by no means another redistribution of land. It is an investigation by the masses themselves of those landlord and rich-peasant elements who have disguised themselves as middle peasants and poor peasants. Not until these elements are discovered and overthrown can the poor and miserable masses be liberated. Moreover, our hired farm hands and poor peasants must ally themselves with all genuine middle peasants to whose interests the Soviets give full protection. The aim of this kind of propaganda is to let all the masses know that the election of delegates by this township and the various [other] districts and townships to attend the conference convened by the central government is for the purpose of launching a big drive for the investigation of class status in the nine hundred townships of the eight counties. [It is expected that] before the return of the delegates there has already been created in the various townships an intense atmosphere favorable to the investigation of class status. Village and hamlet meetings may be held after sunset, and it is the duty of the chairman of the township [Soviet] to take the lead [in those meetings].

Responsible comrades of county Soviets, district Soviets, and township Soviets in the eight counties of Jui-chin, Hui-ch'ang, Yü-tu, Sheng-li, Po-sheng, Shih-ch'eng, Ning-hua, and Ch'ang-t'ing! In order to make both conferences a complete success, you must first of all see to it that: (a) those attending the conferences shall bring faithful reports with them; (b) delegates of the poor-peasant corps shall all be active revolutionary elements rather than passive compromisers; (c) those who expect to attend the conferences shall all be present—and present at the appointed dates; and (d) there shall be a general propaganda for the land investigation drive in all the townships. In regard to these four points, you must exert very great efforts, indeed. If these four points are not well carried out, the conferences will not be able to achieve a complete success. For that you will have to be to blame. Hereby this circular is issued.

Mao Tse-tung
Chairman of the Central Government
Hsiang Ying
Vice-Chairman
Chang Kuo-t'ao
Vice-Chairman

June 1, 1933

DOCUMENT 69

CONCLUSIONS REACHED BY THE CONFERENCE
OF RESPONSIBLE SOVIET AUTHORITIES OF
EIGHT COUNTIES ON AND ABOVE THE DISTRICT
LEVEL ON THE LAND INVESTIGATION DRIVE

Probably a statement originally made by Mao
(As printed in *Red China*, No. 89, June 29, 1933, pp. 5–7)

From June 17 to 21, 1933, the central government has sponsored a conference of the responsible Soviet authorities on and above the district level in the eight counties of Jui-chin, Hui-ch'ang, Yü-tu, Sheng-li, Po-sheng, Shih-ch'eng, Ning-hua, and Ch'ang-t'ing on the land investigation drive. Having heard a report on the land investigation drive made by Comrade Mao Tse-tung, chairman of the central government, and after five days of detailed discussions, the conference has gained a deeper insight into the vital significance of the land investigation drive. It is believed that in the course of the great victory of the Soviet movement, the millions of masses in the Soviet areas have already set up their own regime, confiscated the land of the landlord class for redistribution to the peasant masses, and put restrictions on the exploitation of workers by capitalists. Having had their own activism aroused in the revolutionary victory, the broad masses have participated in the revolutionary war and in Soviet reconstruction. In both respects they have achieved splendid accomplishments, defeated innumerable attacks of the enemy, expanded the Soviet areas, and given a vigorous push to the development of the Soviet movement. All these are the results of the correct leadership of the Communist Party and the Soviet government as well as of the active support given to that leadership by the broad masses.

But this does not mean that there are no more serious problems in the Soviet areas. Precisely because of the rapid development of the Soviet movement, all class enemies both outside and inside the Soviet areas are fanatically engaging themselves in a desperate struggle and resistance. Outside the Soviet areas the enemies have resorted to military attacks. Inside the Soviet areas another method has been adopted. Landlords, rich peasants, and all class heretical elements have managed to conceal their own counterrevolutionary features. Taking advantage of the fact that the land problem in many places in the Soviet areas has not yet been thoroughly solved, many of them have managed to retain some economic bases. For instance, the land and [other] property of many landlord elements have not yet been completely confiscated, and many rich-peasant elements have been allotted good land. In addition, many of these elements have wormed their way into Soviet agencies, mass organizations, and local armed forces. Abusing Soviet authority thus gained, they have sought to obstruct the development of the mass struggle, to deceive, bribe, and threaten a part of the masses, to spread rumors, to set up secret organizations, to falsely accuse and entrap active working personnel in the Soviets, and to undertake all sorts of activities of intrigue and sabotage. Such a situation has often been discovered even in many places in the Central Soviet Area. The Eight-County Conference considers this to be a serious problem. It holds that an extensive and thoroughgoing land investigation drive has to be carried out in order to deal a final blow to the feudal remnant forces, to solve the land problem thoroughly, and to consolidate the Soviet regime as strong as iron. The Eight-County Conference realizes that the land investigation drive is definitely a ruthless and violent class struggle, a great revolutionary movement of the masses, and a most important link in the chain of tasks of today. Therefore, the land investigation drive calls for a large-scale organizational mobilization, for implementation of the firm class line, and for the prosecution of patient and adequate work among the masses.

The Eight-County Conference unanimously supports the instruction of the central government on the land investigation drive and completely endorses the following conclusions:

I. On Organizational Mobilization

1. The various departments of the government must take a concerted action. Not only the land department, the workers' and peasants' prosecution department, the judicial department, and the political

security bureau should take up the principal responsibility of leading the land investigation drive, but also the finance department, the military department, the national economy department, and the education department should carry out various kinds of necessary tasks in the land investigation drive. The chairmen and presidiums of the governments should bear the over-all responsibility of leadership in the land investigation drive. It was a mistake in the past to regard the land investigation drive as the work of the land department alone.

2. Land investigation committees should be organized on the three levels of the county, district, and township to be subordinated to the respective levels of government. These committees should have over-all responsibility for leading the land investigation drive. The members of the committees should include responsible government authorities as well as representatives of mass organizations, and so on.

3. The county Soviet should immediately work out a plan of the land investigation drive for the entire county for the month of July. Thereafter, a plan of the land investigation drive should be worked out at the end of every month for the next month.

4. The district Soviet should call a meeting of the chairmen of the township Soviets and the chiefs of the poor-peasant corps to draw up plans for the work of the entire district for the first seven days. Thereafter, there should be both a plan and a review of the work every seven days. But [representatives from] faraway townships may come to the district Soviet to attend meetings every fourteen days, while [representatives from] nearby townships must come to attend meetings once every seven days so that the land investigation drive may be rapidly pushed forward.

5. In regard to the procedure of mobilization on the township level, attention should be paid to: (*a*) the township congress of delegates; (*b*) the labor unions; (*c*) the poor-peasant corps; (*d*) the congress of women's delegates; (*e*) the Red Guard and the Youth Vanguard; (*f*) other revolutionary organizations; and (*g*) village and hamlet mass meetings. It is only through these agencies, organizations, and mass meetings that the greatest possible force can be mobilized to take part in the land investigation drive. All small-scale and simple methods which do not take the great majority of the masses into consideration are not correct.

6. The county Soviet should open a land investigation drive training class to enroll one trainee from each township who will graduate in ten days. To the second class, each township will also send one trainee

to be chosen from among the most active elements in the township Soviet congress of delegates, the poor-peasant corps, and the labor unions. [After graduation] the trainees will be sent back to their respective townships to lead the land investigation drive. But those who come from advanced districts and townships should be sent to work in the backward districts and townships. Two classes should be opened in each of the three months of July, August, and September.

The provincial Soviet should select active elements from advanced counties and districts to open a land investigation drive training class and send them (after graduation) to backward counties and districts to lead the land investigation drive.

7. In order to carry out the land investigation drive vigorously, the organization of various government departments should be immediately strengthened, mainly by abolishing the holding of concurrent jobs, putting an end to the practice of transferring officials without careful consideration, and increasing the number of necessary working personnel.

8. On the township level there should be organized a confiscation and redistribution committee to be elected by the poor-peasant corps and subordinated to the township Soviet. This committee should be responsible for the confiscation and redistribution of the land and [other] property of landlords and rich peasants.

II. On the Implementation of the Correct Class Line in the Land Investigation Drive

1. To rely on the poor peasants, ally with the middle peasants, and make the hired farm hands play a leading role so as to annihilate the landlord class completely and frustrate the attempt of the rich peasants to steal the benefits of the land revolution and weaken their economic power—these are the correct class line and struggle tactics that should be firmly carried out in the land investigation drive. In the matter of allying with the middle peasants, we should, first of all, refrain from violating their interests. The land of the middle peasants (including the well-to-do middle peasants) must not be equally redistributed without their consent. At the beginning of land investigation, the Soviet policy of allying with the middle peasants and refraining from injuring them should be generally publicized. In the process of carrying out land investigation, care should be taken to determine the doubtful class status between middle peasants and rich peasants, and there should be no mistakes made. In redistributing the confiscated land and [other]

properties, attention must be paid to individual poor and miserable elements among the middle peasants so that they may not suffer. In making the hired farm hands play a leading role, the main point is to make them all join the poor-peasant corps and organize the hired-farm-hand small group, thus through them consolidating the active elements among the poor peasants, developing the poor-peasant corps, and pushing forward the land investigation drive. In redistributing the confiscated land and [other] property, the hired farm hands should be the first beneficiaries.

2. To analyze the class status correctly in the light of practical social relations is an important part [of the work] of carrying out the class line. All the mistakes that have been made with regard to this question in the past must be quickly rectified. In attempting to settle all practical questions relating to class status, we must follow the standards which have just been prescribed in *How to Analyze the Classes*. We must explain these standards to all the masses and primarily educate the cadres to let them understand completely what the standards are.

3. The aim of land investigation is to "investigate the classes," but not to redistribute the land. It is wrong to speak of land investigation as being equivalent to "erecting a wooden board" [in the field to mark the land redistributed to a certain individual]. It is only after the completion of the ruthless struggle of class investigation that a fresh redistribution of land is permitted in certain individual places where the great majority of the masses demand it. This strict distinction [between the investigation of the classes and the redistribution of land] must be made not only for the purpose of reassuring the peasants of their ownership of land so that they may not be afraid of the "uncertainty of land redistribution." It is also for the sake of the success of the struggle of the "investigation of the classes." We must concentrate all our efforts (especially our alliance with the middle peasants) in coping with the resistance of the landlords and rich peasants. At the present time, there must not be any confusion in the ranks of the peasants themselves.

4. All possible clan or local struggles should be avoided. All forces should be united to launch a struggle against landlords and rich peasants. Therefore, it would be an important tactic in the land investigation drive to mobilize the poor and miserable masses bearing a common family name in a village to search out the landlords and rich peasants with the same family name in the same village. Similarly, any struggle against superstitions should also be shelved until after the struggle of the "investigation of the classes."

III. On Mass Work

First of all, it is necessary to correct the [malpractice] that has happened in many places in the past: negligence in winning over the great majority of the masses and the manner of work known as bureaucratism and commandism. We must realize that only through patient and hard work in mobilizing and winning over the masses can we have the support of the great majority of the masses, develop their activism to the greatest extent, and achieve the aim of completely wiping out the feudal remnants. This kind of mass work is the only sure way of carrying out the class line. It should manifest itself completely in the following items of practical action in the land investigation drive:

1. At the beginning of the land investigation drive there must be widespread propaganda in all the villages and hamlets, explaining to the masses that the land investigation drive is essential, that land investigation is an investigation of the classes but not another redistribution of land, and that the investigation of the classes will not injure the middle peasants. It is especially important to make clear to the masses what kind of people the landlords, rich peasants, and middle peasants are. The village and hamlet mass meetings should be held more than once. In particular, they should be held more frequently in the most backward villages and hamlets. None of the revolutionary masses should be allowed to miss a chance to listen to our propaganda on the land investigation drive. In order to attain this objective, it is necessary, first of all, to have the matter explained clearly to all activists in the township congress of delegates, the labor unions, the poor-peasant corps, the congress of delegates of laboring women, and other mass organizations. Through these activists a general and thoroughgoing propaganda campaign will be carried out among the broad masses.

2. After the gathering of reports on the class status of landlords and rich peasants, the actual investigation should be carried out not only by the few people of the land investigation committee, but the work should be done from various angles by the active elements of the township congress of delegates, the poor-peasant corps, and the labor unions. All the intricacies of exploitation and misconduct on the part of the landlords and rich peasants should be unearthed and brought home to the masses. At the same time all false reports at the expense of the middle peasants should be established as untrue.

3. After the poor-peasant corps has decided the class status of the landlords and rich peasants who have been subject to investigation, the matter must also be submitted to the township Soviet for a decision

and to the district Soviet for approval. During this process, attention should be paid to all possible obstruction and resistance on the part of the landlord and rich-peasant elements who are secretly hiding in the poor-peasant corps and the Soviets. A severe blow should be given to those elements. At the same time, attention should be paid to possible mistakes in deciding the class status of genuine middle-peasant elements. Before confiscation and disposition, a mass meeting must be called in the village or hamlet of the person whose land and [other] property are being confiscated. It is only after a detailed explanation and with the approval of the masses that the work of confiscation and disposition may be carried out. In many places in the past, for the sake of convenience, the procedure of holding such a mass meeting to approve [the class status of landlords and rich peasants] has been neglected, thus giving rise to discontent among the masses and even causing serious clan or local struggles. Such mistakes should not be repeated in the future.

4. All confiscated property should be given to the poor and miserable masses, except for cash or its equivalent (such as gold or silver trinkets), which should be handed over to the finance department of the government. The erroneous practice of handing over all confiscated property to the government, a practice which has been prevalent in many places in the past, should be thoroughly corrected. In redistributing property, attention should be paid to redistributing a larger amount of it to the villages where the property has come from, so that the masses in those villages may be satisfied. With the consent of the masses, the rice confiscated at the time of or shortly after the autumn harvest may be temporarily stored up for redistribution to the poor and miserable masses next spring or summer. But once the masses demand a redistribution of such rice, it should be redistributed to them immediately. With the exception of the land reserved for public enterprises and of the public land for the Red Army, all confiscated land should be redistributed to those who have been allotted no or inadequate land in the past. The redistribution of property and land should be made as soon as possible; it should not be held up for a long time after their confiscation. In redistributing land and [other] property, a mass meeting should be called and a list [of the confiscated land and property] should be announced in the form of a proclamation so that everybody may know about it.

5. To win over the backward villages and hamlets, especially the big villages, is an important task in many places. Therefore, special

attention should be paid to the following points: (a) To mobilize the poor and miserable masses of a given village to investigate the landlords and rich peasants of the same village. (b) To hold numerous mass meetings for the "explanation of the classes." (c) To find out active elements and educate them, and it does not matter even if there is only one such element available; and through them, to come into close contact with the local masses, to develop the poor-peasant corps and to unfold the local class struggle. (d) In places where the situation is especially serious, those reactionary elements who are standing in the way of the struggle should, first of all, be captured to be tried and sentenced in public trial meetings and shot with the consent of the masses. Following this, the mass struggle is to be unfolded. (e) In places where there have been struggles between two different clans, there should be signed a "reconciliation pact" at a meeting of delegates of the two clans, admitting their past mistakes and agreeing to substitute the class struggle for their clan struggle.

The above-mentioned points are the necessary methods for winning over backward villages and hamlets, especially the big villages. In this connection, we must object to timidity and surrender to the backward big villages. We must object to the method of commandism which would alienate the masses. We must object to opportunistic toleration of reactionary elements, and to clan struggles and local struggles. Only in this way can we win over the revolutionary masses in all the backward villages and wipe out the feudal remnants there.

6. In the land investigation drive the poor-peasant corps is an organization with very important functions. The poor-peasant corps existed only in name in some places in the past; they should be organized in real earnest. In places where the poor-peasant corps have been organized, efforts should be made to unite the active elements in them, win over the backward elements, and firmly eliminate the class heretical elements, as well as other most wicked elements, who have wormed their way into the corps. We must try to avoid dissolving the entire poor-peasant corps and reorganizing them all over again. The sort of commandism under which a poor-peasant corps is to be dissolved on the pretext that it has failed to hold one or two meetings for lack of the necessary attendance is totally wrong. The best propaganda and agitation should be conducted to encourage the activists to attend meetings. Even if only a few persons come to the meetings, we should still hold meetings with them in order to win over more persons to become members. The poor-peasant corps should include all working masses

in the rural districts who are willing to join the corps, so that these people may form the workers' small group in the corps to play a role of leadership. The middle peasants should not become members of the poor-peasant corps, but may be invited to attend the meetings as observers. They should be invited to attend the meetings as observers especially when decisions on the class status are being made. The three-man executive council of the poor-peasant corps, which has been prevalent in the past, should be reorganized into a five-man committee. The five men should choose a chairman from among themselves. Under this committee there should be small groups which are to be organized by five to fifteen members, each according to the proximity of their residences. When the land investigation drive is in full swing, the poor-peasant corps may meet as often as once every several days. When the land investigation drive is over, it will meet according to the normal schedule. In calling frequent meetings, however, consideration should be given to the moods of the masses of the members of the corps, for any orders [from above] and coercion are harmful. Before every meeting, the chairman of the township Soviet should direct the poor-peasant corps committee to make adequate preparations for the items on the agenda. To hold a meeting without preparation is a very bad habit. During the land investigation drive, the district Soviet should call a meeting of the chairmen of the poor-peasant corps once every seven or fourteen days to discuss problems of strengthening the organization of the poor-peasant corps, devising means for leading the struggle, and so forth. If necessary, an extraordinary congress of the poor-peasant corps of the entire district may be called.

IV. On Consolidating the Soviets

1. It is today an important task during the land investigation drive to reorganize unsound Soviet agencies so that they can fully represent the interests of workers and peasants and become adequately competent Soviets.

2. The reorganization of local Soviet agencies may be divided into two aspects: the purging of bad elements from the Soviets and the absorption of active revolutionary elements into the Soviets. The purging of bad elements should be the chief responsibility of the workers' and peasants' prosecution departments on the county and district levels. The method to be employed for this purpose is the organization of prosecution committees on the township level to carry out prosecutions along with the development of the struggle to "investigate the

classes." The township prosecution committee should be composed of two representatives from the labor union, five from the poor-peasant corps, two from the congress of women's delegates, one from the light mounted troops of the Youth Corps, and one from the Youth Vanguard. The said representatives should choose a chairman from among themselves to be directly subordinated to the district workers' and peasants' prosecution department. The persons to be prosecuted are chiefly class heretical elements who have wormed their way into the township congress of delegates, and those elements who have entirely estranged themselves from the interests of workers and peasants and have surrendered to and come to terms with landlords and rich peasants.

The methods of prosecution are: (a) A list of the names of such elements should be prepared, evidences of their crimes should be gathered, and the masses of the entire township should be notified to express their opinions in regard to the matter. (b) After the opinions of the masses have been collected, the prosecution committee should draw conclusions. (c) The conclusions should be submitted to the township congress of Soviet delegates for discussion, after which votes will be taken to expel [the bad elements involved]. (d) [The results of the votes] will be reported to the workers' and peasants' prosecution department of the district Soviet and, with the approval of the district Soviet presidium, the expulsions will be announced to the masses of the entire township in the name of the workers' and peasants' prosecution department.

In the course of the prosecution campaign, the surprise attack teams, informers, and complaint boxes of the workers' and peasants' prosecution department should each play a full part. Those elements with the most serious crimes should also be handed over to the judicial department to be punished according to law after they have been tried by the mass trial meeting. It is the purpose of prosecutions and public trials to clean out, on the one hand, all the bad elements who are presently in the Soviets, and to educate the broad masses on the other, so that they will realize why the bad elements in the Soviets should be cleaned out and why they should rise up like one man to oversee and support the Soviets in order that such bad elements will no longer be able to emerge in the future. Prosecutions and public trials should not apply to those who were merely not active enough in the past or those who made only slight mistakes. Such elements should be won over chiefly by means of criticism and encouragement. Before a public trial takes place, the masses should be supplied with adequate propaganda, exposing the various crimes of the persons to be tried, in order that they may not be able to deceive some of the backward elements and cause them to make trouble during the public trial. In places where there are struggles between clans, between family branches, or between villages, public trials should not be lightly held. Public trials can be held only when these nonclass struggles have disappeared and when such trials are deemed to be necessary by the masses.

The prosecution of bad elements in the district and county Soviets should be carried out, under the leadership of the workers' and peasants' prosecution departments on the same levels, by a prosecution committee composed of representatives from mass organizations and from middle- and low-ranking comrades working in the governments of the same levels (from section chiefs to cooks). The prosecution committee on the district level should also take in active elements on the township level with one representative from each township. The procedure and substance of the prosecution [on the district and county levels] are somewhat similar to those on the township level as described above.

In the prosecution campaign of the Soviets which will closely follow the development of the land investigation drive, the presidium and the workers' and peasants' prosecution department of the government on a higher level should have plans for leading those of a lower level, examine from time to time whether there are any mistakes in prosecution that may be committed by the lower level government, and, if so, take timely measures to correct those mistakes. At the same time, they should gather actual experience in prosecution for the purpose of educating the presidium and the workers' and peasants' prosecution department of a lower level government as well as its prosecution committee.

3. In absorbing active elements into the Soviets, the township level should do the following: Firstly, there should be held a meeting of electors to elect those elements who have shown themselves to be the most courageous and resolute in the land investigation struggle and make them members of the township congress of delegates to fill up the vacancies left by the bad elements who have been purged. There must be good preparation beforehand for this kind of election. From several to more than a dozen alternate delegates can be elected this time. This is especially necessary in places where there have emerged numerous new active elements, so that the incompetent and backward delegates may be gradually replaced. Secondly, large batches of new active elements should be absorbed into the various committees under the jurisdiction of the township Soviet, such as the committee on land

reconstruction, the committee on forests, the committee on waters, the committee on education, and so on, so that all these committees may be earnestly established and set to work. Thirdly, in the general elections to be held throughout the entire Soviet areas this fall, we must see to it that most of the active elements in the land investigation struggle should be elected to serve in the township Soviets.

On the district level, there are the district Soviets where only a small number of the members of the original district executive committees are bad elements. In such cases, the good elements who remain on the committee may be asked to take up the duties of the bad ones who may be purged. At the same time, the active elements in the township Soviets should be absorbed into the district Soviet to take part in its work. In a few places where the majority of the members of the original district executive committee are bad elements, the county Soviet should, during the land investigation drive, send representatives to sponsor an extraordinary congress of delegates of the entire district for the purpose of re-electing the district Soviet.

On the county level, there are two methods for recruiting supplementary personnel: either the bad elements among the members of the county executive committee may be replaced by good ones, or the good elements may be chosen from the district and township Soviets to take part in the work [of the county Soviet].

V. On Suppressing Counterrevolutionaries

1. Governments on all levels and the entire system of the state political security bureaus should pay great attention to suppressing during the land investigation drive all the activities of counterrevolutionary individuals and organizations sponsored by landlord and rich-peasant elements hidden in various places. Above all, the political security bureaus and their special commissioners on the provincial, county, and district levels should mobilize all their own strength to carry out the task of combating the counterrevolutionaries. They should correct their mistaken views of the past, according to which counterrevolutionary activities in many places have been ignored.

2. In suppressing the counterrevolutionaries in the land investigation drive, it is essential to follow the mass struggle in class investigation, direct the masses to act as informers, trace counterrevolutionary clues, and arrest counterrevolutionary elements. During the period of the land investigation drive, the district special commissioners of the security bureaus are hereby empowered to arrest the criminals. After a

preliminary trial by the special commissioners, the criminals will be sent over to the district judicial department for trial. Important criminals should be publicly tried before the masses by a circuit court organized in the villages of the criminals and should be shot on the spot with the approval of the masses. This is the way to stir up the hatred and alertness of the masses against the counterrevolutionaries. This is in contrast to what has been prevalent in some places in the past: sending the arrested criminals to the county Soviet without further ado, ignoring the indignation of the broad masses against the counterrevolutionaries, and failing to educate the masses by this means in order that they may continue to be on the alert against the counterrevolutionaries. For the purpose of suppressing the counterrevolutionaries, we should make a great effort to improve the techniques we have used in the past in investigation, arrest, trial, and imprisonment.

VI. On Attacking Landlords and Rich Peasants by Means of Fines and Contributions

For the purpose of fundamentally annihilating all the economic bases of the landlord class and weakening the economic power of the rich peasants, it is absolutely necessary to attack them by imposing fines on landlords and extorting contributions from rich peasants. In view of the fact that the majority or great majority of landlords and rich peasants in many places in the eight counties have not yet been found out, there should be no doubt that 800,000 silver dollars can be raised in the three months of July, August, and September. The finance departments on the county and district levels should make the greatest efforts to bring this about. The chief methods to be employed are to direct the township Soviets and mobilize the hired-farm-hand unions, the poor-peasant corps, and other mass organizations to investigate the properties of landlords and rich peasants, to fix appropriate sums as fines or contributions to be paid by each person, and to press severely for payment, and so on. In this connection, care must be taken not to involve the middle peasants. Moreover, there should be some difference in the degree of punishment to be meted out against the rich peasants and landlords. That is to say, the landlords are to be annihilated, while the rich peasants are to be weakened.

VII. Relations of the Land Investigation Drive with War Mobilization and with Economic and Cultural Reconstruction

1. In the midst of the success of the land investigation drive it is

entirely possible to recruit eighty thousand men for the Red Army. And it would not take too long a time to achieve this. If we can launch a widespread and thoroughgoing land investigation drive in July, August, and September, and stir up all the broad masses in the eight counties, it is entirely possible for us to mobilize within six to ten months 80,000 new fighters in the eight counties to be sent to the front. Therefore, this task has to depend upon the development of a thoroughgoing land investigation drive. Not to make any effort [to achieve this objective by utilizing] the land investigation drive but simply to confine our effort to the expansion of the Red Army itself has been the basic reason why the eight counties have shown unsatisfactory results in expanding the Red Army in the past. This point must be clearly understood.

2. In the midst of the success of the land investigation drive the eight counties should set up cooperatives as far as possible. The principal cooperatives should be those of the consumers' goods, those for the adjustment of foodstuffs, those for necessary tools of production (chiefly farm implements), and those for making loans to the poor and miserable masses. These are designed to resist the ruthless exploitation of the broad masses by speculating merchants. For it is one of our important tasks of the moment to develop the economy of all the Soviet areas to resist the enemy's economic blockade. To prosecute the war on the economic front quickly and on a large scale requires the great organizational strength of the Soviets and the masses as well as large amounts of capital. Therefore, the central government is hereby requested to issue three million silver dollars of economic reconstruction bonds to be paid in grain in order that the work can be done quickly. The accomplishment of this task also depends upon the successful outcome of the land investigation drive. If we do not exert great efforts in the sphere of the land investigation drive so as to mobilize the majority of the masses to participate in economic reconstruction, it would be impossible to expect the complete success of this task.

3. The autumn harvesting and the autumn plowing are two big events which are confronting us today. They are crucial to the livelihood of the masses and to the revolutionary war. Therefore, we must try to win the complete success of the autumn harvesting and the autumn plowing this year during the land investigation drive.

4. The widespread development of the cultural and educational movement can also be realized only in the midst of the success of the land investigation drive. With the positive support of the great majority of the masses, for instance, it would not be difficult to accomplish such

cultural and educational reconstruction projects as the establishment of a club for every 1,000 people, a primary school for every 500 people, a night school for every 100 people, and a class in which most people over 16 years old will be taught Chinese characters. The county of Hsing-kuo which now in general has almost attained this achievement is a very good example.

VIII. *In Face of Enemy Attacks*

In the enemy's Fourth "Campaign" against the Central Soviet Area, though the heroic and courageous Red Army has fundamentally broken up the main forces of Chiang Kai-shek on the northern front, the enemy is still attacking us. Though the disintegration and downfall of the enemy is being accelerated every day and though the enemy has his innumerable difficulties, he has not forgotten to attack us. Now the enemy from Kwangtung has pushed forward to Hsün-wu and An-yüan, and the enemy from Fukien is still in occupation of the general area of Shang-hang, Lien-ch'eng, and Ch'ing-liu. This is a great threat to the eight counties and their neighboring areas. In order to exterminate fundamentally the main forces of the enemy and to drive away his remnant troops, we have to rely mainly on a broad mass war in addition to the heroic and courageous fighting of the Red Army. This has added a further urgent fighting task to the land investigation drive. In the face of the approaching enemy, we should not relax our efforts in the land investigation drive, but should redouble them. In the course of the land investigation drive, we must quickly win over several million people of the masses and have them positively aroused and armed, suppress the treacherous elements from within—the remnant forces of landlords and rich peasants—and set up Soviets as strong as iron. Only this can provide an adequate guarantee that the enemy will be defeated.

IX. *Dedicate Our Success in the Land Investigation Drive to the Second National Soviet Congress*

We must thoroughly complete the land investigation drive before the Second National Soviet Congress, which is scheduled to meet on December 11, [1933]. Therefore, we should especially intensify our work in July, August, and September. We will call a conference in October to review the land investigation drive in the eight counties. When the central government sends inspectors to the various counties in August, we must show them concrete achievements. In order to accelerate the land investigation drive, the eight counties have voluntarily signed a "Land Investigation Drive Contest Agreement" and will strive hard for its complete implementation.

X. Severe Punishment of the Elements Who Undermine and Oppose the Land Investigation Drive

In the ruthless struggle of the land investigation drive, the class heretical elements and other wicked elements who have wormed their way into the Soviets would certainly come out to undermine or oppose the drive. Such elements should be given severe punishments according to the instruction of the central government on the land investigation drive. Even in the present conference held under the direct sponsorship of the central government, when all other conferees gave unanimous support to the central government's policy of land investigation and were enthusiastically discussing the progress of work, Huang Yen-p'an, chief of the Land Department, Ho-k'ou District, Ning-hua County, alone expressed an opinion which was basically opposed to the land investigation drive. Though both the small group meeting and the conference itself severely criticized him and attacked him, he refused to admit his error. Believing that Huang Yen-p'an was taking an unequivocal stand to help our class enemy and to oppose the land investigation struggle of the broad masses and that he was slurring the work of the Soviets, this conference has recommended to the central government that he be removed from his position as chief of the Land Department of the Ho-k'ou District, and that he be placed under the surveillance of the Ning-hua County Soviet. It is only by purging such wicked elements that we can purify our revolutionary ranks, overcome all the destruction and resistance of the class enemy, and accomplish the great revolutionary tasks of the land investigation drive.

DOCUMENT 77

INSTRUCTION NO. 7 OF THE STATE POLITICAL SECURITY BUREAU—THE RESPONSIBILITY AND WORK OF THE SECURITY BUREAU AND ITS SPECIAL COMMISSIONERS IN THE LAND INVESTIGATION DRIVE

Issued in late June or early July, 1933
(As reproduced by the Minkan Provincial Branch of the Political Security Bureau, [January] 23, 1934)

I. It has been pointed out in the instruction issued by the central government on the land investigation drive that the land struggle of the past has not yet been thoroughgoing, that the benefits of the land in many places have not yet been completely enjoyed by the poor peasants, hired farm hands, and middle peasants, and that many landlords, village bosses, gentry, and rich peasants have stolen the fruits of the land revolution. Consequently, arousing the activism of the masses has been hindered. Above all, the work of mobilization has proved to be particularly backward and fruitless in the nonintensified struggle areas. Many facts contained in the reports of the representatives of various localities at the Eight-County Conference on the land investigation drive prove incontrovertibly that what has been pointed out and estimated in the instruction of the central government in question is entirely correct and that the land investigation drive is absolutely necessary.

II. The urgent task in the current struggle is to mobilize the broad masses for the prosecution of the land investigation drive so as to make the drive an intense class struggle in the rural districts in order to suppress the feudal forces completely and solve the land problem correctly. Under this task, the political security bureau has the responsibility of eliminating counterrevolutionary political cliques and feudal forces and preventing and suppressing all resistance and sabotage by counterrevolutionaries, landlords, village bosses, gentry, and rich peasants. This is the principal task of the political security bureau in the land investigation drive.

III. In accordance with the above-mentioned task, the state political security bureau hereby instructs its branch bureaus in the various provinces and counties and its special commissioners in the districts to carry out the following assignments earnestly and effectively:

1. Search out class heretical elements, landlords, village bosses, gentry, and rich peasants.

In carrying out the movement of the state political security bureau to investigate the property of the village bosses, gentry, landlords, and counterrevolutionaries in the past, the branch bureaus and special commissioners at their respective levels dealt, indeed, a severe blow to the landlords, village bosses, gentry, rich peasants, and counterrevolutionaries. They also registered the landlords, village bosses, gentry, and rich peasants in various localities. However, this work of registration and investigation was obviously not thoroughgoing. It failed to establish a close link between the complete confiscation of the land of the landlords, village bosses, and gentry, and the good land and surplus farm implements of the rich peasants on the one hand and the over-all program of the work of the Soviets on the other. Now copies [of the lists] of the landlords, village bosses, gentry, and rich peasants should immediately be sent to governments of the same level so that they may check to see if their land has been confiscated and if the rich peasants have been given poor land in exchange. In the case of those who have not previously been discovered, our work net should be mobilized to expose them in accordance with the methods of analyzing the classes as adopted by the central government. The findings on the landlords, village bosses, gentry, and rich peasants thus exposed should be reported to the governments of the same level. The provincial and county branch bureaus should be responsible for finding out whether there are any class heretical elements hiding in the structure of the bureaus; these elements must not be shielded or retained. Those who are found guilty of shielding or retaining [such elements] must be severely punished.

2. Suppress the sabotage and resistance of all counterrevolutionaries, land-lords, village bosses, gentry, and rich peasants against the land investigation drive.

Undoubtedly, the village bosses, gentry, landlords, rich peasants, and all counterrevolutionaries will rise against this drive, because the land investigation drive is the final class struggle designed to destroy the political and economic foundations of the landlords, village bosses, and gentry and to oppose the rich peasants. The security bureaus should particularly expose the rumors of the counterrevolutionaries, landlords, village bosses, gentry, and rich peasants—such as the intimidating rumors: "Overthrow the rich peasants after the landlords are over-thrown; overthrow the middle peasants after the rich peasants are overthrown; overthrow the poor peasants after the middle peasants are overthrown," as well as the argument: "Oppose indiscriminate blows to village bosses." The landlords, village bosses, gentry, and rich peasants must be strictly prevented from calling secret meetings and openly spreading rumors to cause trouble. Should any landlords, village bosses, gentry, and rich peasants rise and resort to sabotage and resistance, they must immediately be put under arrest, in addition to having their land and other property confiscated. Those of them who have previously committed counterrevolutionary and anti-Soviet acts must be turned over to the masses for public trials and executed on the spot in accordance with the wishes and demands of the masses.

3. Step up surprise inspections and Red curfews.

It is believed that after the land investigation drive is set in motion a part of the village bosses, gentry, and landlords will come to realize that they cannot possibly escape the flames of the mass struggle in view of the fact that they have committed counterrevolutionary acts in the past. They will seek to flee, or take advantage of any opportunities offered them to move their personal property and articles to the homes of their relatives for concealment. For this reason, our surprise inspection teams and inspection stations should work all the more closely in keeping with the Red curfew of the locality. Not a single landlord, village boss, gentry, or counterrevolutionary should be allowed to escape.

4. Enlarge the organization of our work net and strengthen its function in the land investigation drive.

In attempting to expose all the landlords, village bosses, gentry, and class heretical elements who have concealed themselves in the revolutionary ranks, and the landlords, village bosses, gentry, and rich peasants who have sabotaged the land revolution, our work net is required to play an extremely large role. Consequently, it is necessary to approach the individual chiefs of our work net at once for detailed conversations, making them understand [the documents]: *How to Analyze the Classes* and *How to Penetrate into the Masses to Carry Out Investigations.* In the meantime, it is necessary to absorb the combat elements who have been active in exposing the landlords, village bosses, gentry, and rich peasants into our work net so as to enlarge the organization of the work net.

5. Give the special commissioners of various districts extraordinary powers to arrest and try [landlords, etc.].

According to their working regulations, the special commissioners have the power to watch and investigate only, but no power to try or arrest [counterrevolutionaries]. But during the current land investigation drive, many village bosses, gentry, and reactionary rich peasants will necessarily have to be arrested. If their arrests have to be delayed until their cases have been reported to the superior organs, this will do the struggle harm. Therefore, except for the cases of political criminals who cannot be arrested until after reports on them have been sent to the superior organs, the special commissioners may, in cooperation with the district and township governments of the same levels, arrest and try landlords, village bosses, gentry, and reactionary rich peasants who have been discovered during the land investigation drive.

6. How to deliver and prosecute landlords, village bosses, gentry, and rich peasants who sabotage and oppose the land investigation drive.

As has been said above, the special commissioners have the power to arrest and try village bosses, gentry, landlords, and reactionary rich peasants. Having been arrested, however, these people may be sent to the district governments for detention, and need not be sent one by one to the superior governments. Following preliminary trials, they may be prosecuted in the district judicial departments of the same level. Notoriously counterrevolutionary landlords, village bosses, and gentry may be handed over to the circuit courts to be tried, sentenced, and executed. The special commissioners may also announce the intrigues and crimes of the counterrevolutionaries in question at the mass trial meetings.

All bureau chiefs and special commissioners are [hereby instructed] faithfully.

Attached is a copy of the Working Program of the Land Investigation Drive. [This program is omitted here.]

TENG FA

Chief of the Bureau

DOCUMENT 78

INSTRUCTION NO. 9 OF THE STATE
POLITICAL SECURITY BUREAU

Issued on July 12 (1933)
(As reproduced by the Minkan Provincial Branch of
the Political Security Bureau, January 23, 1934)

1. The struggle in the current land investigation drive is the most ruthless class struggle. It is a struggle designed to eradicate basically the feudal remnants in the rural districts. The security bureau should exert all its strength and mobilize the strength of the broad masses of workers and peasants in order to prevent and suppress the sabotage and resistance of the landlords, village bosses, gentry, rich peasants, and all counterrevolutionaries!

A recent review of *Instruction No. 7* as enforced by the provincial and county branch bureaus and the special commissioners shows complacency and lack of enthusiasm. This bureau has already sent personnel to the counties of Yü-tu, Hui-ch'ang, An-yüan, and Jui-chin to help [in the land investigation drive]. The provincial bureaus should also send special commissioners to the various counties to supervise the enforcement of the land investigation drive.

2. From the reports of the Jui-chin and Yü-tu branch bureaus, we can see the following facts of sabotage and resistance by the landlords, village bosses, gentry, rich peasants, and counterrevolutionaries: (*1*) They have buried their cash and valuables under the ground or thrown them into fish ponds; (*2*) They have taken advantage of the rising water in the rivers to float downstream with their valuables, gold, and silver aboard bamboo or timber rafts or even wooden planks in the direction of Kan-chou (Yü-tu); (*3*) They have carried their gold, silver, and hidden firearms with them to escape into the mountains to become bandits and offer stubborn resistance! (e.g., Jui-chin [two characters not clear], T'ing-chou, Ch'i-li-ch'iao, and Shih-ch'eng); (*4*) They have falsely accused Soviet personnel in an attempt to injure revolutionary comrades and used all kinds of methods to offer final resistance.

3. The provincial and county branch bureaus and the special commissioners should concentrate all their strength in helping lead the land investigation struggle. This is the very core of our central task. The following important items of work must be carried out immediately:

(1) Mobilize our work net and the masses to launch surprise inspections against the landlords, village bosses, and gentry, and to keep a strict watch on them in order to prevent them from concealing cash or throwing it into ponds or rivers, so that the attainment of the objective of raising 800,000 [silver dollars] may be assured.

(2) Cooperate with the military departments in intensifying the Red curfew and the work of inspection stations at all big and small road crossings and in the border areas. *Not a single* landlord, village boss, or gentry should be allowed to carry cash to escape to the White areas.

(3) With the exception of the old and infirm, and women and children, all *able-bodied* landlords, village bosses, and gentry whose land has been expropriated should be detained through the mobilization of the masses made possible by cooperating with the government. They should be organized into forced-labor corps and sent to areas where the masses are best and where they cannot easily climb the mountains, so that, under the surveillance of the masses, they [may reclaim the] waste

[land and help] the troops in harvesting the rice crops, etc. The strictest precautions should be taken to prevent them from escaping into the mountains to become bandits. . . .

(4) In Shih-ch'eng and Po-sheng, the strictest precautions should be taken to prevent all landlords, village bosses, and gentry from joining the Big Sword Society. The Big Sword Society should be suppressed quickly. The security branch bureau at T'ing-chou should immediately suppress the bandits in the T'ai-yang-shan [mountains] and may not let them have a chance to grow in numerical strength.

(5) *Instruction No. 7* on the land investigation drive and the present instruction are inseparable. It is important that all branch bureau chifs and speciael commissioners must not be in the least negligent, and must spare no effort in enforcing both. Such is the order!

To the bureau chiefs and special commissioners

TENG FA

Chief of the Bureau

12/7 [1933]

DOCUMENT 84

PRELIMINARY CONCLUSIONS DRAWN FROM THE LAND INVESTIGATION DRIVE

Mao Tse-tung

(As printed in *Struggle* (Kiangsi), No. 24, August 29, 1933, pp. 4–12)

1. A Great Victory

In response to the call of the party and the central government, the land investigation drive has been unfolded on a large scale. If we say that the land investigation drive was only in the initial stage in the past, then [we must concede that] the work accomplished in the month of July after the Eight-County Conference on the land investigation [drive] held in June has already exceeded our achievements of almost half a year since last winter.

Generally speaking, the land investigation drive has reached a new situation in the eight counties represented at the conference in question. It has become a great mass movement. The achievements made in Jui-chin and Po-sheng are the greatest of all. In these two counties more than 2,000 households of landlords and rich peasants have been uncovered. Initial achievements have also been made in the counties of Sheng-li, Yü-tu, Hui-ch'ang, T'ing-tung, Ch'ang-t'ing, Shih-ch'eng, and Ning-hua. In all the districts and townships where the land investigation has achieved success, great mass struggles have been launched. Much of the Soviet and party work which was formerly in a stagnant condition has now become dynamic. Many bad elements in the Soviets have been purged, and the counterrevolutionary elements hidden in the villages have been severely suppressed. In a word, the feudal remnant forces have been dismally defeated by the broad masses.

On the basis of this background, various kinds of work have been further stepped up. In regions where the land investigation has been successful, tremendous accomplishments have been made in expanding the Red Army and local armed forces, in selling economic reconstruction bonds, in developing cooperatives, in the autumn harvesting and autumn plowing, in developing labor mutual-help societies, and in enterprises of cultural reconstruction such as clubs, night schools, primary schools, and so on.

[In addition], all work has been going on more smoothly. On the basis of mass dynamism, large numbers of active elements have voluntarily and creatively become cadres in various fields of work. Many worker and peasant activists have joined the party and undertaken work in the Soviets. The best example is furnished by the district of Jen-t'ien in Jui-chin. With the help of the working corps of the central government, the land investigation drive in the district of Jen-t'ien has, within 55 days, successfully mobilized the masses of the entire district, thoroughly eradicated the feudal remnants, uncovered more than 300 households of landlords and rich peasants, shot 12 counterrevolutionary elements who were called "big tigers" by the masses, and put down counterrevolutionary activities. Certain elements among the Soviet working personnel who have committed serious mistakes have been prosecuted before the masses. Certain class heretical elements who have wormed their way into the Soviets have been purged. In the entire district a total amount of land capable of producing 27,000 piculs of rice a year has been uncovered. More than 20,000 toiling and miserable masses in the whole district have each been re-allotted an amount of land capable of producing 1.2 piculs of rice annually. Innumerable pieces of property of the village bosses, gentry, and landlords have been redistributed to the masses. Relying on the unprecedented heightening of the activism of the masses, more than 700 persons have been enlisted in the Red Army within 55 days and have been sent to Jui-chin to join the model division, with none of them deserting on the way. More than 1,900 piculs of rice have been saved for sale to the Red Army, and no other district in the whole county can compare with Jen-t'ien in this respect. At the request of the various townships, the entire district has undertaken to sell 40,000 silver dollars of the economic reconstruction bonds. Fines paid by landlords and contributions made by rich peasants have amounted to 7,500 silver dollars. Another 10,000 silver dollars will be raised. Cooperatives have been rapidly developed. Cultural and educational reconstruction work such as clubs, classes in Chinese characters, and night schools has grown in number. The number of party members has been increased and party leadership strengthened. The labor unions have made good progress. A new atmosphere is prevailing in the entire district, which has been transformed within 55 days from a backward district in Jui-chin to a first-class district like that of Wu-yang.

Now we must ask: why is it that Jen-t'ien district has made such great achievements? In this connection, we must point out that it is because they [comrades in Jen-t'ien] have grasped the importance of the task of land investigation and because they have firmly carried out the correct instructions of the Central Bureau and the central government with respect to the methods of mobilization, the class line, and mass work. They have done really Bolshevik work.

As far as their comprehension of the tasks is concerned, they [comrades in Jen-t'ien] clearly understand the close relationships between the land investigation drive and the revolutionary war. Therefore, they have done their work earnestly. They have been able to assume leadership of the land investigation drive and to make plans for work in the locality.

As to the methods of mobilization, they have been able to select seven of the most backward and relatively backward townships from among the eleven townships of the entire district. In these seven townships they have mobilized the party, the Youth Corps, the township Soviets, the labor unions, the poor-peasant corps, and other mass organizations, through which the broad masses have been mobilized.

With respect to the class line, they have firmly carried out the tactics of relying on the hired farm hands and poor peasants and allying with the middle peasants, and have greatly developed the poor-peasant corps. They have made clear that the investigation of land is not a redistribution of land and that the investigation of the classes is not an investigation of the classes of the middle peasants, poor peasants, and hired farm hands. They have fully carried out the work of "explaining the classes." When the landlords and rich peasants of O-feng township were threatening the middle peasants and some of the latter were becoming panicky, our comrades picked a few middle peasants for individual interviews and, through them, communicated our ideas to the other middle peasants. In this way the middle peasants of O-feng township became steady at once. Following this, they lent their active support to the Soviet policy of land investigation. From being deceived by the landlords and rich peasants, they have moved to an alliance with the poor peasants and workers in an effort to attack the landlords and rich peasants.

The comrades of Jen-t'ien district have also made mistakes in deciding the class status of a few households, but those mistakes have quickly been corrected.

With regard to the task of leading the mass struggle, they [comrades in Jen-t'ien] began by carrying out widespread propaganda. They did not call district or township meetings, but village and hamlet meetings instead. In this way they came into closer contact with the broad masses and made propaganda and agitation to them on numerous occasions. Therefore, the masses of the entire district have come to realize that the work of investigating land and investigating the classes is their own responsibility for their own benefit.

Then, in the investigation of the class status, they have mobilized most of the people to do the investigating. They have carefully collected all available data on the class status of each individual to show to the masses, with the consequence that no instance of dissatisfaction has been found on the part of the masses.

As to the determination of class status, this began with an analysis by the land investigation committee, which submitted its recommendations to the poor-peasant corps for discussion and decision. Finally, this decision was sent to the district Soviet for official approval. Then there was called a mass meeting of the entire village in which the person whose property was to be confiscated lived. The reasons for the confiscation were clearly explained to the masses, who endorsed the confiscation by raising their hands. It was only after all this that the confiscation was carried out.

In redistributing articles and land, the working personnel have all become aware that they should serve as models to others by not taking anything for themselves, but redistributing everything to the masses. The villages under confiscation have received more of such articles than other villages. This has satisfied the masses completely. Also, land has been redistributed quickly. Thus, there has been no delay in redistribution in Jen-t'ien district, which has not been the case in other places. For this reason, it has been possible to rouse the masses to action quickly.

The way they [comrades in Jen-t'ien] have penetrated the big backward villages is also correct. They have not been afraid of those big villages, nor have they used arbitrary methods to deal with them. Their way of dealing with them has been to concentrate all their strength, to carry out more and more propaganda, to begin by winning over the local active elements, uniting them together, educating them, and rousing the other masses to action through them. They have been very patient in doing work in this type of village. Superficially, they seem to have gone slowly, but actually they have been working quickly. They managed to arouse all the big backward villages in Jen-t'ien district in 55 days and do away with their backwardness in a very short time.

A village in Pai-k'eng township was originally difficult to penetrate, because there were two notorious "big tigers" who were lording it over there. [In view of such a situation], they [comrades] adopted a different method by first arresting those two bad eggs and putting them on trial before the local circuit court. With the warm support of the masses, the two men were shot on the spot. Since then, the mass struggle there has been afire like a fierce conflagration. They [comrades] held ten mass trials and three circuit courts. All of these trials were carried out by following the broad mass line. In every trial most of the people of the township concerned were present. Present, too, were representatives of other townships—over ten from each small township and forty to fifty from each big township. Therefore, the results of every public trial and sentence became immediately known to all the villages of the various townships of the entire district. This made the masses of all the townships and villages feel that the man put on trial that day deserved to be punished and killed. Also, it made them immediately think of the equally wicked elements in their own localities who deserved to be similarly punished. The land investigation drive in Jen-t'ien district is really the model for the entire Soviet areas.

The district of Chiu-pao in Jui-chin has also achieved great results. They [comrades in Chiu-pao] began by singling out three townships for the purpose. They got the members of the township land investigation committee to undergo a three-day training in the district Soviet, where the manner of mobilization, the class line, and the method to win over the masses were all explained clearly. They devised a good method for confiscation and redistribution: When they were about to confiscate the property of a certain landlord, they called upon the masses of the village or hamlet to go together to watch it. A mass meeting was held, in which a confiscation and redistribution committee was elected. The work of confiscation was carried out under the supervision of the masses. All the confiscated articles were put on a piece of flat ground and, with the approval of the masses, were immediately redistributed to those who deserved them. Another method was adopted with regard to eatables. It consisted of killing the pigs and preparing rice to entertain the masses. This method achieved great results in Chiu-pao district. The confiscation and redistribution committee there was not a regular, but a temporary, organization, and was very closely related to the masses. (The work of confiscating and redistributing land remained the responsibility of the regular land committee.) Nothing would be carried to the township Soviet. Redistribution was carried out without waiting for the assembling of the properties of several families. This had the advantage of avoiding delays and thefts that might be committed by others.

With respect to other lines and methods, the district of Chiu-pao was also generally right. That was why it was able to arouse the broad masses to investigate the class status all by themselves. They did it so successfully that not a single landlord or rich peasant ever went to the township Soviet or the district Soviet to protest against the class status that had been assigned to him. This was exactly opposite to the situation in the land investigation of former days, during which many landlords and rich peasants subject to investigation had invariably gone to the Soviet to lodge their protests, saying that they had been wrongly investigated. This was done not only by the persons directly involved, but also by township delegates and responsible officials of the poor-peasant corps who came to plead and seek bail for them. This time, however, it was not that the landlords and rich peasants did not want to protest, but that they were in no position to protest. None of the members of their clan and none of their relatives would give them support. The consequence was that the landlords and rich peasants were discouraged and incapable of protesting. This proves that the work of mass mobilization has fully been carried out at Chiu-pao. Otherwise, the above accomplishments would not have been possible.

All these glorious and model examples (which can be found in other places also) are a Bolshevik answer to the call of the party and the central government. They prove that the instructions issued by the Central Bureau and the central government are absolutely correct. Wherever these instructions are followed without reservation, great successes would be achieved at once. On the contrary, wherever these instructions are violated or overlooked, errors of work would follow suit and there would be no or little accomplishment. Let me cite other facts to prove the correctness of what I say.

2. Some Places Have Witnessed the Abandonment of the Leadership of the Land Investigation Drive

The combat task of the land investigation drive which had been launched in the various counties did not spread to all localities [Chinese original not clear here], even after the Central Bureau had issued its resolution on land investigation and after the central government had sent out its instruction on land investigation and convened the Eight-County Conference on the land investigation [drive]. For example, the achievements of land investigation in the whole province of Fukien are only comparable to those of Po-sheng county, and the achievements of each of the counties of Sheng-li, Yü-tu, Hui-ch'ang, and Shih-ch'eng are comparable only to those of one or two of the best districts of Jui-chin. The land investigation committee of many a district has not even held a single meeting. The county land investigation committees in several counties have not yet come to grips with the work of land investigation of their respective counties (such as Hui-ch'ang, Yü-tu, Shih-ch'eng, and Ning-hua). In the case of the land investigation committees of many districts and townships, the district and township chairmen simply refused to become their directors. On the pretext of being otherwise busy, they have given up the work of land investigation altogether.

As for the party leadership in the land investigation drive, the firm and strong leadership of the party has been clearly shown in the places where the investigation of land has achieved good results. Most of the masses of the party members have done courageous Bolshevik combat tasks under the leadership of the party branches and district committees. However, in the places where the investigation of land has achieved no or little success, it is found that the party has looked upon the land investigation drive with disdain. Take, for instance, the Hui-ch'ang county committee, which did not meet to discuss the work of land investigation until almost two months after the Central Bureau had sent along its resolution on land investigation. It was not until the end of July that it met to discuss land investigation for the first time. The Hsia-

hsiao district committee of Jui-chin did not even care about the land investigation drive for quite a while. Though the Jui-chin city district committee met once to discuss land investigation, it did not urge the party branches in the suburban areas to give attention to the leadership of land investigation. None of those party branches have ever held a meeting for the sake of the land investigation drive. In other places such as Yü-tu, Sheng-li, Shih-ch'eng, and Ning-hua, the county committees and many of the district committees have similarly failed to pay great attention to the work of land investigation.

The party and the central government say that "the land investigation drive is an attempt to mobilize the masses to go deep into the villages to wage the class struggle and is an effective method for the thorough solution of the land problem and the liquidation of the feudal and semi-feudal forces" (Resolution of the Central Bureau); "that the land investigation drive is a most urgent task which cannot be delayed for one instant by the Soviets of various places" (Instruction No. 11 of the central government); and that "the land investigation drive is a most important link in the chain of tasks of today" (Conclusions of the Eight-County Conference). But many of our comrades say: "We are too busy to have any time for the land investigation drive." The resolution of the party states: "All dilatory attempts to cope with the land investigation drive by means of bureaucratism and formalism are most harmful." But these comrades still use bureaucratism and formalism to deal with the land investigation drive.

3. Some Places Have Even Witnessed Surrender to the Landlords and Rich Peasants

In the places where the land investigation drive has been unfolded, there are still many individual but serious mistakes. This is due to the fact that in those places there are still many individual comrades in the local party headquarters and in the Soviets who have manifested their opportunistic vacillation when confronted with the violent class struggle of the land investigation drive. Above all, they have not been able to abandon their clan and local relations during the violent development of the land investigation drive, thus giving shelter to the landlord and rich-peasant elements of the same clan or of the same hamlet.

Or there have been cases of wrong analysis of the class status, with the result that landlords have been mistaken for rich peasants, and rich peasants for middle peasants.

Or some comrades working in the judicial department have accepted, out of utmost negligence, the false accusations of landlords and rich peasants who, acting in the name of the masses, have leveled charges against the active elements in the land investigation drive. On the other hand, some of our comrades in the security bureau and the judicial department have not been able to keep pace with the masses in their struggle of class investigation to take positive action against the counterrevolutionaries. There were instances in which the masses demanded the arrest and execution of the landlord and rich-peasant elements who resisted the land investigation, but our comrades did not comply with the demand of the masses. The judicial department of Jui-chin has committed many mistakes of this sort.

4. The Tendency to Injure the Middle Peasants Is a Most Serious Danger

The "Left" opportunist tendency has again shown itself in many places in the land investigation drive of July.

What I want to emphasize here is the tendency to injure the middle peasants. In the resolution of the Central Bureau it is clearly stated:

> We must pay special attention to our alliance with the middle peasant masses. The middle peasants are the broadest basic masses in the Soviet rural communities after the revolution. All of our actions and tactics must have their approval and support. Every decision of the poor-peasant corps and of the Soviets must have the support of the middle-peasant masses in the village and hamlet mass meetings. We must listen attentively to the voice of the middle peasants. We must strictly frustrate all attempts to encroach upon their interests.

It is pointed out in the conclusions of the Eight-County Conference:

> The aim of land investigation is to investigate the classes, but not to redistribute the land. . . .
> In the matter of allying with the middle peasants, we should first of all refrain from violating their interests. . . .
> At the beginning of land investigation, the Soviet policy of allying with the middle peasants and refraining from injuring them should be generally publicized. In the process of carrying out land investigation, care should be taken to determine the doubtful class status between middle peasants and rich peasants, and no mistake should be made.

However, the above instructions have not been heeded by our comrades in many places. The land investigation in the city area of Jui-chin began by investigating one family after another and one *mou* of land after another. This caused panic among the middle peasants, some of whom even went to the Soviet with the request that their class status be changed into that of poor peasants, saying, "To be a middle peasant is dangerous. Just one step higher and I shall become a rich peasant. If my status is changed into that of a poor peasant, I shall be farther away from the rich peasant." Should we not listen to such painful cries? Our comrade in Yang-ku township of Huang-pai district told the masses: "The investigation of the classes is nothing but the investigation of the class [status] of middle peasants, rich peasants, and landlords." The comrades in T'a-ching district erected wooden boards in all the fields for an over-all investigation. The result was that part of the middle peasants got panicky and escaped to the mountains. The same happened to certain townships in Po-sheng county, where the wooden boards were similarly erected in all the fields for an over-all investigation, and the middle peasants similarly got panicky. It is declared in the conclusions of the Eight-County Conference: "It is wrong to speak of land investigation as being equivalent to erecting wooden boards." But this has not received the attention of these comrades. The method of erecting wooden boards for an over-all investigation of land has been used in every county. It has given rise to a very serious situation. It has mixed up land investigation with land redistribution. It is true that land redistribution requires the erection of wooden boards so that the number of plots may be ascertained by counting them one by one before they are redistributed. But if this method is employed in the land investigation drive, it would confuse the objectives of the struggle in the villages.

We have pointed out in the past:

> Land investigation and land redistribution must be strictly distinguished. This distinction must be made not only for the purpose of reassuring the peasants of their ownership of land so that they may not be afraid of the uncertainty of land redistribution. It is also for the sake of the success of the struggle of the investigation of the classes. We must concentrate all our efforts, especially our alliance with the middle peasants, in coping with the resistance of the landlords and rich peasants. At the present time, there must not be any confusion in the ranks of the peasants themselves (Conclusions of the Eight-County Conference).

This kind of tactics is the most important part of our over-all tactics in leading the land investigation struggle, but has been ignored by many comrades.

Any further attempt to ignore the above-mentioned tactics cannot be tolerated for another instant. Those who purposely commit the same mistakes after having been given directions to follow the right path should be severely punished by the local Soviet on a higher level. We must wage an ideological struggle in the party and the Youth Corps and oppose any ideas and actions on the part of the members of the party and members of the Youth Corps that may encroach upon the interests of middle peasants and run counter to the tactics of allying ourselves with them. If any mistakes have been committed in the sense that the land and property of the middle peasants have been confiscated, the Soviet personnel should openly confess their mistakes before the middle-peasant masses of the locality and should return the land and property to them. Last year, the land of many middle peasants was returned [to their original owners] in Hsing-kuo. This satisfied the masses of the middle peasants. This is a precious lesson [for us to take to heart].

5. The Closed-Door Policy of the Poor-Peasant Corps and Its Oversight of the Hired Farm Hands Are Mistaken

"The poor-peasant masses are the mainstay of both the party and the proletariat in the villages and are the firm supporters of a thorough-going land revolution." "To rely upon the poor peasants" is one of our important tactics in our land investigation drive and all land struggles. The poor-peasant corps is an organization with extremely important functions in the land investigation drive. The Conference of Delegates of the Eight-County Poor-Peasant Corps has already pointed out that the tendency of the poor-peasant corps to close its doors in the past was mistaken, that the system of introduction [of new members] should be abolished, that the door should be wide open to poor peasants and workers, and that all poor peasants and workers, irrespective of age or sex, should have the right to register their names and become members.

But people in many places still follow the old method without any change, and still insist that no one can become a member of the poor-peasant corps without introduction. What is worse, when nonmember poor-peasant masses in T'a-ching district of Jui-chin went to attend the meetings of the poor-peasant corps, the responsible officials of the corps had the audacity to reject their attendance. In Chu-tse-jen district of Po-sheng, the poor-peasant corps did not take in one single new member in the whole month of July. Indeed, in all districts and townships where the land investigation has achieved good results, the poor-peasant corps have been greatly developed. But in districts and townships where the land investigation has achieved little or no results, the one distinguishing feature there is the closed-door policy of the poor-peasant corps.

The great leading role of the hired farm hands in the land investigation drive has similarly not been recognized by many comrades. It is stated in the resolution of the party:

> The masses of the hired farm hands are the brothers of the urban proletariat in the rural districts. They are the vanguards of the land revolution. Therefore, the Soviet working personnel must operate in close coordination with the labor union, through which the activism of the masses of the workers is developed and organized so as to make them vanguards of the land investigation drive.

Those of our comrades who have worked according to this directive are by no means in the majority.

The main method to be employed here is to get rural workers to join the poor-peasant corps and set up independent small groups of workers in the corps. Through the instrumentality of the small groups of workers, we are going to pull the poor-peasant activists together, develop the poor-peasant corps, and push the land investigation drive forward. The experience of Shan-ho township in Huang-pai district is valuable. After our comrades had failed twice in calling a meeting of the poor-peasant corps, they went ahead to hold a joint mass meeting of the members of the agricultural-labor union and of the handicraft-labor union. They succeeded in arousing the enthusiasm of scores of workers, each of whom led a poor peasant to join the poor-peasant corps. When the poor-peasant corps held another meeting the next day, all of them were present. In this way the land investigation drive in Shan-ho township was carried out successfully. The experience of Shan-ho township should be applied to all rural districts. In this connection, the superior leading organ of the labor union should give positive guidance to the subordinate labor union and should regard the task of land investigation as one of the most important of its tasks.

6. Misconceptions about the Rich-Peasant Problem

Our whole tactics in the struggle in the villages consists in relying upon the poor peasants, allying ourselves firmly with the middle peasants, and making the hired farm hands play the role of vanguards, thus uniting all revolutionary forces to annihilate the landlord class and oppose the rich peasants.

With regard to the problem of the rich peasants, the party has already stated correctly: "We must clearly differentiate between land-lords and rich peasants, and in our ruthless struggle to annihilate the remnants of landlords any attempt to annihilate the rich peasants must not be permitted." Though, in the course of land investigation in July, there did not appear any theory which openly advocated the annihila-tion of rich peasants, it happened in many places that rich peasant elements were mistaken for landlords and their property was entirely confiscated. This mistake originated in our failure to appreciate the labor power of rich peasants. We say that "one who does not engage in labor or engages in supplementary labor only and who exploits others by means of land rent, and so forth, is a landlord." But in some places, those who engage in a good deal of labor in production are regarded as landlords, because their labor is considered to be "supplementary labor" in nature. In other places, rich peasants who lend out money at usury are regarded as "usurers" and are treated as such according to the *Regulations for the Annihilation of Usurers*. In still other places, old scores are settled and counted back to several years before the revolution. A man who employed a long-term laborer five, or six, or even more than ten years ago, is classified as a rich peasant. Or a well-to-do middle peasant who has only employed a long-term laborer for one or two years but has not done so either before or after [Chinese original not clear] is also classified as a rich peasant.

More serious still is the example of a place in Hsing-kuo, where the landlord and rich-peasant elements have been differentiated by the number of the kinds of exploitation committed. Those who have com-mitted three kinds of exploitation are called landlords, and those who have committed two are called rich peasants. For instance, if an in-dividual has employed long-term laborers, collected rents, and made loans to others, he would be called a landlord, irrespective of how many persons in his family are actually working.

Then there is the problem of "reactionary rich peasants," which has become quite baffling in many places. In Wu-yang district, a house-hold of a rich peasant who is concurrently a businessman has seventeen mouths to feed. One member of that household was executed two years ago on charges of affiliation with the A-B League. Two years later our comrades there want to expropriate the whole household at any rate. Similar incidents have also happened in many other places. Before the uprising a rich peasant engaged in none-too-serious counterrevolution-ary activities like "collecting 30 per cent of the rice harvest as rent" (at Jui-chin). But since the uprising he has not carried on any further counterrevolutionary activities, nor have the majority of the masses demanded his punishment. Nevertheless, some of our comrades are determined to expropriate his property.

To speak accurately, there should be tactical differences in dealing with these [counterrevolutionary] elements in the areas already consolidated and in the border areas not yet quite consolidated. In border areas, we must doubtless take severe measures to suppress all counterrevolutionary elements, including the rich peasants. In central areas, [however], cases will have to be decided according to their merits. Anyone who engaged in serious counterrevolutionary activities before the uprising, or who has still continued to carry on counterrevolutionary activities after the uprising, should of course be expropriated. Otherwise, he should not be expropriated. In some cases, only the rich peasant himself and those of his family members who have been directly connected with his counterrevolutionary activities should be expropriated, while others should not be expropriated. Only this method is the correct one.

7. The Workers' and Peasants' Prosecution Department Has Not Fulfilled Its Own Duties and Has in Some Cases Even Committed Mistakes

Many of our comrades in the workers' and peasants' prosecution department do not realize that the unfolding of the land investigation drive is the best opportunity to launch an ideological struggle, to oppose bureaucratism, corruption, and passive sabotage, and to clear the Soviets of class heretical elements. They have not adequately carried out these tasks. Confronted with this violent class struggle, many of our comrades in the workers' and peasants' prosecution department have betrayed their own passive and wavering attitude and their own bureaucratism and formalism. For example, the chief of the workers' and peasants' prosecution section of the Jui-chin city Soviet helped the chief of the judicial section of the city Soviet to conceal the latter's most serious corrupt practice (embezzlement of more than one thousand silver dollars of public funds). The chief of the workers' and peasants' prosecution section of Tu-t'ou district neither criticized nor prosecuted the chairman of the district Soviet when the latter paid no attention to the land investigation drive.

The prosecution campaign of the workers' and peasants' prosecution department has also erred in another direction in certain other places. Anyone who is involved in love-making is considered to be rotten; anyone who takes away things from landlords is considered to be corrupt. These individuals have been prosecuted and even publicly tried. In certain places those who have committed light mistakes are deprived of their jobs. There has been no attempt to practice systematic self-criticism and unfold an ideological struggle. Such difficult tasks are omitted and the simple expedient of punitivism is resorted to instead. It goes without saying that those elements among the Soviet working personnel who have committed serious mistakes for a long time should be resolutely purged, but it would be too much to cashier those who have not committed such mistakes.

As to the problem of class heretical elements, the general practice is to inquire only into the class status of such an element, but not his work. Anyone who has come of a bad origin is without exception called a class heretical element and expelled without any ceremony, irrespective of whether he has waged a long struggle and whether he has correctly carried out the line and policy of the party and the Soviet in the past and at present. Of course, it would be perfectly right for us to be firm in the elimination of the class heretical elements. No doubt, those who have a bad class status and a bad record of work (including landlords, rich peasants, passive saboteurs, and corrupt and rotten individuals) should be all purged. But if we purge anyone who does not come under the above categories, that would be going too far.

8. The Art of Leadership in the Land Investigation Drive

If we know our task and line but do not have the Bolshevik art to lead the mass struggle, the land investigation drive still cannot be developed.

At the beginning of this statement, I have given a number of good examples of leadership of the struggle in Jen-t'ien district and other places. But in many other places a variety of mistakes has been made in regard to this matter. In some places we have failed to use various methods to launch the struggle in big backward villages where landlords and rich peasants are crowded. In some big villages we should first of all arrest the notoriously wicked village bosses, gentry, and landlords, who are called "big tigers" by the masses, before we launch the local struggle. But our comrades have not done so.

As regards the very good method of launching the mass struggle through redistribution of the confiscated property and articles, it has not yet been adopted in many places. In the township of Wa-tzu in the district of T'a-ching, Jui-chin, the [confiscated] articles were only distributed to the land investigation cadres and the members of the poor-peasant corps, but not to any other persons, on the ground that those who were not activist enough should have no share in the redistribution. In some places, the confiscated things were redistributed very slowly, so much so that they were not even redistributed to the masses more than one month after their confiscation. The confiscated land was redistributed still more slowly.

Our comrades in numerous places do not know how to mobilize the various departments of the Soviets and the various mass organizations. They do not know how to mobilize all the members of the party and the Youth Corps to play a leading role in the various mass organizations and in the various villages and households. Whenever they find it difficult to carry on work, they claim that nothing can be done there at all.

In some places when the mass struggle for the investigation of the classes has already been set in motion and when many people among the masses have come to give information about the landlords and rich peasants and request an investigation of their class [status] and confiscation of their property, our comrades have not been able to take advantage of such enthusiasm among the masses to lead them to go on with the struggle and to carry the work of investigating the classes into the villages.

In some places where the enthusiasm of the masses for the struggle could not continue to mount but remained in a stagnant condition after a round of investigation, our comrades failed to use various methods to encourage the masses to continue their struggle until all the feudal remnants were wiped out.

In many places when the enthusiasm of the masses for the struggle was mounting as a result of the land investigation drive, [our comrades] did not know how to make use of such enthusiasm on other battle fronts. For example, when the masses had been allotted articles and lands, they should have been encouraged, right at the mass meeting or on other propitious occasions, to join the Red Army, to buy public bonds, to become members of the cooperatives, to intensify the work of autumn harvesting and autumn plowing, to set up clubs and classes in Chinese characters, and to develop night schools and primary schools. But they let slip such excellent opportunities and would not begin to carry on propaganda and agitation afresh until they were urged by their superiors to do so. This kind of leadership which falls behind the enthusiasm of the masses for the struggle and which therefore is a leadership of "tailism" is most harmful to the revolutionary work.

In addition, the undesirable phenomenon of arbitrary action on the part of a small section of comrades has occurred in many other places. We have emphatically pointed out that if we wish to object to negligence in winning over the majority of the masses and to the working manner of commandism, we must patiently and painstakingly carry out the work of arousing and winning over the masses. It is only in this way that we can have the support of the majority of the masses and achieve the objective of annihilating the feudal remnants. Such mass work is the only guarantee for the [successful] implementation of the class line.

At the beginning of the land investigation drive, we must carry out widespread propaganda in all the villages and hamlets and explain to the masses the necessity of the land investigation drive, making clear that the investigation of land is not the redistribution of land and that the investigation of class [status] is not the investigation of the class [status] of middle peasants, poor peasants, and hired farm hands. It is especially important to explain clearly to the masses what kinds of people are the landlords, rich peasants, and middle peasants. The village and hamlet mass meeting should not be held only once. In the cases of backward villages and hamlets, the mass meetings should be held more than once. We must not fail to let a single member of the revolutionary masses have a chance to listen to our propaganda. In order to attain this objective, we should first of all explain everything clearly to all the active elements in the district Soviet congress of delegates, the labor union, the poor-peasant corps, the congress of delegates of women workers and farming women, and other mass organizations, and through them carry out propaganda among the broad masses.

The investigation of the classes should not be done by a few people, but by a large number of people. The determination of class status should not only be passed by the poor-peasant corps, the township Soviet, and the district Soviet, but to that end, a mass meeting should also be held in the village or hamlet of the individual whose property is to be confiscated. It is only with the consent of the masses that the confiscation can be carried out. In regard to the redistribution of property and articles, they must be given to the masses of the village or hamlet from which they have come, so that the masses may be satisfied.

All the foregoing [measures] are designed to win over the majority of the masses. In doing any work at any time the working personnel of both the party and the Soviet must not forget the majority of the masses.

If we have to face the masses, we have to face the great majority of the masses. If our work has to be carried deep into the masses, it has to be carried deep into the masses of all villages and hamlets, and all cities and towns, big and small. We must strongly object to the mistaken methods of a closed-door policy and commandism on the part of a small section of people.

However, our comrades in many places have not worked that way. In many districts and townships of Jui-chin, no attempt has ever been made to explain the classes (to analyze what kinds of people the land-lords, rich peasants, and middle peasants are) to the masses. In many places in Jui-chin and other counties, it has been found that [our comrades] began to make investigation without carrying out [the necessary] propaganda, so that the landlords and rich peasants came forward and spread rumors to deceive the middle peasants, saying that there were too many landlords and rich peasants in their respective townships, or that several hundreds of landlord and rich-peasant house-holds in their respective townships would require investigation (as in Jui-chin). But our comrades still did not know how to use the method of "explaining the classes" to counter these rumors. The landlords of Kuang-ch'ang said: "The land investigation drive is a device of the central government to ask all debtors of the past to pay their debts to the central [government]." But our comrades did not come forward immediately to expose the falsity of these unfounded allegations.

In several townships of the district of T'a-ching, aside from the lack of propaganda, the work of land investigation was done by only a few people of the land investigation committee, and decisions on the class status were made neither through mass meetings nor through the poor-peasant corps. They said:

> . . . that the masses are unreliable and do not know how to analyze the classes, that to let the class status be decided by the mass meeting would give rise to trouble, and that therefore it would be safer to let the land investigation committee decide the class status.

This theory of the comrades in the district of T'a-ching is really the strangest thing in the whole world!

In several places the work of expropriating the landlords was not done in the daytime but at night, the only reason given being that it was feared that the landlords might run away. In a certain place a mass meeting was held under the name of "all-district meeting," but it was attended by fewer than 200 people. At the meeting three persons took turns making speeches from morning until afternoon without allowing time for the masses to rest or to drink and eat, the reason given being that it was feared that the masses might run away. Such an arbitrary method is, indeed, another instance of the strangest things we have ever heard of.

9. Unfolding a Two-Front Struggle, Overcoming Our Own Mistakes, and Winning a Thoroughgoing Victory in the Land Investigation Drive

No doubt, the land investigation drive has spread to huge regions. But when the drive is going forward and when we accurately estimate that the results obtained have laid the foundation for the further development of the drive, we must vigilantly pay attention to the obstacles standing in the way of the drive. It is only by generating the fire power of a two-front struggle that those obstacles can be removed and the land investigation drive can be pushed forward more rapidly.

It is the duty of every member of the Communist Party to launch an ideological struggle against the Right deviation, to oppose the underestimation of the great significance of the land investigation drive, to object to compromising with and surrendering to the landlords and rich peasants, and to combat the leadership of tailism in the mass struggle.

Meanwhile, we must call the attention of all the members of our party to the danger of injuring the middle peasants. We must "vigorously attack any attempt to violate the interests of the middle peasants." For this is an extremely serious danger which has clearly manifested itself in the work of land investigation these days. Any misconceptions about the rich peasants would doubtless also exert an adverse influence on the middle peasants. All arbitrary behavior based on commandism would be a very great menace to our alliance with the middle peasants.

The moment the fire power of the two-front struggle wipes away all the obstacles in the way of the land investigation drive, the drive will take great strides forward and its complete success will be fully assured.

DOCUMENT 96

HOW TO ANALYZE THE CLASSES

Adopted by the Eight-County Conference on the Land Investigation Drive, June 17–21, 1933, and Approved by the Central Government of the

Chinese Soviet Republic, October 10, 1933
(As reproduced in *A Guide to the Land Investigation
Drive*, printed by the Central Government, n.d.,
probably sometime during July to October, 1933, pp. 27–30)

1. What is meant by a landlord?

[A landlord] owns land (irrespective of amount), but he does not labor himself or [at best] engages in supplementary labor only. He lives solely on exploitation.

The form of exploitation by a landlord is primarily the form of land rent (including the school-land rent) through which he exploits the peasants. In addition, he may lend money, hire labor, or engage in industry and commerce. But the exploitation of the peasants by means of land rent is the main form of exploitation by a landlord. The management of landholdings of public bodies is also a kind of exploitation through land rent.

The small landlords exploit more ruthlessly than [other] landlords. Some landlords, though having become bankrupt, still do not labor themselves after bankruptcy but live by fraud and robbery or by receiving aid from their relatives and friends—these people shall still be classified as landlords.

Warlords, bureaucrats, village bosses, and bad gentry are the political representatives of the landlord class. They are the most ruthless of the landlords. The landlord class is the principal enemy of the land revolution. The policy of the Soviets toward the landlords is to confiscate all their land and [other] property and to annihilate the landlord class.

Those who help landlords collect rent and manage property and who live on the exploitation of peasants by landlords shall be treated as landlords. Those who live wholly or mainly on exploitation by usury are called usurers. Though these people are not landlords, it is necessary to confiscate all their property in order to suppress usurers, since usury is a sort of feudalistic exploitation.

2. What is meant by a rich peasant?

A rich peasant generally owns land. But in some cases he owns only a part of the land [he cultivates] and rents the other part [from others]. In other cases, he owns no land whatever and rents all the land [from others]. (The last-listed cases are relatively few.) Generally speaking, the rich peasant owns better means of production and circulating capital and engages in labor himself, but he constantly depends on exploitation as a part or, in some cases, even a major part of his means of livelihood.

The form of exploitation by a rich peasant lies primarily in exploitation through the hiring of labor (hiring long-term laborers). Besides, he may rent out a part of his land for extorting land rent, or lend money, or engage in commerce and small-scale industry. Most rich peasants also manage landholdings of public bodies. But there are also rich peasants in China who usually labor themselves and hire no laborers, but who exploit the peasants in the form of land rent, loan interest, and so on. The exploitation by rich peasants is constant and, in many cases, major in character.

The policy of the Soviets toward the rich peasants is to confiscate their land. But only the surplus parts of their draft cattle, farm implements, and houses are to be confiscated. They are still to be assigned labor land allotments of a poorer quality.

3. What is meant by a middle peasant?

Many a middle peasant owns land. In some cases he owns only a part of the land [he cultivates] and rents the other part [from others]. In other cases he owns no land whatever and rents all the land [from others]. Invariably he has suitable implements of his own. He depends entirely or for the most part on his own labor [for his living]. In general, he does not exploit others; in many cases he is exploited by others in the form of a small part of land rent, loan interest, and so on. But the middle peasant generally does not sell his labor power. Some middle peasants (including the well-to-do middle peasants) exploit others in a measure, but such exploitation is by no means constant and major in character. All these people are middle peasants.

The policy of the Soviets toward the middle peasants is to enter into a solid alliance with them. Without their consent, the land of the middle peasants shall not be subject to equal redistribution. Those middle peasants who do not own enough land shall be allotted the same amount of land as the poor peasants and hired farm hands.

4. What is meant by a poor peasant?

In some cases a poor peasant owns a part of the land [he cultivates] and some incomplete implements; in others he owns no land whatever but only some incomplete implements. In general, he has to rent land [from others] to till and is exploited by others through land rent, loan interest, and the hiring out of part of his labor (the poor peasant, in general, has to sell a part of his labor power). All these people are poor peasants.

In land redistribution, the poor peasants should obtain the same benefits as the middle peasants and hired farm hands. The small amount of land and the few farm implements they originally own shall not be confiscated.

5. What is meant by a worker?

[A worker] generally owns no land and implements at all. In some cases he owns a very small part of land and implements. He depends entirely or chiefly on the sale of his labor power for his living. This is the worker (including the hired farm hand).

In the course of land revolution, all workers of the rural districts should be allotted the same amount of land as the poor peasants and middle peasants. The very small part of land and implements which some of the workers may originally own shall not be confiscated. There are cases in which the workers are working in the cities [Chinese original a little involved], leaving their families behind in the countryside with land to let and money to lend. If the families do not rely on the collecting of rent as the main means of subsistence, their land shall not be confiscated and they shall all be allotted land as ordinary peasants. [On the other hand,] their land shall be subject to confiscation if their families rely on the collecting of rent and the lending of money as the main means of subsistence. In the latter case, the wives and children shall be allotted land while the workers themselves are not to receive any land because they are in the cities.

NOTE: Parts of this translation are made with assistance of the English version of the revised text of this document appearing in the supplement to *People's China*, II, No. 8, October 16, 1950, 3–5, and in *Selected Works of Mao Tse-tung*, English edition (New York: International Publishers, 1954), I, 138–40 (Peking: Foreign Languages Press, 1965), I, 137–39.

DOCUMENT 101
DECISIONS CONCERNING SOME PROBLEMS ARISING FROM THE AGRARIAN STRUGGLE

Adopted by the Council of People's Commissars
of the Central Government, October 10, 1933
(As mimeographed in pamphlet form)

DECREE NO. 49 OF THE COUNCIL OF PEOPLE'S
COMMISSARS OF THE CENTRAL GOVERNMENT OF
THE CHINESE SOVIET REPUBLIC

1. The *Decisions concerning Some Problems Arising from the Agrarian Struggle* adopted by this Council on October 10, 1933, is hereby promulgated.

2. Where decisions on class status in various localities prior to October 10, 1933, do not conform with the present *Decisions,* they shall be amended in accordance with the present *Decisions.* In case a change of class status entails a change in the disposal of land and [other] properties: the land, houses, forests, ponds, and gardens of the middle peasants, poor people, and workers, which have been apportioned [to others] in the past, shall all be returned to their original owners, while properties other than land, houses, forests, ponds, and gardens shall be returned to their original owners only in so far as circumstances permit (for example, where there is still some landlord's property to be confiscated, and so on). The land, houses, forests, ponds, gardens, draft cattle, and farm implements which should be owned by rich peasants, as well as the property of the capitalists, shall be returned to their original owners only in so far as circumstances permit.

3. Where judgments rendered by judicial organs in cases brought before them in various localities prior to October 10, 1933, do not conform with the present *Decisions,* the original judgments shall be maintained without change if they have already been executed, while they shall be changed in accordance with the present *Decisions* if they have not been executed or are still under execution.

4. Where decisions on class status and consequently on land and [other] properties made prior to or after October 10, 1933, are in conformity with the present *Decisions* and are found without any mistake, no one shall be allowed to ask for a change in those decisions.

MAO TSE-TUNG
Chairman
HSIANG YING
Vice-Chairman
CHANG KUO-T'AO
Vice-Chairman

October 10, 1933

TABLE OF CONTENTS

DECISIONS OF THE CENTRAL GOVERNMENT CONCERNING SOME PROBLEMS ARISING FROM THE AGRARIAN STRUGGLE

Many practical problems have emerged in the course of the struggle for land redistribution and land investigation. Either because old documents contain no provisions or ambiguous provisions regarding such problems, or because of incorrect interpretations of such provisions by the Soviet working personnel, mistakes have been committed in carrying out [the agrarian struggle]. In order to correct and prevent mistakes in connection with these problems, the Council of People's Commissars, apart from approving *How to Analyze the Classes* concerning the principles for differentiating landlords, rich peasants, middle peasants, poor peasants, and workers, hereby makes the following decisions:

1. Labor and Supplementary Labor

Under ordinary circumstances, a family is considered as engaging in labor if one member of the family is engaged in essential labor for one third of a year; a family is considered as engaging in supplementary labor if one member of the family is engaged in essential labor for less than one third of a year, or if he is engaged in labor, but not in essential labor, for one third of a year.

Explanatory Notes

Attention should be paid to the following:

1. Rich peasants engage in labor themselves, while landlords do not engage in labor themselves or engage only in supplementary labor. Thus labor is the basic criterion for differentiating rich peasants from landlords.

2. It is stipulated that the standard number of persons for labor in a family is one person. Suppose a family has several persons. This family shall be considered as engaging in labor if one of those persons is engaged in labor. Some maintain that a family cannot be considered as engaging in labor unless two or even all of its members are engaged in labor. This is not correct.

3. It is stipulated that the standard length of time for labor is one third of a year, that is, four months. The line of demarcation between labor and supplementary labor (i.e., the line of demarcation between rich peasants and landlords) is whether a person is engaged in essential labor for four months, or less than four months. In some cases, those who have already engaged in essential labor for half a year are still considered as engaging in supplementary labor. This is not correct.

4. Essential labor means labor employed in the main forms of [agricultural] production, such as plowing, planting, reaping, and other major items of labor in production. But it is by no means limited to agricultural production; tasks such as cutting firewood, load carrying, and other major items of labor service are all essential labor.

5. Nonessential labor means various kinds of auxiliary labor which play only a secondary part in production, such as helping with weeding, helping with vegetable growing, taking care of draft cattle, and so on.

6. Since labor is the basic criterion for differentiating rich peasants from landlords, a person shall still be treated as a landlord and may not be allotted land if he merely hires long-term laborers to cultivate land and does not resort to any other exploitation such as land rent,

loan interest, and so on, and if he is responsible for directing production himself but not engaged in essential labor personally.

7. As regards the length of time required for determining the class status of a landlord, any person who had lived the life of a landlord for three consecutive years, counted backward from the time of the uprising, shall be considered as having the status of a landlord.

In the course of the land investigation drive, many mistakes have been committed in connection with the problems of labor and supplementary labor. In cases where labor has been taken for supplementary labor, some have been [wrongly] classified as landlords. Conversely, in cases where supplementary labor has been taken for labor, others have been [wrongly] classified as rich peasants. All this is because there has been in the past no clear-cut line of demarcation between landlords and rich peasants. Such mistakes may be avoided if the above-mentioned provisions are applied.

But the foregoing provisions cover only *ordinary circumstances*. Under *special circumstances*, different measures must be taken. There are two categories of such *special circumstances*:

First, there is the case of a big landlord with someone in his family taking part in production. Suppose a person exploits others by means of land rent and loan interest to such a great extent as collecting more than 100 piculs of grain in rent and lending out more than 1,000 silver dollars. Nevertheless, his family is small and his expenses are by no means great. This person shall still be considered a landlord and not a rich peasant, even though someone in his family is engaged in essential labor for more than four months a year. However, if his family and expenses are all large and someone in his family engages in essential labor, he shall not be considered a landlord but a rich peasant despite the fact that he collects 100 piculs of grain in rent and lends out 1,000 silver dollars.

Second, there is the case where a man should be considered a landlord from the point of view of exploitation, but he cannot be treated as a landlord from the point of view of his living conditions. Suppose a man used to be a rich peasant or a middle peasant. But several years before the uprising his family had suddenly lost its labor power because of the death or sickness [of the family member engaged in essential labor], then all his land has had to be rented out or cultivated with hired labor. As a result, the entire family has led the life of a landlord. In such a case, it would be inappropriate to treat this man as a landlord. Rather, he should be treated according to his original status.

Here is another case [under the second category]. Someone is nominally still a landlord, but in fact his landholdings have been transferred to others. He now practices only slight exploitation, engages in supplementary labor himself, and leads a life even worse than that of a peasant. Certainly, such a man should be allotted poor land as a rich peasant. If his conditions are extremely bad, he may be allotted land as a peasant with the consent of the masses.

Here is still another case. Someone used to be a peasant, but he suddenly became rich by a favorable turn of good luck two years before the uprising and has since remained a landlord. Of course, the land of such a man should be confiscated. But since he was a peasant only two years ago, he may be allotted poor land as a rich peasant with the consent of the masses.

The above-mentioned special circumstances have been neglected in the course of the land investigation drive in some localities. This also is not correct.

2. Well-to-do Middle Peasant

Well-to-do middle peasants are that part of the middle peasants who practice a slight degree of exploitation of others. The amount of income derived from such exploitation should not exceed 15 per cent of the total annual income of the whole family. Under certain circumstances, although the income of a middle peasant from exploitation exceeds 15 per cent but not 30 per cent of the total annual income of the whole family, he shall still be treated as a well-to-do middle peasant if the masses have no objection. Under the Soviet regime, the interests of the well-to-do middle peasants shall receive the same protection as those of the ordinary middle peasants.

Explanatory Notes

Attention should be paid to the following:

1. Well-to-do middle peasants are part of the middle peasants, but they differ from other middle peasants in that they practice a slight degree of exploitation of others, while other middle peasants in general do not.

2. The well-to-do middle peasants differ from the rich peasants in that the annual income of a well-to-do middle peasant from exploitation does not exceed 15 per cent of the total annual income of his whole family, while that of a rich peasant does. Such a line of demarcation is necessary in the actual differentiation of class status.

3. A slight degree of exploitation by well-to-do middle peasants

means the hiring of cowherds, odd-job laborers, or monthly laborers; or the lending out of small amounts of money for interest; or the earning of a little interest derived from landed property given as security for loans; or the collection of small amounts of rent from school land; or the renting out of small tracts of land, and so forth. However, the total income derived from all such acts of exploitation does not constitute the main part of the family's means of livelihood; that is to say, it does not exceed 15 per cent [of the total annual family income]. The main means of livelihood of the whole family is derived from its own labor.

4. The well-to-do middle peasants who, for a period of time prior to the uprising, practiced the same degree of exploitation as the rich peasants in a corresponding period of time shall still be considered as well-to-do peasants, provided that the duration of such exploitation did not exceed two years.

5. [As pointed out above], under certain circumstances, although the income of a middle peasant from exploitation exceeds 15 per cent but not 30 per cent of the total annual income of his family, he shall still be treated as a well-to-do middle peasant if the masses have no objection. By "certain circumstances" are meant such cases where though the income from exploitation exceeds 15 per cent, yet the life of the family is no good, either because it is a large family, few members of which are able to work, or because the family is faced with difficulties caused by flood, drought, famine, sickness, or death. Under such circumstances, the family shall not be considered a rich-peasant family but a middle-peasant family if its income derived from exploitation does not exceed 30 per cent [of the total annual income]. If no such circumstances exist, however, a family whose income from exploitation exceeds 15 per cent of its total annual income shall be considered a rich-peasant family and not a well-to-do middle-peasant family. The right judgment on the right circumstances should be based upon the consensus of opinion of the local masses.

Well-to-do middle peasants constitute a considerable proportion of the population in the rural districts. They have been treated as rich peasants in many localities in the course of the land investigation drive. That is not correct. In most cases where the middle peasants have been injured, it is these well-to-do middle peasants who have actually been injured. This should be corrected immediately.

Illustrations:

(1) A family has 6 mouths to feed, with 2 of its members engaged

in labor. It owns land with a potential [annual] yield of 50 piculs of grain but an actual [annual] yield of 35 piculs (which can fetch 140 silver dollars at the current price of 4 silver dollars per picul). The family's land is cultivated entirely by its own members. The family has a house of 5 rooms, an ox, and a pond which brings in an annual income of 12 silver dollars. The family's annual income from the production of nonstaple grains and the rearing of hogs is about 100 silver dollars. The family has for 4 years been lending out 3 piculs of grain at an annual interest rate of 50 per cent, earning $1\frac{1}{2}$ piculs of grain per annum (worth 6 silver dollars). It has also for 5 years been lending out 100 silver dollars (equivalent to 1,800 dimes of small silver cash) at an annual interest rate of 25 per cent, earning 25 silver dollars per annum. *Decision:* This family depends on its own labor as the principal means of livelihood. Its own production amounts to over 250 silver dollars. It exploits others in the form of interest on loans, but the annual income from interest amounts only to 29 silver dollars, constituting less than 15 per cent of the [annual] total income. After defraying all the family expenses, there is some surplus. The family lives rather well. But because the degree of exploitation is not large, the family should be classified as a well-to-do middle-peasant family and not as a rich-peasant family.

(2) A family has 5 mouths to feed with 1 of its members engaged in full-time labor and another in half-time labor. It owns land with a potential yield of 25 piculs of grain but an actual yield of 17 piculs. It rents from others an amount of land with a potential yield of 75 piculs of grain but an actual yield of 42 piculs, and has been paying an annual rent of 25 piculs of grain for 10 years. The family's annual income from the production of nonstaple grains and the rearing of hogs is 50 silver dollars. It has been hiring a cowherd for 3 years. It has for 4 years been lending out 60 silver dollars at an annual interest rate of 30 per cent, earning 18 silver dollars per annum. It has a house of 5 rooms and an ox. It owns a tea-oil plantation with an annual production of 30 piculs of tea-oil nuts. *Decision:* This family lives mainly by its own labor. It exploits others only slightly, amounting barely to twenty-odd silver dollars a year (including the hiring of the cowherd and the lending out of money), while it is exploited by others in the form of land rent up to 25 piculs of grain a year. After defraying all the family expenses, very little is left. This family should be classified as an ordinary middle-peasant family and not as a well-to-do middle-peasant family.

3. Rich-Peasant Exploitation—Its Duration and Degree

A person is classified as a rich peasant, who for 3 consecutive years, counted backward from the time of the uprising, had engaged in production himself and depended for part or the major part of his family's means of livelihood on exploitation, the income from which exceeds 15 per cent of the total annual income of his whole family. Under certain circumstances, a person whose income from exploitation exceeds 15 per cent but not 30 per cent of the total [annual] income should still be classified as a well-to-do middle peasant and not as a rich peasant if the masses have no objection.

Explanatory Notes

Attention should be paid to the following:

1. The duration of exploitation should be counted from the time of the uprising, but not from any other time. Some want to settle "old scores" and determine the class status on the basis of exploitation committed at intervals long since. This is not correct.

2. Exploitation for three consecutive years is the standard duration required for the establishment of a rich-peasant status. If the duration of exploitation is less than three years or if it is three nonconsecutive years (that is, there are intervals in between), such a person should still be classified as a well-to-do middle peasant even though the degree of his exploitation is the same as that of a rich peasant during a corresponding period.

3. The income from exploitation is adequate to establish a rich-peasant status when it exceeds 15 per cent of the total annual income of the whole family. If the income from exploitation is less than 15 per cent of the total [annual] income, it does not make a rich-peasant status, but still a well-to-do middle-peasant status, even though the duration of exploitation lasts for 3 or more than 3 consecutive years.

4. By the "total annual income of the whole family" is meant the total annual amount of what the family has earned from its own production and what it has gained from exploitation of others. Take, for instance, a family which in a year earns 400 silver dollars from its own production and earns another 100 silver dollars from exploitation of others. The sum total is 500 silver dollars, which constitute the total income [of the family in a year]. As its earnings derived from exploitation constitute 20 per cent of the total income, this family has the status of a rich peasant.

5. By "certain circumstances" are meant such cases where the fam-

ily does not lead a good life because it is a large family, few members of which are able to work, or because it is faced with difficulties caused by natural calamities or by artificial misfortunes. Under such circumstances a family whose income from exploitation exceeds 15 per cent but not 30 per cent [of the total annual income] shall still be classified as a well-to-do middle-peasant family if the masses have no objection. Here the opinion of the masses is very important, and the assessment of the circumstances should also be very careful. Well-to-do middle peasants should not be mistaken for rich peasants to incur the displeasure of the middle peasants. On the other hand, rich peasants should also not be mistaken for middle peasants to incur the displeasure of the poor peasants. Hence, it is essential to consider carefully "the merits of the circumstances" in order to obtain the consent of the masses.

In the course of the land investigation drive there has been a good deal of confusion in connection with the problem of the duration and degree [of exploitation]. This is because there has been no clear-cut line of demarcation between rich peasants and well-to-do middle peasants in the past. Either well-to-do middle peasants have been treated as rich peasants, or rich peasants have been treated as well-to-do middle peasants. Disputes have occurred frequently. Now that a line of demarcation between the kinds of people has been drawn, mistakes in this respect may be avoided.

Illustrations:

(1) A family has 11 mouths to feed, with 2 of its members engaged in labor. It owns land with a potential yield of 160 piculs of grain but an actual yield of 120 piculs of grain (worth 480 silver dollars). It owns 2 tea-oil plantations which bring in an annual income of 30 silver dollars, and also a pond which brings in an annual income of 15 silver dollars. The annual income from the production of nonstaple grains and the rearing of hogs is about 150 silver dollars. For 7 years prior to the revolution, the family had hired a long-term laborer and exploited his surplus labor at the value of about 70 silver dollars a year. For 5 years prior to the revolution, it had lent out 250 silver dollars at an annual interest rate of 30 per cent, earning 75 silver dollars per annum. A son in the family is a *hsiu-ts'ai* [i.e., a successful candidate of the first degree under the old examination system] who can draft statements of accusation and aid and abet others in lawsuits. He takes advantage of his influence to bully others.

Decision: This family has 2 members engaged in labor. But it hired a long-term laborer, made loans to no small amount, and its income from exploitation was more than 15 per cent of the total [annual] income of the whole family. Although the family is a large one, there is still a considerable surplus left after meeting all family expenses. Therefore, this family is a rich-peasant family and should be allotted poor land. A member of the family is one of the bad gentry who should not be allotted any land.

(2) A family has 3 mouths to feed, with 1 of its members engaged in essential labor for 4 months [in a year]. It owns land with a potential yield of 60 piculs of grain, out of which it cultivates with its own labor an area with a potential yield of 30 piculs of grain with the result that it actually obtains 18 piculs of grain [in a year]. The family rents out a part of land with a potential yield of 30 piculs of grain and has been collecting an annual rent of 12 piculs of grain for 5 years. It usually hires a short-term laborer for 20 days a year. It owns an ox which it rents out for an annual charge of 2 piculs of grain. It has for 3 years been lending out 120 silver dollars at an annual interest rate of 30 per cent, earning 36 silver dollars per annum.

Decision: This family's income from exploitation exceeds that which it produces itself. But because one of the members of the family is engaged in essential labor for four months [in a year], the family is therefore a rich-peasant family and should be allotted poor land.

4. Reactionary Rich Peasant

A rich peasant who has engaged in serious counterrevolutionary activities before and especially after the uprising shall be called a reactionary rich peasant. The land and [other] properties of such a reactionary rich peasant and of those members of his family who have taken part in the counterrevolutionary activities shall be confiscated.

The above principle also applies to reactionary capitalists.

Explanatory Notes
Attention should be paid to the following:

1. Only those rich peasants who "have engaged in serious counter-revolutionary activities" are to be called reactionary rich peasants, such as those who during the uprising led the militia in the massacre of workers and peasants and stubbornly resisted the revolutionary government, especially those who after the uprising have continued to lead

others in organizing counterrevolutionary groups and organs, or have individually carried out serious counterrevolutionary activities such as assassination, spying for the enemy, voluntarily serving as guides for the White troops, escaping to the White areas to assist the Kuomintang, or actively sabotaging the land investigation drive and economic reconstruction, and so on. The land and [other] properties of those elements whose rich-peasant origin and serious counterrevolutionary activities have been verified shall be confiscated. The land and [other] properties of other rich peasants who, though having participated in counterrevolutionary activities, have not played a leading or major role in them shall not be confiscated.

2. Only the land and [other] properties of those family members of the reactionary rich peasants who have taken part in serious counterrevolutionary activities shall be confiscated. The land and [other] properties of the rest of the family members may not be confiscated.

3. The rich peasants who temporarily went to the White areas for the purpose of making a living are not reactionary rich peasants and shall not be expropriated as such. But the rich peasants who were unwilling to live in the Soviet areas and went over to the White areas and who have since lived there for more than a year without returning home shall still be expropriated, though they are not reactionary rich peasants.

4. In defining and dealing with reactionary capitalists, the above principles shall apply in full.

In a number of places in the past, the land and [other] properties of the rich peasants who had not engaged in serious counterrevolutionary activities were confiscated. Moreover, the land and [other] properties of those members of the rich-peasant families who had taken no part in counterrevolutionary activities were also confiscated. That was wrong. One of the causes of such mistakes was due to Article 3 of the *Regulations of the Kiangsi [Provincial Government] for the Confiscation and Redistribution of Land,* which stipulated:

> The rich peasants who have joined counterrevolutionary organizations (such as the A–B League, the Social Democratic Party, and so on) shall be expropriated on a whole-family basis.

Thus, it failed to make a distinction between leaders and followers, between actual participants and nonparticipants. As to the question of the dependents [of those rich peasants], the latter part of the said article provided that

. . . their dependents, who have taken no part in counterrevolutionary organizations and counterrevolutionary actions, and who have severed their relations with the counterrevolutionary members of their families, may get back their landholdings, if the local masses have no objection.

Thus, there was confiscation on a whole-family basis first, only to leave a part [of the confiscated land] to be returned [to its original owners] later. This was not a right measure. Accordingly, the article in question must be revised in conformity with the present provisions.

Moreover, in some places in the past, the definition of a reactionary capitalist was stretched so much beyond its proper limits that some commercial firms were illegitimately confiscated. This was not correct either.

Illustration:

A family has 9 mouths to feed, with 1 of its members engaged in labor and another in supplementary labor. It owns land with a potential yield of 160 piculs of grain out of which it cultivates land with a potential yield of 80 piculs of grain but an actual yield of 45 piculs of grain. For 10 years the family has been renting out the rest of the land with a potential yield of 80 piculs of grain, for which it has been drawing an annual rent of 40 piculs of grain. It owns 5 tracts of hilly land, which bring in an annual income of 70 silver dollars. It regularly hires a long-term laborer. It has for 3 years been borrowing 425 silver dollars at an annual interest rate of 25 per cent. It has for 5 years been lending 380 silver dollars at an annual interest rate of 30 per cent. One member of the family was a company commander of the [KMT] "Pacification Corps" for 2 years, and took part in 5 battles against the Red Guards. Another member of the family joined the A-B League and has given himself up to the government. There was no evidence of any counterrevolutionary activities on the part of the other members of the family.

Decision: The status of this family is one of the family of a rich peasant. One member of the family has been engaged in serious counterrevolutionary activities. He is a reactionary rich peasant and his property should be confiscated. The property of all other members of the family should not be confiscated. One of them joined the A-B League, but was not an important member of the League and has given himself up. His property should not be confiscated either.

5. Rich-Peasant Contributions

According to the policy of weakening the rich peasants during the period of civil war, it is necessary to call upon the rich peasants to make extraordinary contributions, in addition to the basic measures of assigning them poor land, confiscating their surplus houses, draft cattle, and farm implements, and imposing on them a higher progressive tax. But the amount of the contributions must not exceed the maximum of 40 per cent of the existing total circulating capital of the rich peasants. The frequency of the contributions should also be restricted.

Explanatory Notes

1. There have recently been two tendencies in the collection of contributions from the rich peasants. One is to provide shelter to rich peasants without asking them to make contributions; the other is to deprive them of all their ready money, like the fines imposed on landlords. Neither tendency is correct. The latter particularly tends to annihilate the rich peasants, and is likely to injure the middle peasants. It is now provided that the maximum amount [of contributions] should not exceed 40 per cent [of the total circulating capital of the rich peasants]. The local authorities may call upon each rich peasant to make a suitable contribution within the limits laid down above, taking into account whether he has made any such contributions in the past and what kind of life he is leading at present.

2. The contributions are extraordinary in character. They differ from the ordinary land tax. Therefore, the frequency of contributions should be restricted. They cannot be extorted many times without a limit.

3. The authority to extort contributions from rich peasants is vested in the financial organs of the State. No other organs are allowed to extort contributions from rich peasants.

6. The Land, Houses, Draft Cattle, and Farm Implements Rightfully Owned by the Rich Peasant

Within the limits of the Soviet laws and decrees, the rich peasants shall have the right to dispose of the land, houses, draft cattle, and farm implements, over which their ownership has been established—and others may not interfere. Only for the convenience of production, and with the consent of the rich peasants, are workers, peasants, and poor people allowed to exchange their houses with the rich peasants.

Explanatory Notes

1. It has recently happened in some localities that workers, peasants, and poor people have exchanged their land, houses, draft cattle, and farm implements for the land, houses, draft cattle, and farm implements which are the rightful property of the rich peasants. There have even been instances of exchanging clothing and fertilizers. This is not correct. There should be limits to "weakening the rich peasants." The policy of "weakening" has already been carried out if the rich peasants have been allotted poor land according to labor power, deprived of their surplus houses, draft cattle, and farm implements, made to pay a higher progressive tax, and persuaded to give a portion of their ready money for contributions. Any attempt to go beyond these limits is a tendency to annihilate the rich peasants, which should not be allowed to happen in the present stage of the revolution. Only for the convenience of production and with the consent of the rich peasants, can their houses be made the subjects of exchange.

2. If the poor land allotted to the rich peasants has been improved to become good land after the correct solution of the land problem, no one shall be allowed to make such land the subject for exchange.

3. The draft cattle, farm implements, and houses which the rich peasants have purchased after the uprising shall not be confiscated or exchanged, even if they are more than sufficient.

7. Compulsory Labor of the Rich Peasant

Rich peasants shall undertake more national and local compulsory labor than that undertaken by the workers, peasants, and poor people, provided that this does not hinder the production of the rich peasants.

Explanatory Note

A distinction should be made between the compulsory labor assigned to rich peasants and the compulsory labor assigned to landlords. All able-bodied men of the landlord family should be enrolled in hard-labor corps to undergo training so as to equip them for national and local labor service and for the reform of their class character in the course of labor, thereby annihilating the landlord class. Rich peasants should undertake more compulsory labor than workers, peasants, and poor people, but should not be subjected to unrestricted compulsory labor like landlords so as to hinder production. It is therefore improper to put rich peasants in the same hard-labor corps with landlords to enable them to undertake a kind of compulsory labor which would separate

them from production for a long time when people are busy in agricultural work and when there is no surplus labor power of the rich peasants to spare, nor can it be compensated. Exceptions should, however,
be made in cases where production is not hindered, or the rich peasants
have surplus labor power to spare, or there are some other compensatory
measures available.

8. Bankrupt Landlord

Any landlord who had, prior to the uprising, lost all or the major
portion of his land and [other] properties which were used for exploitation, but who still does not engage in labor but depends on swindling
or plundering or on the assistance of his relatives or friends as his
principal means of livelihood, is called a bankrupt landlord. Bankrupt
landlords remain a part of the landlord class, and shall not be allotted
land. The class status, however, shall be altered in the case of landlords
who, after going bankrupt, have depended on their own labor as the
principal means of livelihood for one year. Such bankrupt landlords
have the right to land allotments. The landlords who, after going
bankrupt, have depended on their own labor to earn a part of their
livelihood, may be treated as rich peasants, provided that the said part
of their income amounts to one third of their annual living expenses.

Explanatory Note

Some regard the partially bankrupt landlords as bankrupt landlords.
This is not correct. For such landlords still retain a part of their property, which they can use for exploitation. Only the amount of their
income from exploitation is different. Others regard as bankrupt landlords those who, after going bankrupt, have engaged in essential labor
for one year. This is all the more incorrect, because the landlords who,
after going bankrupt, had engaged in essential labor for one year (prior
to the uprising) have already changed themselves from landlords into
workers or poor people or peasants.

Still others have continued to treat as landlords those who, after
going bankrupt, have engaged in labor part of the time. This is not
correct, either, because those who have earned one third of their annual
living expenses by means of their own labor should have been treated
as rich peasants.

9. Poor People

With the exception of workers, peasants, independent producers, and professionals, all those who depend on their own labor to engage in one or several occupations, or who for the most part depend on their own labor for subsistence, or who depend on the management of their extremely small capital to earn their minimum living expenses, are called the poor people. The unemployed among the poor people in the rural districts and small towns should be allotted land. The poor people in the cities who have no houses of their own should be assigned the houses of the landlords in the cities.

Explanatory Note

The poor people constitute a considerable number in the cities. A number of them are also found in the rural districts and small towns. They follow diverse occupations, some of which are irregular and often vary from season to season. The life of the poor people is very hard; their income is always insufficient to meet their expenses.

The poor people who depend on the management of their extremely small capital are peddlers.

Physicians, schoolteachers, lawyers, journalists, writers, artists, and so on, who do not exploit others, are called professionals.

10. Intellectual

1. The intellectuals should not be considered as a class. The class status of intellectuals shall be determined according to the class to which they belong.

2. All intellectuals who come of the landlord and capitalist class should be fully utilized for work for the Soviet [regime], provided they obey the Soviet laws and decrees.

3. When intellectuals are engaged in work which does not involve the exploitation of other people—such as serving as schoolteachers, editors, journalists, clerks, writers, artists, and so forth—they are brainworkers. Such brainworkers should be protected by the Soviet laws.

Explanatory Notes

1. Intellectuals have recently been unconditionally discriminated against in many localities. This is not correct. It is a policy advantageous to the cause of the Soviet revolution to utilize the intellectuals of landlord and capitalist origin for work for the Soviets. During the period of their work for the Soviets, it is necessary to take measures to help solve their problems of livelihood.

2. The class status of intellectuals is to be determined according to

the class to which they belong. For instance, the intellectuals who come of landlord families are landlords; the intellectuals who come of rich-peasant families are rich peasants; the intellectuals who come of middle-peasant families are middle peasants. It is not correct to regard intellectuals as a separate class. It is all the more incorrect to regard those children of the peasants who have studied in schools (the so-called "graduates") as undesirable elements.

3. It is also incorrect to regard teaching, and so on, as anything but labor.

11. Idler-Proletarian

Workers, peasants, and other people who shortly before the uprising lost their occupations and land as a result of the oppression and exploitation by the landlord and capitalist class, and who have resorted to improper methods as their principal means of livelihood for three consecutive years, are called idler-proletarians (customarily they are called vagabonds).

The policy of the Soviets towards idler-proletarians is to win over the rank and file while opposing their leaders and other elements who ally themselves with the exploiting class and take an active part in counterrevolution. The chief method of winning over ordinary idler-proletarians is to help them return to production by giving them land and work just like ordinary revolutionary masses. They shall also be accorded the right to vote. But if they are to be assigned land, they must be domiciled in the villages concerned and must be able to till the land themselves.

Explanatory Notes
Attention should be paid to the following:

1. By resorting to improper methods as the principal means of livelihood is meant living by such improper occupations as theft, robbery, swindling, begging, gambling, prostitution, and so on. Some have listed as vagabonds all these elements who, employed or partly unemployed, have been partly engaged in improper occupations (not as their principal means of livelihood). This is not correct. It is all the more so to list as vagabonds those workers, peasants, and poor people who have contracted bad habits (such as brothel-frequenting, gambling, and opium-smoking).

2. In some localities the leading elements of the idler-proletarians (the so-called ringleaders) who have taken an active part in counter-

revolution are not subjected to punishment but are allotted land instead. This is not correct. In other localities the request of the ordinary idler-proletarians for land is simply rejected. This is not correct either.

12. Religious Practitioner

All those who obtained the main part of their means of subsistence from religious or superstitious professions (such as clergymen, priests, monks, Taoists, lay devotees, geomancers, fortunetellers, diviners, and so on) for three years (shortly before the uprising) are called religious practitioners. Religious practitioners have no right to vote and may not be allotted land.

Explanatory Note

All those who followed such religious or superstitious professions but did not depend on them as their principal means of subsistence, or who depended on them as their principal means of subsistence for less than three years, should not be listed as religious practitioners. Such people should be treated separately according to their respective class status; they may not be disenfranchised or denied land allotments on a uniform basis. That is to say, all those who followed such religious or superstitious professions as their secondary professions, or who depended on them as their primary professions for less than three years, should have the right to vote if they are workers, peasants, or poor people. They should also be allotted land if they are domiciled in the villages concerned. So they are to be treated; even more so are their dependents. Some regard monks, Taoists, geomancers, fortunetellers, and so on, as vagabonds. This is not correct.

13. The Red Army Man of Landlord or Rich-Peasant Origin and the Land

All Red Army men of landlord or rich-peasant origin, including officers and soldiers and their dependents, shall have the right to receive land allotments, provided that they fight determinedly for the interests of the workers and peasants.

Explanatory Notes

1. Article 1 of the "Regulations Governing the Preferential Treatment for the Red Army" reads:

All the Red Army men whose homes are located in the Soviet areas, together with their dependents, shall be entitled to the equal redistribution of land, houses, forests, and ponds like the poor and miserable peasants in the same localities.

This article covers all Red Army men. But recently, in some localities, only the origin [of the Red Army man] has been taken into account, without regard to his political record. As a result, it has happened that the land already assigned to Red Army men of landlord or rich-peasant origin has again been confiscated though they have fought staunchly for the interests of the workers and peasants. This is erroneous.

2. The "dependents of the Red Army men" include parents, wives, sons, and daughters, as well as brothers and sisters under the age of sixteen. Other family members shall not enjoy such rights.

3. The land allotted to Red Army men of landlord or rich-peasant origin may be taken back if they are dismissed from the army.

14. Worker from a Rich-Peasant or Landlord Family

Workers from rich-peasant or landlord families, their wives, and their children shall retain their status as workers. Whether they should be allotted land or not is to be decided according to whether they reside in the villages or cities. The other members of their families shall be treated as landlords or rich peasants in status.

Explanatory Notes

1. If a member of a landlord or rich-peasant family had, shortly before the uprising, sold his labor power for one year, he shall be recognized as a worker in status. The said member himself and his wife and children shall be treated as workers in status and that part of the family's property to which they are entitled shall not be confiscated. If he and his wife and children reside in the countryside, they should be allotted land. If he and his wife and children reside in the city, they should not be allotted land. If he himself resides in the city and his wife and children reside in the countryside, he himself should not be allotted land while his wife and children should. The other members of his family shall be treated as landlords or rich peasants in status, and shall not enjoy the rights of workers. If some members of the family belong to any other class status, they should be treated according to their respective status. (Take one family, for instance. If there is a person in the countryside who has, for three years, depended on land rent and loan interest as his principal means of livelihood, then the said

person is a landlord. If there is another person who has, for one year, sold his labor power [as his principal means of livelihood], then the said person is a worker. If there is still another person who has, for one year, run a small manufactory in a small town, producing and selling goods all by himself [as his principal means of livelihood], then the said person is an independent producer. Each person has his status determined in accordance with the nature of the means he employs to earn a living during a given period. The status of each person, in turn, determines the treatment he receives under the Soviet laws.)

2. There are workers, independent producers, primary schoolteachers, physicians, and so on in the countryside who also own small plots of land. They shall be allotted land as ordinary peasants but not treated as landlords, when they, failing to make a living in the rural districts, go elsewhere to seek a living and rent out their small plots of land, provided that they do not depend on the land rent as their principal means of livelihood.

15. The Class Status of Landlords, Rich Peasants, or Capitalists after Marrying Workers, Peasants [or Poor People], and Vice Versa

1. The act of marriage cannot alter the class status [of the parties concerned].

2. The class status of landlords, rich peasants, or capitalists after their marriage with workers, peasants, or poor people, and vice versa, shall be determined in accordance with their marriage before or after the uprising, their original class status, and their living conditions after the marriage.

3. In cases where the marriage took place before the uprising: The women from the families of landlords, rich peasants, or capitalists who married workers, peasants, or poor people and who have engaged in labor for one year, shall be recognized as having the class status of workers, peasants, or poor people. Those who have not engaged in labor or have engaged in labor for less than one year shall retain their original class status.

The women from the families of workers, peasants, or poor people who married landlords, rich peasants, or capitalists will be recognized as having the class status of landlords, rich peasants, or capitalists only when they have lived for five years the same life as the landlords, rich peasants, or capitalists. Those who have not lived the same life as the landlords, rich peasants, or capitalists but have lived the same life as the workers, peasants, or poor people (i.e., depending on their own labor as their principal means of livelihood), or who have lived the same life [as the landlords, rich peasants, or capitalists] for less than five years, shall retain their original class status.

4. In cases where the marriage took place after the uprising: The women from the families of workers, peasants, or poor people who married landlords, rich peasants, or capitalists shall retain their original class status. The women from the families of landlords, rich peasants, or capitalists who married workers, peasants, or poor people shall be recognized as having the class status of workers, peasants, or poor people, provided that they have been engaged in labor for five years. Those who have not engaged in labor, or have engaged in labor for less than five years, shall retain their original class status.

5. Children shall have the same class status as their fathers, irrespective of the class status of the persons whom their fathers married and when the marriage took place.

6. Claims to land and to civic rights are to be determined by the class status of the claimants.

7. The women from the families of landlords, rich peasants, or capitalists who married workers, peasants, or poor people shall not be enrolled in hard-labor corps. The money brought by such women as dowry in marriage shall not be subjected to fine or contribution if it does not exceed 50 silver dollars.

8. Before the uprising there were cases in which the children of workers, peasants, or poor people were sold to landlords, rich peasants, or capitalists, and also cases in which [the sons of] workers, peasants, or poor people were married to the daughters of landlords, rich peasants, or capitalists through the practice of adopting the sons-in-law as heirs of the wives' families, or vice versa [?]. In determining the class status of, and the treatment for, the children sold and the sons-in-law adopted, the foregoing seven articles shall apply.

9. As regards the adoption before the uprising of the sons of workers, peasants, or poor people by landlords, rich peasants, or capitalists, and vice versa, the adopted sons shall retain their original class status if they are under ten years of age, irrespective of their ages at the time of the adoption. From ten years of age on, the sons of workers, peasants, or poor people who were adopted by landlords, rich peasants, or capitalists as sons, and who have lived the same life as their foster parents for five years, shall have the same class status as their foster parents. If they have not lived the same life as their foster parents but have continued

to live the same life as their own parents, they shall retain their original class status. The sons of landlords, rich peasants, or capitalists who were adopted by workers, peasants, or poor people as sons, and who have lived the same life as their foster parents for three years, shall have the same class status as their foster parents. If they have not lived the same life as their foster parents but have continued to live the same life as their own parents, they shall retain their original class status.

Explanatory Note
Here "labor" includes domestic labor.

16. Landlord or Rich Peasant Who Is Concurrently Merchant

1. Landlords who are concurrently merchants: Their land as well as houses and [other] properties connected with the land shall be confiscated, but the commercial enterprises as well as business premises, dwelling houses, and [other] properties connected with such commercial enterprises shall not be confiscated.

2. Rich peasants who are concurrently merchants: Their land as well as houses and [other] properties connected with the land shall be treated as belonging to those who are of rich-peasant status, but the commercial enterprises as well as business premises, dwelling houses, and [other] properties connected with such commercial enterprises shall not be confiscated.

3. Fines imposed upon, or contributions extorted from, landlords or rich peasants who are concurrently merchants shall be limited to that part of their property which they own as landlords or rich peasants, but should not encroach upon the commercial part.

4. Merchants are not to be enrolled in hard-labor corps.

17. Management of Landholdings of Public Bodies

The management of landholdings of public bodies is an act of exploitation. But a distinction should be made between the management of landholdings of public bodies by landlords, rich peasants, or capitalists on the one hand and by workers, peasants, or poor people on the other.

Explanatory Note
By the management of landholdings of public bodies is meant the management of the land and [other] properties belonging to all kinds

of ancestral shrines, temples, and associations. There is no doubt that the management of landholdings of public bodies is a sort of exploitation. Above all, it has become one of the principal forms of exploitation when the landlord class and rich peasants have concentrated large amounts of land and [other] properties through the medium of this system. As the management of landholdings of public bodies has been monopolized by a handful of people and has accordingly become the source of a large amount of income through exploitation for these people, the act of such management constitutes, of course, one of the factors for the determination of the class status of those who are responsible for the management. However, since some of the smaller public bodies are managed by turns by the masses of workers, peasants, and poor people and accordingly make for very little exploitation, the management of such smaller public bodies should not be taken as one of the factors in determining the class status of those who are responsible for the management. Some maintain that all those who have shared in the management of landholdings of public bodies should for that simple reason be regarded as landlords, rich peasants, or capitalists. That is not correct.

18. The Problem of Livelihood of Some Functionaries

Those who are working in the Soviet organs and other revolutionary organizations but who have not been allotted land and are having great difficulty in making a living may be allotted, together with their dependents, suitable amounts of land. Other means may also be devised to help solve their difficulties.

Explanatory Note

The central government has given orders to solve the problem of the livelihood of the Soviet functionaries who have already been allotted land (i.e., by mobilizing the masses to help cultivate their land). Here involved are only those who have not been allotted land. By dependents are meant parents, wives, sons, and daughters, and younger brothers and sisters under the age of ten.

19. Land for Public Enterprises

In the redistribution of land in the new [Soviet] areas and the land newly discovered in the old [Soviet] areas, suitable amounts of land should be reserved for the use of public enterprises such as bridges, ferryboats, roadside resthouses, experimental farms, and so on.

Explanatory Note

To meet the expenses for such public enterprises as the repair of bridges and ferryboats, the payment of ferrymen's wages, and the construction and repair of roadside resthouses, it is necessary to reserve suitable amounts of land and mobilize the masses to cultivate them. In addition, it is also necessary for the Soviets on the county, district, and township levels to reserve suitable tracts of land in the neighborhood of government organs for the purpose of creating experimental farms. (The county Soviets may reserve land with a potential yield of 50 to 150 piculs of grain, the district Soviets may reserve land with a potential yield of 15 to 25 piculs of grain, and the township Soviets may reserve land with a potential yield of 5 to 10 piculs of grain.) Pending the creation of such experimental farms, the land may be leased to peasants to cultivate at a minimum rent.

20. The Problem of Debts

1. With the exception of the debts incurred to commercial firms as a result of business transactions, the principal and interest of all debts lent in cash or in kind by landlords, rich peasants, or capitalists to workers, peasants, or poor people before the uprising shall be annulled. The principal and interest of all debts lent in cash or in kind by workers, peasants, or poor people to landlords, rich peasants, or capitalists shall be repaid in full.

2. Those who depend on usurious exploitation as the sole or principal means of support for themselves and their families are called usurers. Usurers shall be treated as landlords in class status.

3. Debts incurred after the uprising shall be repaid, provided that they are not in contravention of the "Provisional Regulations Governing the Lending and Borrowing of Debts" promulgated by the central government.

Explanatory Note

Those who practice usurious exploitation (most of the debts in the Kuomintang-ruled areas, incurred in cities or in the countryside, are usurious exploitation) but do not depend on usurious exploitation as the sole or principal means to support themselves and their families, may not be classified as usurers. Therefore, they should not be subjected to the policy of wholesale confiscation but should be treated according to their own status. It is not correct to regard as usurers all those who practice usurious exploitation.

The status of those who lend money on the one hand and borrow money on the other is to be determined by the nature and degree of the difference between the debits and credits, coupled with their other relations of exploitation.

MAO TSE-TUNG
Chairman of the Central Government
Chinese Soviet Republic
HSIANG YING
Vice-Chairman
CHANG KUO-T'AO
Vice-Chairman

October 10, 1933

DOCUMENT 106

ON THE QUESTION OF REOPENING THE LAND INVESTIGATION DRIVE—INSTRUCTION, SERIAL CHARACTER *CHUNG*, NO. 1, OF THE COUNCIL OF PEOPLE'S COMMISSARS, MARCH 15, 1934

(As printed in *Red China*, No. 164, March 20, 1934, p. 1)

The former Council of People's Commissars promulgated the *Decisions concerning Some Problems Arising from the Agrarian Struggle* for the purpose of rectifying some excessively "Left" tendencies during the land investigation drive. Obviously that was correct. But following the promulgation of the *Decisions,* numerous serious problems have once again occurred in various places in the course of the land investigation drive. The Soviet governments in many places have even given up the work of continuing to unfold the land investigation drive, and instead have busied themselves with "rectifying" some excessively "Left" mistakes committed in the land investigation drive of the past, or even before the land investigation drive. Furthermore, they have given the landlords and rich peasants many opportunities to counterattack. Taking advantage of some provisions in the *Decisions* (particularly Articles 1, 2, and 3), the landlords and rich peasants have also become very active in an attempt to substitute class investigation with "class calculation" by playing at figures as a trick to recapture their previously lost land and property. For the sake of suppressing the counterattacks and counterrevolutionary activities of the landlords and rich peasants, and for the sake of further unfolding the land investigation drive and bringing about a thorough solution to the land problem, the Council of People's Commissars hereby makes the following decisions:

1. Landlords and rich peasants whose status was decided as such following the uprising and before the land investigation drive must not be allowed to change their status, no matter what evidence they may produce. Such changes as have already been made are null and void.

2. In rectifying individual mistakes committed in the land investigation drive, only the individual cases of the landlord and rich-peasant elements whose status has been decided as such in the past but is being doubted or criticized by the masses may be reconsidered. If not doubted or criticized by the masses, no status can be changed, no matter what evidence the landlords and rich peasants may produce. Such changes as have already been made are null and void.

3. In examining the status of the landlord and rich-peasant elements as decided in the past, it is absolutely forbidden to adopt the method of calling a meeting for the landlords and rich peasants and letting them argue face to face with the poor and miserable workers and peasants (such as the case in the county of Sheng-li). Such examination should be the responsibility of the local land investigation committee together with the worker and peasant comrades operating under its leadership. Any solution should be obtained through an investigation or interview on an individual basis.

4. If the middle peasants have been wrongly defined as rich peasants in the land investigation drive, the original amounts of land of the former should be made up and returned to them as far as possible. If the rich peasants have been wrongly defined as landlords, they should be reassigned suitable amounts of poor land and waste land. The land allotted to workers in the land investigation drive may not be withdrawn. Difficulties which may occur in this respect should be resolved primarily by going deeply into the land investigation drive.

5. In continuing to unfold the land investigation drive, we must object resolutely to the substitution of "class calculation" for class investigation, to the substitution of percentage figures for class struggle. Articles 2 and 3 and Explanatory Note 7 of Article 1 of the *Decisions* adopted by the former Council of People's Commissars are clauses which can only be invoked with the endorsement of the masses when extraordinarily difficult questions of class status arise in the land investigation drive. They must not be invoked mechanically so as to hinder the rapid unfolding of the land investigation drive. On such occasions

the final authority for deciding upon the class status is vested in the great majority of the local masses.

Meanwhile, in regard to the ambiguous words concerning "labor" as used in Explanatory Note 4 of Article 1 and in the Explanatory Note of Article 15 of the *Decisions,* it must be pointed out in very unmistakable terms that the labor which is used as the principal criterion for distinguishing between peasants and landlords refers to essential labor in agricultural production but not to domestic labor such as cooking and laundry, much less to such labor as bookkeeping, trading, or any other used in nonagricultural production. It is essential to prevent landlords and rich peasants from using any clause of the *Decisions* as a weapon to change their status. All their counterrevolutionary activities should be subject to the severest sanction of Soviet laws.

6. While correcting the individual mistakes made in the land investigation drive, we not only cannot afford to halt the further progress of the land investigation drive, but also we precisely want to carry out more correctly the class line of allying with the middle peasants so that the struggle of the land investigation drive may be more smoothly unfolded. It is essential to give a determined blow to Right opportunism which is calculated to call a halt to the land investigation drive on the pretext of rectifying the excessively Left tendencies of the past. Unfolding the land investigation drive is still the central task of the present. Right opportunism is the main danger today.

7. For the purpose of unfolding the land investigation drive, the various provinces should each maintain a firm hold on a few backward but centrally located counties, and border counties, and townships. In new areas where the land problem has not been fundamentally solved, the land should be redistributed. Land discovered as a result of previous investigations should be immediately redistributed. In some places, where the acreage of public land for the Red Army has been reduced because of road construction or other reasons, a part of the land discovered during investigations should be set aside as public land for the Red Army.

8. A close link must be established between the land investigation drive and the current spring plowing movement. Meanwhile, the land investigation drive should be utilized to develop the activism of the broad masses of workers and peasants and to mobilize and organize them for participating more enthusiastically in the revolutionary war.

CHANG WEN-T'IEN
Chairman

March 15, 1934

DOCUMENT 117

SHOULD WE STAND FIRM IN SUPPRESSING THE COUNTERREVOLUTIONARIES OR GET MAD AND CONFUSED IN FACE OF THEM?

Chang Wen-t'ien, June 25, 1934
(As published in *Red China*, No. 208, June 28, 1934, pp. 1–2)

Through the Instruction of the Council of People's Commissars, serial character *Chung*, No. 3, the party has pointed out in unmistakable terms:

> Under the conditions of the increasingly intense war of the revolution, our methods to deal with the landlords and rich peasants have to undergo a change, but the basic tactics of annihilating the landlord class and opposing the rich peasants remain unchanged.

We have advocated a reign of Red Terror to combat the positive counterrevolutionary activities of the landlords and rich peasants— especially the counterrevolutionary activities of the landlords and rich peasants in the war zones and border areas, which we must at once take the most expeditious steps to suppress. This is because only a reign of Red Terror can possibly stop or paralyze the counterrevolutionary activities of the landlords and rich peasants.

We have never said that we want to use a reign of Red Terror to deal with the landlords and rich peasants who are not engaged in counterrevolutionary activities. The landlords and rich peasants who are not engaged in counterrevolutionary activities can still continue to live in the Soviet areas and rely on their own labor to maintain their subsistence. Also, they can reform themselves through labor.

When we speak of the annihilation of the landlord class, we mean the annihilation of the land and [other] property which make the landlords an exploiting class, but not the killing of all landlords. As regards opposition to the rich peasants, it means to weaken the rich peasants economically, but not to annihilate the rich peasants economically, much less to kill all rich peasants. We are determined to arrest or physically destroy only those who are unwaveringly carrying on counterrevolutionary activities in an attempt to overthrow the Soviets.

This basic policy of the Soviet regime must be known to everybody. But as a result of the tension of the revolutionary war and the stepping up of the counterrevolutionary activities of the landlords and rich peasants, some wavering elements in our party have become mad and confused. They have not only wanted to use a Red Terror to deal with the counterrevolutionary landlords and rich peasants, but also to use it against all landlords and rich peasants. They have wanted to arrest all landlords and rich peasants. A concrete demonstration of this tendency is furnished by the urgent order issued by the Security Bureau of Kiangsi on May 23 [a text of this order is unfortunately unavailable].

This kind of ultraleftist tendency obviously has nothing in common with the basic policy of the Soviet regime towards the landlords and rich peasants. The consequence of such a tendency will not only make it impossible to suppress the counterrevolutionary activities of the landlords and rich peasants, but is also likely to pull all landlords and rich peasants together to resort to a desperate and decisive fight against the Soviet regime. For before them there is no alternative but death. The consequence of such a tendency would be even more dangerous to us. That is to say, we would not only make all landlords and rich peasants present a united front against us, but also put landlords and rich peasants in a favorable position to deceive the masses. For the outcome of the ultraleftist tendency would not merely create a panic among all the landlords and rich peasants but also create a panic among the masses. This kind of panic is exactly what will facilitate the deceptive propaganda of the landlords and rich peasants. It would cause a section of the deceived masses, primarily the masses of middle peasants, to escape to the mountains, or to allow themselves to be utilized by the landlords and rich peasants in opposition to the Soviet regime. Some recent incidents occurring in T'ai-lei, Chih-shui, and Kan-hsien have completely proved the accuracy of this observation.

This kind of ultraleftist tendency appears on the surface to be a resolute struggle against the counterrevolution of the landlords and rich peasants, but objectively it has exactly the reverse effect of helping the counterrevolutionary landlords and rich peasants. In substance, this kind of ultraleftist tendency is not different from Right opportunism which favors a surrender to the landlords and rich peasants.

Regarding the utilization of the labor and material resources of the landlords and rich peasants, the basic principle of the party, as embodied in the Instruction of the Council of People's Commissars, serial character *Chung*, No. 3, calls for the confiscation of all the land and [other] property of the landlords, the organization of the landlords into permanent forced-labor corps, the requisition of the food and capital of the rich peasants, and the organization of the rich peasants into temporary forced-labor corps. Only in special areas, such as the direct war zones (that is, where the "solid breastwork and empty field" policy has been or is about to be enforced), we may organize the landlords and the rich peasants into the same forced-labor corps. Such areas are relatively not very extensive. In places immediately behind the direct war zones (for example, our position in T'ou-p'i during the battle of Kuang-ch'ang), the landlords and rich peasants may be organized into the same forced-labor corps only in case of military necessity. In the absence of such a necessity, they obviously need not be organized into the same forced-labor corps. The places immediately behind the direct war zones, referred to here, are not very extensive, either. These are all exceptions to the basic rules, which we are obliged to make under special circumstances. Regarding the dependents of the landlords, those in the war zones are all to be expelled or evacuated to other places.

The Soviet regime has laid down its basic rules regarding this problem, but at the same time it has specifically made some exceptions. This must also be known to everybody. But some Left-deviating comrades make no distinction between "direct war zones" and "places immediately behind the direct war zones." They enlarge the scope of the "war zones" to such a degree that "war zones" and "basic areas" are made literally identical (e.g., all counties in the whole province of Kiangsi are regarded as war zones). In consequence, our exceptions have been converted into our rules, which fact has enabled us to deal with the landlords and rich peasants without the slightest difference. In these areas they have arrested all the village bosses, gentry, landlords, and rich peasants, irrespective of age, placed all able-bodied persons into the forced-labor corps, and expelled all the old and feeble from these areas or had them imprisoned in one concentration camp.

What is meant by organizing the landlords and rich peasants into the same forced-labor corps, expelling the dependents of the landlords and rich peasants alike or having them imprisoned in one concentration camp? That means that we have adopted the ultraleftist line to annihilate the rich peasants. Such being the case, the distinction between confiscation and requisition is obviously only a matter of language, but not a matter of substance. This kind of erroneous line would basically undermine our alliance with the middle peasants and endanger the foundation of the entire Soviet regime. This is a most dangerous

Trotskyite line, which the party has long denounced. This line is the best help to imperialism, the Kuomintang, landlords, capitalists, and rich peasants.

With reference to the organization of the village bosses and gentry into permanent forced-labor corps, [our policy] is merely, except for the war zones, to have their names registered by the district and township governments, so that the government and the military department may draft them in case of need. We have never wanted to have them all concentrated on a permanent basis. If we want to concentrate all the village bosses, gentry, landlords, and rich peasants in all the Soviet areas on a permanent basis, we shall create for ourselves many a new and unnecessary difficulty in administration and in food supply. To concentrate their wives and children is even more absurd!

The border areas and the areas constantly harassed or occupied by bandits differ also from the war zones slightly. Here, it is necessary to move the village bosses, gentry, and landlords, as well as their dependents, to the rear or to areas not harassed by bandits, while the able-bodied persons will be organized into permanent forced-labor corps in the areas where they have moved. It is not necessary to move the rich peasants and their dependents to other places or organize them into permanent forced-labor corps. If we look upon both the border areas and the areas harassed by bandits as war zones, it will, of course, have the effect of extending the scope of the war zones. Naturally, this kind of extension is uncalled for militarily, and is also likely to produce the above-mentioned unfavorable consequences politically.

As regards the question of requisitioning the foodstuffs of the rich peasants, the idea of the requisition is to collect the surplus foodstuffs of the rich peasants to be handed over to the state without compensation. Confiscation means to confiscate all that is owned by landlords and to turn it over to the state. Accordingly, there is a vast difference between requisition and confiscation. The requisition of five pecks of grain from a rich peasant as decided by the Council of People's Commissars is merely a general stipulation which serves as a reasonable yardstick for our working comrades at the lower echelons. In individual cases, however, specific and separate considerations are called for. For those who really cannot produce five pecks of grain, there may be a certain amount of reduction. This kind of reduction must not be viewed as a compromise with the rich peasants; it is exactly for the purpose of carrying out the correct class line. The ultraleftists make no distinction between confiscation and requisition and apply the same measures against the rich peasants that have been applied against the landlords. Obviously, that is basically wrong.

However, we must always follow the line of mobilizing the masses, working through the masses and relying on the masses, whether we arrest and kill counterrevolutionary landlords and rich peasants, organize landlords and rich peasants into forced-labor corps, or confiscate and requisition the foodstuffs of the landlords and rich peasants. For the problem here is not simply to arrest a few people or kill a few people, or confiscate and requisition some belongings of the landlords and rich peasants. The problem is rather one of how to promote the activism of the masses, raise the degree of the consciousness of the masses, and rally and organize the masses around the Soviet regime, when we carry out our clear and definite class line. In the absence of this condition, even if you should have all landlords and rich peasants killed, counterrevolutionary activities not only would not disappear but, on the contrary, would grow into larger proportions. Arrest, shooting, and imprisonment are relatively all simple. The difficulty of the problem is how we should deal with the positive counterrevolutionary elements correctly and severely and how we should rouse the masses to a struggle against the counterrevolution.

This is also true of other problems. Above all,

> ... we should be all the more cautious in dealing with the rich peasants, because any ineptitude in handling them will affect the middle peasants and make the middle peasants waver. And the middle peasants are [our] staunch allies! All emergency measures we adopt must have the understanding and support of the middle peasant masses (from an editorial in *Red China*, No. 193). [The editorial is a signed article by the same author, entitled "Towards Our Class Enemies There Is Only Hatred but No Mercy!"]

Some of our comrades, especially some of our comrades in the Red Army's management organs or logistic organs, often think that once they have arms and power, everything would become simple. Many measures of the nature of a compulsory order have been invented by these people. In truth, however, not only the measures of the nature of a compulsory order have become bankrupt in the work among the masses, but also the compulsory orders to landlords and rich peasants must likewise follow some definite policy and the line of mass mobilization.

The party must most grimly attack and disprove the idea that only the measures adopted by the ultraleftists to deal with the landlords and rich peasants are revolutionary measures. The party must point out that only the correct implementation of both the class line and the mass line is the really revolutionary Bolshevik method. The revolution of the ultraleftists is a pseudo revolution, and gives a helping hand to the class enemy. Vis-à-vis such comrades, the party should first of all persuade them and educate them to make them realize their own mistakes. To those elements who persist in such mistakes, however, the party must mete out severe organizational decisions and the sanctions of Soviet laws.

On the other hand, the party must make all the comrades remember that the really counterrevolutionary elements also often use these ultra-leftist measures to carry out their counterrevolutionary activities.

The more intense the fighting at the front grows, the more positive become the counterrevolutionary activities in the Soviet areas. The party must severely suppress the counterrevolutionary activities of the landlords and rich peasants. In this struggle, we demand all our party comrades to show the greatest resolution and organization in their unwavering implementation of the party's Bolshevik directives. We must deal a most resolute blow to any panic, flurry, surrender, and compromise resulting from Right opportunism in coping with the counterrevolutionary activities. However, we will have no momentary patience with the madness and confusion of the petty bourgeois ultra-leftism, either. It is only when we put a stop at once to the mistakes of Left deviation which have recently occurred in connection with the question of the landlords and rich peasants that we shall be able to unfold the struggle against Right opportunism in a sound way!

Appendix

A. *Land Law Adopted at Ching-kang-shan in December, 1928* (As printed in Mao Tse-tung, *Investigations of the Rural Districts,* published at Yenan in 1941, reissued by Hsinhua Bookstore, Shantung, 1946, pp. 86-88)

I. All land shall be confiscated and turned over to the ownership of the Soviet government. It shall be redistributed according to the following methods:

1. Redistributed to the peasants for their individual cultivation.
2. Redistributed to the peasants for their common cultivation.
3. Cultivated as model farms to be created by the Soviet government.

The first of the above three methods shall be the main one. The second and third methods are to be employed under special circumstances or when the Soviet government is in a position to do so.

II. No land shall be bought or sold after it has been confiscated and redistributed by the Soviet government.

III. After land has been redistributed, all people shall be subject to compulsory labor except the old, young, or sick who are not able to till land, and those who are performing public services.

IV. The numerical and toiling criteria of land redistribution:

1. To use the number of persons as the criterion: All men and women, old and young, shall be entitled to equal redistribution.
2. To use labor power as the criterion: Those who are able to work shall receive double the amounts of land received by those who are not able to work.

The first of the above two criteria shall be the main one. The second criterion may be adopted in places where special circumstances warrant it.

The reasons for adopting the first criterion are: (*a*) The old and young people cannot possibly make a living if they are allotted too little land, before there are adequate and satisfactory facilities to care for the old and the young. (*b*) It would be easier and more convenient to complete land allotments according to the criterion of the number of persons. (*c*) Few households do not have old and young people. Meanwhile, the old and

291

young people, though incapable of tilling land, may nevertheless be designated by the government to perform some suitable public services, such as communications work, and so on, after they have been allotted land.

V. The regional criteria of land redistribution:

1. To use the township as a unit for redistribution.
2. To use several townships as a unit for redistribution (such as the Hsiao-chiang district in Yung-hsin).
3. To use the district as a unit for redistribution (such as the Huang-yao district in Sui-chuan).

The first of the above three criteria shall be the main one. The second and third criteria may be used under special circumstances.

VI. Methods of redistributing forests:

1. Forests of tea-oil plants and firewood forests shall, following the method of land redistribution, be equally redistributed for cultivation and exploitation with the township as a unit.
2. Bamboo forests shall be owned by the Soviet government, but the peasants may cut and use the bamboo with the approval of the Soviet. Not more than fifty stalks of bamboo may be cut with the approval of the township Soviet government. Not more than a hundred stalks of bamboo may be cut with the approval of the district Soviet government. More than a hundred stalks of bamboo may be cut with the approval of the county Soviet government.
3. All bamboo shall be sold by the county Soviet government. The proceeds therefrom shall be disposed of by the Soviet government at a higher level.

VII. The levying of the land tax:

1. The land tax shall be divided into three kinds according to the condition of production: (*a*) 15 per cent, (*b*) 10 per cent, and (*c*) 5 per cent. The first of the above 3 measures shall be the main one. The second and third kinds may be used under special circumstances with the approval of the Soviet government at a higher level.
2. In the event of natural calamities or other special circumstances the land tax may be exempted with the approval of the Soviet government at a higher level.
3. The land tax shall be levied by the county Soviet government and handed over to the Soviet government at a higher level for disposal.

VIII. A rural handicraft worker who wishes to receive a land allotment may obtain half the amount of land allotted to a peasant.

IX. The officers and soldiers of the Red Army forces and the Red Guards, as well as those who are working in the government and all other public agencies, shall all be allotted the same amount of land as the peasants. The Soviet government will hire people to cultivate such land for them.

In 1941, Mao Tse-tung commented:

This land law was adopted at Ching-kang-shan (the Hunan-Kiangsi Border Soviet Area) in the winter of 1928 [–1929]. This was a product of the experience of the land struggle waged during the whole year from the winter of 1927 [–1928] to that of 1928 [–1929]. There had not been any experience [of this kind] before that time.

This land law contains several mistakes: (1) All land was confiscated, instead of only the land of the landlords. (2) Landownership was in the hands of the government, not the peasantry, who had only the right to use the land. (3) The purchase or sale of land was prohibited.

All these were mistakes of principle, which were duly corrected afterward. As to why the common cultivation and labor power used as a criterion of land redistribution had not been adopted as the main methods but, instead, the individual cultivation and the number of persons used as a criterion of land redistribution had been adopted as the main methods, was due to the fact that at that time the former methods, though considered incorrect, were nevertheless favored by quite a number of comrades and therefore had to be written into the law. But subsequently only the latter methods were adopted as the standard practice.

The policy of hiring people to till land for the Red Army personnel was later changed to mobilizing the peasants to do the tilling for them.

B. *Land Law Adopted at Hsing-kuo County in April, 1929* (As printed in Mao Tse-tung, *Investigations of the Rural Districts,* published at Yenan in 1941, reissued by Hsinhua Bookstore, Shantung, 1946, pp. 89-90)

I. All public land and the land of the landlord class shall be confiscated and turned over to the ownership of the Hsing-kuo Council Government of the Works', Peasants', and Soldiers' Delegates. They shall be redistributed to the peasants who have no or little land, to cultivate and use.

II. No public land and no land of the landlord class shall be bought or sold after it has been confiscated and redistributed by the Workers', Peasants', and Soldiers' Government.

III. The numerical and toiling criteria of land redistribution:

1. To use the number of persons as the criterion: All men and women, old and young, shall be entitled to equal redistribution.

2. To use labor power as the criterion: Those who are able to work shall receive double the amounts of land received by those who are not able to work.

The first of the above two criteria shall be the main one. The second criterion may be adopted in places where special circumstances warrant it.

The reasons for adopting the first criterion are: (*a*) The old and young people cannot possibly make a living if they are allotted too little land, before there are adequate and satisfactory facilities to care for the old and the young. (*b*) It would be easier and more convenient to compute land allotments according to the criterion of the number of persons. (*c*) Few households do not have old and young people. Meanwhile, the old and young people, though incapable of tilling land, may nevertheless be designated by the government to perform some suitable public services, such as communications work, and so on, after they have been allotted land.

IV. The regional criteria of land redistribution:

1. To use the township as a unit for redistribution.
2. To use several townships as a unit for redistribution (such as the Hsiao-chiang district in Yung-hsin).
3. To use the district as a unit for redistribution.

The first of the above three criteria shall be the main one. The second and third criteria may be used under special circumstances.

V. Methods of redistributing forests:

1. Forests of tea-oil plants and firewood forests shall, following the method of land redistribution, be equally redistributed for cultivation and exploitation with the township as a unit.
2. Bamboo forests shall be owned by the Soviet government. But the peasants may cut and use the bamboo with the approval of the Soviet government. Not more than fifty stalks of bamboo may be cut with the approval of the township Soviet government. Not more than a hundred stalks of bamboo may be cut with the approval of the district Soviet government. More than a hundred stalks of bamboo may be cut with the approval of the county Soviet government.
3. All bamboo shall be sold by the county Soviet government. The proceeds therefrom shall be disposed of by the Soviet government at a higher level.

VI. The levying of the land tax:

1. The land tax shall be divided into three kinds according to the condition of production: (*a*) 15 per cent, (*b*) 10 per cent, and (*c*) 5 per cent. The first of the above three measures shall be the main one. The second and third kinds may be used under special circumstances with the approval of the Soviet at a higher level.
2. In the event of natural calamities or other special circumstances the land tax may be removed with the approval of the Soviet government at a higher level.
3. The land tax shall be levied by the county Soviet government and handed over to the Soviet government at a higher level for disposal.

VII. A rural handicraft worker who wishes to receive a land allotment may obtain half the amount of land allotted to a peasant.

VIII. The officers and soldiers of the Red Army forces and the Red Guards, as well as those who are working in the government and all other public agencies, shall all be allotted the same amount of land as the peasants. The Soviet government will hire people to cultivate such land for them.

In 1941, Mao Tse-tung commented:

This law was promulgated at Hsing-kuo in southern Kiangsi four months after the adoption of the land law at Ching-kang-shan, from which the Red Army forces had retreated. There was an important change in content, namely, "confiscation of all land" was changed to "confiscation of public land and the land of the landlord class." This was an improvement of principle. All other points, however, had remained unchanged until 1930, when they were modified. These two land laws have been preserved in order to show how our views on the land struggle have developed.

Chronology

1930

February 7. Mao sponsors a party conference in southern Kiangsi, from which the two principles of land redistribution "draw-on-the-plentiful-to-make-up-for-the-scarce" and "draw-on-the-fat-to-make-up-for-the-lean" allegedly emerge as outstanding features of Mao's land policy.

Establishment of the Southwest Kiangsi Soviet Government results in the unification of the multifarious modes of land redistribution in Kiangsi.

May 31. Provisional land law is adopted under Li Li-san's sponsorship at Shanghai.

June. Chu-Mao group adopts a strong anti-rich-peasant policy in western Fukien, apparently under the impact of the Comintern directive of June 7, 1929.

July. Li Li-sanists in the Second Plenum of the Southwest Kiangsi Special Committee raise objections to Mao's land policies adopted at the February 7 conference.

July 23. Comintern addresses a directive to the CCP, denouncing, *inter alia,* Li Li-san's agrarian and economic policies in the Soviet areas.

September 12. Central Preparatory Commission for the National Soviet Congress convenes with the result that all the traits of Li Li-sanism are removed from the provisional land law according to the wishes of Moscow.

September 24. Third Plenum of the CCP Central Committee opens, in which Li Li-san's land policies, among other things, are attacked.

October-November. Mao made several investigations of the rural districts in western Kiangsi, resulting in the drafting of a number of papers and reports included in his *Investigations of the Rural Districts,* published at Yenan in 1941.

November 15, or thereabouts. Comintern Eastern Department's draft resolution on the land and peasant problems in the Soviet areas is received, which, apart from criticizing Li Li-san's land policies, assigns a fifteen-point program to the CCP for work in the Soviet areas. About the same time a Comintern Eastern Department directive on the economic policies in the Soviet areas is also received.

November 16. Comintern directive to the CCP in denunciation of the Li-san line, including land policies, is received.

November 22. CCP Politburo holds an enlarged meeting in which Li Li-san's land policies, among other things, are criticized.

December. Li Li-san, during his Moscow trial, makes abject confessions about his land policies, which are violently attacked by Comintern officials.

December 8. Fu-t'ien incident occurs in which the clash between land policies of Mao and Li Li-san comes into the open.

Late 1930 (?) Comintern issues a directive to the CCP on the peasant problem that is reproduced by a local Chinese Communist agency on February 18, 1931.

1931

1931. Kiangsi Provincial Government issues a proclamation implying no land allotment to the landlord.

Early January. Fourth Plenum of the CCP Central Committee convenes, and Li Li-san's land policies, among other things, are denounced on the basis of the Comintern directive received on November 16, 1930.

February 8. Central Bureau of the Soviet Areas adopts a resolution on the land problem and anti-rich-peasant tactics that denounces the agrarian policies of both the Chu-Mao group and Li Li-san.

Early August. CCP Central Committee prepares a draft land law for submission to the First National Soviet Congress.

August 21. Central Bureau of the Soviet Areas adopts a resolution to accept the draft land law prepared by the Central Committee, attacking land policies of both the Chu-Mao group and Li Li-san.

November 7. First National Soviet Congress opens, resulting in the adoption of a land law, among other things. Meanwhile, Oyuwan adopts a resolution on the confiscation and redistribution of land, revealing the influence of Li Li-san's land policy there.

November 10. CCP central leadership writes to the Central Bureau of the Soviet Areas, criticizing the latter's resolution of August 21, and throwing considerable light on a number of points in the land law adopted by the First National Soviet Congress.

December 1. Land law adopted by the First National Soviet Congress is proclaimed as the land law of the Chinese Soviet Republic.

December 5. Yang-hsin county adopts a resolution on the land problem, setting forth details of confiscation and redistribution.

Late 1931 or early 1932. Kiangsi Provincial Government establishes regulations for the confiscation and redistribution of land.

1932

March. Central Bureau of the Soviet Areas issues an explanatory statement on the land law of the Chinese Soviet Republic.

March 9. Mao's cabinet writes to authorities in western Fukien, telling them how to carry out land redistribution in newly occupied areas.

June 23. Land department of the central government distinguishes between the rich peasantry and well-to-do middle peasantry, between landlords and rich peasantry.

November. Kiangsi Provincial Government makes known the record of land redistribution in nine counties in Kiangsi.

1933

Late April or early May. Mao's cabinet decides to call a conference of responsible Soviet authorities of eight counties above the district level on the land investigation drive.

June 1. Mao's cabinet orders a general land investigation drive in the Central Soviet Area, aimed at searching out hidden landlords and rich peasants in a ruthless class struggle. To that end, the central government under Mao also orders the convocation of two eight-county conferences in the latter half of the month: one for responsible local government officials and the other for delegates from poor-peasant corps.

June 17. A five-day conference of responsible Soviet authorities of eight counties above the district level on the land investigation drive opens under the auspices of the central government. To mark the occasion, Mao publishes a statement dividing the agrarian revolution into three phases, fitting the land investigation drive in the second phase.

June 17–21. Eight-county conference on the land investigation drive adopts a statement entitled *How to Analyze the Classes,* which is to be approved by the central government on October 10.

June 21. Eight-county conference on the land investigation drive ends after a series of seven speeches by Mao.

June 25–July 1. Conference of delegates of eight-county poor-peasant corps takes place, in which Mao gives a speech on the land investigation drive.

July 15. Central government establishes regulations for the poor-peasant corps, which is required to follow the leadership of both the party and the government.

July 21–25. Conference of nine counties along the northern border of the Communist region is held under the auspices of the Kiangsi provincial government to set the land investigation drive afoot there.

August 29. Mao reviews the land investigation drive of July, complaining of its failures and mistakes.

September 8. Central Bureau of the Soviet Areas reviews the progress of the land investigation drive with particular reference to the mistakes made.

October 10. Central government under Mao's leadership adopts a statement entitled *Decisions concerning Some Problems Arising from the Agrarian Struggle,* introducing an elaborate system of mathematical formulas for the determination of the class status.

December 15. Mao drafts his report on an investigation of Ch'ang-kang township, which is followed by a report on Ts'ai-hsi township. Both statements, according to him, are accounts of the advanced stage of land revolution.

1934

January 23. Two orders of the State Political Security Bureau, which were probably issued in the first weeks of the land investigation drive, are reproduced in Minkan Province. They are designed to eliminate landlords and rich peasants during the course of the drive.

March 15. Chang Wen-t'ien, who replaced Mao as premier more than a month earlier, orders the reopening of the land investigation drive, repudiating Mao's policies contained in the 1933 statement, *Decisions concerning Some Problems Arising from the Agrarian Struggle.*

May 22. Premier Chang Wen-t'ien calls for a reign of Red Terror against all counterrevolutionaries, singling out landlords and rich peasants for attack.

June 24. Premier Chang makes a dramatic policy switch toward the right by calling a halt to the excesses done to the landlords and rich peasants.

June 25. Premier Chang reaffirms his policy shift toward the right, bringing the epoch of land revolution to an end.

Glossary

A-B League (Anti-Bolshevik League)	AB團	A-B t'uan
Abolition of debts	廢除債務	Fei-ch'u chai-wu
Absentees	旅行不在家鄉的	Lü-hsing pu-tsai chia-hsiang ti
Absorb the rich peasants	吸收富農	Hsi-shou fu-nung
Action Committee	行委, 行動委員會	Hsing-wei, hsing-tung wei-yüan-hui
Active revolutionary elements	積極革命份子	Chi-chi ko-ming fen-tzu
Activism of the masses	群衆的積極性	Ch'ün-chung ti chi-chi-hsing
Activists, active elements	積極份子	Chi-chi fen-tzu
Adopt	撫養, 過繼	Fu-yang, kuo-chi
Adopt a son-in-law as heir	招郎	Chao-lang
Advanced and relatively advanced areas	先進的較先進的區域	Hsien-chin ti chiao hsien-chin ti ch'ü-yü
Advanced areas	先進區域	Hsien-chin ch'ü-yü
Advanced struggle area, intensified struggle area	鬪爭深入區域	Tou-cheng shen-ju ch'ü-yü
Adventurism	冒險主義	Mao-hsien chu-i
Aggression of imperialism	帝國主義侵略	Ti-kuo chu-i ch'in-lüeh
Agrarian problem, land problem	土地問題	T'u-ti wen-t'i
Agrarian revolution, land revolution	土地革命	T'u-ti ko-ming
Agrarian struggle, land struggle	土地鬪爭	T'u-ti tou-cheng
Agricultural economy	農業經濟	Nung-yeh ching-chi
Agricultural labor union	農業工會	Nung-yeh kung-hui
Agricultural progressive tax	農業累進稅	Nung-yeh lei-chin-shui

Agricultural socialization	農業社會化	Nung-yeh she-hui-hua
Ah Wei	阿偽(人名)	
Alienate the masses, estrange from the masses	脫離群眾	T'o-li ch'ün-chung
Alliance between the proletariat and middle peasants	無產階級與中農的聯盟	Wu-ch'an chieh-chi yü chung-nung ti lien-meng
All-member congress	會員大會	Hui-yüan ta-hui
All-party executive bureau	全黨執行局	Ch'üan-tang chih-hsing-chü
Ally with the middle peasants	聯合中農	Lien-ho chung-nung
An-yüan	安遠 (地名)	
Analyze the class status	分析階級	Fen-hsi chieh-chi
Ancestral shrine	祠堂	Tz'u-t'ang
An extremely isolated small group of masses	一個極孤立的小群眾	I-ko chi-ku-li ti hsiao-ch'ün-chung
An-fu	安福(地名)	
Annihilate the landlord class	消滅地主階級	Hsiao-mieh ti-chu chien-chi
Annihilate the landlords	消滅地主	Hsiao-mieh ti-chu
Annihilate the rich peasants	消滅富農	Hsiao-mieh fu-nung
Anti-Communist campaigns, bandit-suppression campaigns	勦匪, 圍勦	Chiao-fei, wei-chiao
Anti-imperialism	反帝	Fan-ti
Anti-rich-peasant policy	反富農政策	Fan fu-nung cheng-ts'e
Areas under land investigation	查田區域	Ch'a-t'ien ch'ü-yü
Army corps	軍團	Chün-t'uan
Arrest	逮捕, 拘捕	Tai-pu, chü-pu
Art of leadership	領導藝術	Ling-tao i-shu
Associations	會社	Hui-she
August 7 Conference, August 7 Emergency Conference	八七會議 八七緊急會議	Pa-ch'i hui-i, pa-ch'i chin-chi hui-i
Auxiliary labor	輔助勞動	Fu-chu lao-tung
Backward villages and hamlets	落後村屋	Lo-hou ts'un-wu
Bad gentry	劣紳	Lieh-shen
Bamboo forests	竹木山	Chu-mu-shan

Bankruptcy of rural economy	農業經濟破產	Nung-yeh ching-chi p'o-ch'an
Bankrupt landlords	破產地主	P'o-ch'an ti-chu
Barren hills	荒山	Huang-shan
"Basic areas"	「基本地區」	"Chi-pen ti-ch'ü"
Basic masses	基本群衆	Chi-pen ch'ün-chung
Basic peasant masses	基本農民群衆	Chi-pen nung-min ch'ün-chung
Bela Kun	白臘昆	
Better-off peasants	較富裕的農民	Chiao fu-yü ti nung-min
BIC (Bureau of Investigation Collection)	調查局資料	T iao-ch'a-chü tzu-liao
Big hamlets	大屋子	Ta wu-tzu
Big private owners	大私有主	Ta szu-yu-chu
Big Sword Society	大刀會	Ta-tao-hui
"Big tiger"	大老虎	"Ta lao-hu"
Big villages	大村子	Ta ts'un-tzu
Blind actionism	盲動主義	Mang-tung chu-i
Bolshevik art of leadership	布爾塞維克的領導藝術	Pu-erh-se-wei-k'e ti ling-tao i-shu
Bolshevik line of the party	黨的布爾塞(什)維克路線	Tang ti pu-erh-se (-shih)-wei-k'e lu-hsien
Border region	邊區	Pien-ch ü
Bourgeois-democratic revolution	資產階級民權革命	Tzu-ch'an chieh-chi min-ch'üan ko-ming
Brainworkers	腦力勞働者	Nao-li lao-tung-che
Branch bureaus	分局	Fen-chü
Branches	支部	Chih-pu
Broad masses	廣大群衆	Kuang-ta ch'ün-chung
Burden carriers	挑夫	T'ao-fu
Bureaucratism	官僚主義	Kuan-liao chu-i
Cadres	幹部	Kan-pu
Camp School	隨營學校	Sui-ying hsüeh-hsiao
Canton Commune	廣州公社	Kuang-chou kung-she
Carpenters	木匠工人	Mu-chiang kung-jen
Carry out the land revolution thoroughly and deeply	澈底深入土地革命	Ch'e-ti shen-ju t'u-ti ko-ming
Cart pusher	推車的	T'ui-ch'e ti
Catholic priest	天主教神父	T'ien-chu-chiao shen-fu
CC (Central Committee)	中央委員會	Chung-yang wei-yüan-hui

CEC, Central Executive Committee	中委, 中央執行委員會	Chung-wei, chung-yang chih-hsing wei-yüan-hui
Central Bureau, Soviet Areas, Chinese Communist Youth Corps	中國共產主義青年團蘇區中央局	Chung-kuo kung-ch'an chu-i ching-nien-t'uan su-ch'u chung-yang-chü
Central [Committee or Politburo]	中央	Chung-yang
Central Council of the People's Commissars	中央人民委員會	Chung-yang jen-min wei-yüan-hui
Central Executive Committee of the Chinese Soviet Republic	中華蘇維埃共和國中央執行委員會	Chung-hua su-wei-ai kung-ho-kuo chung-yang chih-hsing wei-yüan-hui
Centrally located county	中心縣	Chung-hsin-hsien
Central (National) Soviet Government	中央(全國)蘇維埃政府	Chung-yang (ch'üan-kuo) su-wei-ai cheng-fu
Central People's Commissariat of Education	中央教育人民委員部	Chung-yang chiao-yü jen-min wei-yüan-pu
Central People's Commissariat of Finance	中央財政人民委員部	Chung-yang ts'ai-cheng jen-min wei-yüan-pu
Central People's Commissariat of Land	中央土地人民委員部	Chung-yang t'u-ti jen-min wei-yüan-pu
Central People's Commissariat of Military Affairs	中央軍事人民委員部	Chung-yang chün-shih jen-min wei-yüan-pu
Central People's Commissariat of National Economy	中央國民經濟人民委員部	Chung-yang kuo-min ching-chi jen-min wei-yüan-pu
Central People's Judicial Commissariat	中央司法人民委員部	Chung-yang szu-fa jen-min wei-yüan-pu
Central Preparatory Commission for the National Soviet Congress	全國蘇維埃大會中央準備委員會, 中準會	Ch'üan-kuo su-wei-ai ta-hui chung-yang chun-pei wei-yüan-hui, chung-chun-hui
Central problem	中心問題	Chung-hsin wen-t'i
Central Revolutionary Military Council, Chinese Soviet Areas	中華蘇維埃區域中央革命軍事委員會	Chung-hua su-wei-ai ch'ü-yü chung-yang ko-ming chün-shih wei-yüan-hui
Central Soviet Area	中央蘇區	Chung-yang su-ch'ü
Central Subbureau	中央分局	Chung-yang fen-chü

Central task	中心任務	Chung-hsin jen-wu
Chang Kuo-t'ao	張國燾	
Chang Wen-t'ien (alias Lo Fu)	張聞天(洛甫)	
Change the class status	改階級	Kai chieh-chi
Ch'ang-kang township	長岡鄉	Ch'ang-kang hsiang
Ch'ang-sheng	長勝 (地名)	
Ch'ang-t'ing	長汀 (地名)	
Ch'en Shao-yü (alias Wang Ming)	陳紹禹(王明)	
Ch'en Tu-hsiu	陳獨秀	
Ch'en Yi	陳毅(人名)	
Ch'eng-shih	城市(地名)	
Chi-an	吉安 (地名)	
Chi-shui	吉水 (地名)	
Ch'i-li-ch'iao	七里橋(地名)	
Ch'i-nan	溪南(地名)	
Chiai-fang-she	解放社	
Chiang Han-po	江漢波(人名)	
Chien-ning	建寧 (地名)	
Chih Fu (alias of Ch'ü Ch'iu-pai)	之夫	
Chih-shui	赤水(地名)	
Chih Ying	稺穎(人名)	
Children's Corps	兒童團	Erh-t'ung-t'uan
Chinese Communist movement	中國共產運動	Chung-kuo kung-ch'an yün-tung
Chinese Communist Party, CCP	中國共產黨, 中共	Chung-kuo kung-ch'an-tang, Chung-kung
Chinese Communist Youth Corps, Communist Youth Corps, CY	中國共產主義青年團, 少共	Chung-kuo kung-ch'an chu-i ch'ing-nien-t'uan, Shao-kung
Chinese Revolutionary Military Council	中國革命軍事委員會	Chung-kuo ko-ming chün-shih wei-yüan-hui
Chinese Soviet Central Revolutionary Military Council	中華蘇維埃中央革命軍事委員會	Chung-hua su-wei-ai chung-yang ko-ming chün-shih wei-yüan-hui
Chinese Soviet Republic	中華蘇維埃共和國	Chung-hua su-wei-ai kung-ho-kuo
Chinese Workers' and Peasants' Red Army	中國工農紅軍	Chung-kuo kung-nung hung-chün

Ch'ing-kang-shan	井岡山(地名)	
Ch'ing-liu	清流 (地名)	
Chiu-pao	九堡(地名)	
Chu Teh	朱德	
Chu-tse-jen	竹崤岈 (地名)	
Ch'ü Ch'iu-pai	瞿秋白	
Chung P'ing	鍾平(人名)	
Chün-ts'un	均村(地名)	
CI, *see* Communist International		
Circuit court	巡迴法庭	Hsün-hui fa-t'ing
Circular, circular note	通告	T'ung-kao
Circular order	通令	T'ung-ling
Circulating capital	活動資本	Huo-tung tzu-pen
Circulation of money	流通金融	Liu-t'ung chin-yung
Civic rights	公民權利	Kung-min ch'üan-li
Clan chief	族長	Tsu-chang
Clan or local struggle	氏族地方鬪爭	Shih-tsu ti-fang tou-cheng
Class	階級	Chieh-chi
"Class calculation"	「算階級」	"Suan chieh-chi"
Class concept	階級觀念	Chieh-chi kuan-nien
Class consciousness	階級意識	Chieh-chi i-shih
Class enemy	階級敵人	Chieh-chi ti-jen
Class for learning Chinese characters	識字班	Shih-tzu-pan
Class heretical elements	階級異己分子	Chieh-chi i-chi fen-tzu
Class investigation, investigation of the classes or class status	查階級	Ch'a chieh-chi
Class line	階級路線	Chieh-chi lu-hsien
Class line of battle	階級火線	Chieh-chi huo-hsien
Class relations	階級關係	Chieh-chi kuan-hsi
Class status	階級成份	Chieh-chi ch'eng-fen
Class struggle	階級鬪爭	Chieh-chi tou-cheng
Clergymen	牧師	Mu-shih
Collaboration with the rich peasants	聯合富農	Lien-ho fu-nung
Collection of Important Documents of Communist Bandits' Land Policy	共匪土地政策重要文件彙編	Kung-fei t'u-ti cheng-ts'e chung-yao wen-chien hui-pien
Collection of Reactionary Documents	反動文件彙編	Fan-tung wen-chien hui-pien

Collection of Red Bandit Documents	赤匪文件彙編	Ch'ih-fei wen-chien hui-pien
Collection of Red Bandit Reactionary Documents	赤匪反動文件彙編	Ch'ih-fei fan-tung wen-chien hui-pien
Collection of Red Bandit Secret Documents	赤匪機密文件彙編	Ch'ih-fei chi-mi wen-chien hui-pien
Collective farm	集體農場	Chi-t'i nung-ch'ang
Collective farming	集合耕種	Chi-ho keng-chung
Collective production	集合生産	Chi-ho sheng-ch'an
Collective production of the type of cooperatives	合作社式的集合生産	Ho-tso-she shih ti chi-ho sheng-ch'an
Collectivization of agriculture	農業集體化	Nung-yeh chi-t'i-hua
Combat counterrevolution	肅反	Su fan
Combat tasks	戰鬪任務	Chan-tou jen-wu
Comintern Eastern Department	國際東方部	Kuo-chi tung-fang-pu
Commandism	命令主義	Ming-ling chu-i
Commercial capital	商業資本	Shang-yeh tzu-pen
Committee on education	教育委員會	Chiao-yü wei-yüan-hui
Committee on forests	山林委員會	Shan-lin wei-yüan-hui
Committee on land reconstruction	土地建設委員會	T'u-ti chien-she wei-yüan-hui
Committee on waters	水利委員會	Shui-li wei-yüan-hui
Common cultivation	共同耕種	Kung-t'ung keng-chung
Common cultivation and common consumption	共耕共費	Kung-keng kung-fei
Communist International, Comintern, CI	共産國際, 國際	Kung-ch'an kuo-chi, kuo-chi
Comparatively retarded struggle areas	鬪爭比較落後區域	Tou-cheng pi-chiao lo-hou ch'ü-yü
Complaint box	控告箱	K'ung-kao hsiang
Compromise-ism	調和主義	T'iao-ho chu-i
Compromising line	調和路線	T'iao-ho lu-hsien
Compulsory labor	義務勞働	I-wu lao-tung
Comrade	同志	T'ung-chih
Comrade Pi	皮同志	Pi t'ung-chih
Concentration of supplies	集中供給	Chi-chung kung-chi
Condition of uneven development	不平衡發展狀態	Pu-p'ing-heng fa-chan chuang-t'ai
Conference of Delegates of the Eight-County Poor	八縣貧農團代表查田運動大會	Pa-hsien p'in-nung-t'uan tai-piao ch'a-

Peasant Corps on the   t'ien yün-tung ta-hui
Land Investigation Drive

"Confiscate all land" or   「没收一切土地」   "Mo-shou i-ch'ieh t'u-ti"
   "Confiscation of all land"

"Confiscate the land of   「没收地主階級土地」   "Mo-shou ti-chu chieh-
   the landlord class"   chi t'u-ti"

Confiscation and redis-   没收分配委員會   Mo-shou fen-p'ei wei-
   tribution committee   yüan-hui

Confiscation of land   土地没收   T'u-ti mo-shou

Confiscation on a whole   全家没收   Ch'üan-chia mo-shou
   family basis

Congress of delegates   代表大會   Tai-piao ta-hui

Congress of delegates   勞働婦女代表大會   Lao-tung fu-nü tai-piao
   of laboring women   ta-hui

Congress of delegates   女工農婦代表會   Nü-kung nung-fu tai-
   of women workers and   piao-hui
   farming women

Congress of women's   婦女代表會   Fu-nü tai-piao-hui
   delegates

Consumers' cooperatives   消費合作社   Hsiao-fei ho-tso-she

"Consuming norm"   吃飯人數原則   Ch'ih-fan jen-shu
                                                            yüan-tse

Contest agreement   競賽條約   Ching-sai t'iao-yüeh

Contractor   包工   Pao-kung

Coolie   苦力   K'u-li

Coolie union   苦力工會   K'u-li kung-hui

Corporation agriculture   公司農業   Kung-szu nung-yeh

Council of People's   人民委員會   Jen-min wei-yüan-hui
   Commissars

Counterrevolution   反革命   Fan ko-ming

Counterrevolution-   肅反機關   Su-fan chi-kuan
   combating agencies

Counterrevolutionaries   反革命派   Fan-ko-ming-p'ai

Counterrevolutionary   反革命組織   Fan ko-ming tsu-chih
   organizations

County   縣   Hsien

County Committee   縣委   Hsien-wei

County Soviet   縣蘇   Hsien-su
   (government)

Cowherd   牧童   Mu-t'ung

Craftsman   手藝匠   Shou-i-chiang

Credit cooperatives   信用合作社   Hsin-yung ho-tso-she

Cultivation permit   耕種證   Keng-chung cheng

CY. *See* Chinese Communist
    Youth Corps

Decisive role of the peasants in the Chinese revolution	農民在中國革命中的決定作用	Nung-min tsai chung-kuo ko-ming chung ti chüeh-ting tso-yung
"Deep plowing and frequent weeding"	「深耕易耨」	"Shen-keng i-nou"
Deliver	押送	Ya-sung
Democratic centralism	民權集中制	Min-ch'üan chi-chung-chih
Democratic dictatorship of the workers and peasants	工農民主專政	Kung nung min-chu chuan-cheng
Democratic revolution	民權革命	Min-ch'üan ko-ming
Democratic revolution of workers and peasants	工農民權革命	Kung-nung min-ch'üan ko-ming
Democratic stage	民權階段	Min-ch'üan chieh-tuan
Dependents of the Red Army men	紅軍戰士家屬	Hung-chün chan-shih chia-shu
Directive	指示, 指令	Chih-shih, chih-ling
"Direct war zone"	「直接戰區」	"Chih-chieh chan-ch'ü"
Directing organs	指導機關	Chih-tao chi-kuan
District	區	Ch'ü
District Committee	區委	Ch'ü-wei
District government	區政府	Ch'ü cheng-fu
Diviner	卜卦	Pu-kua
Domestic labor	家務勞働	Chia-wu lao-tung
Draft cattle	耕牛	Keng-niu
Draw-on and make-up	抽補	Ch'ou pu
Draw-on-the-fat-to-make-up-for-the-lean	抽肥補瘦	Ch'ou-fei pu-shou
Draw-on-the-plentiful-to-make-up-for-the-scarce	抽多補少	Ch'ou-to pu-shao
Drive, campaign, movement	運動	Yün-tung
Duration and degree of exploitation by the rich peasant	富農的剝削時間與剝削份量	Fu-nung ti po-hsüeh shih-chien yü po-hsüeh fen-liang
East River	東江	Tung-chiang
ECCI. *See* Executive Committee of the Communist International		
Education department	教育部	Chiao-yü pu

Egalitarianism	平均主義	P'ing-chün chu-i
Eight-County Conference on the Land Investigation Drive	八縣查田運動大會	Pa-hsien ch'a-t'ien yün-tung ta-hui
Eight Great Land Programs	土地八大政綱	T'u-ti pa ta cheng-kang
Employer	業主	Yeh-chu
Enlarged plenum	擴大全體會議	K'uo-ta ch'üan-t'i hui-i
Equal or egalitarian redistribution of land	土地平均分配 平分土地	T'u-ti p'ing-chün fen-p'ei, p'ing-fen t'u-ti
Equal redistribution	平均分配	P'ing-chün fen-p'ei
Equal redistribution according to the number of persons	按人口平均分配	An jen-k'ou p'ing-chün fen-p'ei
Equal redistribution of all land	平均分配一切土地	P'ing-chün fen-p'ei i-ch'ieh t'u-ti
Equal redistribution of land according to the number of persons in the villages	依照鄉村人口數目 平均分配土地	I-chao hsiang-ts'un jen-k'ou shu-mu p'ing-chün fen-p'ei t'u-ti
"Erect a wooden board"	「插牌子」	"Ch'a-p'ai-tzu"
Essential labor	主要的勞働	Chu-yao ti lao-tung
Excesses	過火	Kuo-huo
Excessively "Left" tendencies	過「左」傾向	Kuo-"tso" ch'ing-hsiang
Executive Committee	執行委員會	Chih-hsing wei-yüan-hui
Executive Committee of the Communist International, ECCI	國際執委, 共產國際執行委員會	Kuo-chi chih-wei, kung-ch'an kuo-chi chih-hsing wei-yüan-hui
Executive council	幹事會	Kan-shih hui
Executive secretary	幹事	Kan-shih
Expand the Red Army	擴大紅軍	K'uo-ta hung-chün
Experimental farm	農業試驗場	Nung-yeh shih-yen-ch'ang
"Explanation of the classes"	「講階級」	"Chiang chieh-chi"
Exploitation	剝削	Po-hsüeh
Exploitative relations	剝削關係	Po-hsüeh kuan-hsi
Exploiting classes	剝削階級	Po-hsüeh chieh-chi
Extensive and intensive drive of land investigation	廣泛深入的查田運動	Kuang-fan shen-ju ti ch'a-t'ien yün-tung
Extorting contributions from rich peasants	富農捐款	Fu-nung chüan-k'uan

Extraordinary contributions	臨時特別捐	Lin-shih t'e-pieh-chüan
Extremely ruthless semi-feudal exploitation	極殘酷的半封建剝削	Chi-ts'an-k'u ti pan-feng-chien po-hsüeh
Farm implements	農具	Nung-chü
Fen-i	分宜 (地名)	
Feudal exploitation	封建剝削	Feng-chien po-hsüeh
Feudal forces	封建勢力	Feng-chien shih-li
Feudal remnants	封建殘餘	Feng-chien ts'an-yü
Feudal system	封建制度	Feng-chien chih-tu
Finance department	財政部	Ts'ai-cheng pu
Firewood forests	柴火山	Ch'ai-huo shan
First Army Corps	第一軍團	Ti-i chün-t'uan
First Conference of Soviet Areas	第一次蘇維埃區域會議	Ti-i-tz'u su-wei-ai ch'ü-yü hui-i
First Front Army	第一方面軍	Ti-i fang-mien chün
First National Congress of the Delegates of the Chinese Workers, Peasants, and Soldiers	中華工農兵蘇維埃第一次全國代表大會	Chung-hua kung nung ping su-wei-ai ti-i-tz'u ch'üan-kuo tai-piao ta-hui
First Route Army	第一路軍	Ti-i-lu chün
First Soviet Conference of the Oyüwan Border Area	鄂豫皖邊蘇維埃第一次代表大會	O-yü-wan pien su-wei-ai ti-i-tz'u tai-piao ta-hui
Forced labor corps	勞役隊	Lao-i tui
Foremen	工頭	Kung-t'ou
Forests	山林, 森林	Shan-lin, shen-lin
Forests of tea-oil plants, tea-oil plantations	木子山, 木梓山	Mu-tzu shan
Formalism	形式主義	Hsing-shih chu-i
Fortuneteller	算命, 八字先生	Suan-ming, pa-tzu hsien-sheng
Foster parents	過繼父母	Kuo-chi fu mu
Fourth Front Army	第四方面軍	Ti-szu fang-mien chün
Fourth Plenum	四中全會	Szu-chung ch'üan-hui
Free contributions	自由捐	Tzu-yu-chüan
Free trade	自由貿易	Tzu-yu mou-i
Freedom in commerce	商業自由	Shang-yeh tzü-yu
Front Committee	前委(前敵委員會)	Ch'ien-wei (Ch'ien-ti wei-yüan-hui)
Fruits of the revolution	革命的果實	Ko-ming ti kuo-shih
Fu Po-ts'ui	傅伯翠(人名)	

Garden	園土	Yüan-t'u
General Action Committee	總行委	Tsung hsing-wei
General Front Committee	總前委	Tsung ch'ien-wei
General line	總路線	Tsung lu-hsien
General Political Commissar	總政委	Tsung cheng-wei
General Political Department	總政治部	Tsung cheng-chih-pu
Geomancer	地理先生,看地先生	Ti-li hsien-sheng, k'an-ti hsien-sheng
Government Administration Council	政務院	Cheng-wu-yüan
Grain association	谷會	Ku-hui
Grain-husking water mills	水碓	Shui-tui
Grains	穀子	Ku-tzu
Guerrilla concept	游擊觀念	Yu-chi kuan-nien
Guerrillas	游擊隊	Yu-chi-tui
A Guide to the Land Investigation Drive	查田運動指南	Ch'a-t'ien yün-tung chih-nan
Hai-lu-feng	海陸豊(地名)	
Han Wen	翰文(人名)	
Handicraftsman	手工業者	Shou-kung-yeh-che
Handicraft labor union	手工藝工會	Shou-kung-i kung-hui
Handicraft worker	手工業工人	Shou-kung-yeh kung-jen
Heartland	腹地	Fu-ti
High flow, rising tide	高漲	Kao chang
High tide	高潮	Kao ch'ao
Highest authority	最高機關, 最高權力機關	Tsui-kao chi-kuan, tsui-kao ch'üan-li chi-kuan
Highest directing body	最高指導機關	Tsui-kao chih-tao chi-kuan
Hillside land for nonstaple grains	雜糧山	Tsa-liang shan
Hills with mineral deposits	礦山	K'uang-shan
Hired farm hand	雇農	Ku-nung
Hired-farm-hand small group	雇農小組	Ku-nung hsiao-tsu
Hired-farm-hand union	僱農工會	Ku-nung kung-hui
Hired labor	僱傭勞働	Ku-yung lao-tung
Ho Kan-chih	何幹之	
Ho-k'ou	禾口(地名)	

How to Analyze the Classes	「怎樣分析階級」	"Tsen-yang fen-hsi chieh-chi"
Hsia-chiang	峽江(地名)	
Hsia-hsiao district	下肖區(地名)	
Hsiangkan Provincial Soviet (Government)	湘贛省蘇	Hsiang-kan sheng-su
Hsiangohsi Central Subbureau	湘鄂西中央分局	Hsiang-o-hsi chung-yang fen-chü
Hsiangokan Soviet Area	湘鄂贛蘇區	Hsiang-o-kan su-ch'ü
Hsiao-chiang district	小江區(地名)	
Hsin-ch'üan	新泉(地名)	
Hsin-feng	信豐(地名)	
Hsin-hsia	新峽 (地名)	
Hsin-p'i	新陂(地名)	
Hsing-kuo	興國 (地名)	
Hsing-yü	新喻 (地名)	
Hsiu-ts'ai	秀才	
Hsü Ke-hsiang	許克祥(人名)	
Hsün-wu	尋鄔(地名)	
Hu Hai	胡海(人名)	
Huang-pai District Soviet	黃柏區蘇	Huang-pai ch'ü-su
Huang-p'i	黃陂 (地名)	
Huang-t'ang	黃塘(地名)	
Huang-yao district	黃坳區(地名)	
Huang Yen-p'an	黃衍半(人名)	
Hui-ch'ang	會昌(地名)	
Hui Wen	會文(人名)	
I-huang	宜黃(地名)	
Ideological struggle	思想鬥爭	Szu-hsiang tou-cheng
Idle talk	清談	Ch'ing-t'an
Idler-proletarian	遊民無產者	Yu-min wu-ch'an-che
"Illusions of the petty bourgeoisie"	「小資產階級的幻想」	"Hsiao tzu-ch'an chieh-chi ti huan-hsiang"
"Illusory hopes of equality"	「妄想平均」	"Wang-hsiang p'ing-chün"
Immigrants	移民	I-min
Immovable property	不動產	Pu-tung-ch'an
Imposing fines on landlords	地主罰款	Ti-chu fa-k'uan
"Impossible of penetration"	「打不進去」	"Ta-pu-chin-ch'ü"
Imprisonment	監禁	Chien-chin

Independent laborer	獨立勞働者	Tu-li lao-tung-che
Independent political role of the peasants	農民的獨立政治作用	Nung-min ti tu-li cheng-chih tso-yung
Independent producer	獨立生產者	Tu-li sheng-ch'an-che
"Indiscriminate blows to village bosses"	「亂打土豪」	"Luan-ta t'u-hao"
Individual cultivation	個別耕種, 私人耕種	Ko-pieh keng-chung, szu-jen keng-chung
Informer	通信員	T'ung-hsin-yüan
Infringe on the interests of the middle peasants	侵犯中農的利益	Ch'in-fan chung-nung ti li-i
Injure the middle peasants	侵犯中農	Ch'in-fan chung-nung
Inspection station	檢查站	Chien-ch'a-chan
Instruction	訓令	Hsün-ling
Insurrection, uprising	暴動	Pao-tung
Intellectuals	知識份子	Chih-shih fen-tzu
Intensified struggle areas	鬪爭深入區域	Tou-cheng shen-ju ch'ü-yü
Intensify the class struggle in villages	加深農村中階級鬪爭	Chia-shen nung-ts'un chung chieh-chi tou-cheng
Intensifying land struggle	深入土地鬪爭	Shen-ju t'u-ti tou-cheng
Interest on land given as security for a loan	典租	Tien-tsu
Intimidating rumors	恐嚇造謠	K'ung-ho tsao-yao
Investigation	偵察	Ch en-ch'a
"Investigation of the classes"	「查階級」	"Ch'a-chieh-chi"
IOU	債券借約	Chai-ch'üan chieh-yüeh
Jan-chih	然之(人名)	
Jen-t'ien district	壬田區(地名)	
Jobless idler	無業遊民	Wu-yeh yu-min
Jobless masses	失業群衆	Shih-yeh ch'ün-chung
Joint production	共同生產	Kung-t'ung sheng-ch'an
Judicial Department	裁判部	Ts'ai-p'an pu
Jui-chin	瑞金 (地名)	
Jui-lin	瑞林(地名)	
Kan-chou	贛州 (地名)	
Kan-hsien	贛縣 (地名)	
Kao Tsu-li	高自立	
Kiangsi Provincial	江西省政治保衞局	Chiang-hsi-sheng cheng-

Political Security Bureau		chih pao-wei-chü
Kiangsi Provincial Soviet (Government)	江西省蘇, 江西省蘇維埃政府	Chiang-hsi sheng-su, chiang-hsi-sheng su-wei-ai cheng-fu
Ku-kiang	固江(地名)	
Kuang-ch'ang	廣昌 (地名)	
Kuchumov	苦秋莫夫	
Kung-lüeh	公略(地名)	
"Labor land allotment"	「勞働份地」	"Lao-tung fen-ti"
Labor law	勞働法	Lao-tung fa
Labor mutual-help society	勞働互助社	Lao-tung hu-chu-she
Labor power	勞働力	Lao-tung li
Labor power unit	勞働力單位	Lao-tung-li tan-wei
Labor service	勞働工作	Lao-tung kung-tso
Labor union	工會	Kung-hui
Land and [other] properties	土地財産	T'u-ti ts'ai-ch'an
Land department	土地部	T'u-ti pu
Land for public enterprises	公共事業田	Kung-kung shih-yeh-t'ien
Land investigation	查田	Ch'a-t'ien
Land investigation committee	查田委員會	Ch'a-t'ien wei-yüan-hui
Land investigation drive	查田運動	Ch'a-t'ien yün-tung
"Land investigation drive propaganda team"	「查田運動宣傳隊」	"Ch'a-t'ien yün-tung hsüan-chüan tui"
Land investigation drive training class	查田運動訓練班	Ch'a-t'ien yün-tung hsün-lien pan
Land investigation surprise attack drive	查田突擊運動	Ch'a-t'ien t'u-chi yün-tung
Land law	土地法, 土地法令	T'u-ti fa, t'u-ti fa-ling
Landlord	地主	Ti-chu
Landlord class	地主階級	Ti-chu chieh-chi
Land nationalization	土地國有	T'u-ti kuo-yu
Land problem	土地問題	T'u-ti wen-t'i
Land program	土地政綱	T'u-ti cheng-kang
Land reconstruction	土地建設	T'u-ti chien-she
Land redistribution	分地, 平地	Fen-ti, p'ing-ti
Land Reform Law	土地改革法	T'u-ti kai-ko fa
Land registration	土地登記	T'u-ti teng-chi
Land registration committee	土地登記委員會	T'u-ti teng-chi wei-yüan-hui
Land relations	土地關係	T'u-ti kuan-hsi

Land rent	地租	Ti-tsu
Land tax	土地稅, 田賦	T'u-ti-shui, t'ien-fu
Lay devotee	齋公	Tsai-kung
Leadership of rural workers	農村工人領導	Nung-ts'un kung-jen ling-tao
Lease contract	租約	Tsu-yüeh
Lease land and pay rent in unhusked rice	租田交穀	Tsu-t'ien chiao-ku
Lease of land	租田	Tsu-t'ien
Left deviation	左傾	Tso-ch'ing
Left line	左傾路線	Tso-ch'ing lu-hsien
Left opportunism	左傾機會主義	Tso-ch'ing chi-hui chu-i
Left-wing infantile disorder	左的幼稚病	Tso ti yu-chih-ping
Li-chia-fang	李家坊 (地名)	
Li-ch'uan	黎川(地名)	
Li Li-san	李立三	
Li Li-sanism	李立三主義	Li-li-san chu-i
Li-san line	立三路線	Li-san lu-hsien
Li Wei-han (alias Lo Mai)	李維漢	
Lien-ch'eng	連城 (地名)	
Light mounted troops of the Youth Corps	青年團輕騎隊	Ch'ing-nien-t'uan ch'ing-ch'i-tui
Line	路線	Lu-hsien
Liquidation	清算	Ch'ing-suan
Liu meng (vagabond)	流氓	
Livestock	牲畜	Sheng-ch'u
Livestock and farm implement station	牲畜農具經理處	Sheng-ch'u nung-chü ching-li-ch'u
Lo-an	樂安 (地名)	
Lo Fu (alias of Chang Wen-t'ien)	洛甫(張聞天)	
Lo Mai (alias of Li Wei-han)	羅邁(李維漢)	
Load carrying	挑擔	T'iao-tan
Loan interest	債利	Chai-li
Localism	地方主義	Ti-fang chu-i
Long-term laborer	長工	Ch'ang-kung
"Loot the grains"	「搶穀」	"Ch'iang-ku"
Low ebb	低潮	Ti-ch'ao
Lower echelon responsible persons (cadres)	下級負責人	Hsia-chi fu-tse-jen
Lower poor peasants	下層貧農	Hsia-ts'eng p'in-nung

Madyar, L.	馬其亞爾	
Main content of the Chinese revolution	中國革命的主要內容	Chung-kuo ko-ming ti chu-yao nei-yung
Main labor	主要的勞働	Chu-yao ti lao-tung
Make the hired farm hands play a leading role	使雇農起領導作用	Shih ku-nung ch'i ling-tao tso-yung
Management of land-holdings of public bodies	管公堂	Kuan kung-t'ang
Manual of Political Instruction	政治課講授大綱	Cheng-chih-k'o chiang-shou ta-kang
Manual worker	手工業工人	Shou-kung-yeh kung-jen
Marxism-Leninism	馬列主義	Ma-lieh chu-i
Masses who have deserted to the enemy	反水群衆	Fan-shui ch'ün-chung
Mass line	群衆路線	Ch'ün-chung lu-hsien
Mass meeting	群衆大會	Ch'ün-chung ta-hui
Mass movement	群衆運動	Ch'ün-chung yün-tung
Mass organizations	群衆團體	Ch'ün-chung t'uan-t'i
Mass struggle	群衆鬪爭	Ch'ün-chung tou-cheng
Mass work	群衆工作	Ch'ün-chung kung-tso
Master workmen	師傅	Shih-fu
Means of livelihood	生活來源	Sheng-huo lai-yüan
Means of production	生産工具	Sheng-ch'an kung-chü
Meeting of electors	選民大會	Hsüan-min ta-hui
Mei-hsien	梅縣(地名)	
Method of using labor power as the criterion for land redistribution	以勞働力爲標準的分配土地方法	I lao-tung-li wei piao-chun ti fen-p'ei t'u-ti fang-fa
Middle peasants	中農	Chung-nung
Mif, Pavel	米夫	
Migration	移民	I-min
Military Council of the Oyüwan Soviet Area	鄂豫皖蘇區軍事委員會, 鄂豫皖軍委	O-yü-wan su-ch'ü chün-shih wei-yüan-hui, O-yü-wan chün-wei
Military department	軍事部	Chün-shih pu
Militia	保衞團, 民團	Pao-wei t'uan, min-t'uan
Minkan	閩贛	
Mixed principle of labor power and the number of persons	勞働力與人口混合原則	Lao-tung-li yü jen-kou hun-ho yüan-tse
Mobilization of the organization	組織上的動員	Tsu-chih shang ti tung-yüan
Model division	模範師	Mu-fan shih

Model farm	模範農場	Mu-fan nung-ch'ang
Money association	錢會	Ch'ien-hui
Monk	和尚	Ho-shang
Monthly laborer	月工	Yüeh-kung
Mortgage	典押	Tien-ya
Mortgage paper	押據	Ya-chü
Most active elements	最積極分子	Tsui chi-chi fen-tzu
Mou	畝	Unit of land measurement, about one sixth of an acre
Movable property	動産	Tung-ch'an
Mu-k'ou-ts'un	木口村（地名）	
Mulberry field	桑田	Sang-t'ien
Mutual-aid enterprise	互濟事業	Hu-chi shih-yeh
Nan-feng	南豐（地名）	
National Conference of Delegates from the Soviet Areas	全國蘇維埃區域代表大會	Ch'üan-kuo su-wei-ai ch'ü-yü tai-piao ta-hui
National economy department	國民經濟部	Kuo-min ching-chi pu
Neutralize the rich peasants	使富農中立	Shih fu-nung chung-li
New Communist Party	新共産黨	Hsin kung-ch'an-tang
Newly developed areas	新發展區域	Hsin fa-chan ch'ü-yü
New Soviet areas	新蘇區	Hsin su-ch'ü
New unhusked-rice system	新穀制	Hsin-ku chih
Nine-County Conference on the Land Investigation Drive	九縣查田運動大會	Chiu-hsien ch'a-t'ien yün-tung ta-hui
Ning-hua	寧化（地名）	
Ning-tu Conference	寧都會議	Ning-tu hui-i
Nonessential labor	非主要勞働	Fei-chu-yao lao-tung
Non-Soviet areas	非蘇維埃區域	Fei su-wei-ai ch'ü-yü
Nonstaple grains	雜糧	Tsa-liang
"No redistribution of unripe rice"	"青苗不分"	Ch'ing-miao pu-fen
"Not to entertain any illusory hopes of equality"	「不得妄想平均」	"Pu te wang-hsiang p'ing-chün"
"Not to keep fat land for oneself"	「不得把持肥田」	"Pu-te pa-ch'ih fei-t'ien"
Number of persons	人口, 人口數目	Jen-k'ou, jen-k'ou shu-mu

O-feng	鵝鳳（地名）	
Obligatory labor of the rich peasants	富農的義務勞働	Fu-nung ti i-wu lao-tung
"Object to absolute egalitarianism"	「反對絕對平均主義」	"Fan-tui chüeh-tui p'ing-chün chu-i"
"Obtain land without compensation and redistribute both land and unripe rice"	無償得田分畝 分青	Wu-shang te-t'ien fen-mou fen-ch'ing
Odd-job laborer	零工	Ling-kung
Oil-pressing mill	油糟	Yu-tsao
One thousand cash	一串	I ch'uan
Opened or closed to the public for exploitation	公禁, 公採	Kung-chin, kung-ts'ai
Opportunism	機會主義	Chi-hui chu-i
Opportunistic vacillation	機會主義的動搖性	Chi-hui chu-i ti tung-yao-hsing
"Oppose indiscriminate blows to village bosses"	「反對亂打土豪」	"Fan-tui luan-ta t'u-hao"
Oppose the rich peasants	反富農	Fan fu-nung
Organizational mobilization	組織上的動員	Tsu-chih-shang ti tung-yüan
Organization department	組織部	Tsu-chih pu
Organizations	團體	T'uan-t'i
Owner-peasant	自耕農	Tzu-keng-nung
Oyūwan Soviet Area	鄂豫皖蘇區	O-yü-wan su-ch'ü
Pacification corps	靖衞團	Ching-wei t'uan
Pai-k'eng township	柏坑鄉(地名)	
Pang Hua	邦華(人名)	
Paper mill	紙坊	Chih-fang
Party headquarters	黨部	Tang-pu
Party line	黨的路線	Tang ti lu-hsien
Passive compromisers	消極妥協分子	Hsiao-chi t'o-hsieh fen-tzu
Passivists, passive elements	消極分子	Hsiao-chi fen-tzu
Paupers, poor people	貧民	P'in-min
Peasant association	農民協會	Nung-min hsieh-hui
Peasant consciousness	農民意識	Nung-min i-shih
Peasant economy	農民經濟	Nung-min ching-chi
Peasant mentality	農民意識	Nung-min i-shih
Peasant regime	農民政權	Nung-min cheng-ch'üan
Peasant struggle	農民鬪爭	Nung-min tou-cheng

Peasants with no or little land	無地與少地的農民	Wu-ti yü shao-ti ti nung-min
People's Commissariat of Judicial Affairs	司法人民委員部	Szu-fa jen-min wei-yüan pu
People's Commissariat of Workers' and Peasants' Prosecution	工農檢察人民委員部	Kung-nung chien-ch'a jen-min wei-yüan pu
Per capita land redistribution	計口授田	Chi-k'ou shou-t'ien
Permanent labor corps	永久勞役隊	Yung-chiu lao-i tui
Petty bourgeoisie	小資產階級	Hsiao-tzu-ch'an chieh-chi
Petty bourgeois ultra-leftism	小資產階級的極左主義	Hsiao tzu-ch'an chieh-chi ti chi-tso chu-i
P'i-t'ou	陂頭 (地名)	
Plowing	犁田	Li-t'ien
Po Chao	伯釗(人名)	
Po Shan (alias of Li Li-san)	伯山	
Po-sheng	博生 (地名)	
Political Bureau, Politburo	政治局	Cheng-chih chü
Political Commissar	政委, 政治委員	Cheng-wei, cheng-chih wei-yüan
Political department	政治部	Cheng-chih pu
Political resolution	政治決議案	Cheng-chih chüeh-i-an
Political Secretariat	政治秘書處	Cheng-chih Mi-shu-ch'u
Political security bureau	政治保衛局	Cheng-chih pao-wei chü
Poor and miserable laboring masses	貧苦勞働群眾	P'in-k'u lao-tung ch'ün-chung
Poor and miserable masses	貧苦群眾	P'in-k'u ch'ün-chung
Poor and miserable peasants	貧苦農民	P'in-k'u nung-min
Poor and miserable worker and peasant masses	貧苦工農群眾	P'in-k'u kung-nung ch'ün-chung
Poor land	壞田	Huai-t'ien
Poor-Peasant Association	貧農會	P'in-nung hui
"Poor-peasant consciousness"	「貧農意識」	"P'in-nung i-shih"
Poor-peasant corps	貧農團	P'in-nung t'uan
Poor peasants	貧農	P'in-nung
Poor people	貧民, 窮人, 貧民分子	P'in-min, ch'iung-jen, p'in-min fen-tzu
Poor petty merchants	貧苦小商人	P'in-k'u hsiao shang-jen
Preliminary trial	預審	Yü-shen
Premature measures	過早辦法	Kuo-tsao pan-fa

Presidium	主席團	Chu-hsi-t'uan
Presidium of the Action Committee	行委主席團	Hsing-wei chu-hsi-t'uan
Presidium of the First National Soviet Congress	第一次全國蘇維埃大會主席團	Ti-i-tz'u ch'üan-kuo su-wei-ai ta-hui chu-hsi-t'uan
Priest	神父	Shen-fu
Private landownership	土地私有	T'u-ti szu-yu
Proclamation	佈告	Pu-kao
Producers' cooperatives	生產合作社	Sheng-ch'an ho-tso-she
Productive power	生產力	Sheng-ch'an-li
Professionals	自由職業者	Tzu-yu chih-yeh-che
Programs of struggle	鬥爭綱領	Tou-cheng kang-ling
Progressive tax	累進稅	Lei-chin-shui
Prohibition of the purchase, sale, lease, or mortgage of land	禁止土地買賣租佃典押	Chin-chih t'u-ti mai-mai tsu-tien tien-ya
Proletariat	無產階級	Wu-ch'an chieh-chi
Propaganda and agitation	宣傳鼓動	Hsüan-ch'uan ku-tung
Propaganda department	宣傳部	Hsüan-ch'uan pu
Propaganda slogan	宣傳口號	Hsüan-ch'uan k'ou-hao
Prosecute	檢察, 檢舉, 公訴	Chien-ch'a, chien-chü, kung-su
Prosecution committee	檢舉委員會	Chien-chü wei-yüan-hui
Protestant pastor	基督教牧師	Chi-tu-chiao mu-shih
Provide shelter to rich peasants	包庇富農	Pao-pi fu-nung
Provincial Action Committee	省行委	Sheng hsing-wei
Provincial Committee	省委	Sheng-wei
Provincial Committee Correspondence	省委通訊(雜誌名)	Sheng-wei t'ung-hsün
Provincialism	地方主義	Ti-fang chu-i
Provincial Soviet (Government)	省蘇	Sheng-su
Provisional Central Government	臨時中央政府	Lin-shih chung-yang cheng-fu
Provisional Land Law	土地暫行法	T'u-ti tsan-hsing fa
Pu-ch'ien District	舖前區	
Public body	公堂	Kung-t'ang
Public enterprises	公共事業	Kung-kung shih-yeh
Public land	公田, 公共土地	Kung-t'ien, kung-kung t'u-ti

Public land for Red Army	紅軍公田	Hung-chün kung-t'ien
Public property	官産	Kuan-ch'an
Public trial	公審	Kung shen
Public trial meeting	公審大會	Kung-shen ta-hui
Public welfare fee	公益費	Kung-i-fei
Public welfare work	公益事業	Kung-i shih-yeh
Punitivism	懲辦主義	Ch'eng-pan chu-i
Purchase and sale of land	土地買賣	T'u-ti mai-mai
"Put on red ribbons and call each other comrades"	「掛紅帶子稱同志」	"Kua hung tai-tzu ch'eng t'ung-chih"
Raise funds	籌經済	Ch'ou ching-chi
Reactionaries	反動派	Fan-tung-p'ai
Reactionary capitalists	反動資本家	Fan-tung tzu-pen-chia
Reactionary rich peasants	反動富農	Fan-tung fu-nung
Receive and care for	收容	Shou-yung
"Reconciliation pact"	「團結公約」	"T'uan-chieh kung-yüeh"
Reconstruction of the party	黨的建設(雜誌名)	Tang ti chien-she
Red areas	紅色區域	Hung-se ch'ü-yü
Red Army	紅軍	Hung-chün
Red Army men of land-lord origin	地主出身的紅軍戰士	Ti-chu ch'u-shen ti hung-chün chan-shih
Red Army men of rich peasant origin	富農出身的紅軍戰士	Fu-nung ch'u-shen ti hung-chün chan-shih
Red Army School	紅軍學校	Hung-chün hsüeh-hsiao
Red Bandits	赤匪	Ch'ih-fei
Red China	紅色中華, 紅中(報名)	Hung-se chung-hua, hung-chung
Red curfew	赤色戒嚴	Ch'ih-se chieh-yen
Red Documents	紅色文獻	Hung-se wen-hsien
Red Guards	赤衞隊, 赤衞軍	Ch'ih-wei-tui, ch'ih-wei-chün
Redistribution of land	土地分配	T'u-ti fen-p'ei
Redistribution of land according to labor power	以勞働力爲標準分田	I lao-tung-li wei piao-chun fen-t'ien
Redistribution of land according to the number of persons	以人口爲標準分田	I jen-k'ou wei piao-chun fen-t'ien
Redistribution of land according to the tools of production	以生産工具爲標準分田	I sheng-ch'an kung-chü wei piao-chun fen-t'ien

Redistribution of unripe rice	分青	Fen-ch'ing
Red Terror	赤色恐怖	Ch'ih-se k'ung-pu
Red Vanguard	赤色先鋒隊	Ch'ih-se hsien-feng-tui
Regime of the council of the peasant delegates in the rural districts	農村中農民代表會議的政權	Nung-ts'un chung nung-min tai-piao hui-i ti cheng-ch'üan
Regulations Governing the Preferential Treatment for the Red Army	優待紅軍條例	Yu-tai hung-chün tiao-li
Religious feelings	宗教感情	Chung-chiao kan-ch'ing
Religious practitioners	宗教職業者	Chung-chiao chih-yeh-che
Rely on the poor peasants	依靠貧農	I-k'ao p'in-nung
"Rent-collecting system"	收租制	Shou-tsu chih
Rent from school land	學租	Hsüeh-tsu
Rent in cash	錢租	Ch'ien tsu
Reopen the land investigation drive	繼續開展查田運動	Chi-hsü k'ai-chan ch'a-t'ien yün-tung
Reorganizationists	改組派	Kai-tsu-p'ai
Represent the hired farm hands	代表僱農	Tai-piao ku-nung
Reproduction	翻印本	Fan-yin-pen
Residue of residues	殘餘的殘餘	Ts'an-yü ti ts'an-yü
Resolution	決議, 決議案	Chüeh-i, chüeh-i-an
Resolution on the land problem	土地問題決議案	T'u-ti wen-t'i chüeh-i-an
Resolution on the peasant problem	農民問題決議案	Nung-min wen-t'i chüeh-i-an
Responsible Soviet authorities	蘇維埃負責人員	Su-wei-ai fu-tse jen-yüan
Retarded struggle areas	鬥爭落後區域	Tou-cheng lo-hou ch'ü-yü
"Revenge of personal grudges in the name of the public"	「公報私仇」	"Kung-pao szu-ch'ou"
Revolt	反水	Fan-shui
Revolutionary character of the peasants	農民的革命性	Nung-min ti ko-ming hsing
Revolutionary Committee	革命委員會	Ko-ming wei-yüan-hui
Revolutionary high tide	革命高潮	Ko-ming kao-ch'ao
Revolutionary Military Council of the Workers'	工農紅軍革命軍事委員會	Kung nung hung-chün ko-ming chün-shih

and Peasants' Red Army | | wei-yüan-hui
Revolutionary provisional regime | 革命的臨時政權 | Ko-ming ti lin-shih cheng-ch'üan
Revolutionary rising tide | 革命高漲 | Ko-ming kao-chang
Revolutionary situation | 革命形勢 | Ko-ming hsing-shih
Revolutionary war | 革命戰爭 | Ko-ming chan-cheng
Rich peasant | 富農 | Fu-nung
"Rich-peasant consciousness" | 「富農意識」 | "Fu-nung i-shih"
Rich-peasant contributions | 富農捐款 | Fu-nung chüan-k'uan
Rich-peasant problem | 富農問題 | Fu-nung wen-t'i
Rich peasants of a capitalistic character | 資本主義性富農 | Tzu-pen chu-i hsing fu-nung
Rich peasants of an initial-stage character | 初期性富農 | Ch'u-chi hsing fu-nung
Rich peasants of a semifeudal character | 半封建性的富農 | Pan-feng-chien hsing ti fu-nung
Rich peasants of a semi-landlord character | 半地主性富農 | Pan ti-chu hsing fu-nung
Rich peasants who lead revolts | 領導反水的富農 | Ling-tao fan-shui ti fu-nung
Right deviation | 右傾 | Yu-ch'ing
Right of being elected | 被選舉權 | Pei hsüan-chü-ch'üan
Right opportunism | 右傾機會主義 | Yu-ch'ing chi-hui chu-i
Right to vote | 選舉權 | Hsüan-chü-ch'üan
Riverbank | 河堤 | Ho-t'i
Roadside resthouse | 茶亭 | Ch'a-t'ing
Rudimentary cooperatives | 初步合作社 | Ch'u-pu ho-tso-she
Rural class | 農村階級 | Nung-ts'un chieh-chi
Rural revolutionary base | 農村革命根據地 | Nung-ts'un ko-ming ken-chü-ti
Rural workers | 農村工人 | Nung-ts'un kung-jen
Russian Returned Student group | 留俄派 | Liu-o-p'ai
Ruthless class struggle | 殘酷的階級鬥爭 | Ts'an-k'u ti chieh-chi tou-cheng
Safarov | 薩活洛夫 |
San Hsiang | 三湘(人名) |
Second National Soviet Congress | 第二次全國蘇維埃代表大會, 第二次全蘇大會 | Ti-erh-tz'u ch'üan-kuo su-wei-ai tai-piao ta-hui, ti-erh-tz'u ch'üan-su ta-hui

Second Soviet Conference of the Oyüwan Area	鄂豫皖區蘇維埃第二次代表大會	O-yü-wan-ch'ü su-wei-ai ti-erh-tz'u tai-piao ta-hui
Secretariat of the Central Government	中央政府秘書處	Chung-yang cheng-fu mi-shu-ch'u
Self-criticism	自我批評	Tzu-wo p'i-p'ing
Semifeudal character	半封建性質	Pan-feng-chien hsing-chih
Semifeudal exploitation	半封建剝削	Pan feng-chien po-hsüeh
Semilandlords	半地主	Pan ti-chu
Semiproletariat	半無產階級	Pan wu-ch'an chieh-chi
Serious counterrevolutionary action	重大反革命行爲	Chung-ta fan-ko-ming hsing-wei
Service fee	使用金	Shih-yung chin
Sha-hsin	砂心(地名)	
Shan-ho	山河(地名)	
Shang-hang	上杭 (地名)	
Shao Shih-p'ing	邵式平	
Sheng-li	勝利 (地名)	
Sheng Yung	盛榮(人名)	
Shih-ch'eng	石城(地名)	
Shop proprietor	老板	Lao-pan
Short-term laborer	短工	Tuan-kung
Short-term training classes for the land investigation drive	短期查田運動訓練班	Tuan-ch'i ch'a-t'ien yün-tung hsün-lien-pan
Shui-nan District	水南區	Shui-nan ch'ü
Shui-tung District Committee	水東區委	Shui-tung ch'ü-wei
Shun-hua	純化 (地名)	
Silver dollar	花邊	Hua-pien
Sixth National Congress	六次大會	Liu-tz'u ta-hui
Slogan	口號	K'ou-hao
Small group	小組	Hsiao-tsu
Small groups of workers	工人小組	Kung-jen hsiao-tsu
Small hamlets	小屋子	Hsiao wu-tzu
Small market town	小圩坊	Hsiao yü-fang
Small merchants in the villages	鄉村小商人	Hsiang-ts'un hsiao shang-jen
Small villages	小村子	Hsiao ts'un-tzu
Social Democratic Party	社會民主黨	She-hui min-chu-tang
"Socialist joint production"	「社會主義的共同生產」	"She-hui chu-i ti kung-t'ung sheng-ch'an"
Socialist revolution	社會革命, 社會主義	She-hui ko-ming, she-

	革命	hui chu-i ko-ming
Socialization	社會化	She-hui-hua
Social relief	社會救濟	She-hui chiu-chi
Southwest Kiangsi Soviet Government	贛西南蘇維埃政府	Kan-hsi-nan su-wei-ai cheng-fu
Southwest Kiangsi Special Area	贛西南特區	Kan-hsi-nan t'e-ch'ü
Soviet agencies	蘇維埃機關	Su-wei-ai chi-kuan
Soviet areas	蘇區	Su-ch'ü
Soviet farm	蘇維埃農場	Su-wei-ai nung-ch'ang
Soviet laws and decrees	蘇維埃法令	Su-wei-ai fa-ling
Soviet model farm	蘇維埃的模範農場	Su-wei-ai ti mu-fan nung-ch'ang
Soviet movement	蘇維埃運動	Su-wei-ai yün-tung
Soviet personnel on various levels	各級蘇維埃人員	Ko chi su-wei-ai jen-yüan
Soviet regime	蘇維埃政權	Su-wei-ai cheng-ch'üan
Soviet state farm	蘇維埃國立農場	Su-wei-ai kuo-li nung-ch'ang
Special commissioners	特派員	T'e-p'ai-yüan
Special Committee	特委	T'e-wei
Speculating merchants	投機商人	T'ou-chi shang-jen
SPSB. *See* State Political Security Bureau		
SPSB Branch in Kiangsi Province	江西省政治保衛分局	Chiang-hsi sheng cheng-chih pao-wei fen-chü
SPSB Branch in Min-kan Province	閩贛省政治保衛分局	Min-kan sheng cheng-chih pao-wei fen-chü
SSC, Shih Sou Collection	石叟資料室	Shih-sou tzu-liao shih
Stage of land confiscation and redistribution	沒收分配土地的階段	Mo-shou fen-p'ei t'u-ti ti chieh-tuan
Stage of land investigation	檢查土地的階段	Chien-ch'a t'u-ti ti chieh-tuan
Stage of land reconstruction	土地建設的階段	T'u-ti chien-she ti chieh-tuan
Standing committee	常委會	Ch'ang-wei-hui
State farm	國立農場	Kuo-li nung-ch'ang
State Political Security Bureau	國家政治保衛局	Kuo-chia cheng-chih pao-wei-chü
Status	成份	Ch'eng-fen
Step up the struggle against the rich peasants	加緊對富農的鬥爭	Chia-chin tui fu-nung ti tou-cheng
Storehouse	倉庫	Ts'ang-k'u

Struggle	鬪爭	Tou-cheng
Struggle against the rich peasants	反富農鬪爭	Fan fu-nung tou-cheng
Struggle between family branches	房界鬪爭	Fang-chieh tou-cheng
Struggle for an equal redistribution of grains	平穀鬪爭	P'ing-ku tou-cheng
Struggle for an equal redistribution of land	平田鬪爭	P'ing-t'ien tou-cheng
Struggle on two fronts, two-front struggle	兩條戰線鬪爭	Liang-t'iao chan-hsien tou-cheng
Subjective strength	主觀力量	Chu-kuan li-liang
Supplementary labor	附帶勞働	Fu-tai lao-tung
Supplementary land	補充土地	Pu-ch'ung t'u-ti
Supplementary personnel	補充人員	Pu-ch'ung jen-yüan
Suppress the counterattack of landlords and rich peasants	鎮壓地主富農的反攻	Cheng-ya ti-chu fu-nung ti fan-kung
Surplus farm implements	多餘農具	To-yü nung-chü
Surplus labor	剩餘勞働	Sheng-yü lao-tung
Surprise Attack Team	突擊隊	T'u-chi-tui
Surprise inspection	突擊檢查	T'u-chi chien-ch'a
Surprise Inspection Post	突擊檢查站	T'u-chi chien-ch'a chan
Surprise inspection team	突擊檢查隊	T'u-chi chien-ch'a-tui
Szu Mei (alias of Chang Wen-t'ien)	思美	
Ta-pu	大埔(地名)	
T'a-ching	蹈跧 (地名)	
Tactics	策略	Ts'e-lüeh
T'ai-ho	泰和 (地名)	
T'ai-lei	太雷(地名)	
T'ai-yang-shan	太陽山 (地名)	
Tailism	尾巴主義	Wei-pa chu-i
Tang Sheng-chih	唐生智(人名)	
Taoist priest	道士	Tao-shih
T'ao-huang	桃黄(地名)	
Tea-oil nuts	木桃, 茶子	Mu-t'ao, ch'a-tzu
Temple	廟宇	Miao-yü
Temporary forced labor corps	臨時的勞役隊	Lin-shih ti lao-i-tui
Third Party	第三黨	Ti-san-tang
Third Plenum	三中全會	San-chung ch'üan-hui

T'ing-chou (Ch'ang-t'ing)	汀州(地名)	
T'ing-tung	汀東 (地名)	
Title deed	田契	T'ien-ch'i
Title-deed duties	契稅	Ch'i-shui
Toiling and miserable peasants	勞苦農民	Lao-k'u nung-min
"Toiling norm," "labor norm"	勞働力原則	Lao-tung-li yüan-tse
Toiling peasants	勞働農民	Lao-tung nung-min
Tools of labor	勞働工具	Lao-tung kung-chü
T'ou-p'i	頭陂 (地名)	
Township	鄉	Hsiang
Township congress of delegates	鄉民代表	Hsiang-min tai-piao
Trial	審訊	Shen-hsün
Trotsky-Ch'en Tu-hsiu group	托陳派	T'o-ch'en-p'ai
Trotskyites	托派	T'o-p'ai
True Words	實話(雜誌名)	Shih-hua
True Words of Youth	青年實話(雜誌名)	Ch'ing-nien shih-hua
Ts'ai Ho-shen	蔡和森	
Ts'ai-hsi Township	才溪鄉	Ts'ai-hsi hsiang
Tseng Shan	曾山(曾珊)(人名)	
Tu-t'ou	渡頭(地名)	
Tung-t'ang	東塘 (地名)	
Tung-ku	東固 (地名)	
Two extremes of the peasant economy	農民經濟兩極化	Nung-min ching-chi liang chi-hua
Ultraleftism	極左主義	Chi-tso chu-i
Ultraleftist policy	過左政策	Kuo-tso cheng-ts'e
Ultrarightism	極右主義	Chi-yu chu-i
"Uncertainty of land redistribution"	「分田不定」	"Fen-t'ien pu-ting"
"Unconditional redistribution of unripe rice"	無條件分青	Wu-t'iao-chien fen-ch'ing
Uneven development	不平衡發展	Pu-p'ing-heng fa-chan
Unhusked-rice-dividing system	分穀制	Fen-ku chih
Uniform agricultural progressive tax	單一農業累進稅	Tan-i nung-yeh lei-chin-shui
Uncut rice	禾	Ho
Unusual revolutionary	農民特殊革命性	Nung-min t'e-shu ko-

character of the peasants		ming-hsing
Unwadded coverlet	單被	Tan-pei
Upper poor peasants	上層貧農	Shang-ts'eng p'in-nung
Uprising	暴動	Pao-tung
Usurer	高利貸者	Kao-li-tai-che
Usurious loan, usury	高利貸	Kao-li-tai
Vagabonds	流氓	Liu-meng
Vanguard of the proletariat	無産階級先鋒隊	Wu-ch'an chieh-chi hsien-feng-tui
Vegetable gardens	菜園	Ts'ai-yüan
Village and hamlet mass meeting	村屋群衆大會	Ts'un-wu ch'ün-chung ta-hui
Village bosses	豪, 土豪	Hao, t'u-hao
Village congress of the poor peasants	村貧農大會	Ts'un pin-nung ta-hui
Villages	村	Ts'un
Villages and hamlets	村屋	Ts'un-wu
Wa-tzu township	瓦子鄉(地名)	
Wage	工資	Kung-tzu
Wan-t'ai Ho-tung Committee	萬泰河東委員會	Wan-t'ai ho-tung wei-yüan-hui
Wan-tsai	萬載 (地名)	
[Wang] Hsiu	[王]秀(人名)	
Wang Huai	王懷(人名)	
Wang Kuan-lan	王觀瀾	
Warlord	軍閥	Chün-fa
"War zone"	「戰區」	"Chan-ch'ü"
Waste land	荒地	Huang-ti
Watchword	標語	Piao-yü
Water facilities	水利	Shui-li
Weaken rich peasants	削弱富農	Hsüeh-jo fu-nung
Well-to-do middle peasants	富裕中農	Fu-yü chung-nung
Well-to-do peasants	富裕農民	Fu-yü nung-min
Western Fukien	閩西	Min-hsi
Western Fukien Special Committee	閩西特委	Min-hsi t'e-wei
White areas	白區, 白色區域	Pai-ch'ü, pai-se ch'ü-yü
White Army	白軍	Pai-chün
White Terror	白色恐怖	Pai-se k'ung-pu
Wickedest elements	最壞的分子	Tsui-huai ti fen-tzu

Woodwork shop	木店	Mu-tien
Workers	工人	Kung-jen
Workers' and Peasants' Inspectorate	工農檢察部	Kung-nung chien-ch'a pu
Working corps	工作團	Kung-tso t'uan
Work net	工作網	Kung-tso wang
"Write off all debts"	「廢除一切債務」	"Fei-ch'u i-ch'ieh chai-wu"
"Write off usuries"	「廢除高利貸」	"Fei-ch'u kao-li-tai"
Wu-p'ing	武平(地名)	
Wu-yang	武陽(地名)	
Yang Ch'eng-fu	楊成芙(人名)	
Yang-hsin County Soviet Executive Committee	陽新縣蘇執行委員會	Yang-hsin hsien-su chih-hsing wei-yüan-hui
Yang-ku	洋古（地名）	
Yeh-p'ing	葉坪(地名)	
Yen-fu township	延福鄉(地名)	
Youth Corps	青年團	Ch'ing-nien t'uan
Youth Vanguards	少先隊	Shao-hsien tui
Yung-feng	永豊（地名）	
Yung-hsin	永新（地名）	
Yung-ting	永定(地名)	
Yü-tu	雩都（地名）	
Yüan Wen-tsai	哀文才(人名)	
Yün-chi	雲集(地名)	

Alphabetical List of Documents

(Page numbers refer to the discussion in the text; when a second page number is given, it refers to the translation)

Bibliography

(*Annotated in this volume. †Annotated and translated in this volume.
‡All entries indicated as a part of the Shih Sou collection (SSC) are available
on microfilm in the United States.)

Barnett, A. Doak. *Communist China and Asia*. New York: Harper and Brothers,
1960.

Bland, J. O. P. *China: The Pity of It*. London: W. Heinemann, 1932.

Bolshevik (布爾塞維克 *Pu-erh-se-wei-k'e*) (Shanghai), organ of the CCP central
leadership, published in Shanghai. On file in Bureau of Investigation
Collection, Taiwan (BIC), 300.805/804; Vol. IV, No. 3 (May 10, 1931).
Generally known as *Pu-pao* 布報.

‡*Bolshevik* (布爾塞維克 *Pu-erh-se-wei-k'e*) (Kiangsi), organ of the CCP central
leadership, published by the Central Bureau, n.p., probably in Jui-chin.
No. 1 dated July, 1934, 008.105/4913, SSC.

Brandt, Conrad, Benjamin Schwartz, and John K. Fairbank. *A Documentary
History of Chinese Communism*. Cambridge: Harvard University Press, 1952.

Carr, Edward Hallett. *The Bolshevik Revolution, 1917–1923. A History of Soviet
Russia*. 3 vols. New York: The Macmillan Company, 1951–1960.

Central Correspondence (中央通訊 *Chung-yang t'ung-hsin*), a periodical issued irreg-
ularly by the CCP leadership for intraparty circulation, n.p., probably
first at Hankow in August–September, 1927, and then at Shanghai until
July, 1928. Beginning with No. 14 (probably December, 1927), it was
renamed *Central Political Correspondence* (中央政治通訊 *Chung-yang cheng-chih
t'ung-hsin*). Scattered issues available.

"The Central Soviet Area in Kiangsi" (江西的中央蘇區 *Chiang-hsi ti chung-
yang su-ch'ü*), a special correspondence printed in *The Red Flag Weekly*,
No. 24 (November 27, 1931), pp. 39–50.

Chamberlin, William Henry. *The Russian Revolution, 1917–1921*. 2 vols. New
York: The Macmillan Company, 1960.

Ch'en Shao-yü 陳紹禹. *Struggle for the More Complete Bolshevization of the Chinese
Communist Party* (爲中共更加布爾塞維克化而鬥爭 *Wei chung-kung keng-chia pu-*

337

erh-se-wei-k'e hua erh tou-cheng). 1st ed., Shanghai, February, 1931, under the title *Two Lines;* 2nd ed., Moscow, March, 1932; 3rd ed., Yenan, July, 1940, under the present title; 224.07/372, BIC.

The Chinese Soviet Political Program (中國蘇維埃的政綱 *Chung-kuo su-we-ai ti cheng-kang*), taken from the Political Resolution of the Conference of Delegates from the Soviet Areas, May, 1930; reproduced in *A Collection of Red Bandit Secret Documents*, Vol. II, leaves 1–2, in *A Collection of Red Bandit Reactionary Documents*, III, 655–56, and in Hsiao Tso-liang, *Power Relations within the Chinese Communist Movement, 1930–1934: Vol. II, The Chinese Documents*.

The Chinese Soviets, Vol. I (中國蘇維埃, 第一集 *Chung-kuo su-wei-ai, ti-i-chi*). Compiled and printed by the Central Preparatory Commission for the National Soviet Congress, November 7, 1930, n.p., probably Shanghai; mimeographed; 952.2/804, BIC. A collection of documents adopted by the Central Preparatory Commission or prepared by it for adoption by the National Soviet Congress originally scheduled to be held in November, 1930.

A Collection of Important Documents of Communist Bandits' Land Policy (共匪土地政策重要文件彙編 *Kung-fei t'u-ti cheng-ts'e chung-yao wen-chien hui-pien*). Compiled and printed by Chung-lien Publishing House 中聯出版社, December, 1947; 554.2821/804, BIC.

A Collection of Reactionary Documents (反動文件彙編 *Fan-tung wen-chien hui-pien*). Compiled by the KMT Headquarters, Fourteenth Division of the Army 陸軍第十四師特別黨部, March 1, 1932; 4 vols. bound in 2 tomes, mimeographed; 008.2129/7120/V.1, Nos. 1–2, 3–4, SSC.

A Collection of Red Bandit Documents (赤匪文件彙編 *Ch'ih-fei wen-chien hui-pien*). Compiled by the Fourth and later the Second Department, Nanchang Headquarters, Chairman of the (Nationalist) Military Council 軍事委員會委員長南昌行營第二, 第四廳, July, 1933—October, 1934; 4 vols. (I, VII, VIII, XI) on file; 008.2129/4070, SSC.

A Collection of Red Bandit Reactionary Documents (赤匪反動文件彙編 *Ch'ih-fei fan-tung wen-chien hui-pien*). Compiled under the sponsorship of General Ch'en Ch'eng, June, 1935; reprinted May, 1960; 6 vols.; 008.2129/4072, SSC.

A Collection of Red Bandit Secret Documents (赤匪機密文件彙編 *Ch'ih-fei chi-mi wen-chien hui-pien*). Compiled by the First Bandit Suppression Propaganda Department, Headquarters of the Commander-in-Chief of the Land, Sea, and Air Forces 陸海空軍總司令部第一勦匪宣傳處, June–October, 1931; 6 vols. bound in 1 tome, mimeographed; 008.2129/4074, SSC.

A Collection of Reference Materials on the Land Laws of the Chinese People's Republic (中華人民共和國土地法參攷資料彙編 *Chung-hua jen-min kung-ho-kuo t'u-ti fa ts'an-k'ao tzu-liao hui-pien*). Edited by the Center for the Instruction and Study of Civil Law of the Peking Political and Law College, published by the Law Publishing House, Peking, 1957.

Compton, Boyd. *Mao's China: Party Reform Documents, 1942–44*. Seattle: University of Washington Press, 1952. Washington Paperback—4, 1966.

†*Decisions concerning Some Problems Arising from the Agrarian Struggle* (關於土地鬥爭中一些問題的決定 *Kuan-yü t'u-ti tou-cheng chung i-hsieh wen-t'i ti chüeh-ting*). Adopted by the Central Council of People's Commissars, October 10, 1933, 008.743/4037, SSC; mimeographed; reproduced in *A Collection of Red Bandit Reactionary Documents*, III, 989–1010.

**Definitions of the Rich Peasants, Middle Peasants, Poor Peasants, Hired Farm Hands, Shop Proprietors, Master Workmen, Foremen, Independent Laborers, and Workers, and Tactics to Oppose the Rich Peasants, Shop Proprietors, Master Workmen, and Foremen, and to Ally with the Middle Peasants and Independent Laborers* (富農, 中農, 貧農, 雇農與老板, 師父, 工頭, 獨立勞働者, 工人之解釋以及反對富農, 老板, 師父, 工頭與聯合中農, 獨立勞働者之策略 *Fu-nung, chung-nung, p'in-nung, ku-nung, yü lao-pan, shih-fu, kung-t'ou, tu-li lao-tung-che, kung-jen chih chiai-shih, i chi fan-tui fu-nung, lao-pan, shih-fu, kung-t'ou, yü lien-ho chung-nung, tu-li lao-tung-che chih ts'e-lüeh*). Compiled and mimeographed by the CCP Ning-tu County Committee, January 18, 1932, 008.2122/2715, SSC.

"Discussion of the Li-san Line by the Presidium of the ECCI" (共產國際執委主席團對於立三路線的討論 *Kung-ch'an kuo-chi chih-wei chu-hsi-t'uan tui-yü li-san lu-hsien ti t'ao-lun*). December, 1930; Chinese version printed in *Bolshevik* (Shanghai), IV, No. 3 (May 10, 1931), 1–75, 300.805/804, BIC, and in Hsiao Tso-liang, *Power Relations within the Chinese Communist Movement, 1930–1934: Vol. II, The Chinese Documents*.

**Draft Resolution on the Land and Peasant Problems in Soviet Areas* (蘇維埃區域土地農民問題議決案草案 *Su-wei-ai ch'ü-yü t'u-ti nung-min wen-t'i i-chüeh-an ts'ao-an*), by the Comintern Eastern Department 共產國際東方部, n.d. Reprinted by the CCP Central Secretariat, November 20, 1930, five days after it had been received; a pamphlet printed in lead type, 008.751/4424/C.1, SSC; reprinted by the CCP Wan-t'ai Ho-tung Committee 萬泰河東委員會, April 22, 1931, mimeographed, 008.751/4424/C.2, SSC; reproduced in *A Collection of Red Bandit Secret Documents*, Vol. III, leaves 38–45; in *A Collection of Reactionary Documents*, Vol. IV, leaves 1–8, and in *Power Relations within the Chinese Communist Movement, 1930–1934: Vol. II, The Chinese Documents*.

Draft Resolutions Introduced by the CCP Central Committee to the First National Soviet Congress (中國共産黨中央委員會提出全國蘇維埃第一次代表大會草案 *Chung-kuo kung-ch'an-tang chung-yang wei-yüan-hui t'i-ch'u ch'üan-kuo su-wei-ai ti-i-tz'u tai-piao ta-hui ts'ao-an*). Reprinted by the Political Department, Third Army Corps, First Route Army, Chinese Workers' and Peasants' Red Army, n.d., probably 1931; 008.631/8064.2, SSC, and in Hsiao Tso-liang, *Power Relations within the Chinese Communist Movement, 1930–1934: Vol. II, The Chinese Documents*.

Fairbank, John King. *The United States and China.* Rev. ed. Cambridge: Harvard University Press, 1962.

"A General Survey of Land Redistribution—Report of the Kiangsi Provincial Soviet" (土地分配概況—江西省蘇報告 *T'u-ti fen-p'ei kai-k'uang—chiang-hsi sheng-su pao-kao*). Printed in *Red China,* November 21, 1932, p. 5.

A Guide to the Land Investigation Drive (查田運動指南 *Ch'a-t'ien yün-tung chih-nan*). Printed and issued by the Central Government, n.d., probably sometime between July and October, 1933; 008.743/4063-3/C.1, 2, SSC.

Guide Weekly (嚮導週報 *Hsiang-tao chou-pao*), organ of the Chinese Communist Party, 1922-1927. A total of 201 issues in photo-reproduction.

Ho Kan-chih 何幹之. *History of the Contemporary Chinese Revolution* (中國現代革命史 *Chung-kuo hsien-tai ko-ming-shih*). Hongkong, 1958.

†*How to Analyze the Classes* (怎樣分析階級 *Tsen-yang fen-hsi chieh-chi*). Adopted by the Eight-County Conference on the Land Investigation Drive, June 17-21, 1933; printed in: *Red China,* No. 89 (June 29, 1933), p. 8; *A Guide to the Land Investigation Drive,* pp. 27-30; appendix to *Decisions concerning Some Problems Arising from the Agrarian Struggle; Selected Works of Mao Tse-tung,* I, 121-24; *A Collection of Red Bandit Reactionary Documents,* III, 946-49.

*How to Redistribute Land (怎樣分配土地 *Tsen-yang fen-p'ei t'u-ti*). Released by the General Political Department of the Military Council of the Oyuwan Soviet Area; reprinted by the General Political Department of the Fourth Front Army of the Chinese Workers' and Peasants' Red Army, on the anniversary of the October Revolution (November 7), 1931; reproduced in *A Collection of Red Bandit Documents,* III, 934-46.

Hsiao Tso-liang 蕭作梁. *Power Relations within the Chinese Communist Movement, 1930-1934.* Seattle: University of Washington Press, 1961.

―――. *Power Relations within the Chinese Communist Movement, 1930-1934: Vol. II, The Chinese Documents.* Seattle: University of Washington Press, 1967. This volume includes the original (Chinese) version of translated documents numbers 1, 9, and 34, annotated documents numbers 2, 7, 8, 31, 35, and 36. References to other documents that are reproduced in this volume are indicated.

†*Instruction No. 11 of the Council of People's Commissars of the Provisional Central Government of the Chinese Soviet Republic—Launching an Extensive and Intensive Land Investigation Drive* (中華蘇維埃共和國臨時中央政府人民委員會訓令第十一號—實行廣泛深入的查田運動 *Chung-hua su-wei-ai kung-ho-kuo lin-shih chung-yang cheng-fu jen-min wei-yüan-hui hsün-ling ti shih-i hao—shih-hsing kuang-fan shen-ju ti ch'a-t'ien yün-tung*), June 1, 1933. Printed in *Red China,* No. 87 (June 20, 1933), p. 5, and in *A Guide to the Land Investigation Drive,* pp. 7-10.

The International Line (國際路線 *Kuo-chi lu-hsien*), printed by the Central Bureau, Soviet Areas, CCP, December, 1932, n.p., probably Jui-chin; 009.54/6076, SSC. Probably the first volume of a three-volume collection of documents of the same title; the second volume is unavailable.

International Press Correspondence, Vol. VI, No. 40 (May 13, 1926).

Kung Ch'u 龔楚. *The Red Army and I* (我與紅軍 *Wo yü hung-chün*). Hongkong: South Wind Publishing Company, 1954.

†*Land Law* (土地法 *T'u-ti fa*). Promulgated by the Chinese Revolutionary Military Council 中國革命軍事委員會, n.d. Reprinted by the General Political Department, First Army Corps, 1930 紅軍第一軍團總政治部; reproduced in 1931 in *A Collection of Red Bandit Secret Documents*, Vol. V, leaves 1–4, in 1935 in *A Collection of Red Bandit Reactionary Documents*, III, 912–18, and in Hsiao Tso-liang, *Power Relations within the Chinese Communist Movement, 1930–1934: Vol. II, The Chinese Documents*.

Land Law, adopted by the CCP National Land Conference, September 13, 1947.

†*Land Law of the Chinese Soviet Republic* (中華蘇維埃共和國土地法 *Chung-hua su-wei-ai kung-ho-kuo t'u-ti fa*). Adopted by the First National Soviet Congress 第一次全國蘇維埃大會, November, 1931; an original copy of the proclamation by the Presidium of the First National Soviet Congress and the Central Executive Committee of the Chinese Soviet Republic on December 1, 1931, 008.742/4043, SSC; reproduced in: (1) *The Soviet Code*, II, 41–47; (2) *The Red Flag Weekly*, No. 29 (January 15, 1932), pp. 67–72, on file in Hoover Library; (3) *A Collection of Red Bandit Documents*, I, 2–9; (4) *A Collection of Red Bandit Reactionary Documents*, III, 922–27; (5) Hsiao Tso-liang, *Power Relations within the Chinese Communist Movement, 1930–1934: Vol. II, The Chinese Documents*.

*The Land Problem (土地問題 *T'u-ti wen-t'i*). Compiled by the Propaganda Department of the Central Bureau of the Soviet Areas; Lenin Bookstore ed., Western Fukien, lithographed, March, 1932, 12 leaves, 008.741022/4047/C.1, SSC; Red Army School ed., n.p., n.d., 14 leaves, 008.741022/4047/C.2, SSC; reproduced in *A Collection of Red Bandit Reactionary Documents*, III, 890–910.

*The Land Problem (土地問題 *T'u-ti wen-t'i*), *Manual of Political Instruction in Camp Schools*. Compiled by the Political Department of the 12th Army of the Chinese Workers' and Peasants' Red Army, April, 1932, 008.741022/4947-2, SSC.

*The Land Problem and the Anti-Rich-Peasant Tactics (土地問題與反富農策略 *T'u-ti wen-t'i yü fan fu-nung ts'e-lüeh*). Circular No. 9 of the Central Bureau, Soviet Areas, CCP, February 8, 1931; 008.741022/4047-3, SSC, mimeographed; also reproduced in *A Collection of Red Bandit Secret Documents*, Vol. V, leaves 19–28.

*The Land Program of the Chinese Communist Party (中國共產黨土地政綱 *Chung-kuo kung-ch'an-tang t'u-ti cheng-kang*). Taken from chap. V, sec. 20, of the resolution on the land problem adopted by the CCP Sixth National Congress in 1928; issued as an official proclamation by the Political Department of the First Army Corps of the Chinese Workers' and Peas-

ants' Red Army, n.d., probably sometime before September 1, 1931, 008.743/4041, SSC; reproduced in: *A Collection of Red Bandit Secret Documents,* Vol. V, leaves 6–7; *A Collection of Red Bandit Reactionary Documents,* III, 910–12; and *A Collection of Red Bandit Documents,* I, 10–11.

Land Reform Law, adopted by the Central People's Government of the Chinese People's Republic, June 28, 1950.

**Letter from the ECCI to the CCP Central Committee* (共產國際執行委員會給中國共產黨中央委員會的信 *Kung-ch'an kuo-chi chih-hsing wei-yüan-hui kei chung-kuo kung-ch'an-tang chung-yang wei-yüan-hui ti hsin*), received November 16, 1930. Chinese version, reprinted in *Red Documents,* pp. 362–75, and reproduced in *A Collection of Red Bandit Reactionary Documents,* II, 434–47.

**Letter from the ECCI to the CCP on the Peasant Problem* (共產國際執行委員會與中國共產黨書—關於農民問題 *Kung-ch'an kuo-chi chih-hsing wei-yüan-hui yü chung-kuo kung-ch'an-tang shu—kuan-yü nung-min wen-t'i*), June 7, 1929. Reprinted in *The International Line,* pp. 43–57, and *Red Documents,* pp. 319–33.

**Letter of the ECCI Presidium to the Chinese Communist Party* (共產國際執委主席團給中國共產黨的信 *Kung-ch'an kuo-chi chih-wei-chu-hsi-t'uan kei chung-kuo kung-ch'an-tang ti hsin*), adopted by the enlarged session of the ECCI Presidium, July, 1931. Chinese version reprinted in *Bolshevik* (Kiangsi), No. 1 (July, 1934), pp. 1–41; in *Red Documents,* pp. 376–404; and in Hsiao Tso-liang, *Power Relations within the Chinese Communist Movement, 1930–1934: Vol. II, The Chinese Documents.*

Lu Ch'iang 盧強. *The "Hero" on the Ching-kang-shan* (井崗山上的"英雄" *Ching-kang-shan shang ti "ying-hsiung"*). Hongkong: Liberty Press 自由出版社, 1951; subtitled *Romances of Mao Tse-tung* (毛澤東外史 *Mao Ts-təung wai-shih*).

Mao Tse-tung 毛澤東. *Investigations of the Rural Districts* (農村調查 *Nung-ts'un t'iao-ch'a*). Yenan, 1941; reissued in Shantung: Hsinhua Bookstore, 1946.

†———. "The Land Investigation Is the Central Task of Great Magnitude in Vast Areas" (查田運動是廣大區域的中心重大任務 *Ch'a-t'ien yün-tung shih kuang-ta ch'ü-yü ti chung-hsin chung-ta jen-wu*), printed in *Red China,* No. 86 (June 17, 1933), p. 3.

———. *Report on the Investigation of the Peasant Movement in Hunan* (湖南農民運動考察報告 *Hu-nan nung-min yün-tung k'ao-ch'a pao-kao*), February 18, 1927, *Guide Weekly (Hsiang-tao chou-pao),* No. 191, March 12, 1927, pp. 2061–66; reprinted with revisions and additions in *Selected Works of Mao Tse-tung,* Chinese ed., I, 13–46; English ed., I, 21–59.

———. *Selected Works of Mao Tse-tung* (毛澤東选集 *Mao Tse-tung hsüan-chi*), compiled by the Mao Tse-tung Selected Works Publishing Committee, CCP Central Committee (中共中央毛澤東选集出版委員會). Chinese ed., Peking: People's Publishing Co., 1953–57 (3 vols.); English ed., New York: International Publishers, 1954–56 (4 vols.).

*————. "Soviet Work in Ch'ang-kang Township, Hsing-kuo" (興國長岡鄉的蘇維埃工作 *Hsing-kuo ch'ang-kang-hsiang ti su-wei-ai kung-tso*), December 15, 1933. Published in *Struggle* (Kiangsi), No. 42 (January 12), pp. 10–16, No. 43 (January 19), pp. 15–20, No. 44 (January 26), p. 16, 1934.

*————. "Soviet Work in Ts'ai-hsi Township, Shang-hang" (上杭才溪鄉的蘇維埃工作 *Shang-hang ts'ai-hsi-hsiang ti su-wei-ai kung-tso*). Published in *Struggle* (Kiangsi), No. 45 (February 2), pp. 15–16, No. 46 (February 9), pp. 15–16, No. 48 (February 23), pp. 18–29, 1934.

————. *The Struggle in the Ching-kang Mountains* (井崗山上的闘爭 *Ching-kang-shan shang ti tou-cheng*), November 25, 1928; reprinted in *Selected Works of Mao Tse-tung*, Chinese ed., I, 59–86; English ed., I, 71–104.

Mif, Pavel 米夫. *Heroic China: Fifteen Years of the Communist Party in China.* New York, 1937; Chinese version entitled 英勇奮闘的十五年 *Ying-yung fen-tou ti shih-wu nien*, 1936, 291/906, BIC.

†*On the Question of Reopening the Land Investigation Drive—Instruction, Serial Character* Chung, *No. 1, of the Council of People's Commissars* (關於繼續開展查田運動的問題——人民委員會訓令, 中字第一號 *Kuan-yü chi-hsü k'ai-chan ch'a-t'ien yün-tung ti wen-t'i—Jen-min wei-yüan-hui hsün-ling chung-tzu ti-i hao*), March 15, 1934. Printed in *Red China*, No. 164 (March 20, 1934), p. 1.

†*An Outline of the Land Problem* (土地問題提綱 *T'u-ti wen-t'i t'i-kang*). Adopted by the Joint Meeting of the Chairmen of County and District Soviet Governments, Kiangsi, sometime before September 1, 1931; reproduced in *A Collection of Red Bandit Secret Documents*, Vol. V, leaves 7–11.

Peffer, Nathaniel. "Chinese Idea of Communism," *Current History*, XXXVI (July, 1932), pp. 400–404.

Political Resolution Adopted by the First Party Congress of the [Central] *Soviet Area* (蘇區黨第一次代表大會通過政治決議案 *Su-ch'ü tang ti-i tz'u tai-piao ta-hui t'ung-kuo cheng-chih chüeh-i-an*), printed by the Central Bureau, Soviet Areas, November, 1931; 008.235/1833/C.1–2, SSC; reprinted in Hsiao Tso-liang, *Power Relations within the Chinese Communist Movement, 1930–1934: Vol. II, The Chinese Documents.*

Political Resolution of the Sixth National Congress (六次大會政治決議案 *Liu-tz'u ta-hui cheng-chih chüeh-i-an*), July 9, 1928; reprinted in *The International Line*, pp. 58–94, and *Red Documents*, pp. 136–72.

†*Proclamation of the Kiangsi Provincial Government on the Land Problem* (江西省政府關於土地問題的布告 *Chiang-hsi sheng cheng-fu kuan-yü t'u-ti wen-t'i ti pu-kao*), 1931; reproduced in *A Collection of Reactionary Documents*, Vol. I, Book IV, leaves 8–10.

Provincial Committee Correspondence (省委通訊 *Sheng-wei t'ung-hsün*), issued by the Kiangsi Provincial Committee of the CCP, 1933–34, n.p.; 008.2105/9025, SSC. Scattered issues bound in 1 vol., mimeographed. Published every three or four days. The earliest number on file (No. 11) is dated July 6, 1933, and the last issue available (a special edition) is dated May 15, 1934.

†*Provisional Land Law* (土地暫行法 *T'u-ti chan-hsing fa*), adopted by the National Conference of Delegates from the Soviet Areas 全國蘇維埃區域代表大會, May, 1930; printed in *The Red Flag*, No. 107 (June 4, 1930), pp. 2–3, on file in the Hoover Library, Stanford University; reproduced in *A Collection of Red Bandit Documents*, I, 11–17, in *A Collection of Red Bandit Reactionary Documents*, III, 918–21, and in Hsiao Tso-liang, *Power Relations within the Chinese Communist Movement, 1930–1934: Vol. II, The Chinese Documents.*

**Provisional Land Law* (土地暫行法 *T'u-ti chan-hsing fa*), adopted by the National Conference of Delegates from the Soviet Areas, May, 1930, and revised by the Central Preparatory Commission for the National Soviet Congress, September, 1930; printed in *The Chinese Soviets*, I, 10–12, and in Hsiao Tso-liang, *Power Relations within the Chinese Communist Movement, 1930–1934: Vol. II, The Chinese Documents.*

Räte-China, documents on the Chinese revolution, published by Verlagsgenossenschaft Ausländischer Arbeiter in der Udssr, Moscow-Leningrad, 1934. Part I: Soviet movement in China; Part II: Materials and documents; Part III: Enemies of the Chinese Soviets. Also published in Russian in 1934 as Johanson i Taube, *Soviety v Kitae*, translated from German, Partiinoe Izdatel'stvo, Moscow, 1934.

Red China (紅色中華 *Hung-se chung-hua*). Organ of the Provisional Central Government of the Chinese Soviet Republic. Founded in Jui-chin, December 11, 1931, published until the evacuation of the Chinese Communists from Kiangsi, the last available issue dated October 20, 1934. Appeared first once a week, then every ten days, then every three days. For the most part, one issue consists of four pages, sometimes six, very often up to eight. Bound in 8 vols. with some scattered issues missing. Bearing the call number 008.1052/2125, SSC, the newspaper is the richest and most complete store of information about the Kiangsi Soviet known.

Red Documents (紅色文獻 *Hung-se wen-hsien*). Printed by *Chiai-fang-she* 解放社, February, 1938; 008.2129/2703, SSC.

The Red Flag (紅旗 *Hung-ch'i*). Organ of the CCP central leadership, published in Shanghai every Wednesday and Saturday. Scattered numbers on file in the Hoover Library, Stanford University.

The Red Flag Weekly (紅旗週報 *Hung-ch'i chou-pao*). Published in Shanghai by the Central Department of Propaganda, CCP. Nos. 10–58 and 63 on file in BIC, call number 052.1/809; Nos. 1–9 and 59–62 not available. No. 10 appeared July 20, 1931, and No. 63 on January 1, 1934.

Reference Items of the Third Plenum (三中全會材料 *San-chung ch'üan-hui ts'ai-liao*). An official collection of 22 documents of and concerning the Third Enlarged Plenum of the CC, CCP; printed by the Central Bureau, Soviet Areas(?), October 6, 1930(?); some items reproduced in *A Collection of Red Bandit Secret Documents*, Vol. III, leaves 2–55, others not available.

†*Regulations of the Kiangsi Provincial Government for the Confiscation and Redistribution of Land—Approved by the Provisional Central Government* (江西省政府對於 沒收和分配土地的條例—臨時中央政府批准 *Chiang-hsi sheng cheng-fu tui-yü mo-shou han fen-p'ei t'u-ti ti t'iao-li—lin-shih chung-yang cheng-fu p'i-chun*). Probably adopted sometime between December 1, 1931, and April 1, 1932; reproduced in *The Land Problem—Manual of Political Instruction in Camp Schools*, April 1, 1932, leaves 3–6, 008.741022/4047-2, SSC; *A Collection of Red Bandit Reactionary Documents*, III, 927–34.

"Report of the Comintern Eastern Department on the Errors of the Chinese Party Third Plenum and of Comrade Li Li-san" (國際東方部關於中國黨 三中全會與李立三同志的錯誤的報告 *Kuo-chi tung-fang-pu kuan-yü chung-kuo tang san-chung ch'üan-hui yü li-li-san t'ung-chih ti ts'o-wu ti pao-kao*), dated December, 1930, Moscow; Chinese version as appendix to "The Discussion of the Li-san Line by the Presidium of the ECCI," printed in *Bolshevik* (Shanghai), IV, No. 3 (May 10, 1931), 66–75; and in Hsiao Tso-liang, *Power Relations within the Chinese Communist Movement, 1930–1934: Vol. II, The Chinese Documents*.

"Report on the Plenum of the Central Preparatory Commission for the National Soviet Congress" (全國蘇維埃大會中央準備委員會全體會議經過 *Ch'üan-kuo su-wei-ai ta-hui chung-yang chun-pei wei-yüan-hui ch'üan-t'i hui-i ching-kuo*), printed in *The Red Flag Daily*, No. 36 (September 19, 1930); also in the appendixes to *The Chinese Soviets*, Vol. I; and in Hsiao Tso-liang, *Power Relations within the Chinese Communist Movement, 1930–1934: Vol. II, The Chinese Documents*.

*"Resolution concerning the Land Problem Adopted by the Third Plenary Session of the Yang-hsin County Soviet Executive Committee" (陽新縣蘇 第三次全體執行委員會議土地問題決議 *Yang-hsin hsien-su ti-san-tz'u ch'üan-t'i chih-hsing wei-yüan hui-i t'u-ti wen-t'i chüeh-i*), December 5, 1931. Reproduced in *A Collection of Red Bandit Documents*, I, 56–97.

*"Resolution of the Central Bureau on the Land Investigation Drive" (中央 局關於查田運動的決議 *Chung-yang-chü kuan-yü ch'a-t'ien yün-tung ti chüeh-i*), June 2, 1933. Printed in *Red China*, June 20, 1933, p. 2, and *A Guide to the Land Investigation Drive*, pp. 1–5.

"Resolution of the Enlarged Fourth Plenum of the CCP Central Committee" (中國共產黨中央委員會擴大會第四次全體會議議決案 *Chung-kuo kung-ch'an-tang chung-yang wei-yüan-hui k'uo-ta-hui ti-szu-t'zu ch'üan-t'i hui-i i-chüeh-an*), January, 1931, 008.235/5048/C.1, SSC. Reprinted by Wan-t'ai Ho-tung Committee, CCP, April 21 (1931), 008.235/5948/C.2, SSC; *Red Documents*, pp. 235–44; also reproduced in *A Collection of Red Bandit Reactionary Documents*, III, 424–34, and in Hsiao Tso-liang, *Power Relations within the Chinese Communist Movement, 1930–1934: Vol. II, The Chinese Documents*.

"Resolution of the Sixth National Congress on the Land Problem" (六次大會 土地問題決議案 *Liu-tz'u ta-hui t'u-ti wen-t'i chüeh-i-an*), July 9, 1928. Reprinted in *The International Line,* pp. 118–44, and *Red Documents,* pp. 196–222.

"Resolution of the Sixth National Congress on the Peasant Problem" (六次大會農民問題決議案 *Liu-tz'u ta-hui nung-min wen-t'i chüeh-i-an*), July 9, 1928. Reprinted in *The International Line,* pp. 145–55, and *Red Documents,* pp. 228–34.

"Resolution on Some Historical Problems" (關於若干歷史問題的決議 *Kuan-yü jo-kan li-shih wen-t'i ti chüeh-i*). Adopted by the Seventh Enlarged Plenary Session of the CCP Sixth Central Committee, April 20, 1945; reprinted in *Selected Works of Mao Tse-tung,* Chinese ed., III, 955–1022; English ed., IV, 171–218, and in Hsiao Tso-liang, *Power Relations within the Chinese Communist Movement, 1930–1934: Vol. II, The Chinese Documents.* One-volume reprint published by the People's Publishing Company, Peking, 1953.

"Resolution on the Chinese Problem" (中國問題決議案 *Chung-kuo wen-t'i chüeh-i-an*). Adopted by the Seventh Enlarged Session of the ECCI, November, 1926; Chinese version reprinted in *The International Line,* III, 1–21; and *Red Documents,* pp. 245–66.

"Resolution on the Chinese Problem" (中國問題決議案 *Chung-kuo wen-t'i chüeh-i-an*). Adopted by the Eighth Plenum of the ECCI, May, 1927; Chinese version reprinted in *The International Line,* III, 22–43, and *Red Documents,* pp. 267–88.

*"Resolution on the Chinese Problem" (中國問題決議案 *Chung-kuo wen-t'i chüeh-i-an*). Adopted by the ECCI Political Secretariat, July 23, 1930; Chinese version reprinted in *Red Documents,* pp. 346–61, and in Hsiao Tso-liang, *Power Relations within the Chinese Communist Movement, 1930–1934: Vol. II, The Chinese Documents;* reproduced in *A Collection of Red Bandit Secret Documents,* Vol. III, leaves 3–12, mimeographed.

*"Resolution on the Land Problem" (關於土地問題的決議案 *Kuan-yü t'u-ti wen-t'i ti chüeh-i-an*). Adopted by the CCP Central Bureau of the Soviet Areas, August 21 [1931]; printed by the General Political Department, Central Revolutionary Military Council 中央革命軍事委員會, n.d., and reprinted by the CCP Shui-tung District Committee 水東區委, September 7, 1931; mimeographed, 008.743-4047-3, SSC.

†*The Rich-Peasant Problem* (富農問題 *Fu-nung wen-t'i*), Resolution No. 2 adopted by a joint meeting of the Front Committee and the Western Fukien Special Committee; printed by the General Political Department, First Front Army, Red Army, June 1930; 008.7511/3057, SSC.

Schwartz, Benjamin. *Chinese Communism and the Rise of Mao.* Cambridge: Harvard University Press, 1951.

———. "The Legend of the 'Legend of "Maoism,' " " *The China Quarterly,* No. 2 (April–June, 1960).

Snow, Edgar. *Random Notes on Red China (1936–1945).* ("Chinese Economic and Political Studies," special series.) Cambridge: Harvard University,

1957.

———. *Red Star over China*. New York: Modern Library, 1944.

The Soviet Code, Vol. II (蘇維埃法典, 第二集 *Su-wei-ai fa-tien, ti-erh chi*). Compiled by the People's Judicial Commissariat, July, 1934; 008.542/ 4424/V.2, SSC.

Struggle (鬥爭 *Tou-cheng*) (Kiangsi), organ of the Central Bureau, Soviet Areas, published by the Party Press Committee 黨報委員會, Central Bureau, Soviet Areas, February 4, 1933—September 30, 1934, n.p., probably Jui-chin; 73 numbers bound in 6 vols. (18 scattered numbers missing); 008.2105/7720, SSC.

Thornton, Richard. "The Comintern and the Chinese Communists: 1928–1931." Unpublished Ph.D. dissertation, University of Washington, 1966.

Treadgold, Donald W. *Twentieth-Century Russia*. Chicago: Rand McNally, 1959.

True Words of Youth (青年實話 *Ch'ing-nien shih-hua*), organ of the Central Bureau of the Soviet Areas of the Chinese Communist Youth Corps 中國共產主義青年團蘇區中央局. Published by the Chinese Communist Youth Corps, July, 1931—September, 1934, at Yung-feng, Jui-chin, or T'ing-chou at different times; scattered issues bound in 7 vols., 008.2105/5083, SSC.

*Wang Kuan-lan. "Reopening the Land Investigation Drive and Suppressing Ruthlessly the Counterattack of Landlords and Rich Peasants" (繼續開展查田運動與無情的鎮壓地主富農的反攻 *Chi-hsü k'ai-chan ch'a-t'ien yün-tung yü wu-ch'ing ti chen-ya ti-chu fu-nung ti fan-kung*). Printed in *Red China*, No. 164 (March 20, 1934), p. 1.

Wilbur, C. Martin (ed.). *Chinese Sources on the History of the Chinese Communist Movement*. ("Columbia University East Asian Institute Studies," No. 1.) New York, 1950.

Wittfogel, Karl A. "A Short History of Chinese Communism." Unpublished manuscript on file in the Far Eastern and Russian Institute, University of Washington, 1956.

———. "The Legend of 'Maoism,'" *The China Quarterly*, Nos. 1, 2 (January–March, April–June), 1960.

Yakhontoff, Victor A. *The Chinese Soviets*. New York: Coward-McCann, 1934.

Index

A–B League (Anti-Bolshevik League), 143, 144, 182, 191, 197, 204, 248, 268, 269
Advanced struggle area, 80, 83–85 *passim*
Agricultural socialization, 147, 162–63
Ah Wei, 118
An-fu, 147, 184, 199
An-yüan, 198, 205, 229, 235

Big Swords, 92, 236
Blind actionism, 157, 165
Bolshevik (Kiangsi), 57
Bourgeoisie, 29
Bureaucratism: opposed, 94, 98, 220, 249; in Workers' and Peasants' Prosecution Department, 97; in Ch'ang-kang township, 101; in land investigation drive, 243
Bureaucrats: lands confiscated, 187; as political representatives of landlord class, 255

Capitalism: future in China, 55; development in rural areas, 154; in villages, 156; effect on peasants, 167–68
Capitalists: in class analysis, 110, 112; houses not confiscated, 140; to be overthrown, 167, 168; exploitation by restricted, 215; reactionary, 267–69 *passim;* intellectuals, 273; and interclass marriage, 277–79; management of public lands, 279–80; payment of debts and annulment of loans, 281; helped by ultraleftist tendency, 288
Cattle, draft: confiscation of, 51, 104, 105, 112, 145; confiscation and redistribution of, 73, 140, 151–52, 195, 200; rightfully owned by rich peasant, 110, 270–71; redistribution of, 161

Central Bureau of the Soviet Areas: set up to check Mao, 38–39, 50; resolution on rich-peasant problem, 38–39; on land problem, 48–50, 67; asked to correct its errors, 50; on land investigation drive, 80–82 *passim,* 97–98
Central People's Commissariat of Land: on land allotments, 61; on differentiation between landlord, rich peasant, and well-to-do middle peasant, 69; instruction on land struggle and landlord policy, 72; and land registration, 75–76, 113; on rich-peasant situation, 106–7; on land investigation drive, 106–7
Central Preparatory Commission for the National Soviet Congress, 6, 12
Central Soviet Area: scene of struggle between agrarian ideas of Mao and Li Li-san, 49; general land investigation drive in, 79; comparatively retarded struggle area in, 80, 205; land problem not thoroughly solved in, 198; landlord and rich-peasant intrigue in, 216
Central Soviet Government: planning of, 6; and land law of Chinese Soviet Republic, 52; direction on how to redistribute land in western Fukien, 66; investigation of leftist excesses in Jui-chin, 67; ordered mobilization of masses, 74; located at Yeh-p'ing, 85; called Eight-County and Poor-Peasant Corps conferences, 85–86, 210–14; on organization of poor-peasant corps, 91; on unfolding the land investigation drive, 97; on how to analyze classes, 107–8
Chamberlin, William Henry, 19
Chang-kang township, 100–101
Chang Kuo-t'ao: commenting on relation-

349

37–38

Owner-peasants. *See* Rich peasants
Oyuwan Soviet Area: and Li Li-sanism, 7, 10, 62; confiscation and redistribution of land in, 61–62

Pai-k'eng township, 240
Pang Hua, 115–16
P'eng Teh-huai, 14
Petty bourgeoisie, 13–14
Petty merchants, 141
P'i-t'ou Conference, 148
Po Chao, 67–68
Ponds: redistribution of, 13, 60, 71, 140, 144–45, 189–90, 195, 258; and land registration, 76; confiscated and given to public ownership, 130; operated or leased out by Soviets, 133
Poor-peasant corps: formation of urged, 37, 41–43 *passim*, 45, 56, 182; to combat rich peasants, 39; role in hired-farm-hand union, 41; functions of, 42, 44, 91, 175, 180, 184–86; organization of, 43–44, 91, 176–80, 183–84; membership of, 43, 44, 175–76, 184, 247; in liquidation of landlords, 72; in confiscation and redistribution of property, 73; in land investigation drive, 80, 96, 217–24, 227, 238, 239, 250–51, 252; conference at Yeh-p'ing, 85, 86, 88–89, 200, 212–14; closed door policy, 96, 246–47; excesses committed by, 99; in Ch'ang-kang township report, 101; executive committee, 176, 177, 178–80, 181, 223; congress of delegates, 176, 177–78, 179, 181; members' duties, 176; members' rights, 176; discipline within, 180–81; financing of, 181; use of confiscated and redistributed houses, 189; importance recognized, 190, 201; labor unions to participate in, 207; and Eight-County Conference, 211; executive council, 223
Poor peasants: percentage of land owned by, 25, 30, 136; percentage of population, 25, 30, 137, 155; attitude toward revolution as seen by Mao, 29; in class analysis, 28, 65, 66, 103, 110, 112, 256–57; as mainstay of land revolution, 40, 43, 75, 80, 218; in relation to middle peasant, 41, 50, 65, 113; and poor-peasant corps, 43, 246; in land redistribution, 49, 51–52, 59–61 *passim*, 63, 130, 141, 143, 147, 148, 163–64, 167–68, 187, 188, 192, 195, 197, 200, 202, 257, 258; special protection of, 51, 105, 127–28; as division of rural population, 62; role in land investigation drive, 98, 200, 231, 238–39, 246, 247; debts canceled,

133–34, 154, 155, 185, 189, 281; and land tax, 134–35; to be liberated in land revolution, 137; mills not confiscated, 140; farm implements redistributed to, 151–52, 189, 195, 200; and lease of land, 151–52; draft cattle redistributed to, 151–52, 189, 195, 200; in relation to rich peasant, 153–55, 157, 159, 160, 166–67; and progressive agricultural tax, 166; to establish leadership of in villages, 168, 169; and hired-farm-hand union, 173; houses redistributed to, 189, 195, 200; lease of waste land, 197–98; exchange of houses with rich peasants, 270, 271; interclass marriage, 277–79; management of public lands, 279–80
Po-sheng County: in Eight-County Conference, 80, 200, 210, 211, 214, 215; progress in land investigation drive, 94–95, 96, 98, 99, 198, 199, 205, 242, 245, 246; fight against Right and Left deviations in, 99; suppression of landlords, village bosses, and gentry, 236
Power Relations within the Chinese Communist Movement, 1930–1934, 1, 3, 6, 12, 15–17 *passim*, 35, 38, 44–45, 47, 52, 55–57 *passim*, 77
Presidium of the Action Committee, 14–15
Proletarian hegemony, 29
Proletariat: as antonym to bourgeoisie, 29; leading land revolution struggle, 147, 159, 186, 202; all peasants eventually will be, 167; as leaders of land investigation drive, 207
Provincial Committee Correspondence, 90, 93–95 *passim*, 107
Public enterprises, 280–81
Public lands: redistributed, 23, 138–39, 162–63; owned by rich peasants, 25; reserved for Red Army men, 60; confiscation of, 127, 191; surrendered to government, 132; in land distribution in old China, 136; transferred to peasants, 188; management by landlords, rich peasants, and capitalists, 279–80; management by the masses, 279–80
Public welfare, 129–30
Pu-ch'ien, 115–16

Räte-China, 47, 48
Red Army: maneuvers in Changsha, 4, 31; role in land revolution, 5, 187; land allotments to members, 5–9 *passim*, 23, 57, 60, 62, 70, 129, 131, 187, 195–96, 275–76, 284; organization of called for, 57; in confiscation and redistribution of property, 73, 201; and land registration, 76; ex-

Far Eastern and Russian Institute Publications on Asia

1. Compton, Boyd (trans. and ed.). *Mao's China: Party Reform Documents, 1942–44.* 1952. Reissued 1966. Washington Paperback-4. 330 pp., map.
2. Chiang, Siang-tseh. *The Nien Rebellion.* 1954. 177 pp., bibliog., index, maps.
3. Chang, Chung-li. *The Chinese Gentry: Studies on Their Role in Nineteenth-Century Chinese Society.* Introduction by Franz Michael. 1955. Reissued 1967. Washington Paperback on Russia and Asia-4. 277 pp., bibliog., index, tables.
4. *Guide to the Memorials of Seven Leading Officials of Nineteenth-Century China.* Summaries and, indexes of memorials to Hu Lin-i, Tseng Kuo-fan, Tso Tsung-tang, Kuo Sung-tao, Tseng Kuo-ch'üan, Li Hung-chang, Chang Chih-tung. 1955. 457 pp., mimeographed. Out of print.
5. Raeff, Marc. *Siberia and the Reforms of 1822.* 1956. 228 pp., maps, bibliog., index. Out of print.
6. Li Chi. *The Beginnings of Chinese Civilization: Three Lectures Illustrated with Finds at Anyang.* 1957. Reissued 1968. Washington Paperback on Russia and Asia-6. 141 pp., illus., bibliog., index.
7. Carrasco, Pedro. *Land and Polity in Tibet.* 1959. 318 pp., maps, bibliog., index.
8. Hsiao, Kung-chuan. *Rural China: Imperial Control in the Nineteenth Century.* 1960. Reissued 1967. Washington Paperback on Russia and Asia-3. 797 pp., illus., bibliog., index.
9. Hsiao, Tso-liang. *Power Relations within the Chinese Communist Movement, 1930–1934.* Vol. I: *A Study of Documents.* 1961. 416 pp., bibliog., index, glossary. Vol. II: *The Chinese Documents.* 1967. 856 pp.
10. Chang, Chung-li. *The Income of the Chinese Gentry.* Introduction by Franz Michael. 1962. 387 pp., tables, bibliog., index.
11. Maki, John M. *Court and Constitution in Japan: Selected Supreme Court Decisions, 1948–60.* 1964. 491 pp., bibliog., index.
12. Poppe, Nicholas, Leon Hurvitz, and Hidehiro Okada. *Catalogue of the Manchu-Mongol Section of the Toyo Bunko.* 1964. 391 pp., index.
13. Spector, Stanley. *Li Hung-chang and the Huai Army: A Study in Nineteenth-Century Chinese Regionalism.* Introduction by Franz Michael. 1964. 399 pp., maps, tables, bibliog., glossary, index.
14. Michael, Franz, and Chung-li Chang. *The Taiping Rebellion: History and Documents.* Vol. I: *History.* 1966. 256 pp., maps, index. Vols. II and III: *Documents and Comments.* In press 1969.
15. Shih, Vincent Y. C. *The Taiping Ideology: Its Sources, Interpretations, and Influences.* 1967. 576 pp., bibliog., index.
16. Poppe, Nicholas. *The Twelve Deeds of Buddha: A Mongolian Version of the Lalitavistara; Mongolian Text, Notes, and English Translation.* 1967. 241 pp., illus. Paper.
17. Hsia, Tsi-an. *The Gate of Darkness: Studies on the Leftist Literary Movement in China.* Preface by Franz Michael. Introduction by C. T. Hsia. 1968. 298 pp., index.
18. Hsiao, Tso-liang. *The Land Revolution in China, 1930–1934: A Study of Documents.* 1969. 378 pp., tables, glossary, bibliog., index.